Best Buy Bargain Plus Books

Skills & Practice

Grade 2

Frank Schaffer Publications®

Editor: Karen Thompson

Frank Schaffer Publications®

Send all inquiries to:
Frank Schaffer Publications
8720 Orion Place
Columbus, OH 43240-2111

Best Buy Bargain Plus Books: Skills & Practice Grade 2

ISBN 0-7682-3792-0

1 2 3 4 5 6 7 8 9 10 MAZ 09 08 07

Table of Contents

Language Arts 1–80

Math 81–173

Science 174–230

Social Studies 231–288

Answer Key 289–320

Name ______________________________

Food for Gregory

Print Gregory's food in ABC order. Then draw each meal on the plate.

Breakfast

tin can juice
eggs ham

____
____
____
____

Lunch

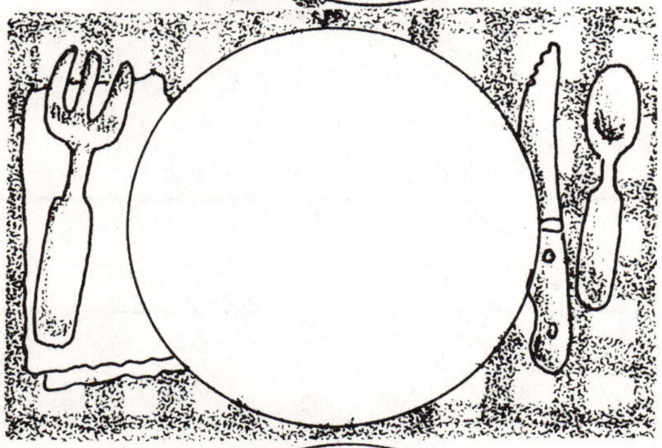

milk rubber boot
hot dog apple

____
____
____
____

Dinner

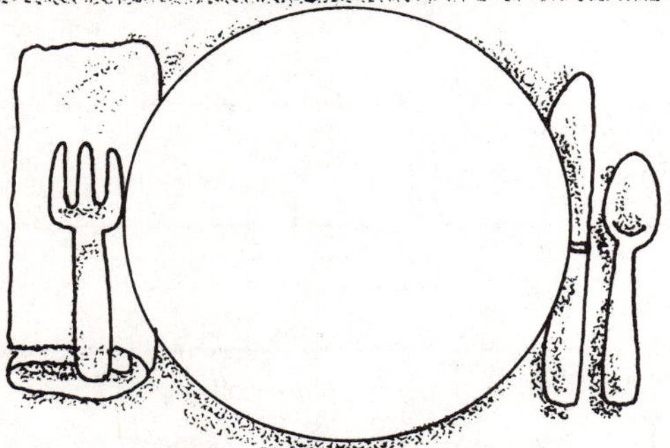

shoe fish
carrots bread

____
____
____
____

Draw what you ate yesterday for breakfast, lunch and dinner on these plates.

Breakfast

Lunch

Dinner

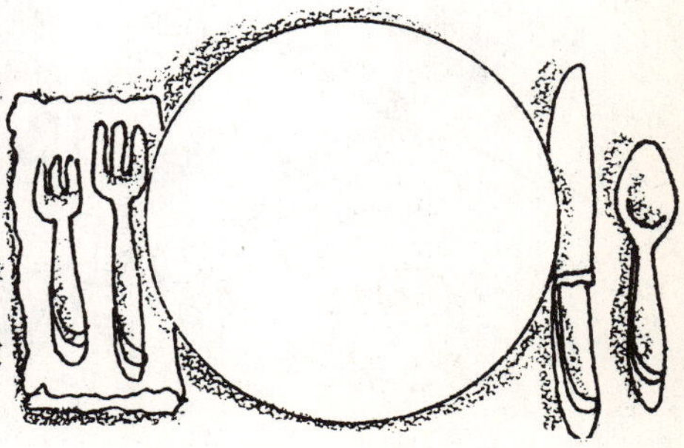

Name ______________________

Which Part Shall I Play?

Grace loves to act out stories. Read the list of characters. Then write them in alphabetical order.

Joan of Arc
Anansi
Peter Pan
Juliet
Captain Hook
Hiawatha
Wendy
Romeo
Mowgli
Aladdin

1. ______________________
2. ______________________
3. ______________________
4. ______________________
5. ______________________
6. ______________________
7. ______________________
8. ______________________
9. ______________________
10. ______________________

Name ______________________________

Which Way?

Read the words in the Word Bank. Write them in alphabetical order on the lines.

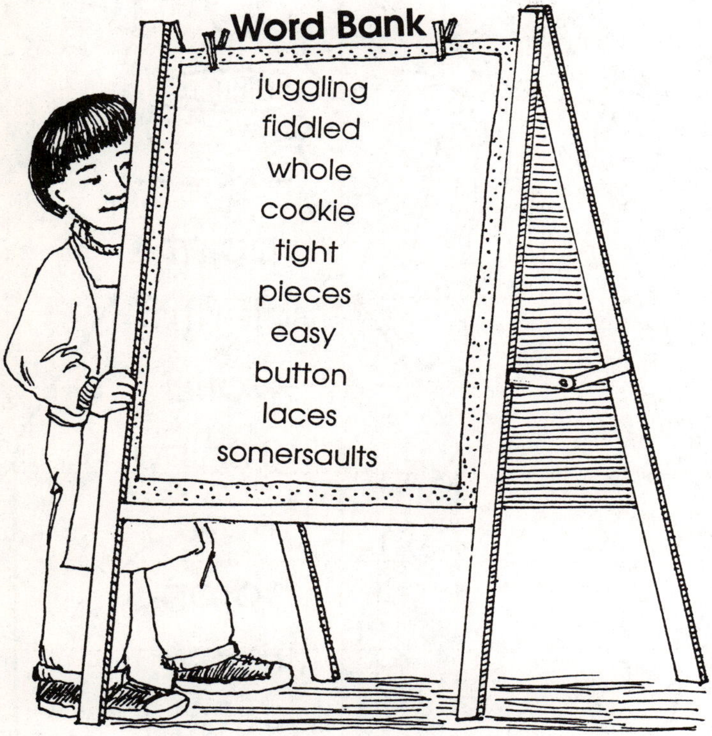
Word Bank
juggling
fiddled
whole
cookie
tight
pieces
easy
button
laces
somersaults

1. ______________________________
2. ______________________________
3. ______________________________
4. ______________________________
5. ______________________________
6. ______________________________
7. ______________________________
8. ______________________________
9. ______________________________
10. ______________________________

Write the missing lowercase letters in alphabetical order.

___ ___ c ___ ___ ___ ___ h ___ ___ k ___ ___

___ o ___ ___ ___ ___ ___ u ___ ___ x ___ ___

Name ______________________

ABC Potion

Write the words in alphabetical order.

1. ______________________
2. ______________________
3. ______________________
4. ______________________
5. ______________________
6. ______________________
7. ______________________
8. ______________________
9. ______________________
10. ______________________
11. ______________________
12. ______________________
13. ______________________
14. ______________________
15. ______________________

point
scientist
world
lightning
hard
baron
flashed
monster
rumbled
control
ketchup
overhead
drink
thunder
always

Name ______________________

Crazy Creatures

Draw a line to each letter in ABC order to finish this dot-to-dot picture.

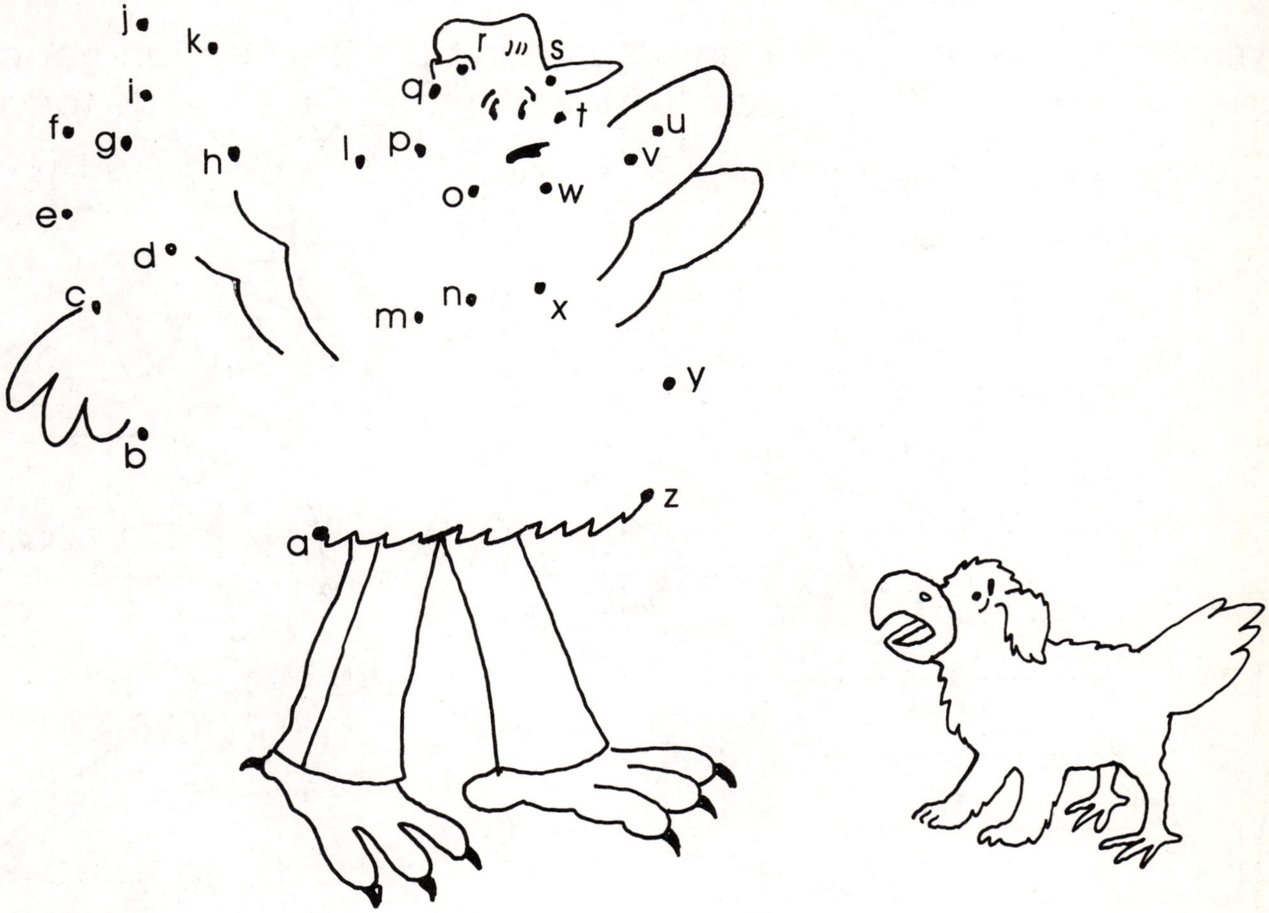

Now color and add details to the picture. Then write all the consonants in order on these lines.

1. ________ 5. ________ 9. ________ 13. ________ 17. ________ 21. ________

2. ________ 6. ________ 10. ________ 14. ________ 18. ________

3. ________ 7. ________ 11. ________ 15. ________ 19. ________

4. ________ 8. ________ 12. ________ 16. ________ 20. ________

Name ____________________

Alphabet Soup

Nan Cook has a special way of making alphabet soup. She mixes two boxes of soup together. Then she adds two secret ingredients — mystery and fun. After the soup is cooked, a strange thing happens. All the vowels rise to the top of the pot.

Write the consonant that can be used in both the front and back of each vowel or pair of vowels to make a word. One is done for you.

peep
__ a __
__ o __
__ o __
__ a __
__ ee __
__ oo __
__ i __
__ u __
__ o __
__ o __
__ i __
__ u __
__ o __
__ u __
__ u __
__ i __
__ oo __
__ e __
__ ee __
__ a __
__ i __

Name ______________________

Stretch and Grow

Goofy Gladys got new glasses. The glasses had springs on them which stretched words out and then added another vowel to each one.

Add a vowel to each word below to see what words Gladys saw through her glasses.

1. pal pa__l
2. fed fe__d
3. chin ch__in
4. ran ra__n
5. cat c__at
6. Jon jo__n
7. shut sh__ut
8. bran bra__n
9. lid l__id
10. hat h__at
11. bad b__ad
12. flat fl__at
13. bit b__it
14. pin p__in
15. men me__n

Name ______________________________

Motorcycle Maze

Help Ralph move through the maze to the Mountain View Inn by tracing over the path in which all of the words have two syllables.

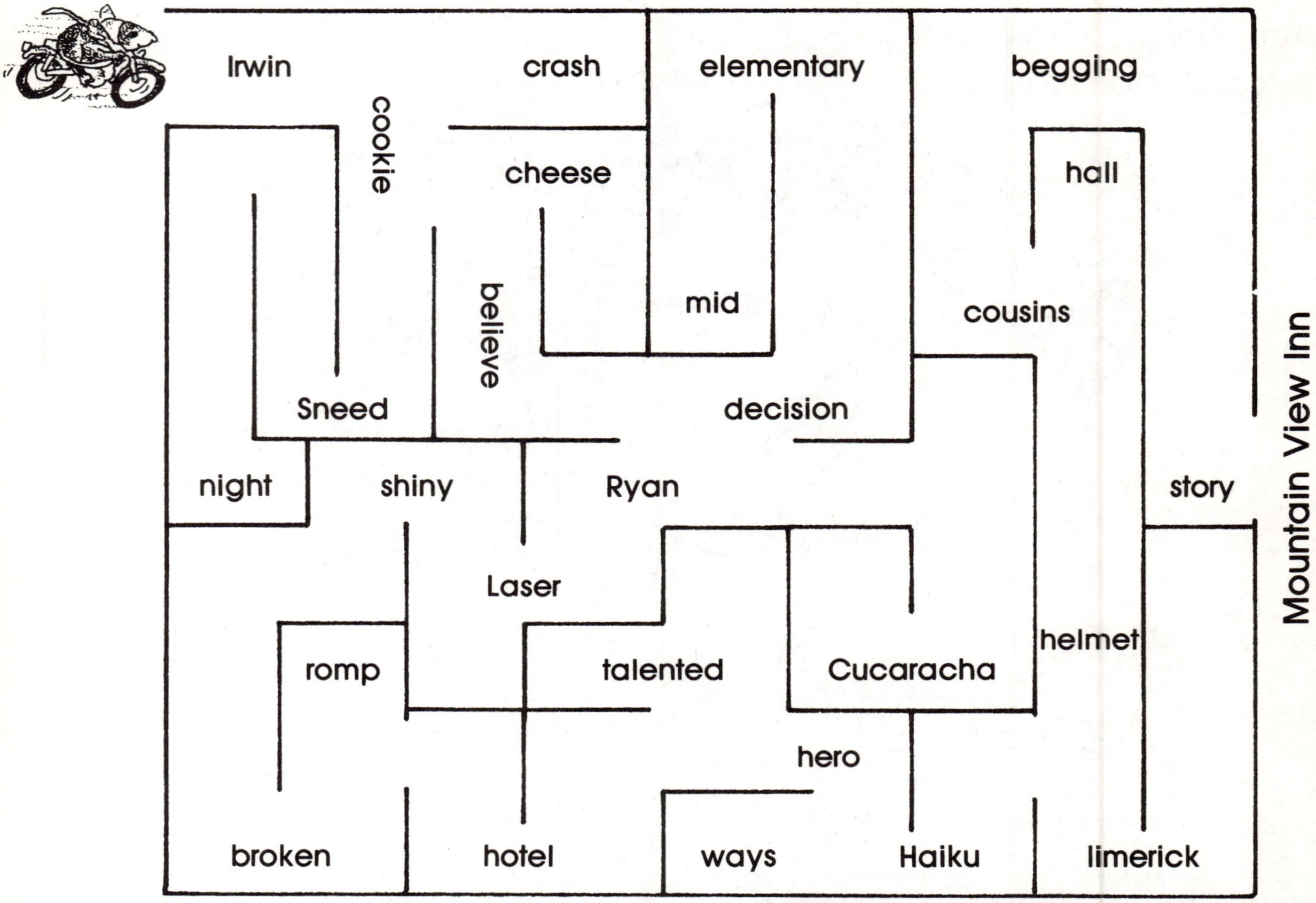

Now write the words from the correct path in alphabetical order on the lines below.

1. ______________________ 8. ______________________
2. ______________________ 9. ______________________
3. ______________________ 10. ______________________
4. ______________________ 11. ______________________
5. ______________________ 12. ______________________
6. ______________________ 13. ______________________
7. ______________________ 14. ______________________

Name ______________________

Trick or Treat Syllables

2
3

Think about how many syllables are in each word in the Word Bank. Then write each word on the correct jack-o'-lantern.

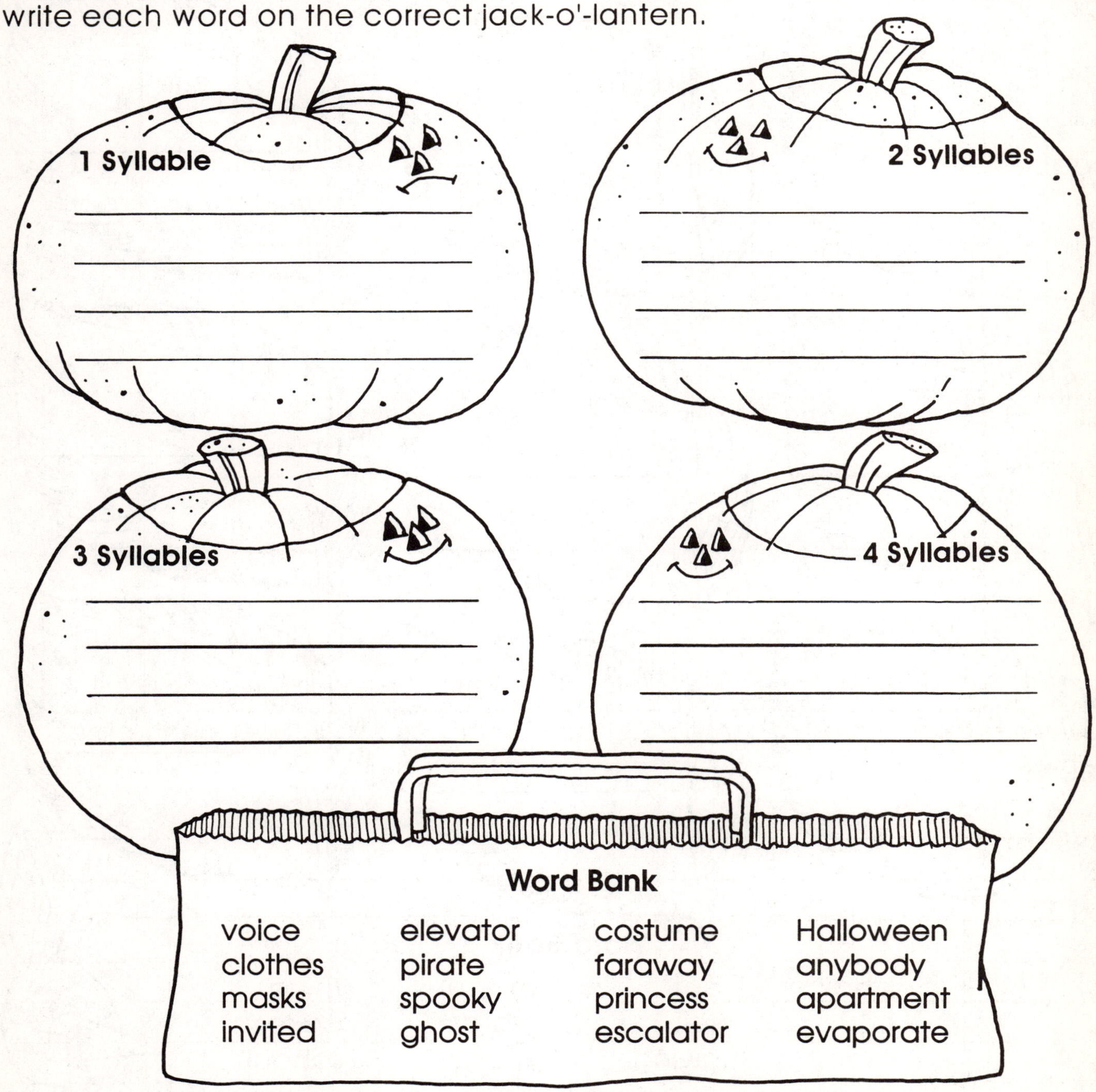
1 Syllable
2 Syllables
3 Syllables
4 Syllables

Word Bank

voice	elevator	costume	Halloween
clothes	pirate	faraway	anybody
masks	spooky	princess	apartment
invited	ghost	escalator	evaporate

Name ______________________________

All Together Now

Match a word in the Word Bank with a word on a feather to make a compound word. Then write it on the line.

space ____________
cup ____________
out ____________
Thanks ____________
with ____________
on ____________
news ____________
your ____________
some ____________

Word Bank

back	out	paper	thing
fit	self	yard	cakes
man	giving	stage	school

Name ______________________________

Word Magic

Maggie Magician announced, "One plus one equals one!" The audience giggled. So Maggie put two words into a hat and waved her magic wand. When she reached into the hat, Maggie pulled out one word and a picture. "See," said Maggie, "I was right!"

Look at each picture below. Use the Word Bank to help write a compound word for each.

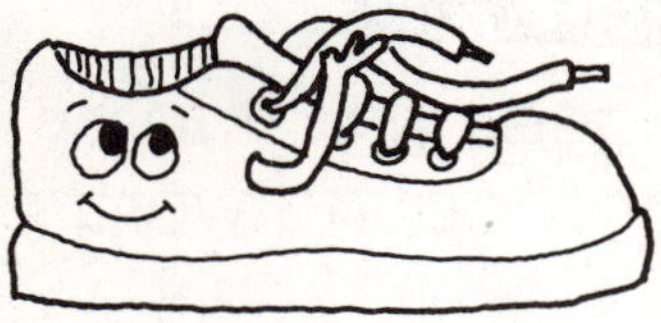
____

____

____

____

____

____

____

____

____

____

____

____

Word Bank

ball	door	rain
basket	ear	shirt
bell	fish	shoe
book	foot	star
bow	lace	stool
box	light	sun
cake	mail	tail
cup	phone	worm

Name ______________________________

Compound Your Effort

IS BUZZARDLIPS
A COMPOUND
WORD?

Read each word. Find the word in the Word Bank that goes with it to make a compound word. Cross it out. Then write the compound word on the line.

1. coat ______________________
2. snow ______________________
3. home ______________________
4. waste ______________________
5. tip ______________________
6. chalk ______________________
7. note ______________________
8. grass ______________________
9. school ______________________
10. with ______________________

Look at the words in the Word Bank you did not use. Use those words to make your own compound words.

1. ______________________
2. ______________________
3. ______________________
4. ______________________
5. ______________________

Word Bank

board	room	thing	side
writing	book	hopper	toe
bag	ball	class	where
work	out	basket	

Name ______________________

Mystery Word Mix-Up

Put on your detective hat! How many words can you make using only the letters in the words:

N a t e t h e G r e a t

1. ____________
2. ____________
3. ____________
4. ____________
5. ____________
6. ____________
7. ____________
8. ____________
9. ____________
10. ____________
11. ____________
12. ____________
13. ____________
14. ____________
15. ____________
16. ____________
17. ____________
18. ____________
19. ____________
20. ____________
21. ____________
22. ____________

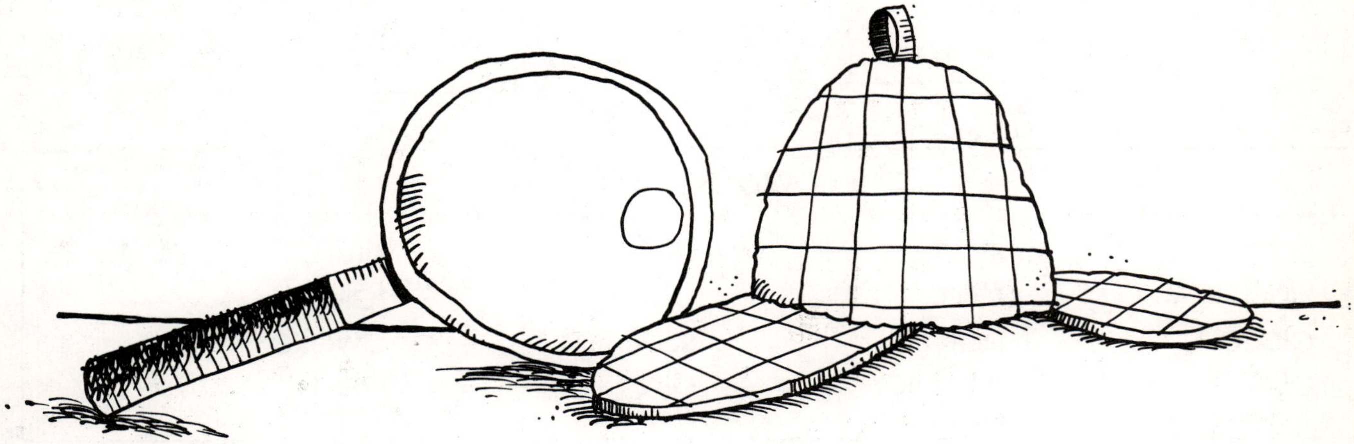

Name ______________________

Flower Fun

Find words in the Word Bank that are synonyms for the words in the leaves. Write them on the leaves.

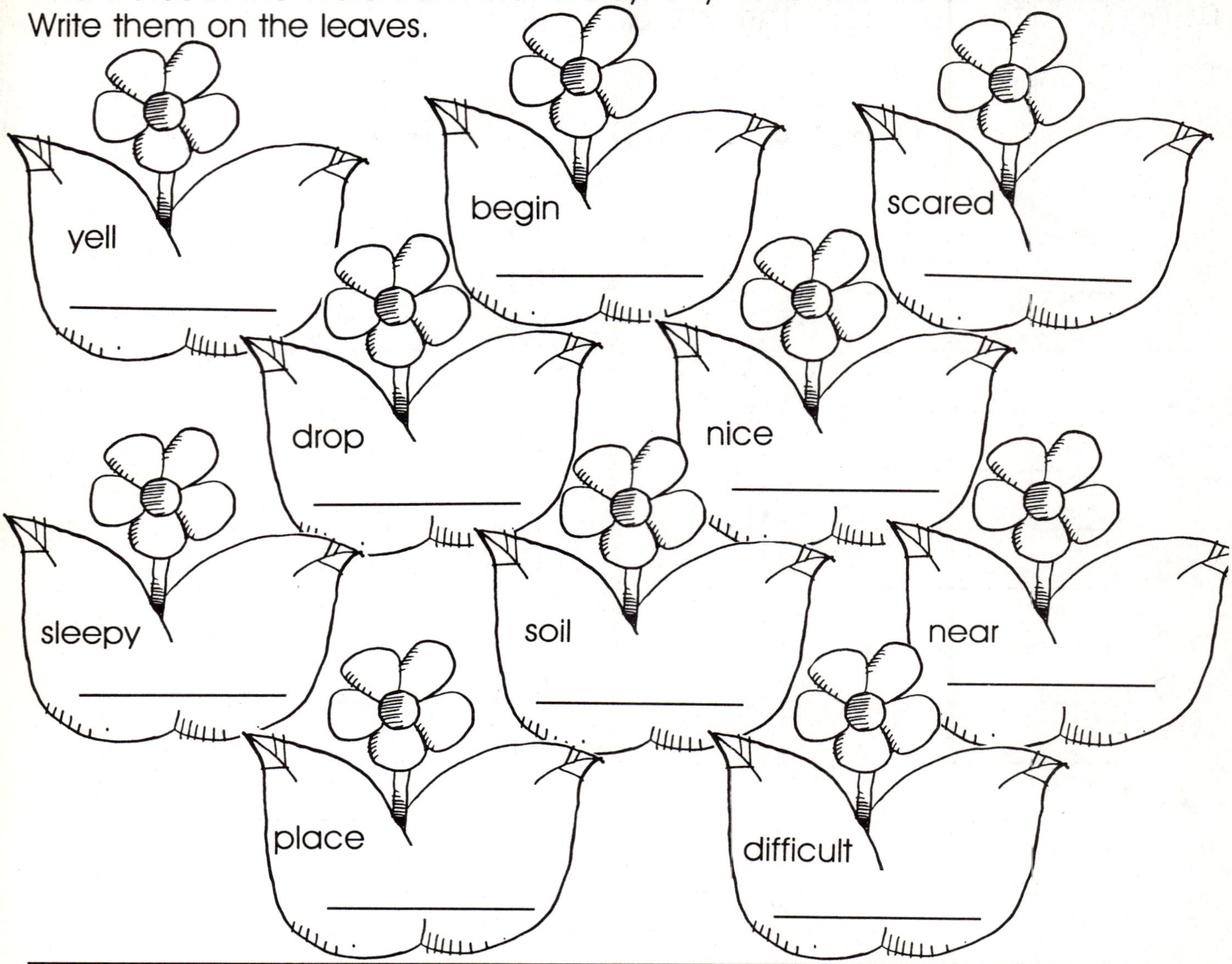
yell
begin
scared
drop
nice
sleepy
soil
near
place
difficult

Word Bank

pick	start	easy	sky
kind	rain	afraid	fall
close	hard	scream	awake
put	whisper	dirt	tired

Where?

Name ______________________

Read each word on the left. Find its synonym in the Word Bank and write it on the line.

1. below ______________
2. drummed ______________
3. hear ______________
4. scrambled ______________
5. over ______________
6. close ______________
7. slipped ______________
8. woods ______________
9. spring ______________
10. cleaned ______________
11. sturdy ______________
12. paths ______________
13. perhaps ______________
14. house ______________
15. evening ______________

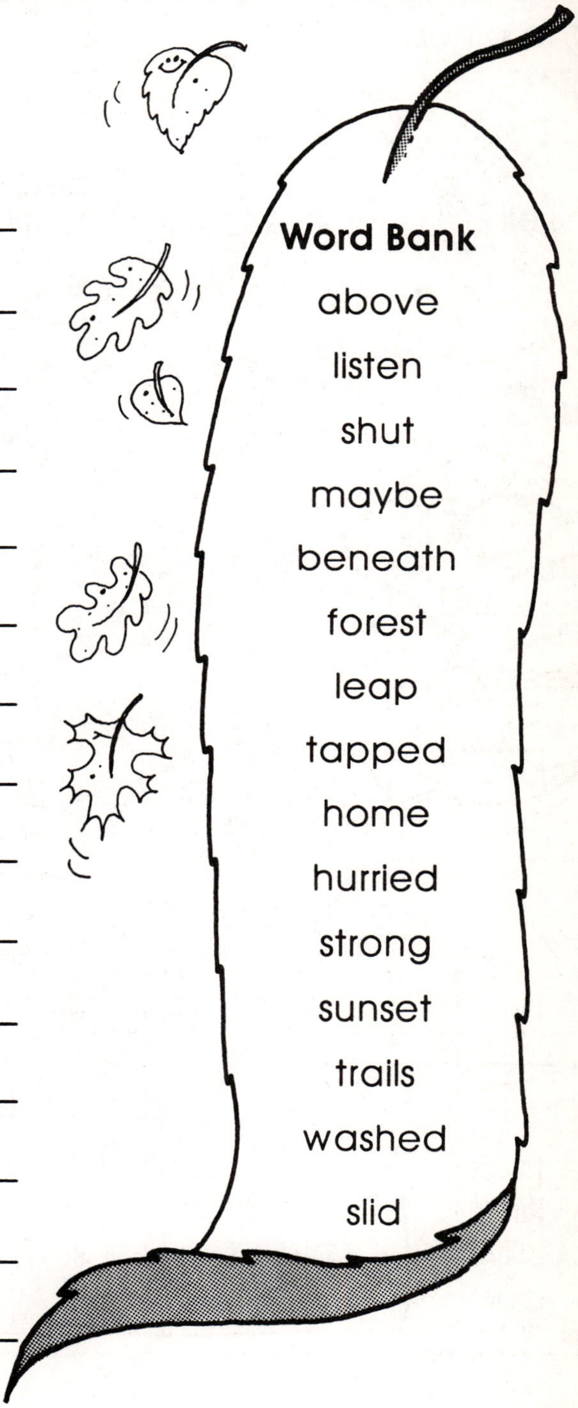

Word Bank

above
listen
shut
maybe
beneath
forest
leap
tapped
home
hurried
strong
sunset
trails
washed
slid

Name ______________________

Who's Afraid?

Help Frog and Toad escape from the snake. Read the two words in each space. If the words are antonyms, color the space green. Do not color the other spaces.

go stop
large small
wide narrow
dinner supper
scared afraid
shut close
happy sad
brave afraid
fall rise
dark light
outside inside
higher lower
leap jump
tremble shake
none all
fast quick
happy glad
look see
stones rocks
top bottom
covers blankets
friend pal
down up
shout whisper
loud soft
under over
Toad's House

Name ____________________

Should We Wake Them?

Read the words on each of the pillows. Find a word in the Word Bank that means the opposite and write it on the line.

sold ________	off ________	first ________
hated ________	warm ________	front ________
remembered ________	small ________	to ________
yours ________	everybody ________	early ________

Word Bank

bought	on	all	tiny
nobody	big	last	late
ahead	mine	from	cool
forgotten	loved	back	

Name ____________________

Flying Free Like an Eagle

Read the beginning of each sentence. Draw a line to the words on the feather that best complete each sentence.

1. The strong stallion fought like...
2. The bolt of lightning lit the sky like...
3. The wild horses roamed the hills as free as...
4. The thunder roared like...
5. The running herd crossed the land like...
6. The stallion's eyes were as cold as...
7. The hills were as dark as...
8. The rising sun was like...

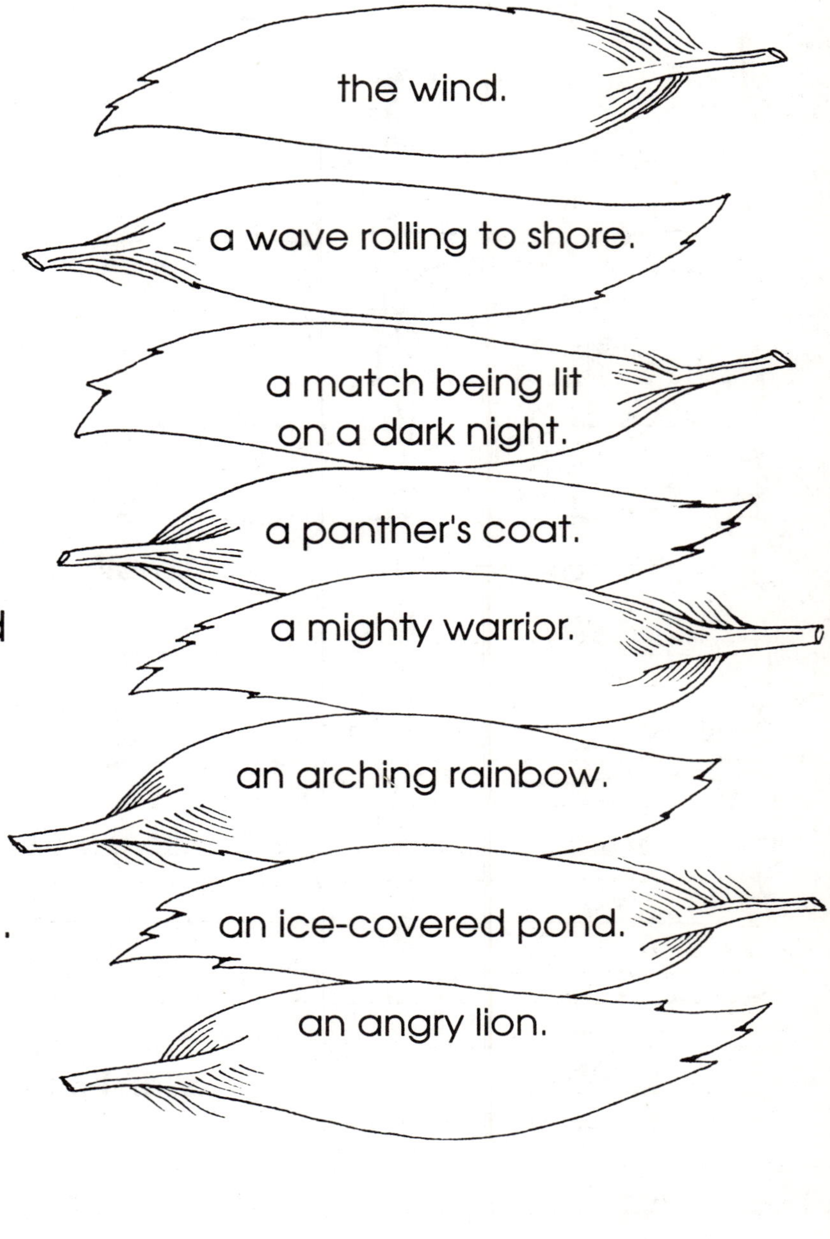
the wind.
a wave rolling to shore.
a match being lit on a dark night.
a panther's coat.
a mighty warrior.
an arching rainbow.
an ice-covered pond.
an angry lion.

Name ______________________________

Rain, Rain Go Away!

Read the naming parts in the tent.
Write one of the naming parts to begin each sentence.

Rain
Black clouds
A big wind
The campfire
Todd and Clint
The old green tent

1. ______________________ went camping.

2. ______________________ was hard to set up.

3. ______________________ blew the trees.

4. ______________________ filled the sky.

5. ______________________ ran off the tent.

6. ______________________ went out.

Name ______________________

It Takes Many Colors

Read the words in the Word Bank. If the word means one, write it on the paint jar. If the word means more than one, write it on the paintbrushes.

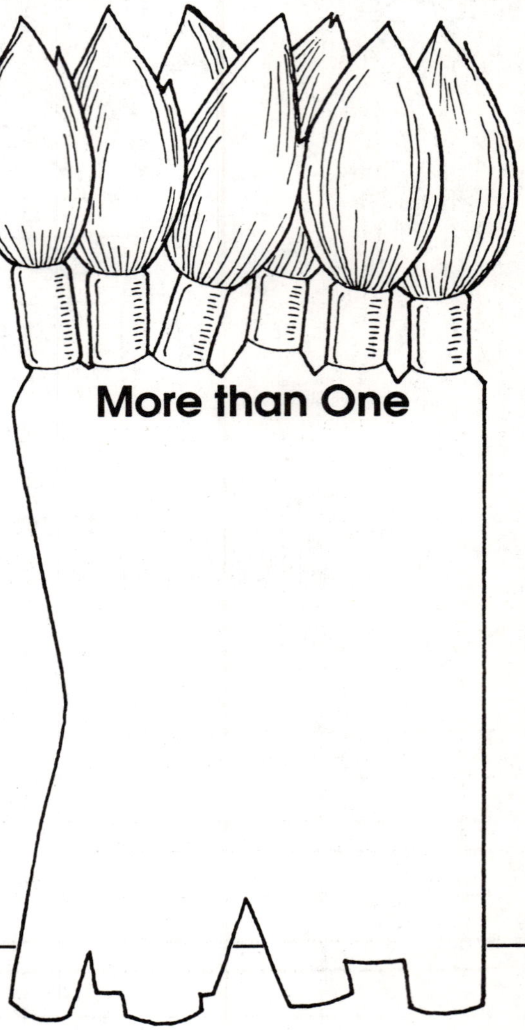

Word Bank

deed people berries child brushes
visions paintbrush boy flowers
children warrior picture

LANGUAGE ARTS

Name ______________________

Fun Around the Campfire

Word Bank

beat	sang	told
danced	sat	wore

 a verb in each sentence below. Use the word bank to help you.

1. The boys and girls ______________ around the campfire.

2. They ______________ songs.

3. Brian ______________ a drum.

4. Jerry and Helen ______________ costumes.

5. They ______________ around the campfire.

6. The teacher ______________ stories.

Name ____________________

It's Time ✎ these verbs in the correct Time Machine.

play	pull	barked	jumped	danced
looked	laugh	walk	listen	lived

Now
In the Past

Name ____________________

I Was. Were You?

Use "was" and "were" to tell about something that happened in the past. Use "was" to tell about one person or thing. Use "were" to tell about more than one person or thing. Always use "were" with the word "you."

"was" or "were" in each sentence below.

1. Lois __________ in the second grade last year.

2. She __________ eight years old.

3. Carmen and Judy __________ friends.

4. They __________ on the same soccer team.

5. I __________ on the team, too.

6. You __________ too young to play.

Name ______________________

Playing in the Summer Sun

Look at the picture. Read the sentence. Circle the missing word. Then write it on the line.

It is ______________________.

rain **raining**

He can ______________________ the boat.

row **rowing**

The kite is ______________________.

fly **flying**

He is ______________________.

swing **swinging**

He is ______________________.

pick **picking**

0-7682-3792-0 *Skills & Practice Gr. 2*

Name ________________________________

An Owlish Activity

Write the words where they belong.

Word Bank

bite	school	children	skip	donkey	house
jump	lunchbox	kitten	write	hop	run

Nouns | **Verbs**

Flip Fun! Draw a picture of one of the nouns.

Name ______________________

Tic-Tac-Toe

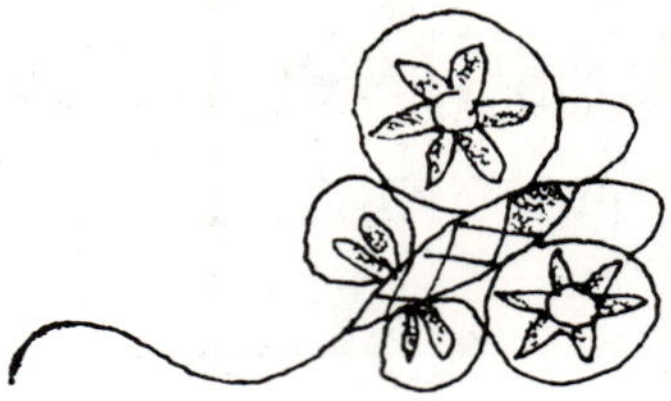

Circle all of the naming words (nouns).
Put an **X** on all of the doing words (verbs).
Under each game, write the **X** words that scored a tic-tac-toe.

boy	well	fell
mother	wished	ladder
ran	man	cake

____
____
____

fished	water	book
told	stone	lamp
pumped	people	shoe

____
____
____

child	sent	house
tree	ate	China
Chang	raced	body

____
____
____

paper	bear	bridge
Tikki	table	flower
read	yelled	jump

____
____
____

Name ____________________

Picking Pronouns

The words *he, she, it,* and *they* can be used in place of a noun.

Read the sentence pairs. Write the correct pronoun in each blank.

1. John won first place. ________ got a blue ribbon.	
2. Janet and Gail rode on a bus. ________ went to visit their grandmother.	
3. Sarah had a birthday party. ________ invited six friends to the party.	
4. The kitten likes to play. ________ likes to tug on shoelaces.	
5. Ed is seven years old. ________ is in the second grade.	

Name ______________________

Marvelous Me!

You are a very special person!

Draw hair and eyes on the body below to make it look like you. Then use the describing words listed in the box to label your beautiful body parts. Be sure to label each part with a describing word that begins with the same letter. Write a story about how each part of your body is special.

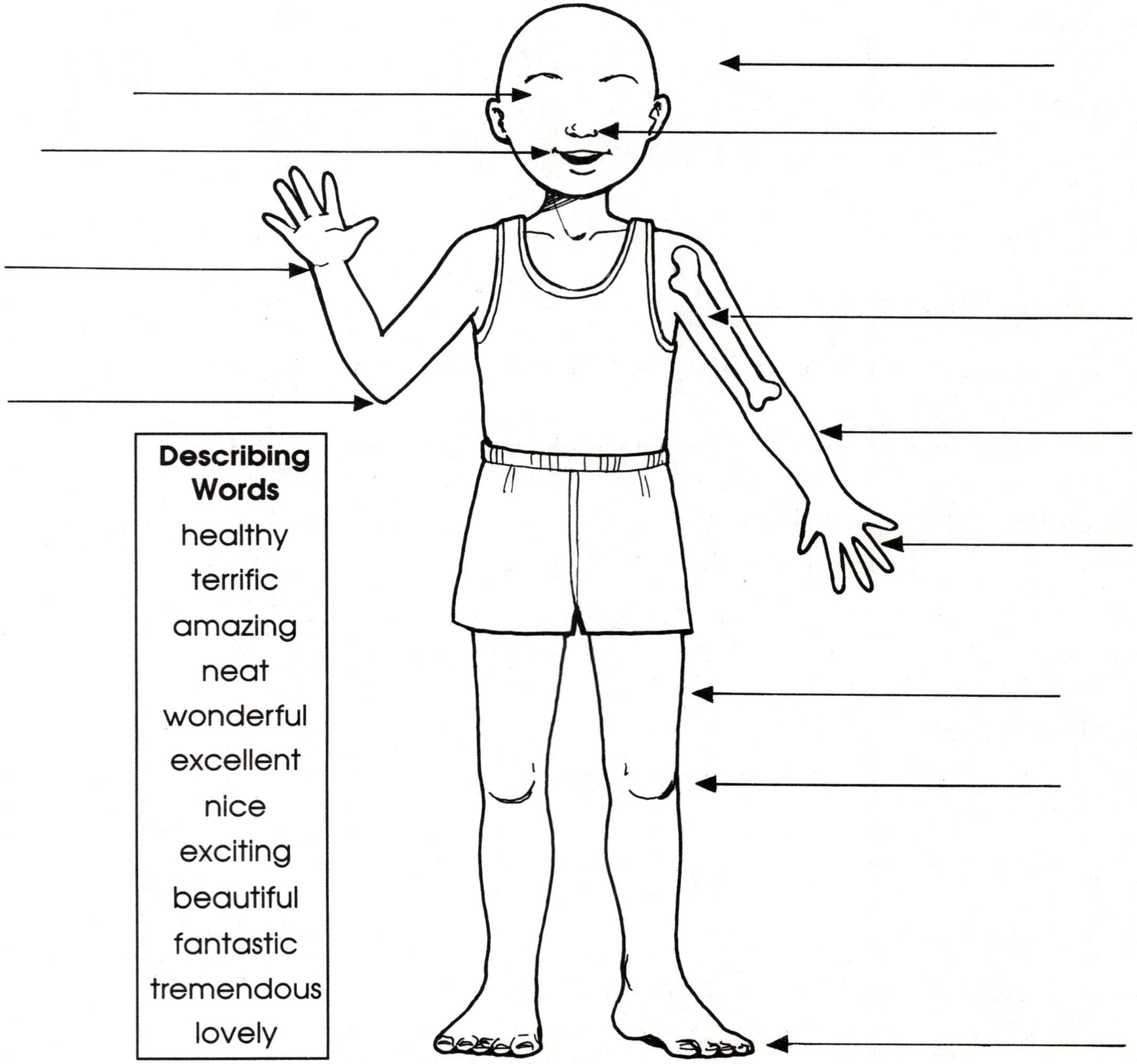

Describing Words
healthy
terrific
amazing
neat
wonderful
excellent
nice
exciting
beautiful
fantastic
tremendous
lovely

Name ______________________________

Add the Adjectives

Read each sentence. Write a describing word on each line. Draw a picture to match each sentence.

The ______________ flag waved over the ______________ building.

A ______________ lion searched for food in the ______________ jungle.

We saw ______________ fish in the ______________ aquarium.

Her ______________ car was parked by the ______________ van.

The ______________ dog barked and chased the ______________ truck.

The ______________ building was filled with ______________ packages.

Wordy Treats

Name ______________________________

Write the word from the Word Bank on the correct trick or treat bag. If the word **names** a person, place or thing, write it on the bag marked **Nouns**. If the word **describes** something, write it on the bag marked **Adjectives**.

Nouns

1. ______________________
2. ______________________
3. ______________________
4. ______________________
5. ______________________
6. ______________________
7. ______________________
8. ______________________
9. ______________________

Adjectives

1. ______________________
2. ______________________
3. ______________________
4. ______________________
5. ______________________
6. ______________________
7. ______________________
8. ______________________
9. ______________________

Word Bank

costumes	elevator	pirate	fifth
ghosts	spooky	robot	bossy
party	squeaky	scary	stairs
special	wings	high	crown
	heavy	silly	

0-7682-3792-0 *Skills & Practice Gr. 2*

Name ______________________

Summer Camp

A telling sentence begins with a capital letter and ends with a period. Write each telling sentence correctly on the lines.

1. everyone goes to breakfast at 6:30 each morning

____

2. only three people can ride in one canoe

____

3. each person must help clean the cabins

____

4. older campers should help younger campers

____

5. all lights are out by 9:00 each night

____

6. everyone should write home at least once a week

____

Name ______________________________

Tell-a-vision

Look at each TV picture. Write a telling sentence about each program.

Name ____________________

Telephone Talk

An asking sentence is called a question. A question begins with a capital letter and ends with a question mark.

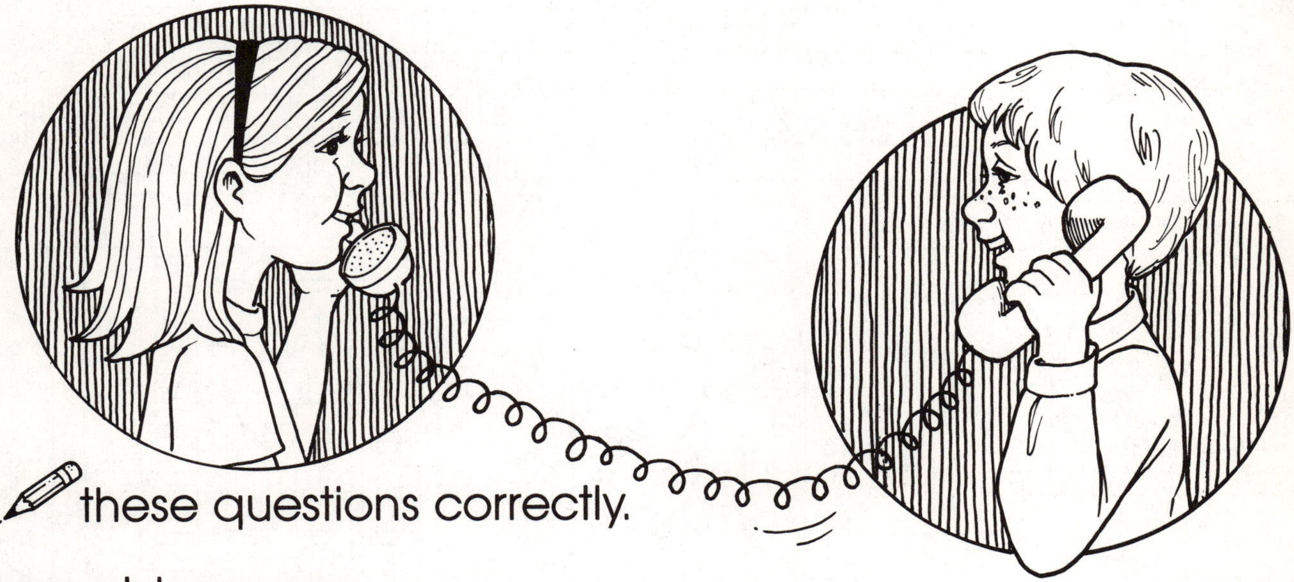

(pencil) these questions correctly.

1. how old are you

2. are you in second grade

3. who is your teacher

4. did you read that book

5. where do you live

Name ___________________________

Asking Questions

Look at the picture. Write **five** asking sentences about the picture.

____

____

____

____

____

Name ______________________

That Doesn't Make Sense!

A sentence must make sense. Read each sentence. Put an **X** on the **two** words which do not belong. Write the corrected sentence on the lines below.

My neighbor is orange having a yard very sale.

1. ____

____

She is snow selling lots of old things phone.

2. ____

____

A man until is buying five candle old books.

3. ____

____

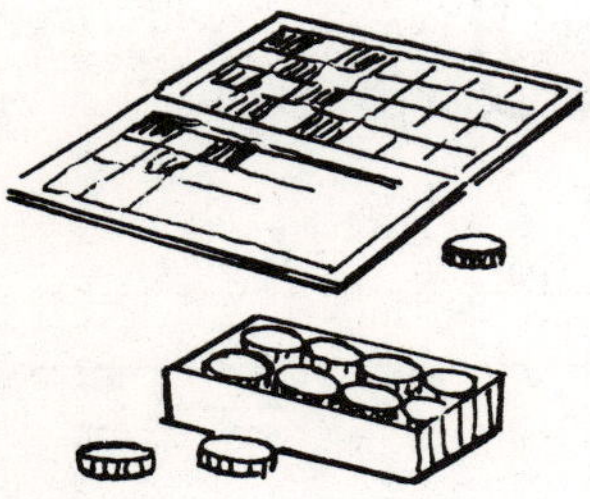

My brother is buying an salt old checkers it game.

4. ____

____

Two ladies pull are buying an old touch toy chest.

5. ____

____

Name ______________________

Flight to Fun

Would you like to fly away for a fun trip? Write words about a trip on the plane. Use the words to write five sentences about the trip.

1. ______________________
2. ______________________
3. ______________________
4. ______________________
5. ______________________

Name ______________________

About Me

Sentences can tell much about you. Begin at the **START** sign and write sentences that tell all about you—how you look, your age, things you like to do, etc. Write as many sentences as you can going around and around the circle.

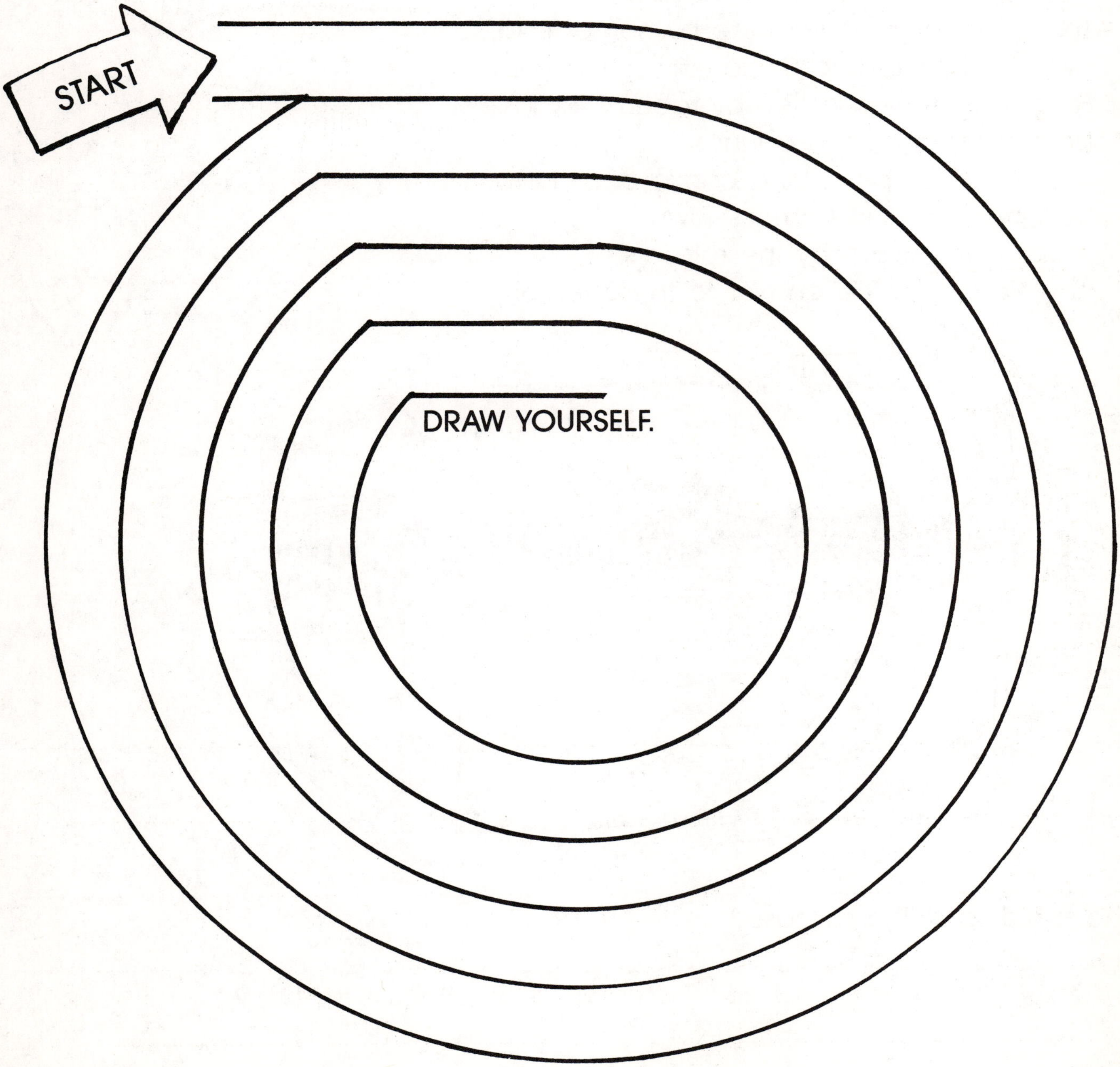
START
DRAW YOURSELF.

Name ______________________

A Sensational Scent

Circle the letters that should be capital letters. Then write them in the matching numbered blanks to answer the question.

1. eddie, Homer's friend, lives on elm Street.
2. Homer's aunt lives in kansas City, kansas.
3. are you sure Aunt aggie is coming?
4. old Rip Van Winkle came to town.
5. The doughnuts were made by homer Price.
6. Miss terwillinger and Uncle telly saved yarn.
7. Homer Price was written by robert McCloskey.
8. Uncle ulysses owned a lunch room.
9. The super – Duper was a comic book hero.
10. Doc pelly lived in Homer's town.
11. money was stolen by the robbers.
12. now you have the answer to the question.

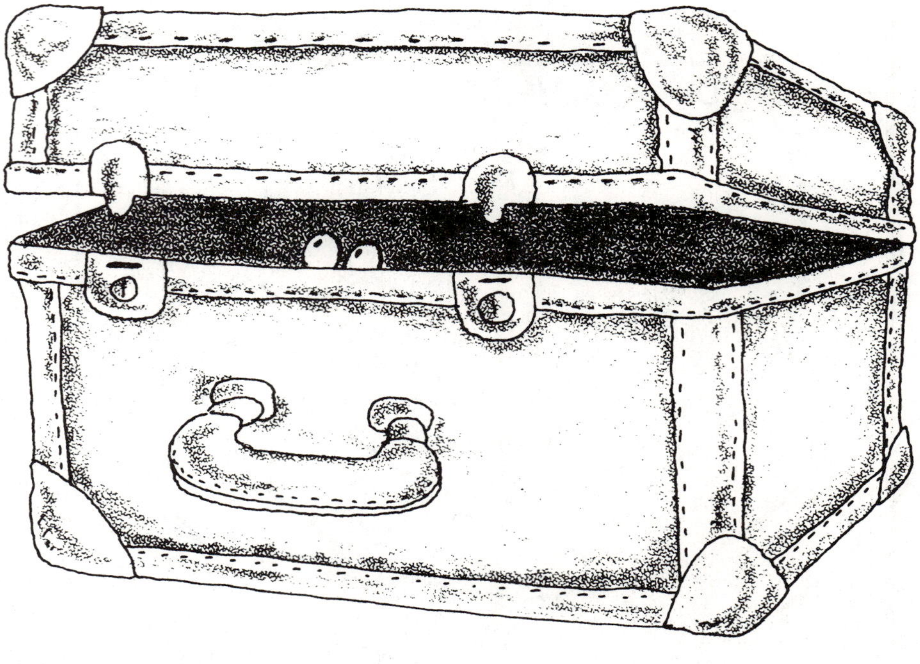

Who is hiding in the suitcase?

_ _ _ _ _   _ _ _   _ _ _   _ _ _ _ _
3 7 4 11 3   6 5 1   10 1 6   9 2 8 12 2

Name ________________________

Now, How Does That Go?

Write the sentences correctly. Be sure to put capital letters, periods and exclamation marks where they belong.

1. muffy spoke the words very quietly

2. buster said that the pilgrims sailed on a ship named the mayflower

3. francine said, "i will not play the part of a turkey "

4. arthur thought about turkeys while he and d w did dishes

5. arthur worried about finding a turkey

6. everyone looked at the audience and said, "happy thanksgiving "

Name ______________________

Punctuation Magic

POWERFUL
PUNCTUATION
Gives sentences
PIZZAZ!

Write the sentences correctly. Be sure to put capital letters, periods and question marks where they belong.

1. mrs paris talked to richard, alex, matthew and emily about the trip to the museum

___

___

___

2. the children read a story about a king who was greedy

___

___

3. everyone but richard drew a picture about the story

___

___

4. why was drake sick

___

___

5. mrs gates asked matthew to take homework to drake

___

___

6. did richard's wish make drake sick

___

___

Name ____________________

An Excellent Exercise

The words *a* and *an* help point out a noun. Use *a* before a word that begins with a consonant. Use *an* before a word that begins with a vowel or a vowel sound.

1. Our class visited _____ farm.
2. We could only stay _____ hour.
3. A man let us pick eggs out of _____ nest.
4. We saw _____ egg that was cracked.
5. We watched _____ lady milk a cow.
6. We got to eat _____ ice cream cone.

Name ____________________

Add an Apostrophe

Add **'s** to a noun to show who or what **owns** something.

the correct word under each picture.

The ____ nose is big.
clown clowns clown's

This is ____ coat.
Bettys Betty's Betty

I know ____ brother.
Burt's Burt Burts

The ____hat is pretty.
girls girl girl's

That is the ____ ball.
kitten's kitten kittens

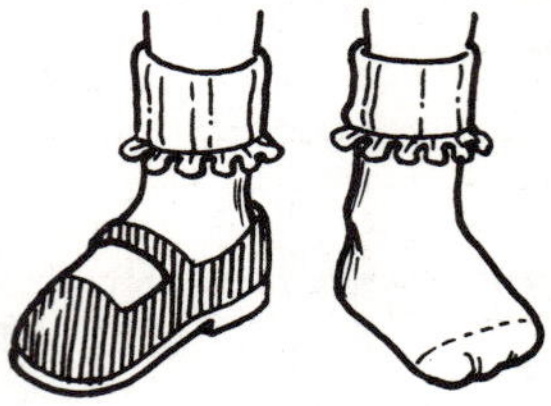

My ____ shoe is missing.
sisters sister sister's

The ____ coach is Mr. Hall.
teams team's team

The ____ cover is torn.
book's books book

Name ______________________

Fish for Plurals

Write the words on the fish in the correct tank.

kites	mitten	star	cats	chick	matches	foxes	lunch

One

More Than One (Plural)

Name ______________________

Who Is Hungrier?

Use the pictures to help you complete each sentence with the correct word.

Sludge Fang Big Hex

sleepy sleepier sleepiest

1. Fang is ____________ than Big Hex.
2. Big Hex is ____________.
3. Sludge is the ____________ of all.

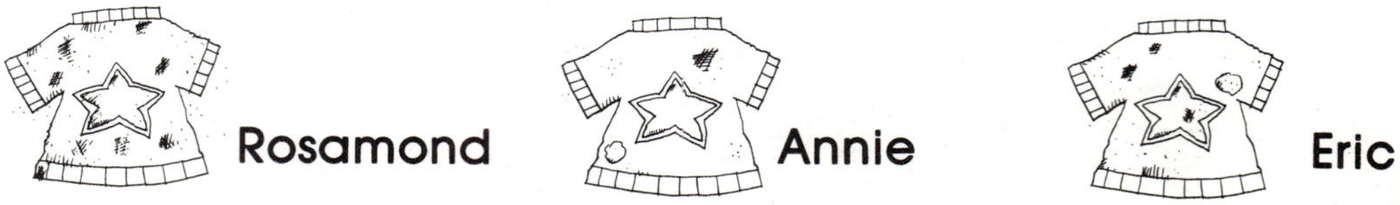
Rosamond
Annie
Eric

dirty dirtier dirtiest

1. Rosamond's shirt is the ____________ of all.
2. Eric's shirt is ____________ than Annie's.
3. Annie's shirt is ____________.

Marshmallow cotton ball pillow

soft softer softest

1. The pillow is ____________.
2. The cotton ball is the ____________.
3. The marshmallow is ____________ than the pillow.

Nate Finley Pip

hungry hungrier hungriest

1. Pip is ____________ than Nate.
2. Nate is ____________.
3. Finley is the ____________.

Name ____________________

Is It a World Record?

Read each sentence. Choose the correct word and write it on the line.

big
bigger
biggest

1. The town made the ____________ snowball on record.
2. Emmett made a ____________ snowball.
3. Sara helped him make it even ____________ .

fast
faster
fastest

1. The snowball started to roll very ____________ .
2. It was the ____________ rolling snowball anyone had ever seen.
3. It rolled ____________ than they could run.

white
whiter
whitest

1. As the snowball rolled closer, Mr. Wetzel's face became even ____________ .
2. After it snowed all night, the town was the ____________ it had ever been.
3. Mr. Wetzel's face turned ____________ when he saw the snowball rolling toward his candy store.

Name ______________________

Can I, or Can't I?

Read each sentence. Write **can** or **can't** on the line.

1. The day is warm so I ____________ wear my mittens.

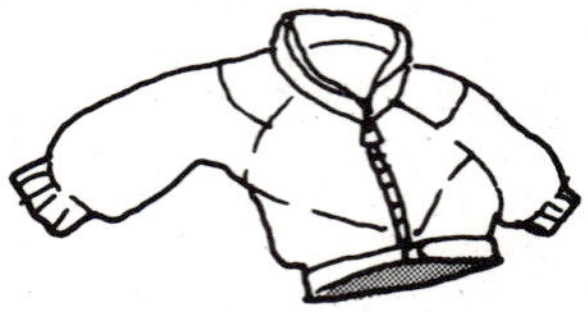

2. It is snowing so I ____________ wear my snowsuit.

3. My boots are too big so I ____________ wear them.

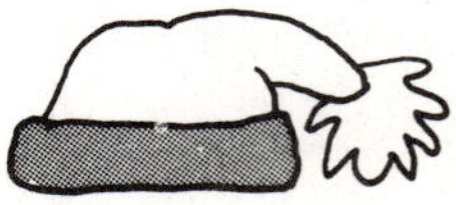

4. My hat is too little so I ____________ wear it.

5. It snowed so I ____________ make a snowman.

6. The shade will not open so I ____________ see if it has snowed.

Bunny Bunch

Name ____________________

There are ten bunnies in this family. Each one is special.

Read the clues and fill in the blank with the word that rhymes and makes sense.

1. I like to hop
   and drink ______________ .

2. I can run fast,
   but still I am always ______________.

3. I like to run and jump,
   but sometimes I fall and get a ______________.

4. I like to help Mom and Pop
   by scrubbing the floor with a ______________.

5. After I feed the cat,
   I take out my baseball and ___________ .

6. I like to go on a hike
   or ride my ______________ .

7. I like to dig in the sand
   and play the drums in a ______________ .

8. I like to play with a toy car
   while I eat a candy ______________.

9. I can walk in the fog
   and also chop a ______________ .

10. I can fly my kite
    but not during the ______________.

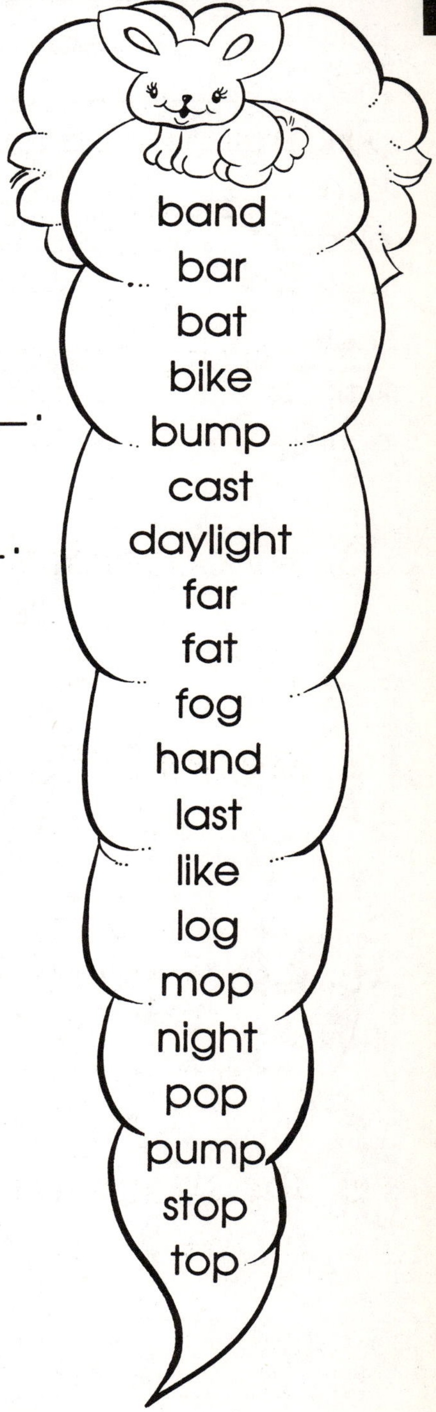
band
bar
bat
bike
bump
cast
daylight
far
fat
fog
hand
last
like
log
mop
night
pop
pump
stop
top

Name ____________________

Loosey Goosey

Find the names of the birds at the bottom of the page that will rhyme with the words given. For example: Loose goose

narrow ____________________
hairy ____________________
men ____________________
pork ____________________
love ____________________
pleasant ____________________
perky ____________________
soon ____________________
luck ____________________
darling ____________________

bobbin ____________________
dark ____________________
pinch ____________________
muffin ____________________
beagle ____________________
frail ____________________
hull ____________________
lay ____________________
howl ____________________

dove
stork
canary
wren
robin
jay
starling
sparrow
pheasant
eagle
turkey
owl
gull
quail
loon
puffin
duck
lark
finch

Name ______________________

Do You Know a Boa?

Print a rhyming word under each word on the boa's body. Slither down from the head to the tail. Sssssssssssss.

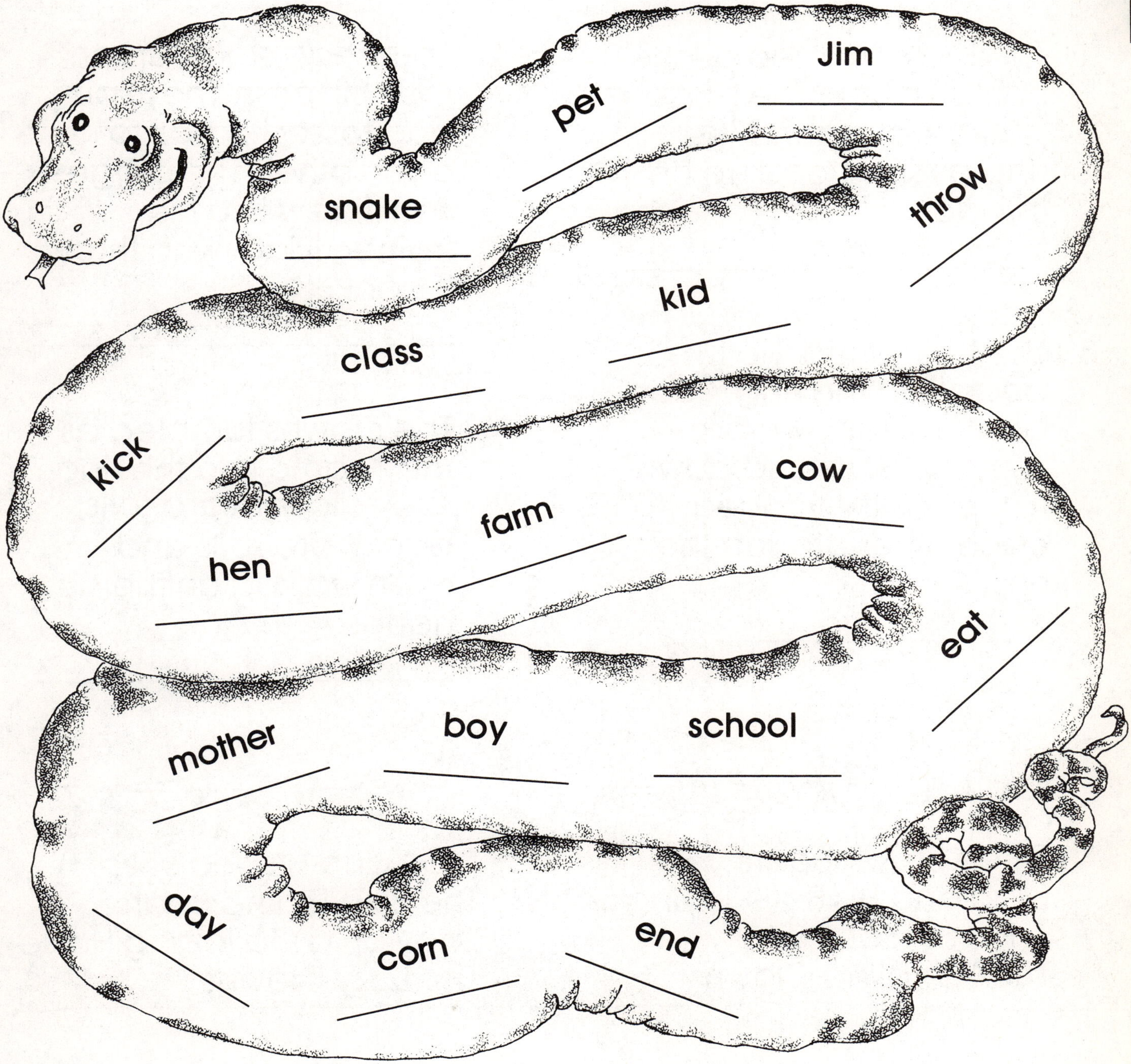

snake
pet
Jim
throw
kid
class
kick
hen
farm
cow
eat
school
boy
mother
day
corn
end

Name ______________________

What an Act!

Read about each act. Read the titles in the Word Bank. Write the best title for each act.

1. The lady climbed on the horse's back. The horse galloped around the ring as she stood up on its back.

   ____

2. Four seals stood up on their flippers. They spun and tossed a ball to each other. The biggest seal threw it to his trainer, Mac, who threw it back.

   ____

3. The trainer led the five bears into the ring. Each bear had its own bike. They rode up and down ramps as they raced each other around the ring.

   ____

4. The clowns tumbled as they came into the ring. They did forward rolls, backward rolls and even walked on their hands.

   ____

Word Bank

Three Brown Bears
Mac and His Ball-Playing Seals
A Horse Rider
The Tumbling Clowns
Mac and His Seals
The Bike-Riding Bears
Lady on a Galloping Horse
The Lazy Clowns

Name ____________________

High-Flying Acts

L-A-A-A-DIES AND GENTLEMEN...

Read each sentence. Look at the underlined words. Write **who, what, when, where or why** to show what the underlined words tell.

1. Clifford and Emily Elizabeth spent the day at the circus. ____________
2. The biggest elephant couldn't lead the parade because he had a cold. ____________
3. The circus owner was afraid there would not be a show. ____________
4. Clifford shot a tent pole at the hot air balloon. ____________
5. Clifford caught the diver before he landed in the empty tank. ____________
6. The clowns needed help because some had quit. ____________
7. Clifford liked the cotton candy. ____________
8. The poster said there would be a circus today. ____________
9. The human cannon ball landed on top of a haystack. ____________
10. The lions and tigers didn't listen to the lion tamer. ____________

Name ______________________

Donuts, Anyone?

Write who, what, when, where or why to show what the underlined words in each sentence tell you.

1. The Pee Wee Scouts went to Mrs. Peter's house on Tuesday. ____________
2. The Scouts turned in the money they had received for selling the boxes of donuts. ____________
3. Roger and Rachel sold the most boxes of donuts. ____________
4. Sonny's mother sold many boxes at work. ____________
5. Rachel sold the donuts to her relatives. ____________
6. Rachel was angry at Molly because she was making fun of her relatives. ____________
7. Sonny and Rachel would win badges because they sold the most boxes of donuts. ____________
8. If people eat a lot of donuts, they might get fat. ____________
9. Everyone was happy that they had earned enough money to go to camp in two weeks. ____________
10. The scout meeting started after three o'clock. ____________

0-7682-3792-0 *Skills & Practice Gr. 2*

It's a Surprise!

Name ____________________

Read the clues. Find the answers in the Word Bank.

1. You need snow to do this. You can go fast or slow. You can turn corners. You need a pair of something to do this. What is it?

   ____

2. This can be soft or hard. It can be made of paper or metal. You need it when you want to buy something. What is it?

   ____

3. It is a place where you can buy sweet treats to eat. Many of the treats that can be bought there have to be baked in an oven. What is it?

   ____

4. In larger cities these come out every day. It can have a few pages or many pages. It tells you what is happening in the world. What is it?

   ____

5. It can be large or small. It smells very good. It is green. It is very special and people like to decorate it at one time of the year. What is it?

   ____

6. It needs gas. It is very big. Its driver stops a lot at people's houses to pick up things. What is it?

   ____

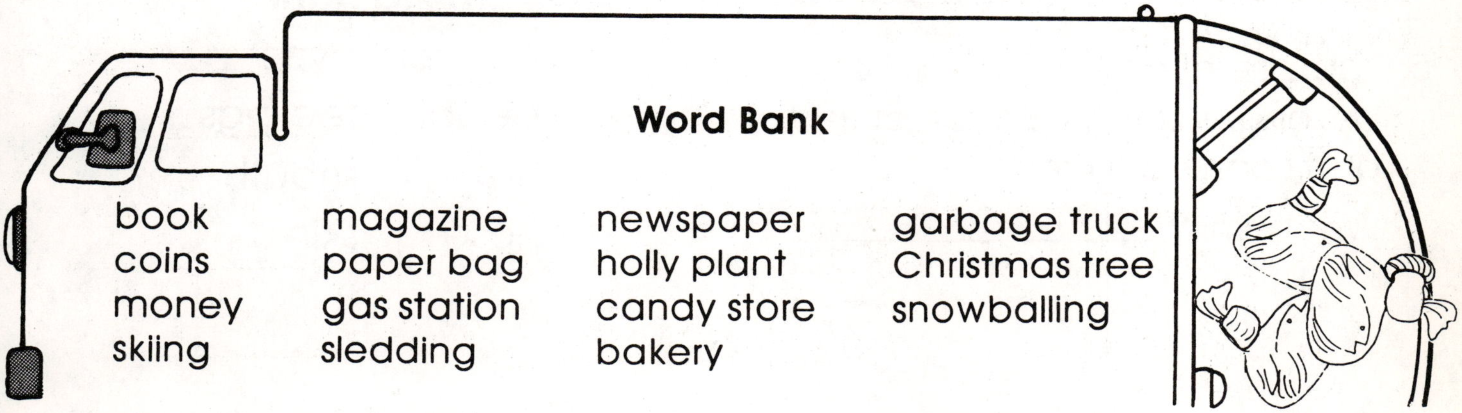

Word Bank

book	magazine	newspaper	garbage truck
coins	paper bag	holly plant	Christmas tree
money	gas station	candy store	snowballing
skiing	sledding	bakery	

Name ____________________

Reflect on the Riddles

Read each riddle. Find the answer in the Word Bank and write it on the line.

1. There are two of me. We can blink. We can see. We can wink. We can weep.

   What are we? ____________

2. There is one of me. I can sing. I can form words. I can eat. I can even blow a big bubble. I can eat ice cream, too.

   What am I? ____________

3. There is one of me. If I tickle, I will sneeze. I like to sniff flowers. I like the whiff of hot dogs, also.

   What am I? ____________

4. We need to bend and stretch. We need rest. We need to work and we need to play. We are all different.

   What are we? ____________

5. I can be almost any color. I can be long or short. I can be curled and I can be spiked.

   What am I? ____________

6. We can change. We can be happy or sad. We can be worried or excited. We can even be scared.

   What are we? ____________

7. I cover a lot. I keep muscles, bones, and blood inside your body. I let you know if it is hot or cold. I tell you if something is wet or dry.

   What am I? ____________

8. We all have feelings. We all have bodies. We all like to do many of the same things. But, we also are all very different.

   Who are we? ____________

Word Bank

bodies	eyes
people	feelings
hair	mouth
nose	skin

0-7682-3792-0 *Skills & Practice Gr. 2*

Name ____________________

It's a Fact!

Read each sentence. If it states a fact, write the word **fact** on the line. If it states an opinion, write the word **opinion** on the line.

1. An opera is a play that is sung. ____________
2. Many operas are terribly boring. ____________
3. Opera stars wear costumes on stage. ____________
4. People who have trunks filled with jewels are robbers. ____________
5. In many cities people dial 911 for emergency help. ____________
6. It is fun to check the mailbox every day. ____________
7. Seventy is a very old age. ____________
8. Second and third grade are about the same. ____________
9. Many operas are recorded on records. ____________
10. It is all right to snoop in other people's things if you have a reason. ____________

Name ____________________

Is This for Real?

Read each sentence. If it tells something that could really happen, draw a pumpkin on the line.

1. Spiders spin cobwebs. ____________
2. Robots are people. ____________
3. Cats have nine lives. ____________
4. Bats hang upside down. ____________
5. Ghosts haunt houses. ____________
6. There really are spooks. ____________
7. A mask can hide your face. ____________
8. Boys and girls can run in high heels. ____________
9. Owls have wings. ____________
10. Witches ride on brooms. ____________
11. Some people buy costumes. ____________
12. Pirates sail on ships. ____________

Name ______________________________

Elephant Dressing

Mrs. Marsh's kids need your help dressing. First color all of the elephants' skin gray. Then follow the directions to color their clothes.

Mollie
Jason
Gary
Megan
Robbie
Lisa

1. Color Robbie's pants brown and his shirt yellow. His shoes are brown.
2. Color Mollie's dress pink polka dots. Put a pink bow in her hair. Her shoes are black.
3. Color Lisa's dress blue, green and purple stripes. Her bow and shoes are purple.
4. Color Jason's jeans blue and his shirt red. His shoes are red.
5. Color Gary's pants orange. His shirt is orange and white stripes. His shoes are black.
6. Color Megan's dress red with pink flowers. Her shoes are red.

Name ______________________________

Top or Bottom?

Read and follow the directions.

1. Paste the dog in the middle of the bottom shelf.
2. Paste the cat on the right side of the bear.
3. Paste the rabbit on the left side of the top shelf.
4. Paste the elephant on the shelf below the rabbit.
5. Paste the frog on the left side of the bottom shelf.
6. Paste the horse on the middle shelf below the cat.
7. Paste the giraffe on the middle shelf above the dog.
8. Paste the turtle on the right side of the bottom shelf.

Cut _

elephant
cat
giraffe
frog
horse
dog
rabbit
turtle

0-7682-3792-0 *Skills & Practice Gr. 2*

Name ______________________

Where Is It?

Follow the directions. **Hint:** Read through all of the directions before starting.

1. Draw a brown mound in the middle of the box.
2. Draw a red car on top of the mound.
3. Draw apartments behind and to the left of the mound.
4. Draw a bird nest, with four blue eggs inside, on top of the car.
5. Draw three yellow birds flying away from the nest.
6. Draw two tin cans at the bottom of the mound.
7. Put an **X** on one of the tin cans.
8. Draw you and your friend looking at the car.

Name ______________________________

I'll Try Another Way

Help the little mole find his way to Percy's hut. Read and follow the directions. Write each word that tells what blocks his path as he looks for the loose floorboard. Then draw a line to show where the mole traveled.

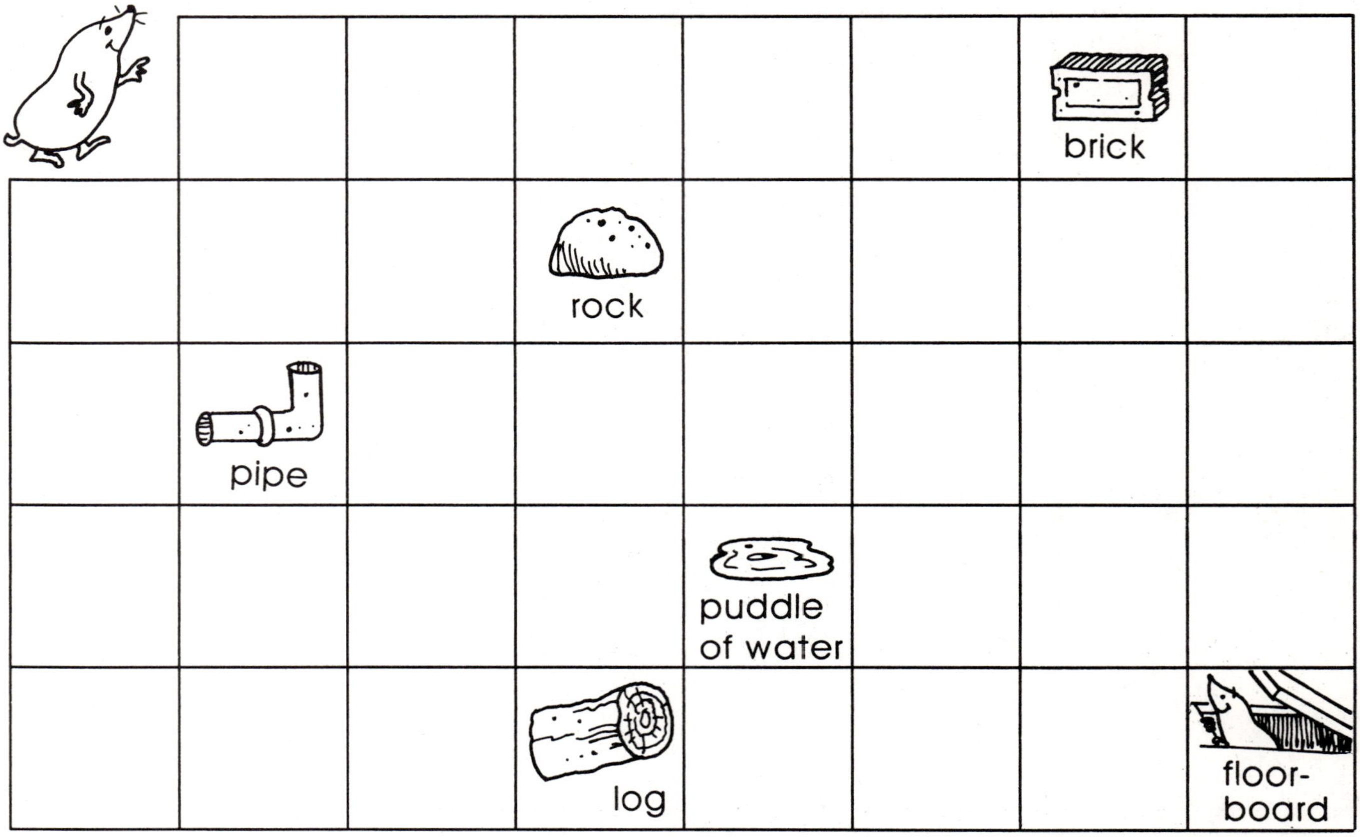

Go right 1 space, then down 1 space. There is a ______________.

Go left 1 space, down 3 spaces,
then right 2 spaces. There is a ______________________.

Go up 1 space, right 1 space, then up 1. There is a ______________.

Go left 1 space, up 2, then right 3 spaces. There is a ______________.

Go down 1 space, right 2 spaces,
down 2, then left 2 spaces. There is a ______________.

Go down 1 space, then right 1 space. Hooray! It's the ______________.

Name ______________________

What Did I Say?

Unscramble the words in each  .  each sentence on the line.

in
the I'm
woods
hiking

birthday
my
is friend's
Today

solve
this
I
mystery
will

my
bee
stung
The finger

nurse
enjoy
a
being
I

Name ____________________

The One in the Middle

Print the words in order to make a sentence. The word in the middle is there to help you. Print the sentences.

1. good Dissel jumper Freddy a
   ____________________ was ____________________
2. was Gumber teacher Ms.
   ____________________ Freddy's ____________________
3. and one sister had Freddy one
   ____________________ brother ____________________
4. Freddy play going in was to a
   ____________________ be ____________________
5. green They face on painted his
   ____________________ dots ____________________
6. break Gumber to a told leg Ms.
   ____________________ Freddy ____________________

Now color this picture.

Name ______________________

What Do I Do First?

Look at the pictures. Number them in the correct order. Then read and number the sentences in the correct order.

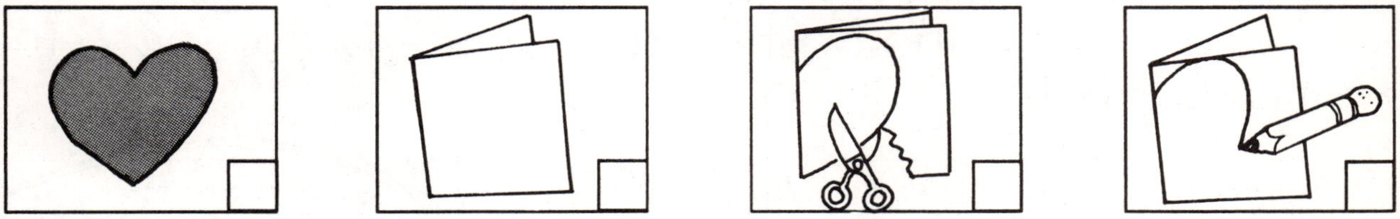

___ Cut along the line.
___ Fold a piece of paper in half.
___ Draw one half of a heart on the paper.
___ Open the heart.

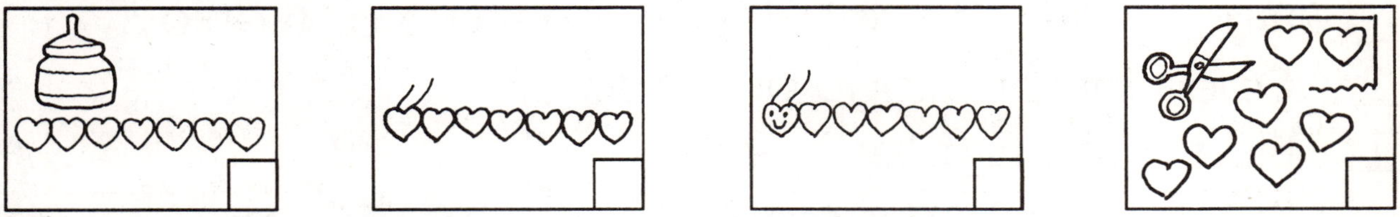

___ Draw two antennas on the first heart.
___ Paste the hearts in a line.
___ Then draw two eyes and a mouth on the first heart.
___ Cut out seven small hearts.

What did you make? ______________________

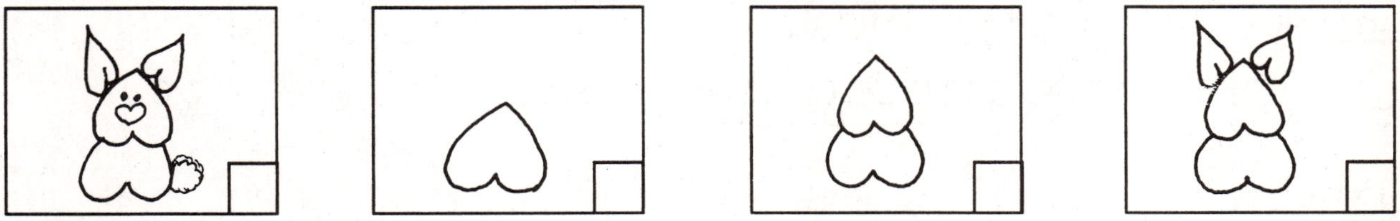

___ Draw two eyes and a nose. Paste a cotton ball on the big heart.
___ Paste a big heart upside down on a piece of paper.
___ Glue a smaller heart upside down on top of the big heart.
___ Paste two long skinny hearts upside down on the smaller heart.

What did you make? ______________________

Name ______________________

Terrific Toast

Lionel said he made the best toast in the world! Number the sentences to show the best order to make terrific toast. The first two are done.

____ Close the jar of jam.
____ Close the package of bread.
____ Push down on the toaster button.
____ Put butter on the hot toast.
____ Place the plate of toast on the table and enjoy.
__2__ Open the package of bread.
__1__ Plug in the toaster.
____ Put the toast on a plate.
____ Take out two slices of bread.
____ Place the two slices of bread in the toaster.
____ Open the jar of jam.
____ Wait for the toast to pop up.
____ Put jam on the toast.
____ Take the toast out of the toaster.

What do you like to put on your toast? ______________________

____

What is your favorite flavor of jam? ______________________

Name ____________________________

What's What?

Write the words from the Word Bank in the correct category.

Living	Non-Living
1. ______________	1. ______________
2. ______________	2. ______________
3. ______________	3. ______________
4. ______________	4. ______________
5. ______________	5. ______________
6. ______________	6. ______________

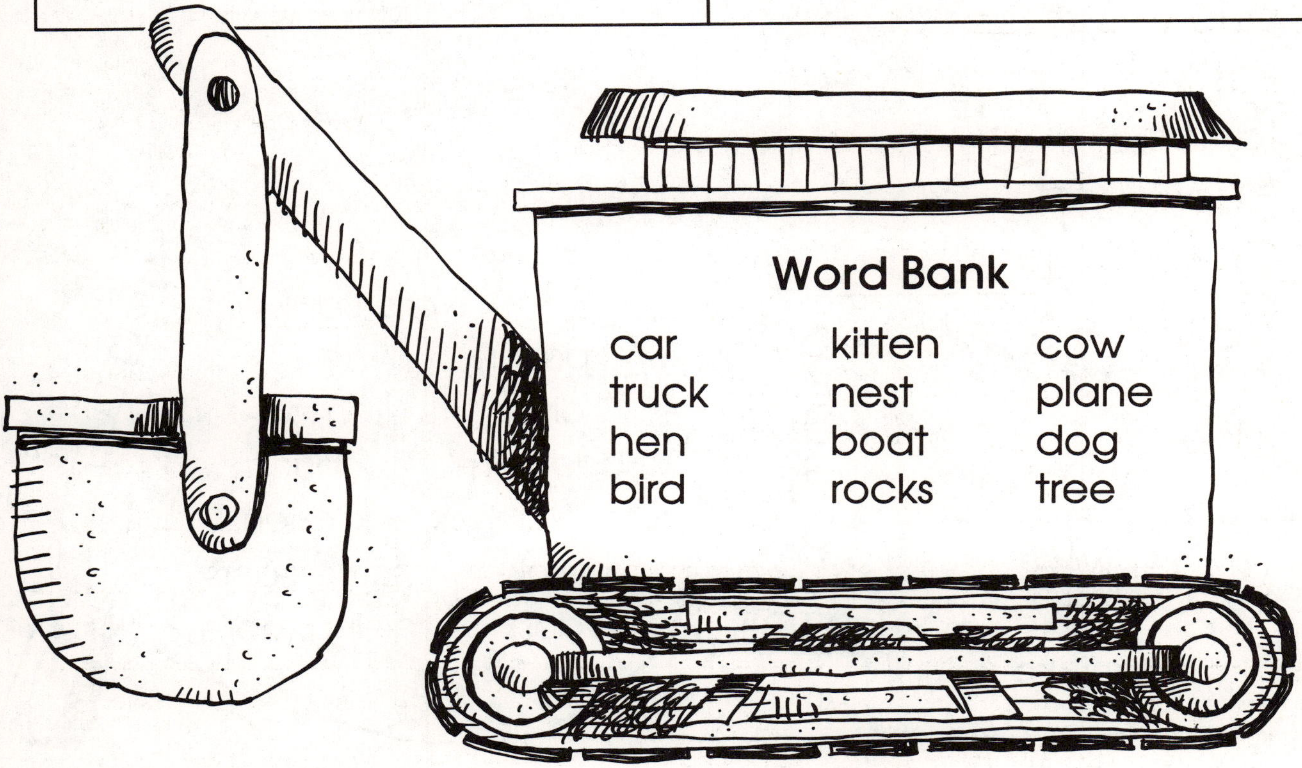

Word Bank

car	kitten	cow
truck	nest	plane
hen	boat	dog
bird	rocks	tree

Name ______________________

Tidying Up

Write the words from the Word Bank in the correct category.

Household Chores

Rooms in a House

Furniture

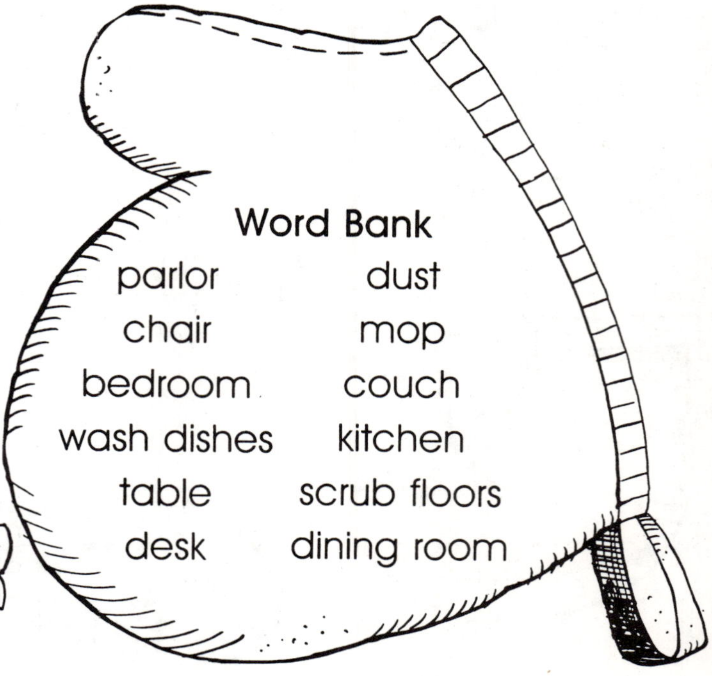
Word Bank
parlor
dust
chair
mop
bedroom
couch
wash dishes
kitchen
table
scrub floors
desk
dining room

Name ____________________

Cookie Jar

Read the categories on the jars. Cut and paste the cookies in the correct jar.

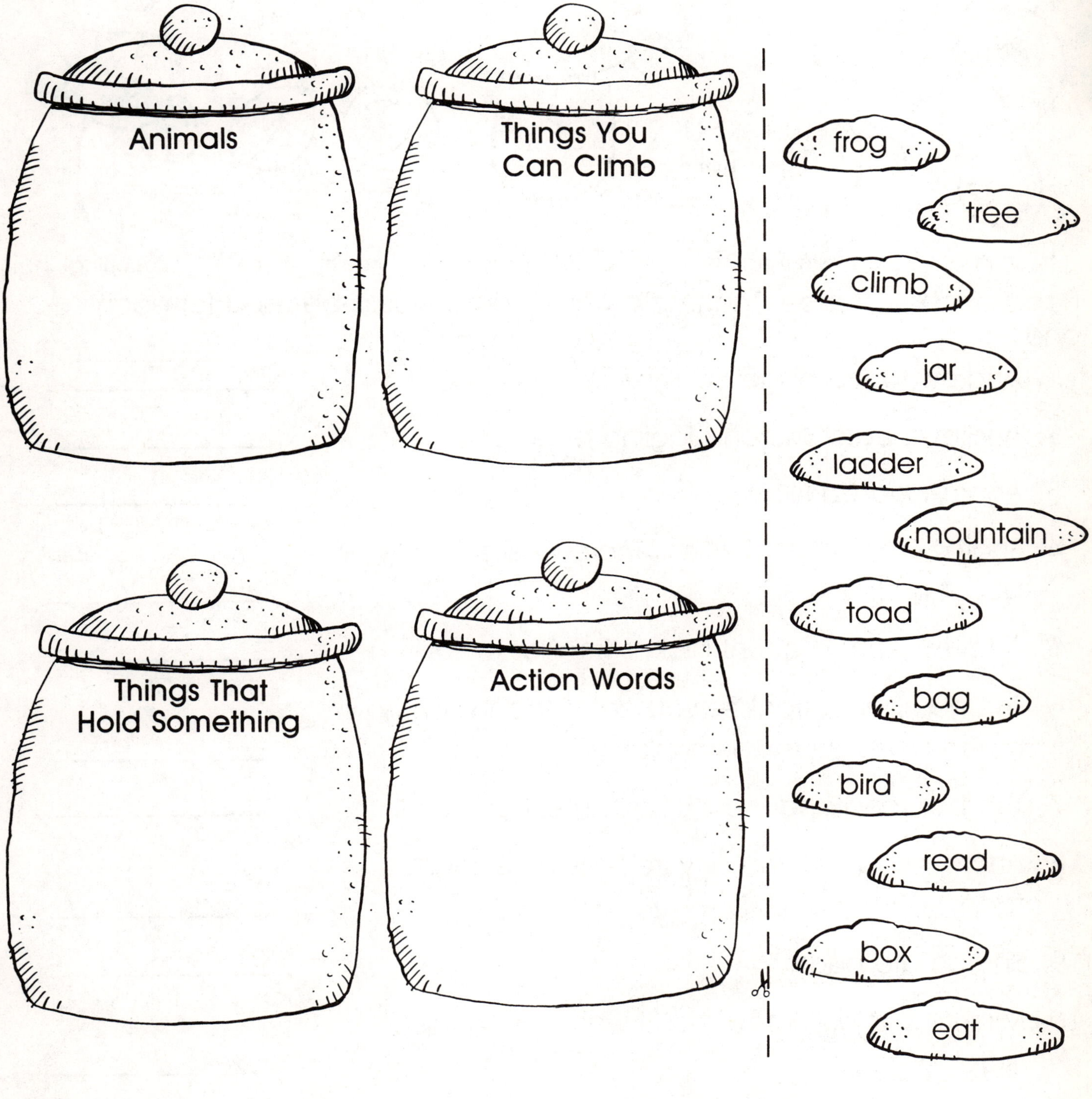
Animals
Things You Can Climb
Things That Hold Something
Action Words
frog
tree
climb
jar
ladder
mountain
toad
bag
bird
read
box
eat

Name ____________________

Sense-ational!

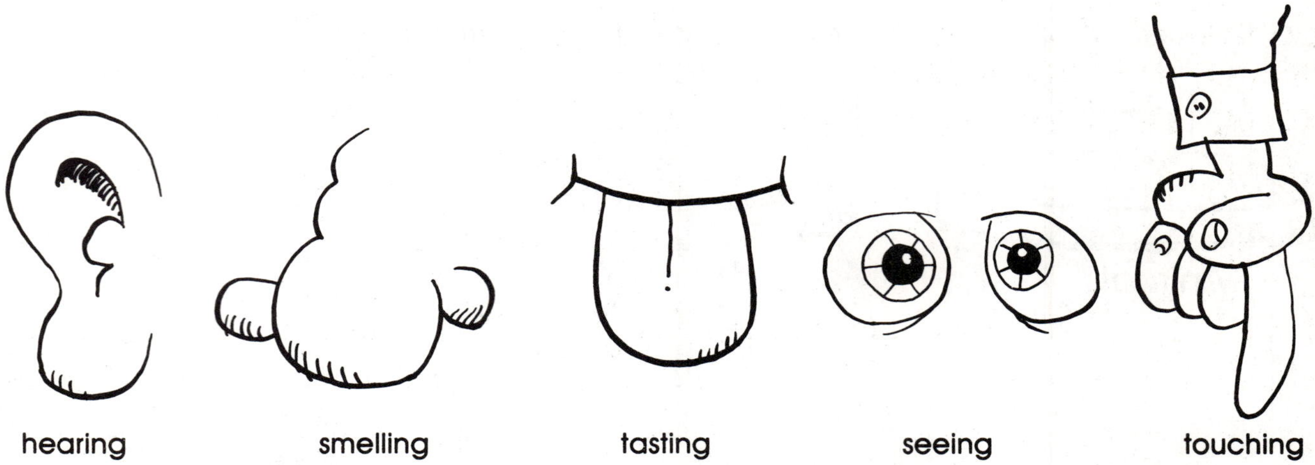
hearing
smelling
tasting
seeing
touching

Read each sentence. Then write which sense would be used for each one.

1. Andrew found page 64 in his reading book. ____________
2. Andrew heard Sharon giggling at him. ____________
3. Andrew poked Nicky. ____________
4. Sharon was listening when Andrew asked Nicky about his freckles. ____________
5. Andrew liked to count Nicky's freckles. ____________
6. The number of freckles you get depends on how much of the juice you drink. ____________
7. The bell rang and the students lined up. ____________
8. Andrew couldn't find any freckles on Sharon's face. ____________
9. Sharon ate bugs. ____________
10. Miss Kelly told Andrew that it was time for his reading group. ____________

Name ______________________

What's Going On?

Look at the pictures. Find the sentence in the Word Bank that explains each one. Write it on the lines.

____

____

____

____

____

____

____

____

Word Bank

The team was treated to hot dogs after their win.

They won the big Thanksgiving game.

Coach Swamp made them practice hard.

The team had lost every game.

Name ______________________

Just Rolling Along!

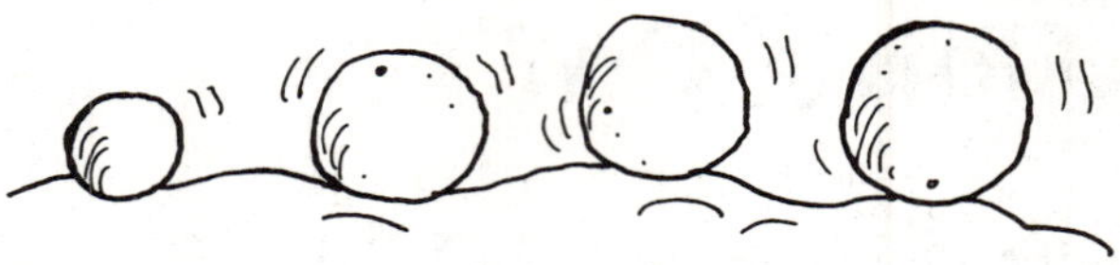

Help Emmett roll the snowball down the hill. Read the clues. Then find the words in the Word Bank and write them in the correct spaces. **Hint:** The last letter of each answer is the first letter of the next answer.

1. Boasting
2. Very, very good
3. Many moving cars and trucks
4. A little cold
5. Paid attention
6. Twice an amount
7. Comes after seventh
8. One of two equal parts
9. Very well-known
10. Not crooked

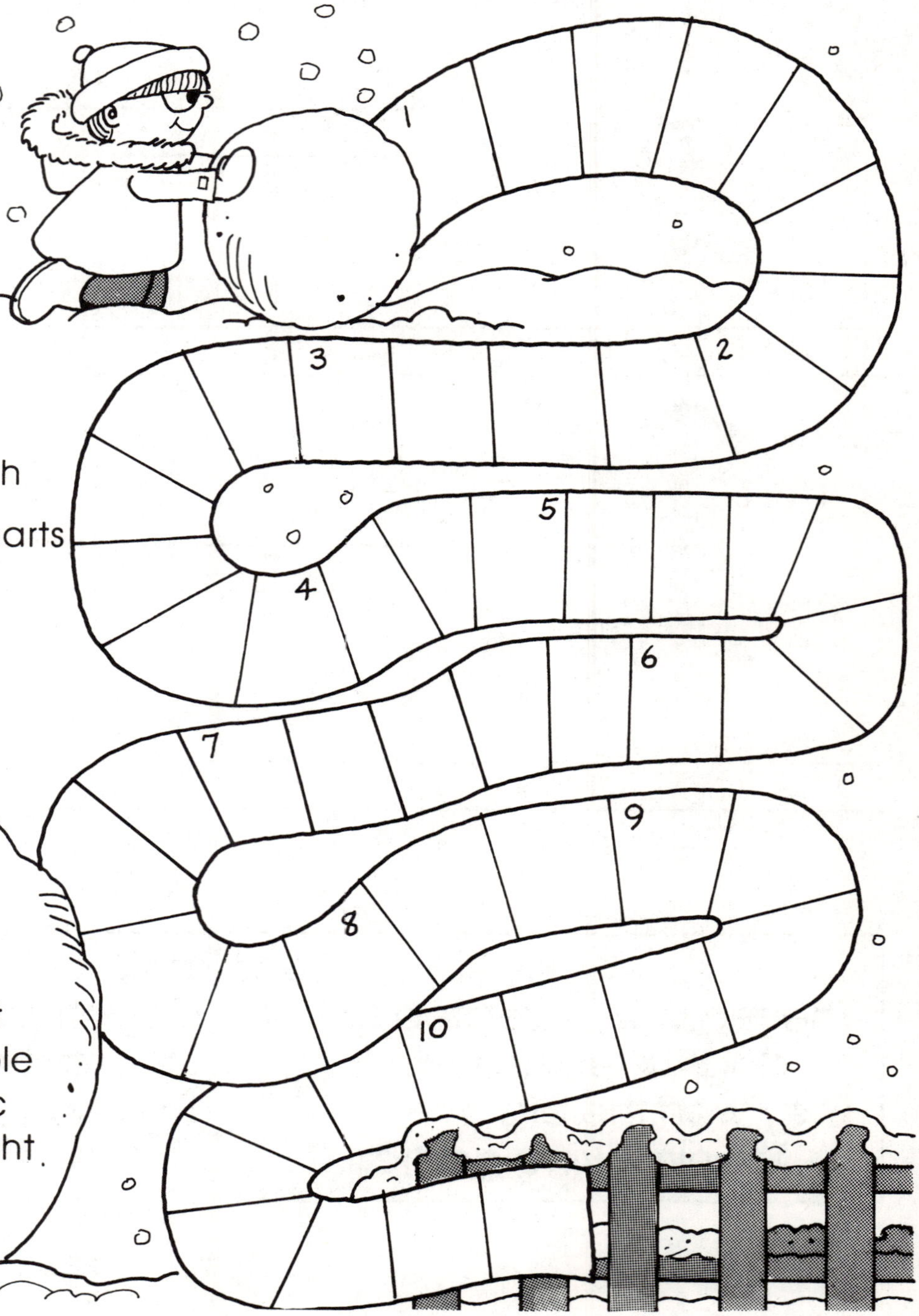

Word Bank

listened	half
bragging	great
cool	double
famous	traffic
eighth	straight

Name ______________________________

A-maze-ing

Draw a line through the maze in the order of the clues to help baby bird find his way back to his nest.

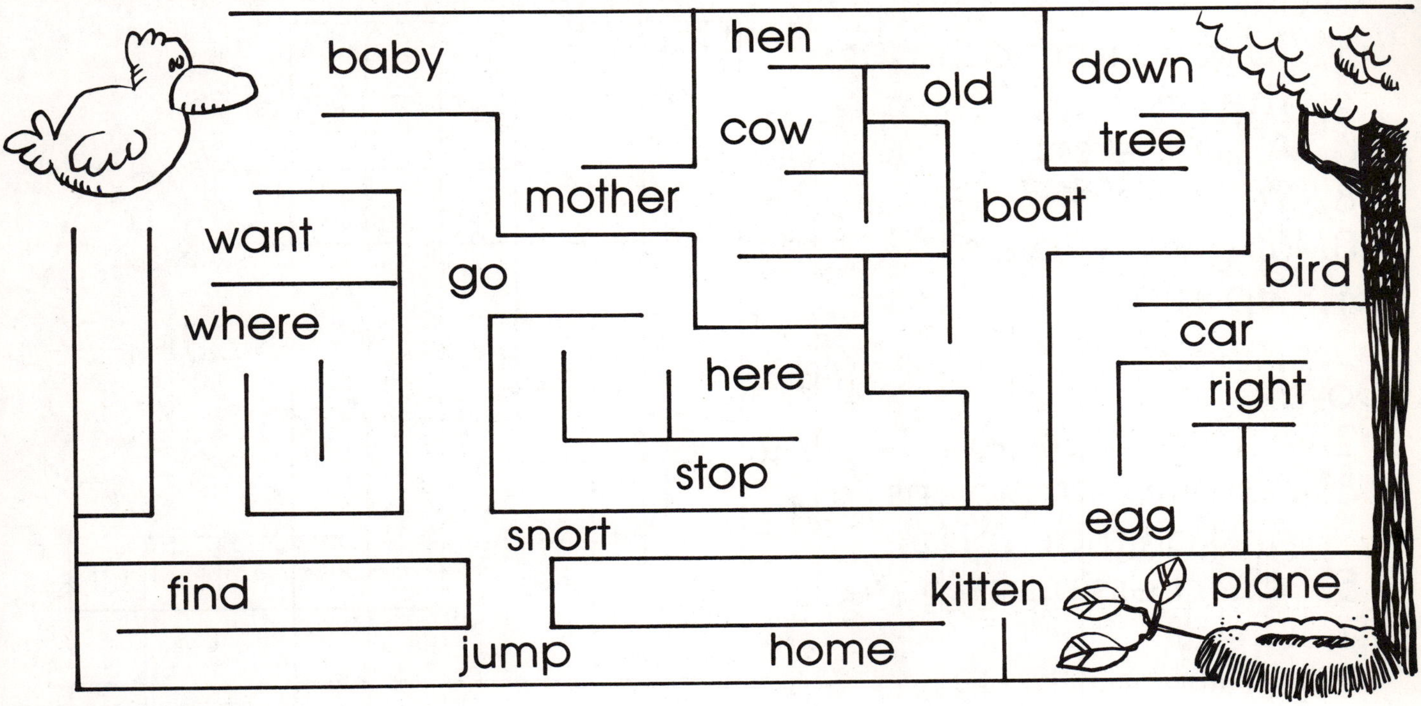

Clues

1. A very young child
2. Opposite of father
3. A large farm animal
4. A bird that lives on a farm
5. Opposite of new
6. Something that can float
7. A very large plant
8. Opposite of up
9. An animal that can fly
10. Something you can drive
11. Opposite of left
12. A bird hatches out of it
13. A sound
14. To leap
15. Your house
16. A baby cat
17. A machine that flies

Name ______________________

Circus Sights

Find the answers to the puzzle in the Word Bank.

Across
1. To save from danger
4. The last act
6. A silly person
8. Your mistake
10. To give an order
11. A poster

Down
2. A large weapon
3. A show with clowns and animal acts
5. You dress up in these
7. Great
9. A person who trains animals
11. A trick

1
2
3
4
5
6
7
8
9
10
11

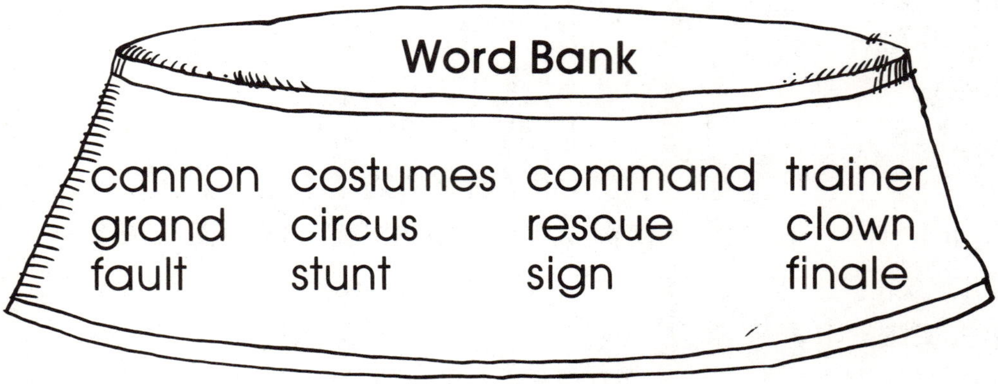
Word Bank
cannon
costumes
command
trainer
grand
circus
rescue
clown
fault
stunt
sign
finale

Name ____________________

Hidden Mystery

Read the clues. Find the matching words in the Word Bank and write them on the lines. Then find each two-letter mystery word by circling the letters that are the same in each set of matching words. Write each mystery word on a magnifying glass.

1. Something you put on a hot dog ____________
2. Outside part of bread ____________
3. Dance or sing to . . . ____________
4. Someone who might be guilty ____________

The hidden mystery word is 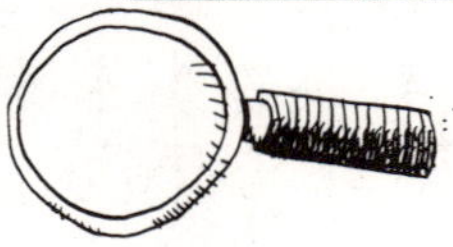

1. Words you can sing ____________
2. Not weak ____________
3. A small rock ____________
4. A round fastener ____________

The hidden mystery word is 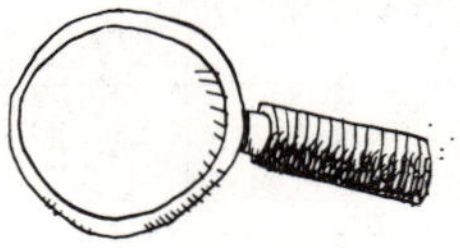

1. A note asking you to a party ____________
2. Start ____________
3. The meal you eat at night ____________
4. A part of a fish ____________

The hidden mystery word is 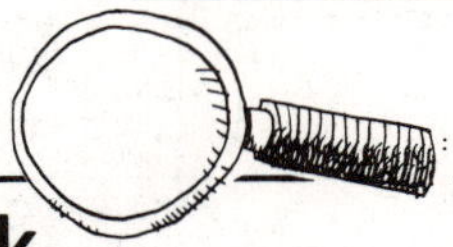

Word Bank

strong	dinner	fin	stone
invitation	begin	crust	song
button	music	mustard	suspect

Name ______________________

We're Just Hopping!

Find and circle the words in the puzzle.
Look → and ↓ .

b	c											k	l	
n	o	w									g	m		
d		e	d							f	i	n		
		g	l	o	a	d	h	o	i	i	e			
			f	p	o	s	s	u	m	e				
			l	e	f	t	f	a	p	l	y			
	c	a	r	t	s	g	p	e	y	d	h	r		
	a	n	i	m	a	l	s	z	k	s	x	p	y	
d	m	o	u	n	t	a	i	n	s	a	t	j	m	
r	q	o	t	m	k	c	l	b	o	w	p	a	o	i
u	b	a	s	k	e	t	t	f	h	l	a	o	u	h
l	a	d	y	b	u	g	d	a	r	e	r	a	s	t
w	o	o	d	s	n	s	g	r	p	a	a	e	e	
	v	w	a	k	e	s	s	m	y	v	d	v	n	
		a	e	h	e		a	o	a	e	e	v		

mouse	mountains	load	parade
basket	ladybug	carts	possum
leave	animals	left	wakes
farm	fields	now	woods

0-7682-3792-0 *Skills & Practice Gr. 2*

Name ______________________

Lazy One Liners

Use your laziest imagination to finish these lazy lines. An example would be, "The lion was so lazy that . . . he made his mate roar for him." Choose three of your best one liners and illustrate them on another paper.

1. The doctor was so lazy that ______________________
2. The baker was so lazy that ______________________
3. The teacher was so lazy that ______________________
4. The fireman was so lazy that ______________________
5. The dentist was so lazy that ______________________
6. The truck driver was so lazy that ______________________
7. The vet was so lazy that ______________________
8. The plumber was so lazy that ______________________
9. The house builder was so lazy that ______________________
10. The principal was so lazy that ______________________
11. The astronaut was so lazy that ______________________
12. The football player was so lazy that ______________________
13. The zookeeper was so lazy that ______________________
14. The TV repairman was so lazy that ______________________
15. The traffic cop was so lazy that ______________________

Name ______________________

A Story for the People

Look carefully at the picture on the buckskin. Write a story on the lines to tell what is happening in the picture.

Name ______________________

Using Descriptive Language

Stories are always more exciting when you can picture them happening in your mind. Descriptive words help make the story imaginable. Use these categories to think of words that describe a walk along the beach. Pretend you are barefoot walking close to the water. With a partner, write three words in each area. Then, use all the words in a story.

What I smell:
1. ______________
2. ______________
3. ______________

What I taste:
1. ______________
2. ______________
3. ______________

What I hear:
1. ______________
2. ______________
3. ______________

What I see:
1. ______________
2. ______________
3. ______________

What I feel on my feet:
1. ______________
2. ______________
3. ______________

My Walk Along the Beach

____

____

____

____

____

____

____

____

Name ______________________

Writing Haiku Poetry

Haiku poetry is originally from the country of Japan. It is a very simple form of poetry and does not have to rhyme.

Example	**Poem Pattern**
The polar bear cubs	5 syllables
learn to swim and dive for fish	7 syllables
in the cold, blue sea.	5 syllables

Write your own haiku poem by yourself or with a partner. Give it a title and illustrate it.

____
Title

____

____

____

By a Beary Special Poet ______________________
Name

Name ______________________

Ready to Mail

Read the envelope Tilly addressed to Mr. Bunny.

tilly mole
102 garden road
forest maine 25136

mr bunny
523 sweet potato lane
forest maine 25136

Address the envelope correctly. Be sure to use capital letters, periods and commas where they belong.

Draw and color a stamp on the envelope.

Name ______________________

Write, Please

Read the thank you letter Louis wrote to his Uncle McAllister.

october 5 1990

dear uncle mcallister

thank you for the tadpole i named him alphonse he likes to eat cheeseburgers this is the best gift you ever sent me

thank you again

love

louis

Write the letter correctly. Be sure to use capital letters, periods and commas where they belong.

Name ______________________

Which Book?

Read the questions. Write which book you would use to find the answer.

Dictionary **Encyclopedia** **Telephone Book**

1. What makes rain? ______________________
2. What does purify mean? ______________________
3. When does the waterworks plant allow visitors? ______________________
4. Where would you find glaciers? ______________________
5. What is a water cycle? ______________________
6. What are impurities? ______________________
7. Where is your town's waterworks located? ______________________
8. What chemicals are put into the water on its way to the storage tank? ______________________
9. How do you pronounce the word evaporation? ______________________
10. What time does the waterworks open? ______________________
11. How do you pronounce the word reservoir? ______________________
12. How are clouds formed? ______________________

Name ______________________

Let's Get Cooking!

Read each phrase.
If you would need a **dictionary** to find the information, color the space **yellow**.
If you would need an **encyclopedia** to find the information, color the space **white**.
If you would need a **cookbook** to find the information, color the space **brown**.

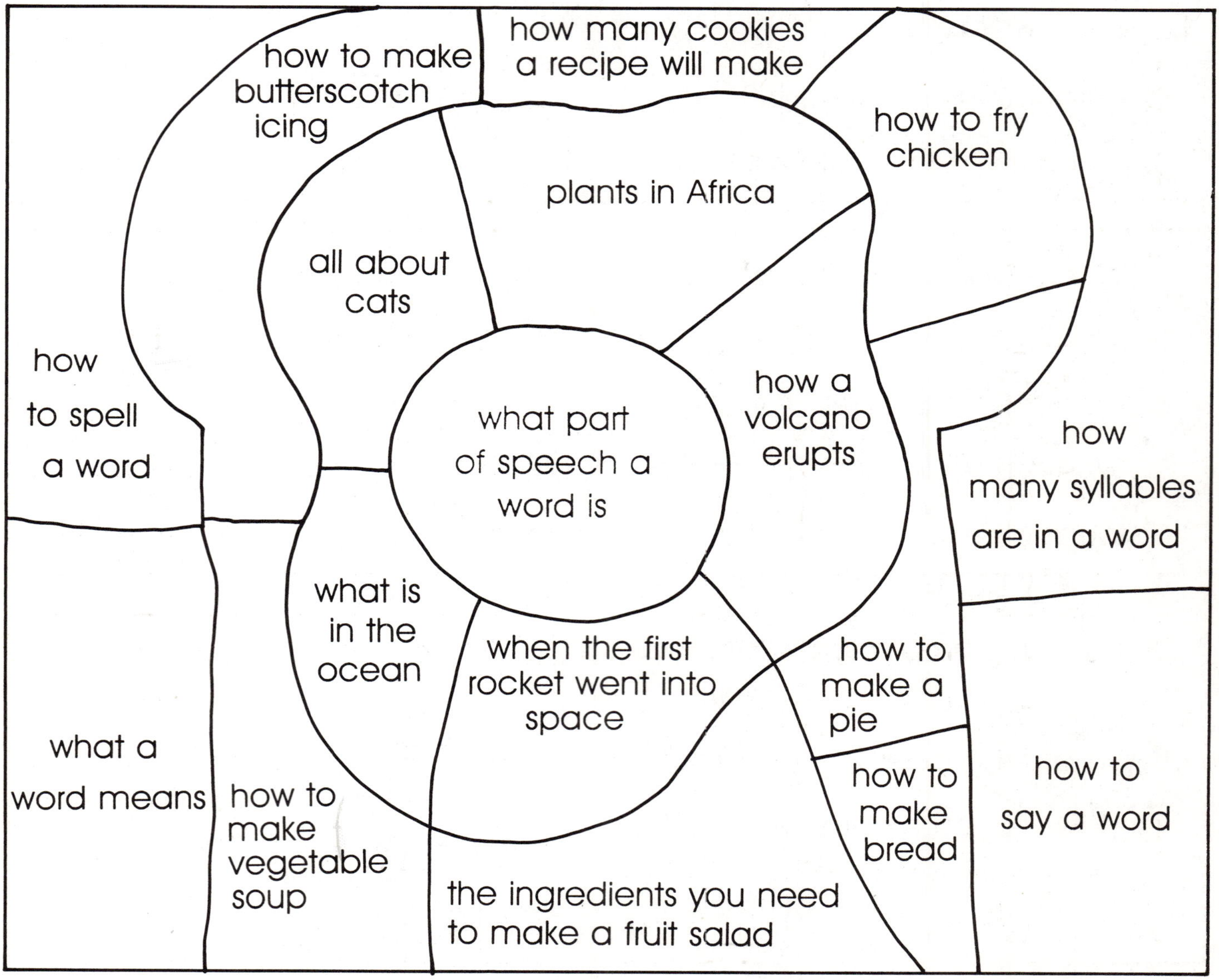
how to make butterscotch icing
how many cookies a recipe will make
how to fry chicken
plants in Africa
all about cats
how to spell a word
what part of speech a word is
how a volcano erupts
how many syllables are in a word
what is in the ocean
when the first rocket went into space
how to make a pie
what a word means
how to make vegetable soup
how to make bread
how to say a word
the ingredients you need to make a fruit salad

Name ______________________________

Pottery Patterns

Before beginning a project, an artist who makes pottery must think about how the piece will be used, what type of clay to use, and what color and patterns to use.

This talented artist does something special with all the pottery he makes. Here are some examples of his pottery.

The pottery here is not his. Something is different.

Circle the pottery below that the talented artist might have made.

What is special about his pottery? ______________________________

Name ___________________________

Dressing the Part

People who act in plays are called actors and actresses. For each play, costumes are chosen that make the characters in the story seem more realistic.

Below is the inside of a costume closet.

Pretend that you want to act in some silly plays. Look at the titles of each play below. Write the names of the two costumes you would combine to fit the main character of each play.

1. "The Strong, Flying Ape" ________________ ________________
2. "The Invisible Man on His Horse" ________________ ________________
3. "The Cat Who Squeaked" ________________ ________________
4. "Her Royal Highness Barks up the Wrong Tree"
   ________________ ________________
5. "Flying Animal-like Man Saves Building from Fire" ________________
   ____

Name ______________________

Everyone Is Welcome

Cut out the pictures of the people at the bottom of the page. Read the clues carefully. Paste the people where they belong at the table.

1. Robert already has his hamburger.
2. Kioko will pass the plate of hamburgers to the others at the table.
3. Mike asks Teresa to please pass the pitcher of lemonade so that he may fill his glass.
4. Pablo likes sitting between his friends Kioko and Teresa.
5. Sue likes hot dogs better than hamburgers.

Cut -

Pablo
Kioko
Robert
Sue
Mike
Teresa

Name ______________________________

Comparing the Seasons

Each of the four seasons (winter, spring, summer, autumn) has certain characteristics. Choose two of the seasons and write their names on the lines above each shape below. Then, complete the other lines with words that describe the season. In the center area, write words that describe both seasons. This is called a Venn diagram.

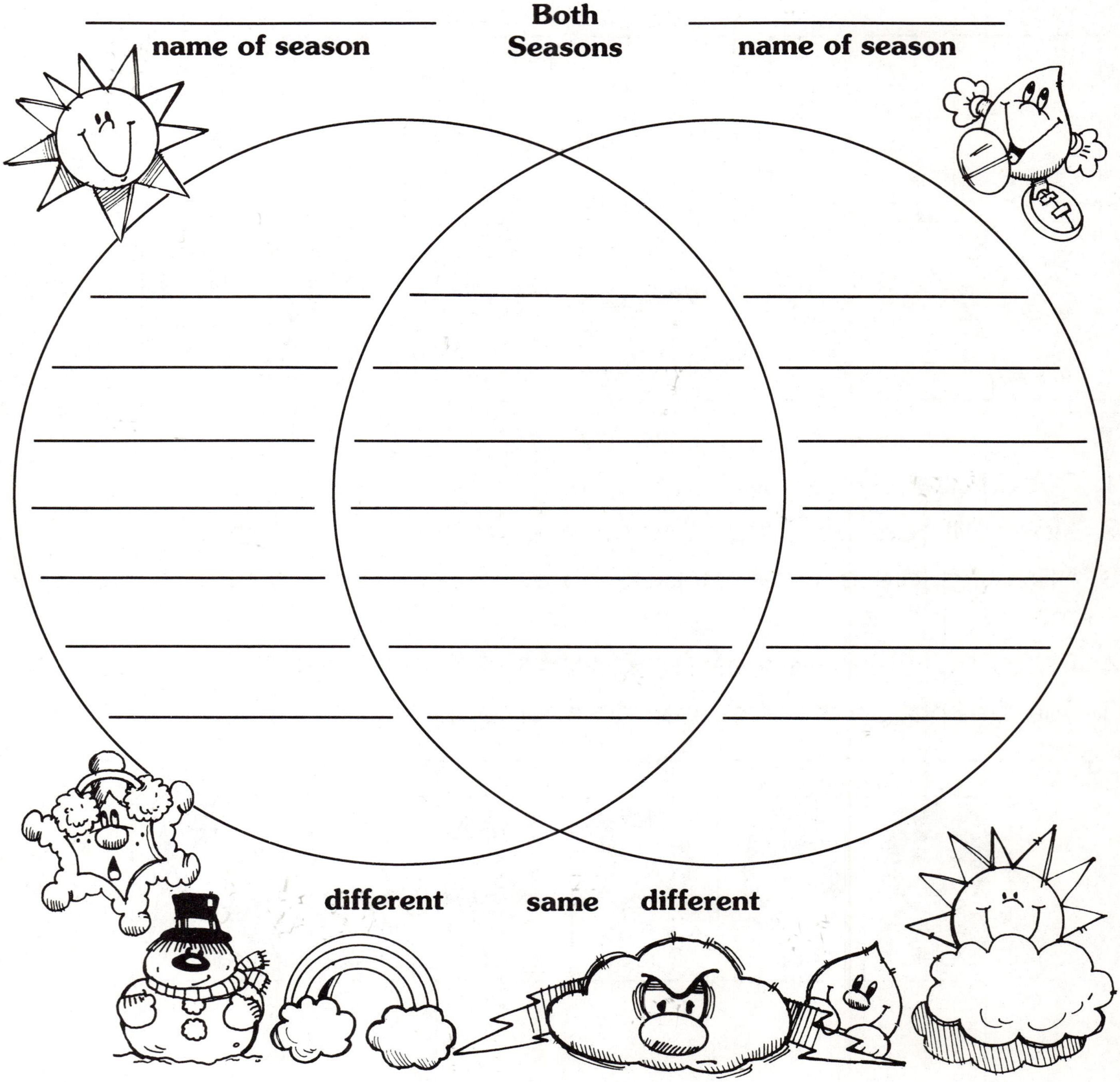
name of season
Both Seasons
name of season
different
same
different

Name ____________________

Just Napping

Count. Write the correct number of cats in the box on each cat bed.

MATH

Name ____________________

Plump Piglets

Pigs like to eat corn. These little pigs just ate lunch.

Read the clues to find out how many ears of corn each pig ate. Write the number on the line below each pig.

I ate the number that comes before 26.
Patsy
25
I ate the number that comes between 87 and 89.
Horace
88
I ate the number that comes after 92.
Portly
93
I ate the number that comes before 57.
Hilda
56
I ate the number that comes between 39 and 41.
Pesky
40

Who ate the most and was really piggy? ____________________

Who ate the least? Portly ____________________

Patsy

Name ____________________

Unpack the Teddy Bears

Cut out the bears at the bottom of the page. Paste them where they belong in numbered order.

Cut ✂ -

Name ______________________

Air Bear Addition

Help Buddy off the ground. Solve the problems. Then color the clouds with sums of 9 to find the right path.

$5 + 5$

$7 + 4$

$3 + 7$

$4 + 4$

$8 + 1$

$6 + 3$

$6 + 4$

$2 + 7$

$2 + 5$

$10 + 1$

$5 + 4$

$6 + 5$

$3 + 4$

$3 + 2$

$2 + 5$

$4 + 5$

$0 + 9$

$9 + 0$

$2 + 6$

$8 + 2$

$3 + 6$

Name ____________________

Math-Minded Mermaids

Each mermaid sits upon her own special rock.

Look at the number on each shell. Then look → and ↓ in the number boxes. Circle each pair of numbers that can be added together to equal the number in the shell the mermaid is holding.

7	5	3	6
9	6	8	6
3	9	1	8
10	2	11	4

1	9	6	3
8	0	4	7
5	9	5	2
3	2	7	5

10	7	8	3
5	4	4	8
6	3	6	5
2	9	3	8

3	7	9	1
10	5	5	9
0	8	6	4
8	2	3	7

Name Smelly Sophia

Domino Math

wrong

Write the number that tells how many dots are on the greater side of each domino. Then, "count on" to find the sum of both sides.

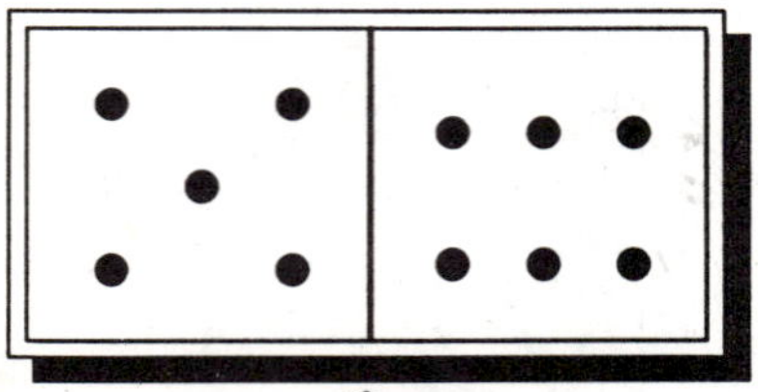

5

sum 6

11

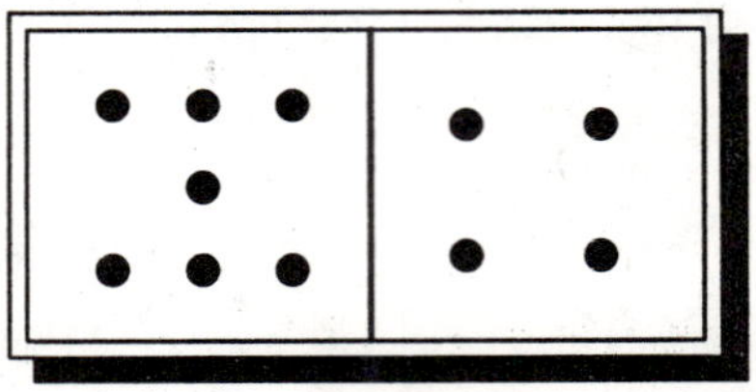

7

sum 4

11

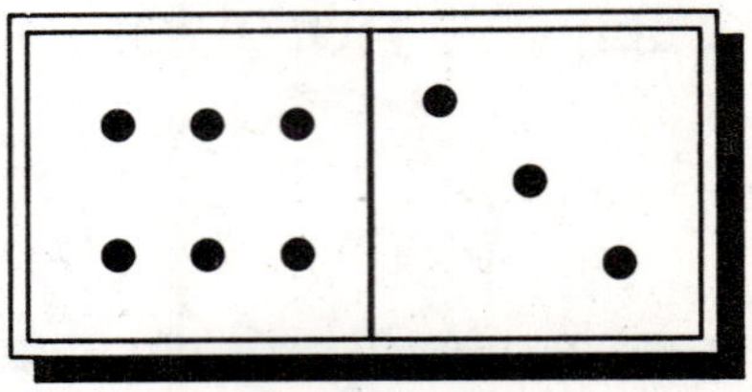

______

sum ______

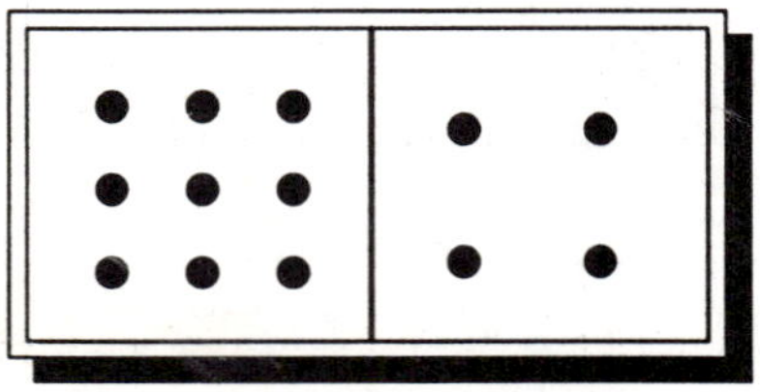

______

sum ______

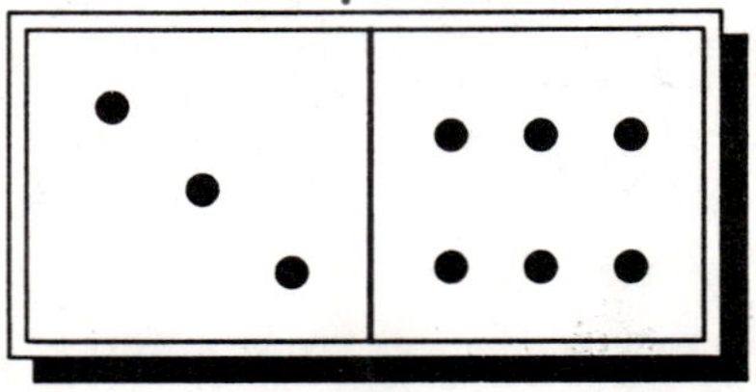

______

sum ______

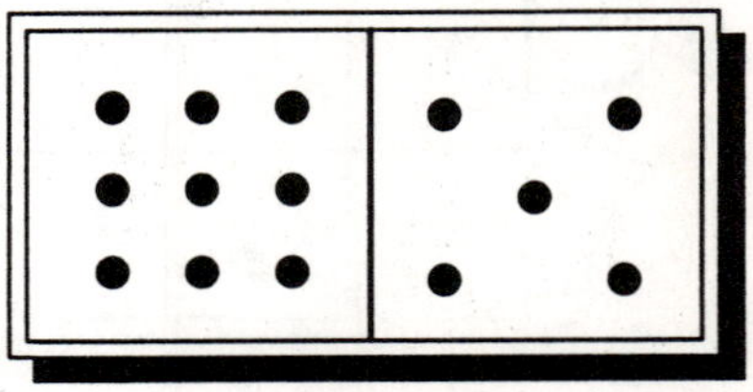

______

sum ______

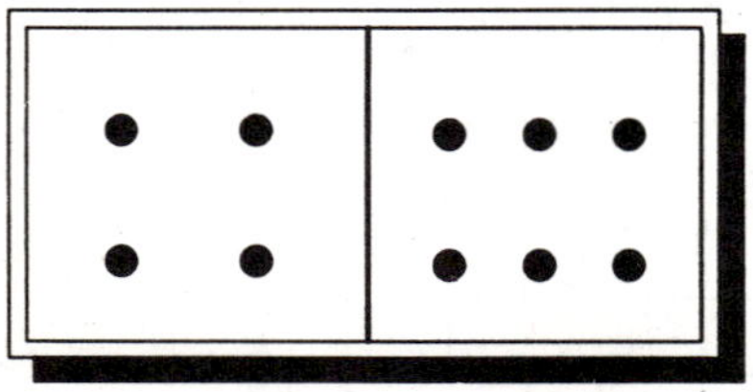

______

sum ______

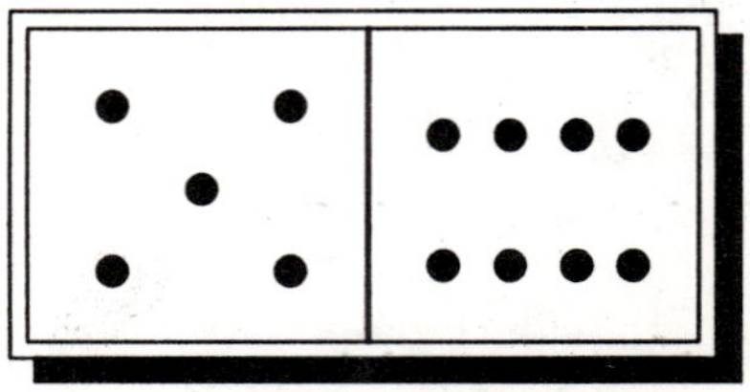

______

sum ______

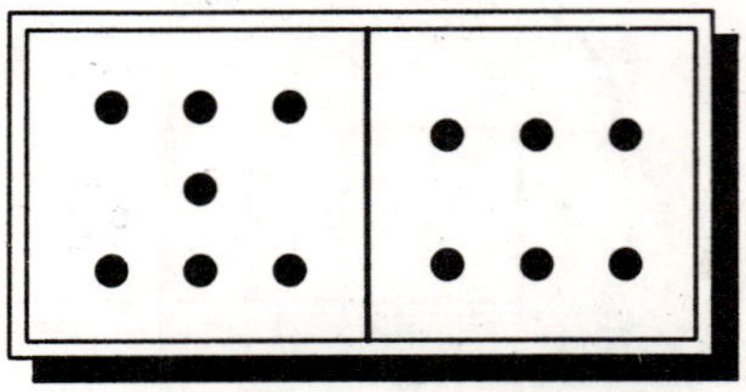

______

sum ______

0-7682-3792-0 *Skills & Practice Gr. 2*

Name ______________________

Ride the Rapids

Write each problem on the life jacket with the correct answer.

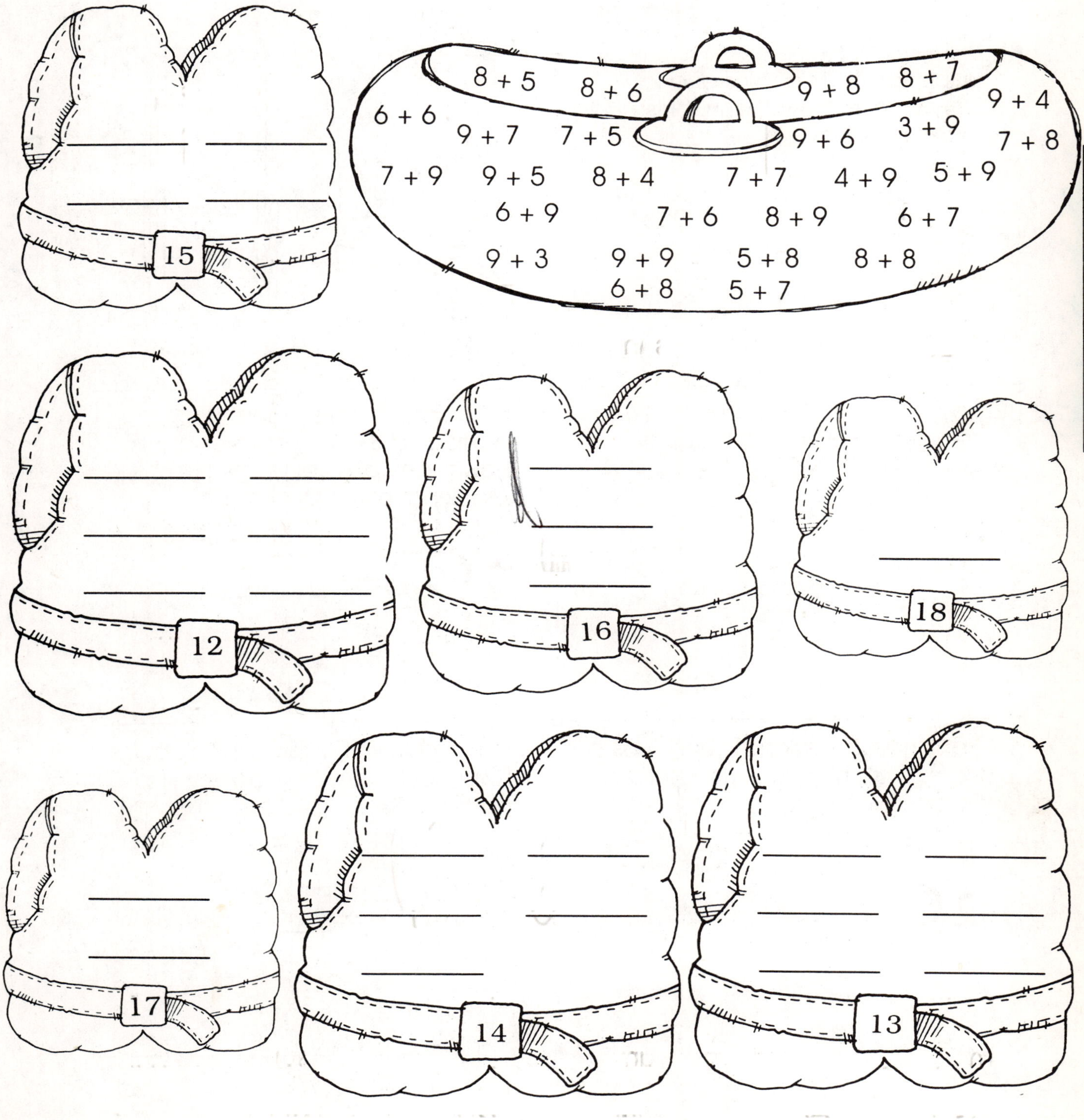
15
8 + 5
8 + 6
9 + 8
8 + 7
9 + 4
6 + 6
9 + 7
7 + 5
9 + 6
3 + 9
7 + 8
7 + 9
9 + 5
8 + 4
7 + 7
4 + 9
5 + 9
6 + 9
7 + 6
8 + 9
6 + 7
9 + 3
9 + 9
5 + 8
8 + 8
6 + 8
5 + 7
12
16
18
17
14
13

Name ______________________

Story Problems

The key words **in all** tell you to add. Circle the key words **in all** and solve the problems.

1. Jack has 4 white shirts and 2 yellow shirts. How many shirts does Jack have in all?

   4 ⊕ 2 = ______

2. Joan has 4 pink blouses and 6 red ones. How many blouses does Joan have in all?

   4 ○ 6 = ______

3. Mack has 3 pairs of summer pants and 8 pairs of winter pants. How many pairs of pants does Mack have in all?

   3 ○ 8 = ______

4. Betsy has 2 black skirts and 7 blue skirts. In all, how many skirts does Betsy have?

   2 ○ 7 = ______

5. Willis has 5 knit hats and 5 cloth hats. How many hats does Willis have in all?

   5 ○ 5 = ______

0-7682-3792-0 *Skills & Practice Gr. 2*

Name ______________________

Additional Story Problems

Circle the addition key words **in all** and solve the problems.

1. On the block where Cindy lives there are 7 brick houses and 5 stone houses. How many houses are there in all?

$7 + 5 = $ ______

2. One block from Cindy's house there are 7 white houses and 4 gray houses. How many houses are there in all?

3. Near Cindy's house there are 3 grocery stores and 5 discount stores. How many stores are there in all?

4. Children live in 8 of the two-story houses, and children live in 2 of the one-story houses. How many houses in all have children living in them?

5. In Cindy's neighborhood 4 students are in high school and 9 are in elementary school. In all, how many children are in school?

MATH

Name ______________________________

Problems in the Park

Circle the addition key words **in all** and solve the problems.

1. At the park there are 3 baseball games and 6 basketball games being played. How many games are being played in all?

2. In the park 9 mothers are pushing their babies in strollers, and 8 are carrying their babies in baskets. How many mothers in all have their babies with them in the park?

3. On one team there are 6 boys and 3 girls. How many team members are there in all?

4. At one time there were 8 men and 4 boys pitching horseshoes. In all, how many people were pitching horseshoes?

5. While playing basketball, 4 of the players were wearing gym shoes and 6 were not. How many basketball players were there in all?

0-7682-3792-0 *Skills & Practice Gr. 2*

Name ______________________________

Solving Stories

Write a number sentence to solve each problem.

1. Brad ate five slices of pizza. Todd ate three. How many slices of pizza did both boys eat?

2. Sam scored four points for the team. Dave scored eight points. How many points did Sam and Dave score?

3. Missy bought six dresses. Dot bought two. How many dresses did they buy in all?

4. Three bears are having a picnic. Two more bears join the fun. How many bears are having a picnic now?

5. Matt has a barn. In the barn are four horses, three cows and five pigs. How many animals are in the barn?

0-7682-3792-0 *Skills & Practice Gr. 2*

Name ____________________

Daisy Subtraction

Work problems.
Use code to color.

2—green	**7**—orange	**10**—pink
3—blue	**8**—red	**11**—red
4—yellow	**9**—purple	**12**—purple

5 – 2
6 – 3
13 – 1
12 – 2
14 – 11
13 – 3
9 – 6
15 – 12
15 – 3
14 – 2
14 – 4
10 – 7
15 – 6
12 – 1
12 – 4
14 – 7
14 – 3
12 – 3
15 – 5
15 – 8
13 – 5
11 – 3
10 – 6
13 – 2
13 – 4
15 – 11
11 – 4
13 – 6
15 – 4
14 – 5
11 – 9
15 – 7
12 – 5
14 – 6
13 – 11
8 – 6
9 – 7
15 – 13
14 – 12
5 – 3
4 – 2
6 – 4
7 – 5
10 – 8

Name ______________________

Pick a Picnic

Subtract. Write each answer. Then draw a line to show where three answers are the same in a row.

12 – 9 = ____	11 – 2 = ____	9 – 8 = ____
8 – 6 = ____	7 – 4 = ____	7 – 5 = ____
7 – 3 = ____	10 – 1 = ____	11 – 8 = ____

10 – 7 = ____	12 – 3 = ____	11 – 2 = ____
12 – 7 = ____	9 – 0 = ____	8 – 5 = ____
11 – 4 = ____	9 – 2 = ____	12 – 5 = ____

10 – 4 = ____	8 – 3 = ____	8 – 4 = ____
12 – 4 = ____	12 – 8 = ____	8 – 2 = ____
11 – 7 = ____	10 – 3 = ____	11 – 3 = ____

9 – 7 = ____	11 – 9 = ____	10 – 2 = ____
11 – 5 = ____	9 – 3 = ____	12 – 6 = ____
8 – 1 = ____	12 – 7 = ____	9 – 5 = ____

7 – 7 = ____	11 – 6 = ____	9 – 1 = ____
10 – 3 = ____	9 – 4 = ____	10 – 0 = ____
8 – 8 = ____	10 – 5 = ____	12 – 4 = ____

Name ______________________________

Connect the Facts

Subtract. Write the answer.

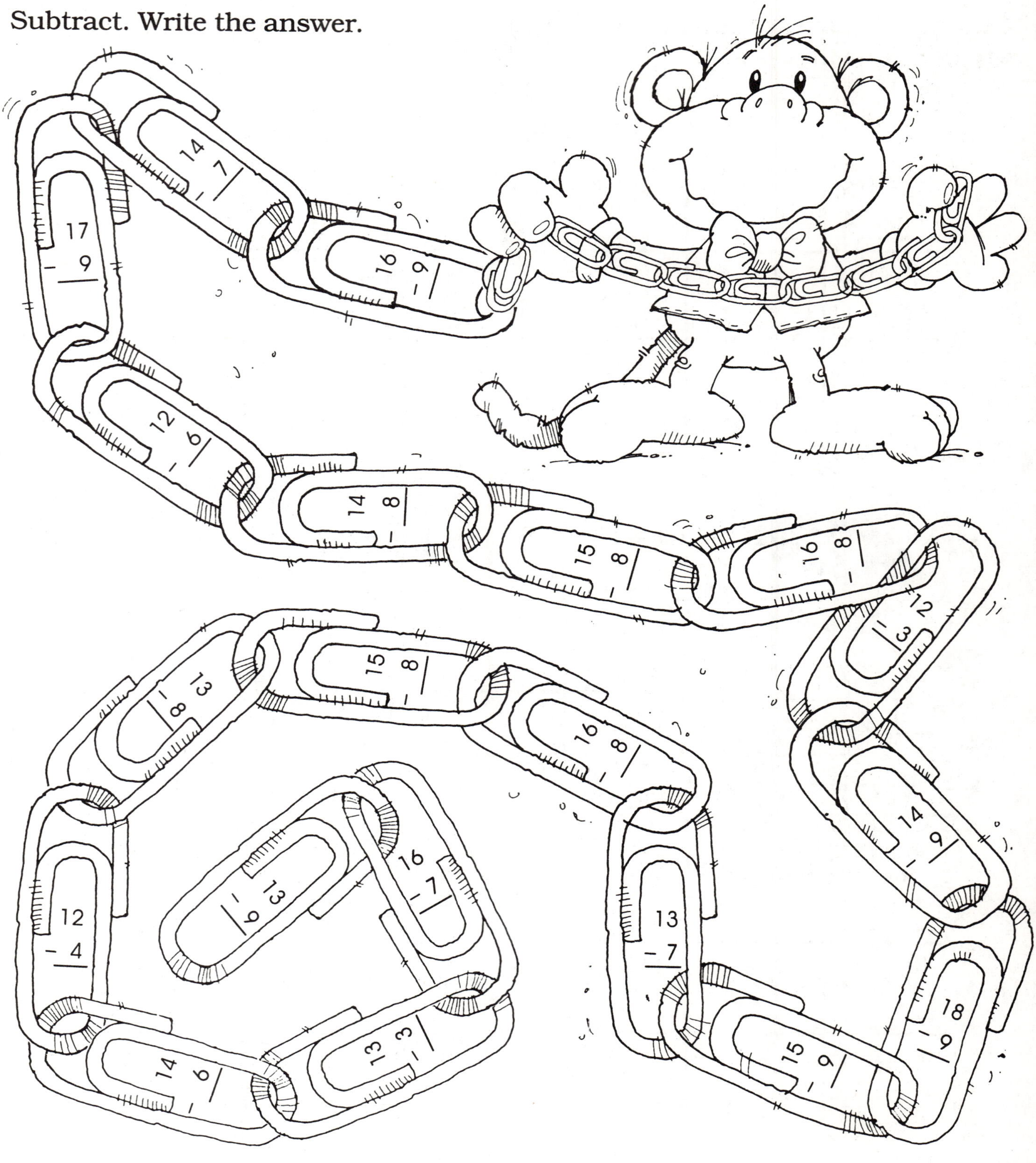
14 − 7
17 − 9
16 − 9
12 − 6
14 − 8
15 − 8
16 − 8
12 − 3
15 − 8
13 − 8
16 − 8
14 − 9
16 − 7
13 − 6
12 − 4
13 − 7
13 − 3
14 − 6
15 − 9
18 − 9

Name ______________________

How Many Animals Are Left?

The key word **left** tells you to subtract. Circle the key word **left** and solve the problems.

1. Bill had 10 kittens, but 4 of them ran away. How many kittens does he have left?

$10 - 4 =$ ______

2. There were 12 rabbits eating clover. Dogs chased 3 of them away. How many rabbits were left?

3. Bill saw 11 birds eating from the bird feeders in his back yard. A cat scared 7 of them away. How many birds were left at the feeders?

4. There were 14 frogs on the bank of the pond. Then 9 of them hopped into the water. How many frogs were left on the bank?

5. Bill counted 15 robins in his yard. Then 8 of the robins flew away. How many robins were left in the yard?

MATH

Name ______________________

Maggy at School

Circle the subtraction key word **left** and solve the problems.

1. In Maggy's classroom there are 12 girls. One day 4 of the girls went home with the flu. How many girls were left in school that day?

2. Maggy is in 10 different clubs. This week 5 of them will not meet. How many of Maggy's clubs are left to meet this week?

3. Maggy had 16 crayons. She broke 9 of them. How many crayons does Maggy have left?

4. There are 13 boys in Maggy's classroom. One morning 8 of the boys went to the gym. How many were left in the classroom?

5. One day 4 of the 13 boys were called in from the playground. How many of the boys were left on the playground?

0-7682-3792-0 *Skills & Practice Gr. 2*

Name ____________________

A Hidden Message

Add or subtract. Use the code to find out your new motto!

Code:

9	18	6	15	13	12	16	11	8	7	14	17
H	Y	D	E	V	T	S	O	A	M	N	I

9 + 8

16 - 7	14 - 6	8 + 5	6 + 9

14 - 7	9 + 9

17 - 8	15 - 7	9 + 5	13 - 7	8 + 8

4 + 7	6 + 8

12 - 5	17 - 9	6 + 6	15 - 6

MATH

0-7682-3792-0 *Skills & Practice Gr. 2*

Name ______________________

All Aboard!

Add or subtract. Match the related facts.

5 + 9 = 14 •	• 6 + 9 = ___
8 + 7 = ___ •	• 14 − 9 = 5
15 − 9 = ___ •	• 15 − 7 = ___
17 − 8 = ___ •	• 14 − 7 = ___
7 + 7 = ___ •	• 9 + 8 = ___

Add or subtract. Color spaces with answers greater than 12 brown. Color the rest green.

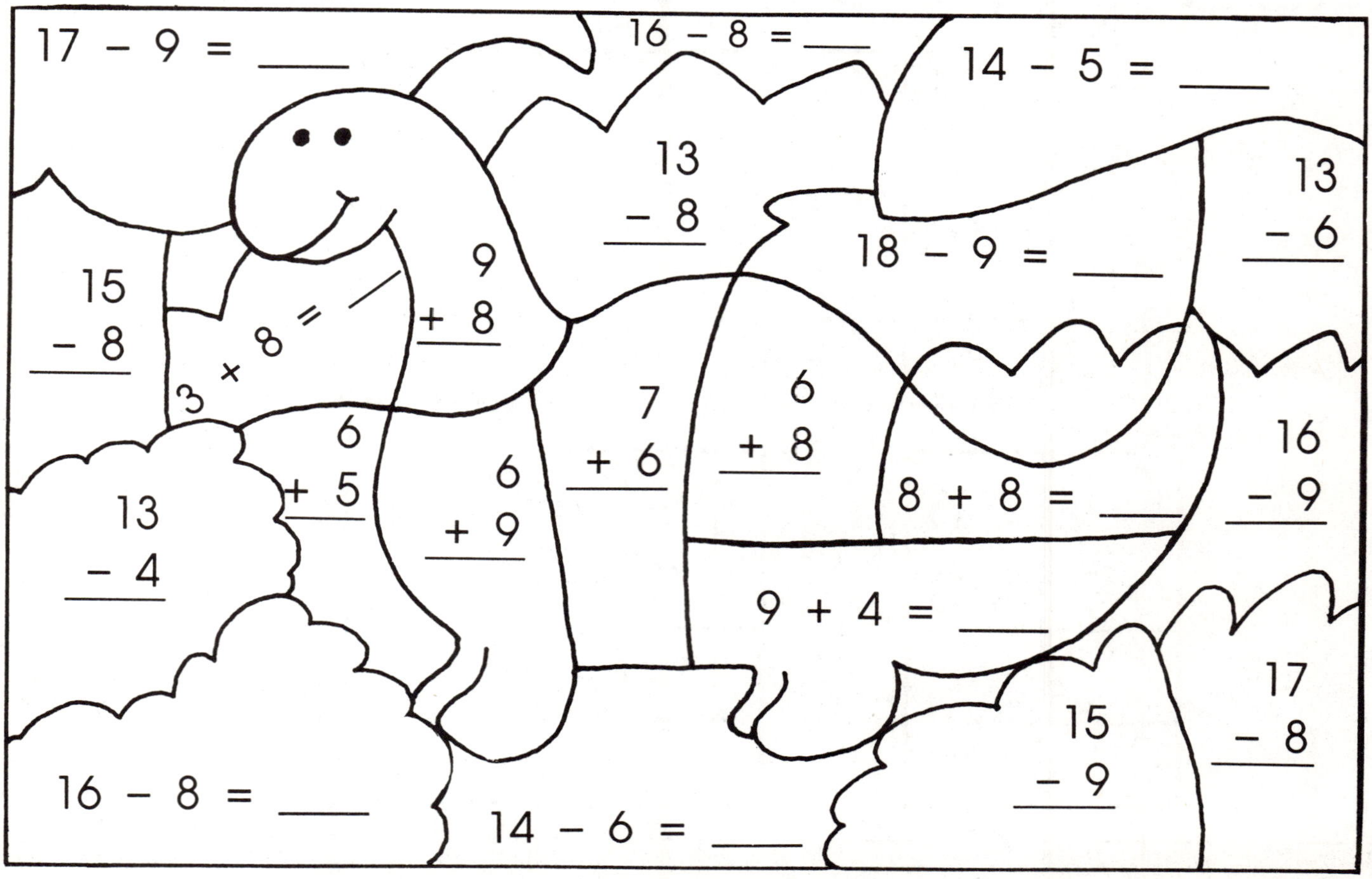
17 − 9 = ___
16 − 8 = ___
14 − 5 = ___
13 − 8
13 − 6
15 − 8
9 + 8
3 + 8 = ___
18 − 9 = ___
6 + 5
7 + 6
6 + 8
6 + 9
13 − 4
16 − 9
8 + 8 = ___
9 + 4 = ___
17 − 8
15 − 9
16 − 8 = ___
14 − 6 = ___

Name ______________________

Add or Subtract?

The key words **in all** tell you to add. The key word **left** tells you to subtract. Circle the key words and solve the problems.

1. The pet store has 3 large dogs and 5 small dogs. How many dogs are there in all?

3 ⊕ 5 = ______

2. The pet store had 9 parrots and then sold 4 of them. How many parrots does the pet store have left?

9 ○ 4 = ______

3. The pet store gave Linda's class 2 adult gerbils and 9 young ones. How many gerbils did Linda's class get in all?

2 ○ 9 = ______

4. At the pet store 3 of the 8 myna birds were sold. How many myna birds are left in the pet store?

8 ○ 3 = ______

5. The monkey at the pet store has 5 rubber toys and 4 wooden toys. How many toys does it have in all?

5 ○ 4 = ______

Name ____________________

Training with Facts

Use the numbers on each train to write the fact families.

___ + ___ = ___

___ + ___ = ___

___ − ___ = ___

___ − ___ = ___

___ + ___ = ___

___ + ___ = ___

___ − ___ = ___

___ − ___ = ___

___ + ___ = ___

___ + ___ = ___

___ − ___ = ___

___ − ___ = ___

___ + ___ = ___

___ + ___ = ___

___ − ___ = ___

___ − ___ = ___

Name ______________________________

Adding Strategies

When adding three numbers, add two numbers first, then add the third to that sum. To decide which two numbers to add first, try one of these strategies.

Look for doubles.

8	4 ⟩ 8	2
3 ⟩ 6	4	9 ⟩ 4
+ 3	+ 5	+ 2
14	13	13

Look for a ten.

7 ⟩ 10	8	1
3	4 ⟩ 10	5 ⟩ 10
+ 4	+ 6	+ 9
14	18	15

Try these. Look for a 10 or doubles.

5	2	7	3	6
5	6	1	7	2
+ 4	+ 8	+ 7	+ 4	+ 6

7	7	6	5
6	8	7	5
+ 6	+ 3	+ 4	+ 3

MATH

Name ____________________

Sum Ice Cream

Add. If the sum is 11 or more, color the cone brown. If the sum is less than 11, color the cone yellow.

Name ______________________

Path Problems

Add. Show the detective the correct path. Color the path with sums of 13.

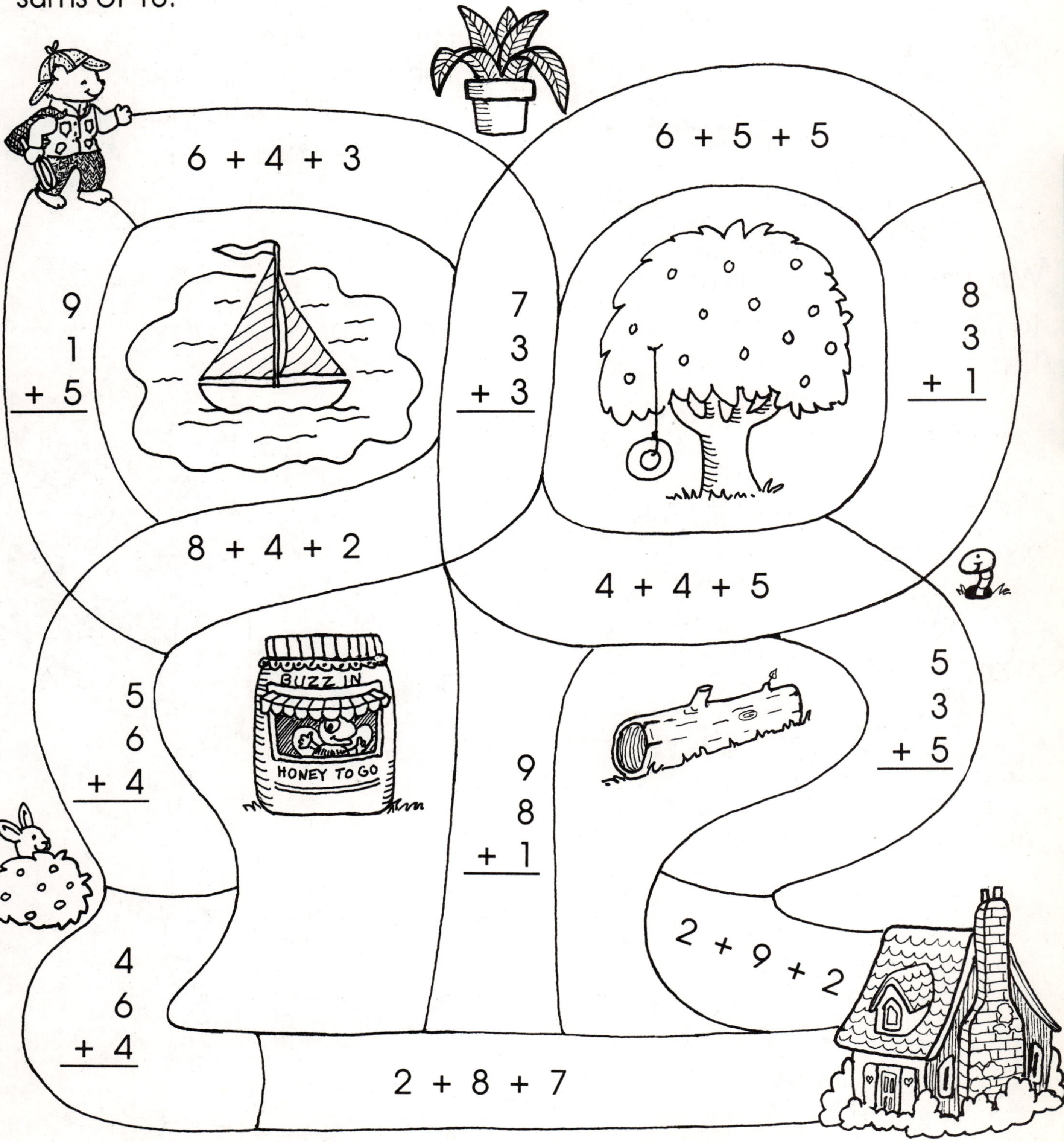
6 + 4 + 3
6 + 5 + 5
9
1
+ 5
7
3
+ 3
8
3
+ 1
8 + 4 + 2
4 + 4 + 5
BUZZ IN
HONEY TO GO
5
6
+ 4
5
3
+ 5
9
8
+ 1
2 + 9 + 2
4
6
+ 4
2 + 8 + 7

Name ____________________

Something's Missing

In the forest, 13 animals have a picnic. Skunk brings 8 sandwiches. How many sandwiches should Raccoon bring so that each animal can have one?

$$8 + \underline{\ ?\ } = 13$$

What number added to 8 equals 13?

To find the missing addend, find the difference of 13 and 8. That is, subtract the given addend (8) from the sum (13).

$$13 - 8 = \underline{\ 5\ }$$

Since 13 – 8 = 5, then 8 + __5__ = 13.

Raccoon should bring __5__ sandwiches.

Try these. Find the missing addends.

____ + 6 = 15

____ + 7 = 13

9 + ____ = 14

8 + ____ = 14

____ + 8 = 16

9 + ____ = 18

Name ______________________

Food Fun

The table below tells what each animal brought to the picnic.
Fill in the missing numbers.

Animal	Vegetables	Fruits	Total
Skunk	8	6	14
Raccoon	9		17
Squirrel		8	15
Rabbit	6		13
Owl	7		16
Deer		9	18

Write the name of the animal that answers each question.

1. Who brought the same number of vegetables as fruits?

   ____

2. Who brought two more fruits than vegetables? ______________
3. Who brought two more vegetables than fruits? ______________
4. Which two animals brought one more fruit than vegetables?

   ______________ and ______________

5. Which two animals brought the most vegetables?

   ______________ and ______________

6. Which two animals brought the most fruit? ______________ and

   ____

7. Which animal brought the least vegetables? ______________
8. Which animal brought the least fruit? ______________
9. Who brought more fruit, Skunk and Squirrel, or Raccoon and Rabbit? ______________________

Name ______________________

Circus Fun

Add. Remember to add the ones first.

	tens	ones
	2	5
+	1	4

	tens	ones
	5	3
+	3	2

	tens	ones
	7	1
+	2	8

	tens	ones
	4	4
+	3	2

	tens	ones
	5	1
+	3	7

	tens	ones
	2	6
+	5	2

	tens	ones
	2	6
+	4	2

	tens	ones
	3	7
+	5	1

	tens	ones
	1	9
+	3	0

Name ______________________________

Anchors Away

Add. Use the code to find the answer to this riddle:

What did the pirate have to do before every trip out to sea?

48	36	58	96	69	75	89	29
O	H	G	B	T	E	N	A

42 + 16	34 + 41	60 + 9
58		
G		

17 + 31	55 + 34

26 + 43	14 + 22	52 + 23

83 + 13	24 + 24	5 + 24	52 + 17

Name ______________________

Digital Addition

Add ones first.
4 + 2 = 6

tens	ones
2	4
+ 3	2
	6

Then, add tens.
2 + 3 = 5

tens	ones
2	4
+ 3	2
5	6

tens	ones
1	7
+ 2	1

tens	ones
3	4
+ 5	2

tens	ones
	5
+ 6	2

tens	ones
	6
+ 5	2

tens	ones
2	0
+ 4	0

tens	ones
5	1
+	8

tens	ones
7	2
+ 1	7

tens	ones
4	7
+ 2	1

tens	ones
2	5
+ 6	2

tens	ones
4	2
+ 2	4

tens	ones
8	3
+ 1	4

tens	ones
3	2
+ 2	5

tens	ones
4	4
+ 3	1

tens	ones
	8
+ 3	1

tens	ones
6	2
+ 1	7

tens	ones
8	2
+	7

Name ____________________

Nutty Addition

Sam Squirrel and his friend Wendy were gathering acorns. When they got 10 acorns, they put them in a bucket. The picture shows how many acorns Sam and Wendy each gathered. Write the number that tells how many.

tens	ones

______

tens	ones

______

How many acorns did Sam and Wendy gather in all? To find out:

1. Put numbers on ten's and one's table.

tens	ones
3	6
+ 2	7

2. Add ones first.

tens	ones
1	
3	6
+ 2	7
	3

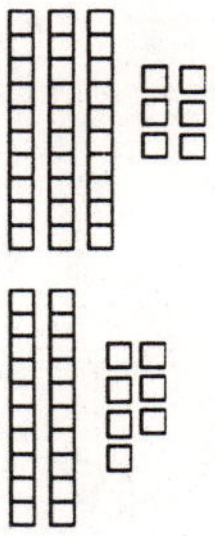

Ring 10.
Regroup 13 ones as 1 ten 3 ones.

3. Add tens.

tens	ones
1	
3	6
+ 2	7
6	3

Sam and Wendy gathered 63 in all.

Try this. Add. Regroup as needed.

tens	ones
3	8
+ 4	6

tens	ones
5	4
+ 2	7

tens	ones
4	9
+ 1	3

tens	ones
2	6
+ 1	7

MATH

Name ______________________________

Keep On Truckin'

Write each sum. Connect the sums of 83 to make a road for the truck.

	17 + 66	58 + 25	42 + 19	38 + 25
26 + 57	17 + 75	48 + 26	28 + 38	65 + 29
58 + 37	64 + 19	48 + 35	65 + 16	37 + 39
39 + 59	59 + 27	55 + 28	39 + 44	

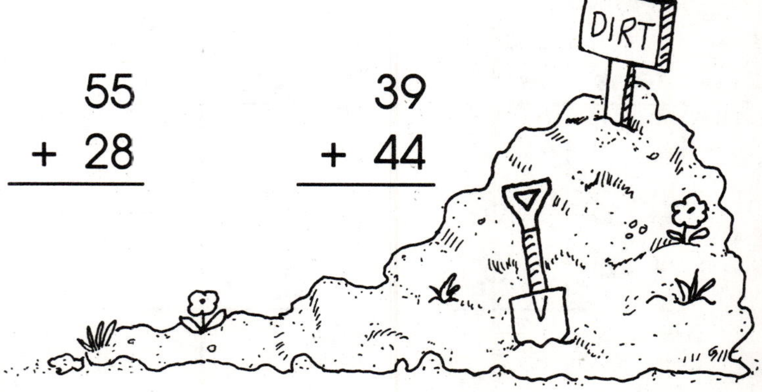

Name ______________________

Just Like Magic

Add. Write each answer.

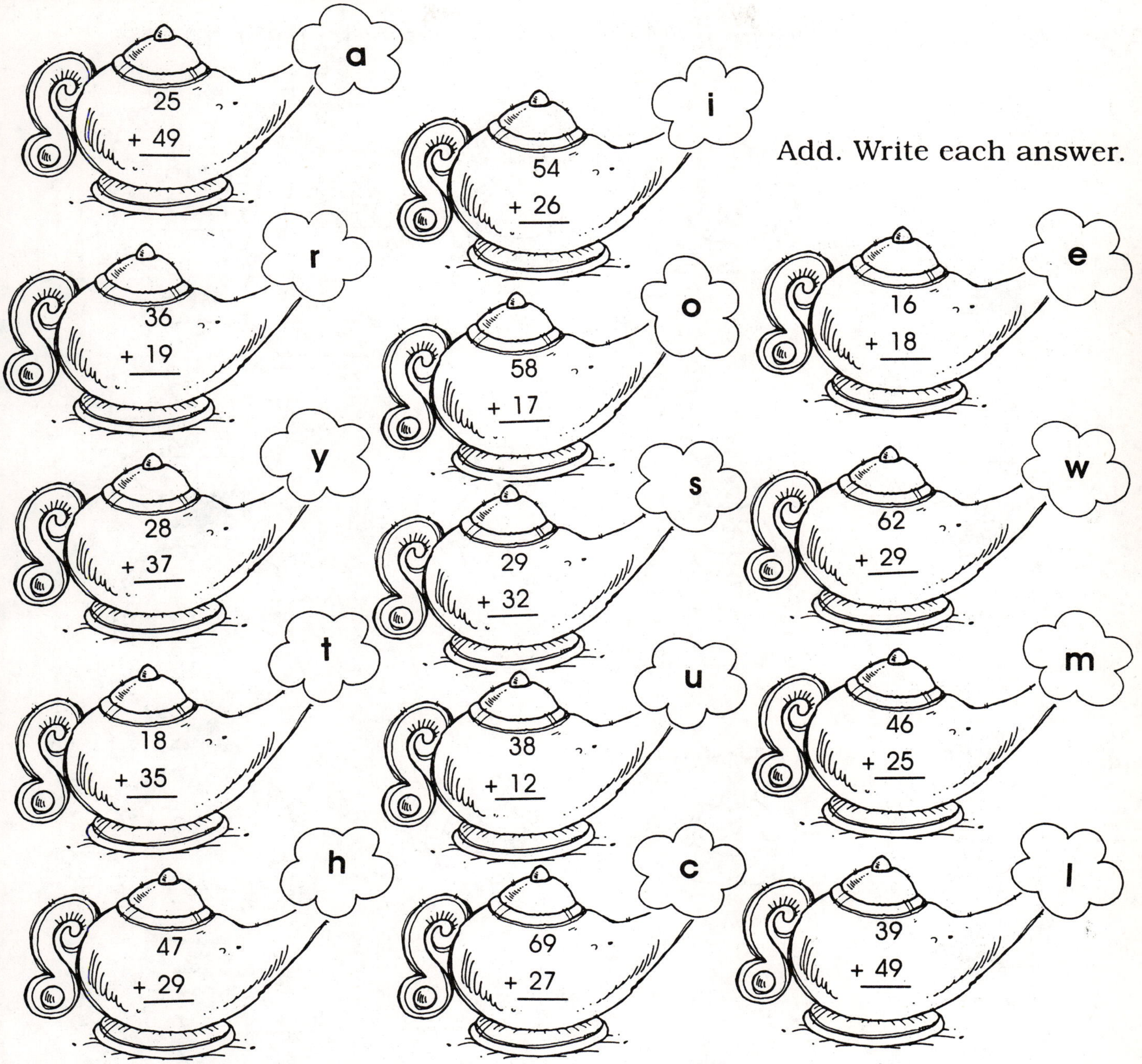
a
25
+ 49
i
54
+ 26
r
36
+ 19
o
58
+ 17
e
16
+ 18
y
28
+ 37
s
29
+ 32
w
62
+ 29
t
18
+ 35
u
38
+ 12
m
46
+ 25
h
47
+ 29
c
69
+ 27
l
39
+ 49

Use the answers and the letter on each lamp to solve the code.

__ __ __   __ __ __   __ __ __ __

71 74 65   74 88 88   65 75 50 55

__ __ __ __ __ __   __ __ __ __   __ __ __ __ !

91 80 61 76 34 61   96 75 71 34   53 55 50 34

Name ____________________________

Squirrelly Fun

Add. Regroup as needed. Match the squirrels to their trees.

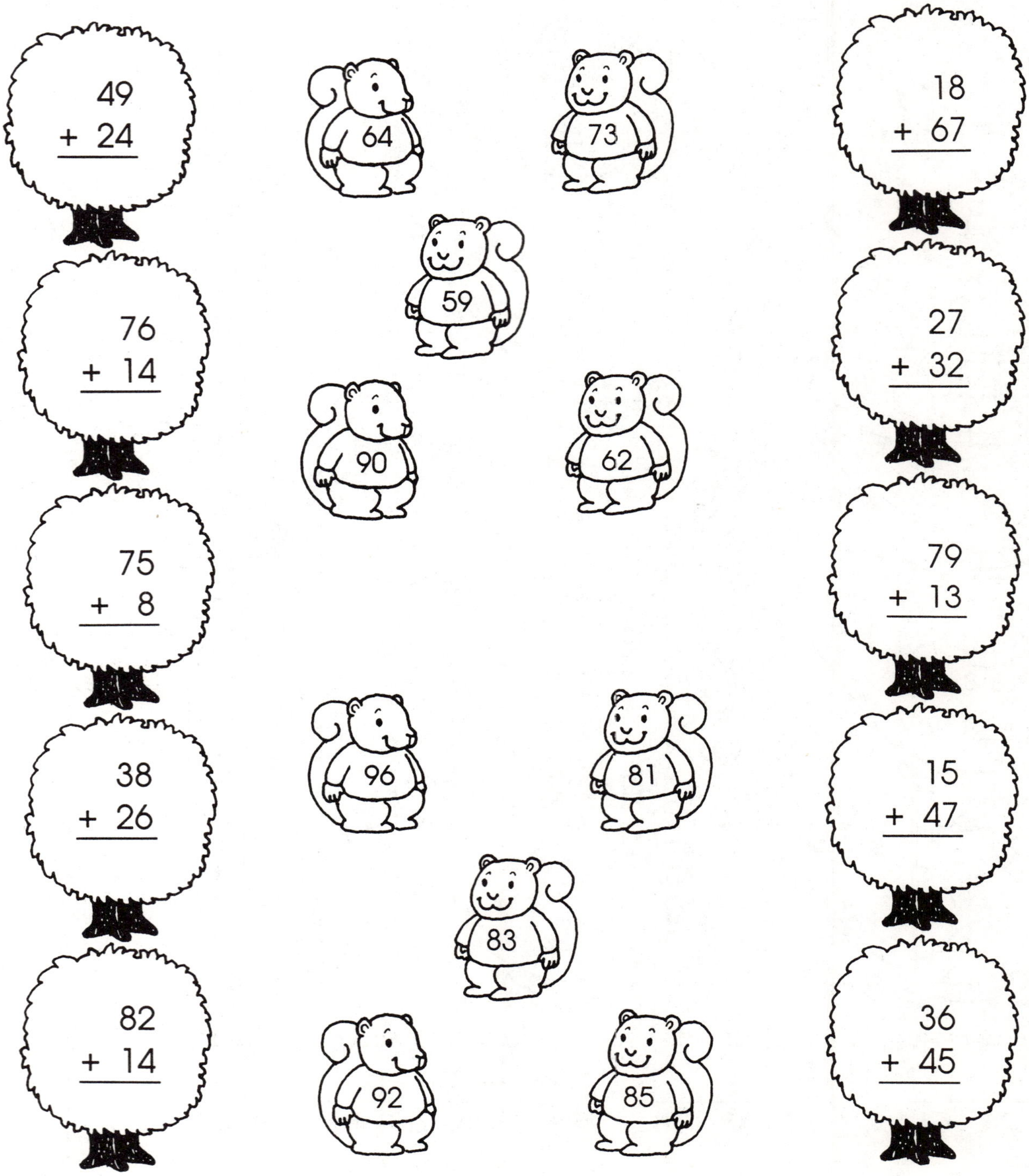

Name ____________________________

Fishy Business

Write the numbers and subtract.

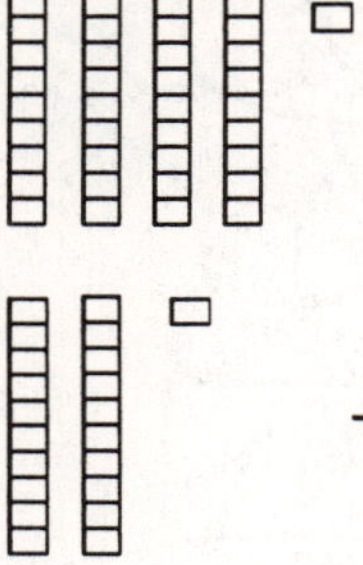

	tens	ones
	4	2
−	2	1

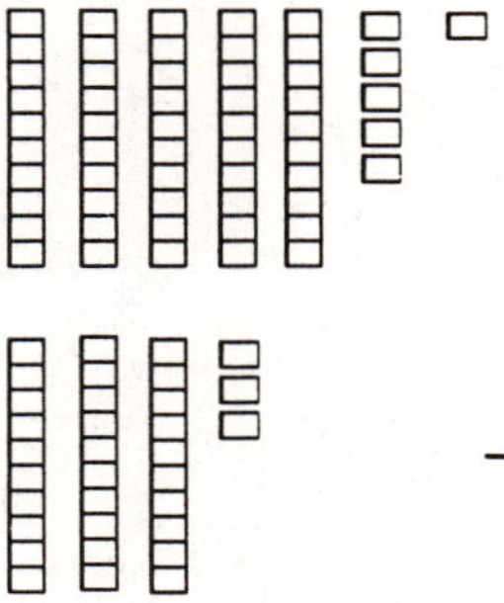

	tens	ones
−		

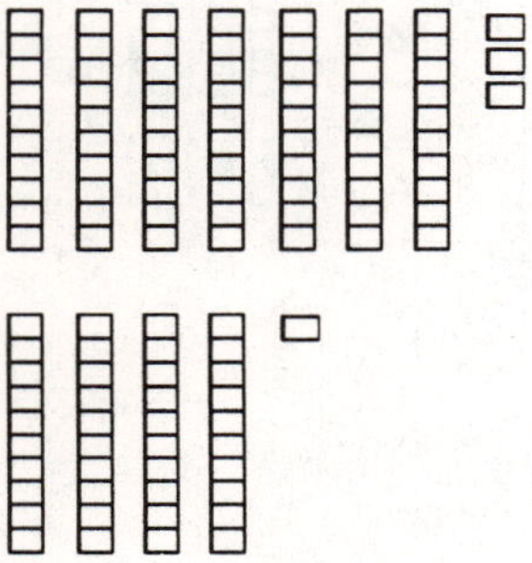

	tens	ones
−		

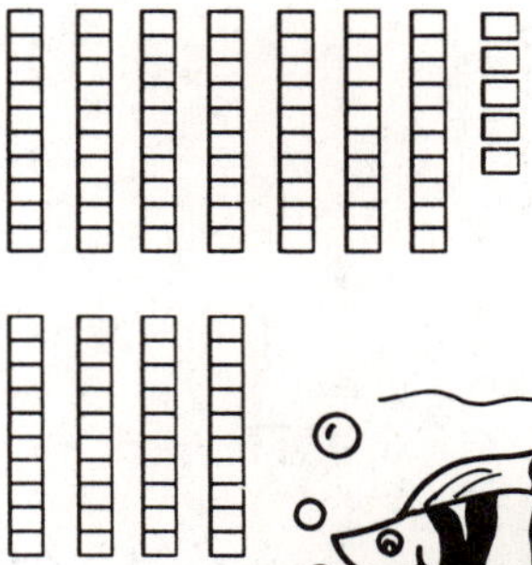

	tens	ones
−		

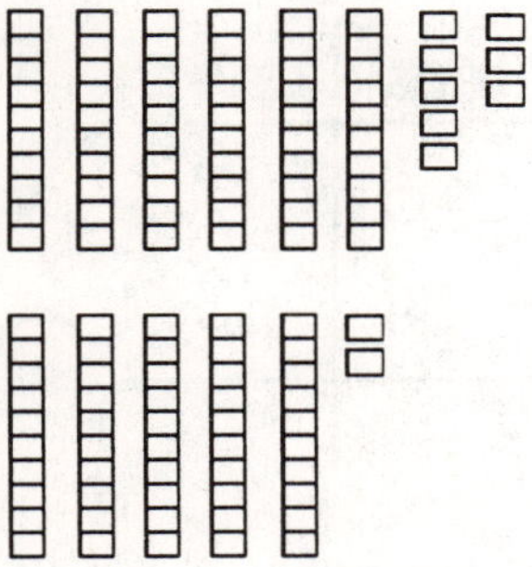

	tens	ones
−		

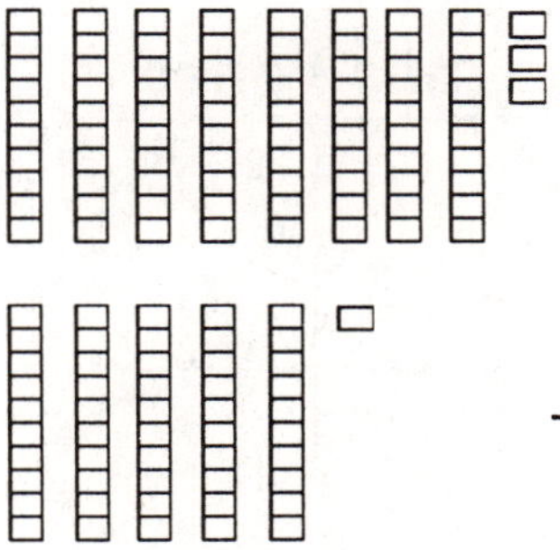

	tens	ones
−		

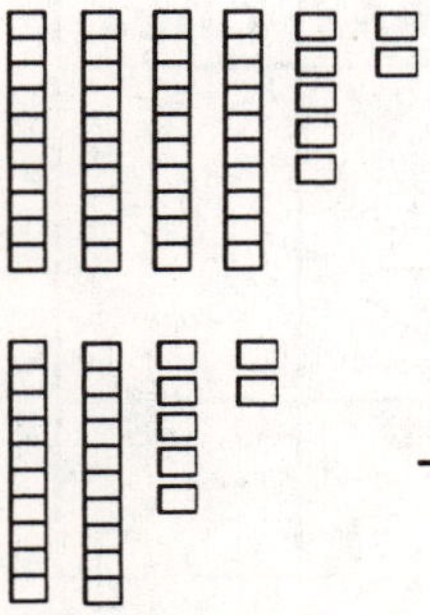

	tens	ones
−		

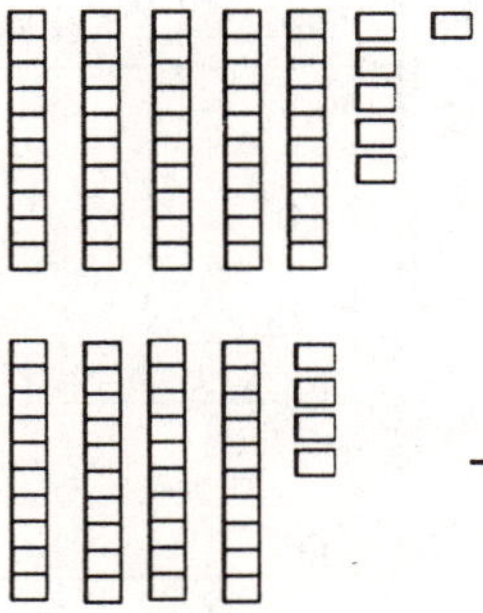

	tens	ones
−		

MATH

Name ______________________________

Cookie Mania

There are 46 cookies.
Bill eats 22 cookies.
How many are left?

$$\begin{array}{r} 46 \\ -\ 22 \\ \hline \end{array}$$

1. Put numbers on ten's and one's table.

tens	ones
4	6
– 2	2

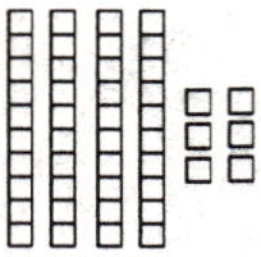

2. Subtract ones.

tens	ones
4	6
– 2	2
	4

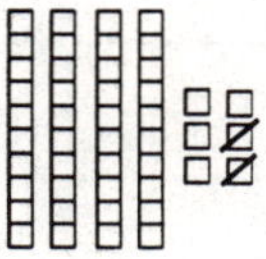

3. Subtract tens.

tens	ones
4	6
– 2	2
2	4

There are 24 cookies left.

Try these. Subtract the ones first. Then subtract the tens.

tens	ones
7	8
– 2	5

tens	ones
5	9
– 3	6

tens	ones
8	3
– 6	1

tens	ones
6	7
– 4	3

Rewrite in column form. Subtract ones, then tens.

97 – 14 = ____

tens	ones
–	

54 – 30 = ____

tens	ones
–	

Name ____________________

Prehistoric Problems

Work problems. Use color code. **25**—blue, **31**—yellow, **57**—green, **14**—orange, **21**—brown, **11**—red

47
− 22
52
− 21
62
− 31
25
− 11
77
− 20
51
− 40
55
− 34
98
− 41
69
− 12

Name ______________________

Cookie Craze!

Subtract. Circle the difference. Color the cookies with differences greater than 30.

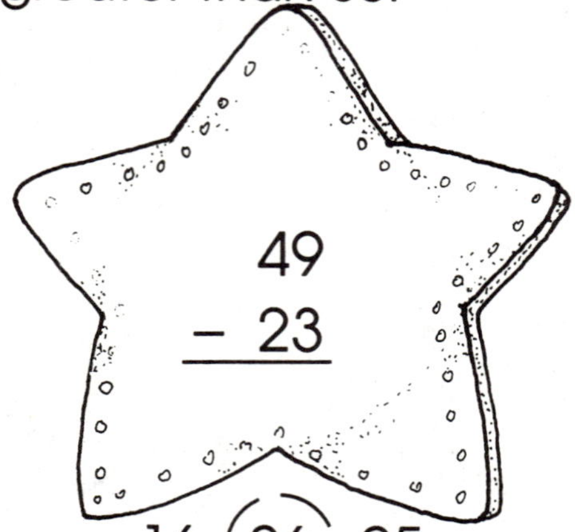

16 (26) 25

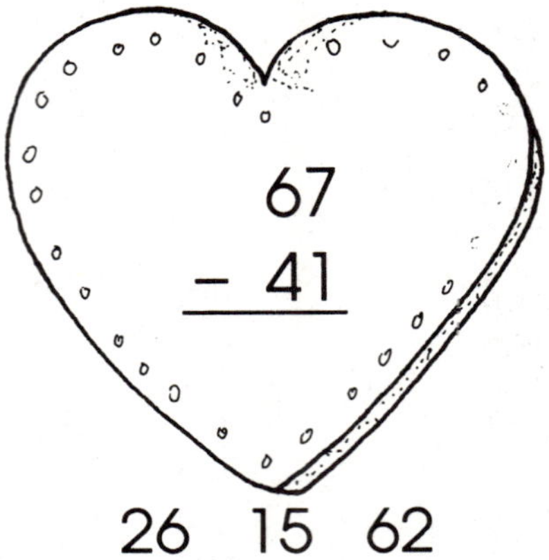

26 15 62

81 11 21

20 25 35

67 86 65

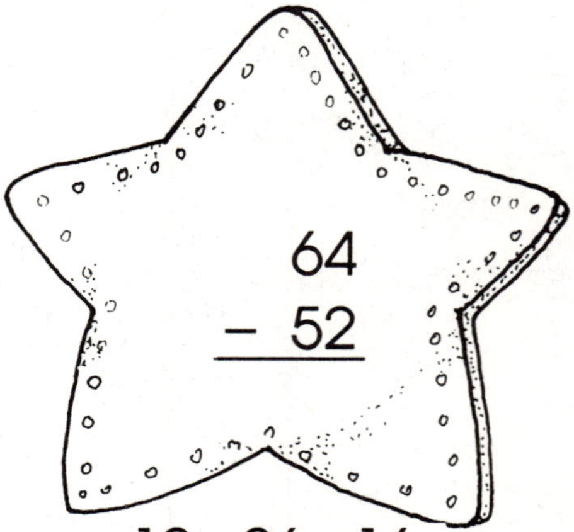

12 26 16

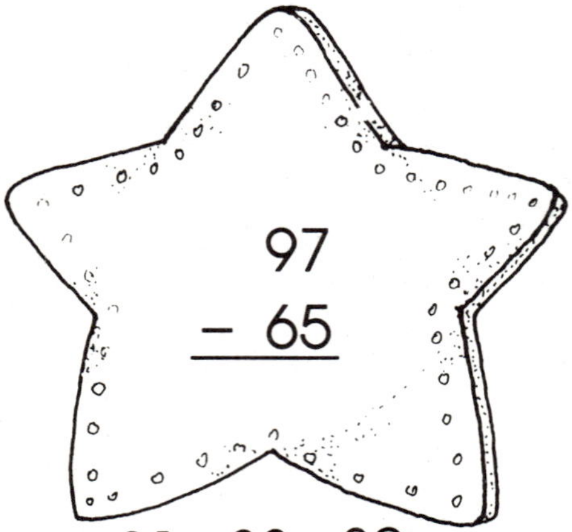

31 33 32

34 43 39

56 36 37

Name ______________________

Shell Subtraction

Ellen found 32 shells on the beach. She gave 15 shells to Cindy. How many shells does Ellen have now? To find out:

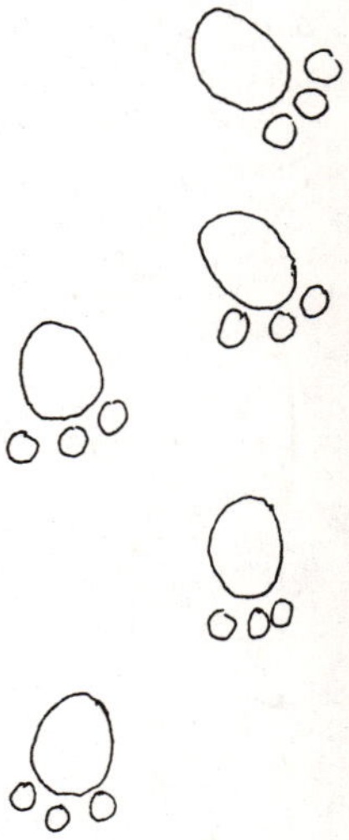

1. Put numbers on ten's and one's table.

tens	ones
3	2
– 1	5

2. Subtract ones. Ask: Do I need to regroup?

tens	ones
2	12
~~3~~	~~2~~
– 1	5
	7

regroup

32 = 2 tens and 12 ones

3. Subtract tens.

tens	ones
2	12
~~3~~	~~2~~
– 1	5
1	7

Ellen has 17 shells now.

Try this. Subtract. Regroup as needed.

tens	ones
4	1
– 1	7

tens	ones
7	5
– 3	8

tens	ones
5	0
– 2	6

tens	ones
3	6
– 1	9

MATH

Name ______________________________

Driving You Crazy

Match the drivers to their cars.

84

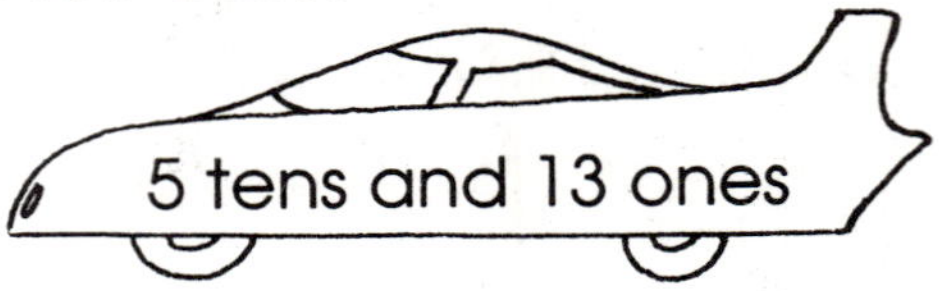
5 tens and 13 ones

20

4 tens and 18 ones

16

3 tens and 17 ones

58

0 tens and 16 ones

63

7 tens and 14 ones

47

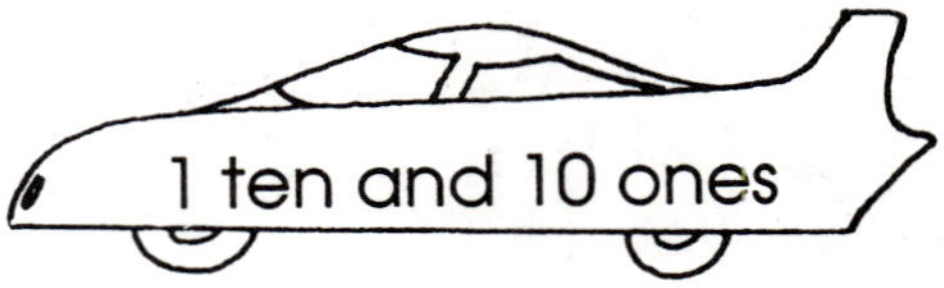
1 ten and 10 ones

Regroup. Write how many tens and ones.

40

_____ tens and _____ ones

35

_____ tens and _____ ones

21

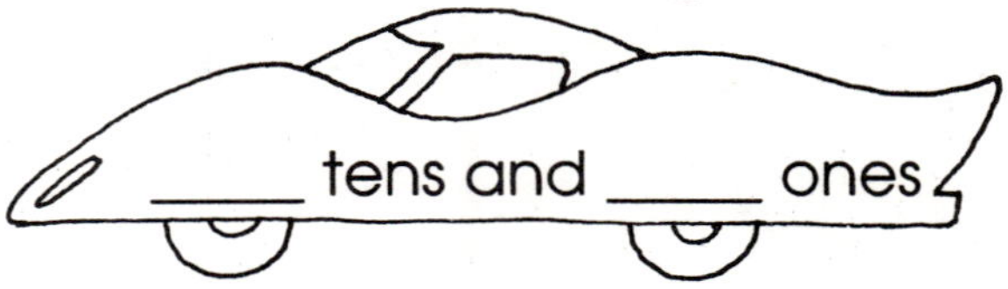
_____ tens and _____ ones

Name ______________________

Hatta Boy!

Subtract. Regroup as needed. Write your answers on the hats.

66 – 49
43 – 25
34 – 16
42 – 29
52 – 17
72 – 34
46 – 28
67 – 28

Name ____________________

Subtraction on the Beach

Subtract. Regroup as needed. Color the spaces with differences of:

10-19	red	30-39	green
50-59	brown	20-29	blue
40-49	yellow	60-69	orange

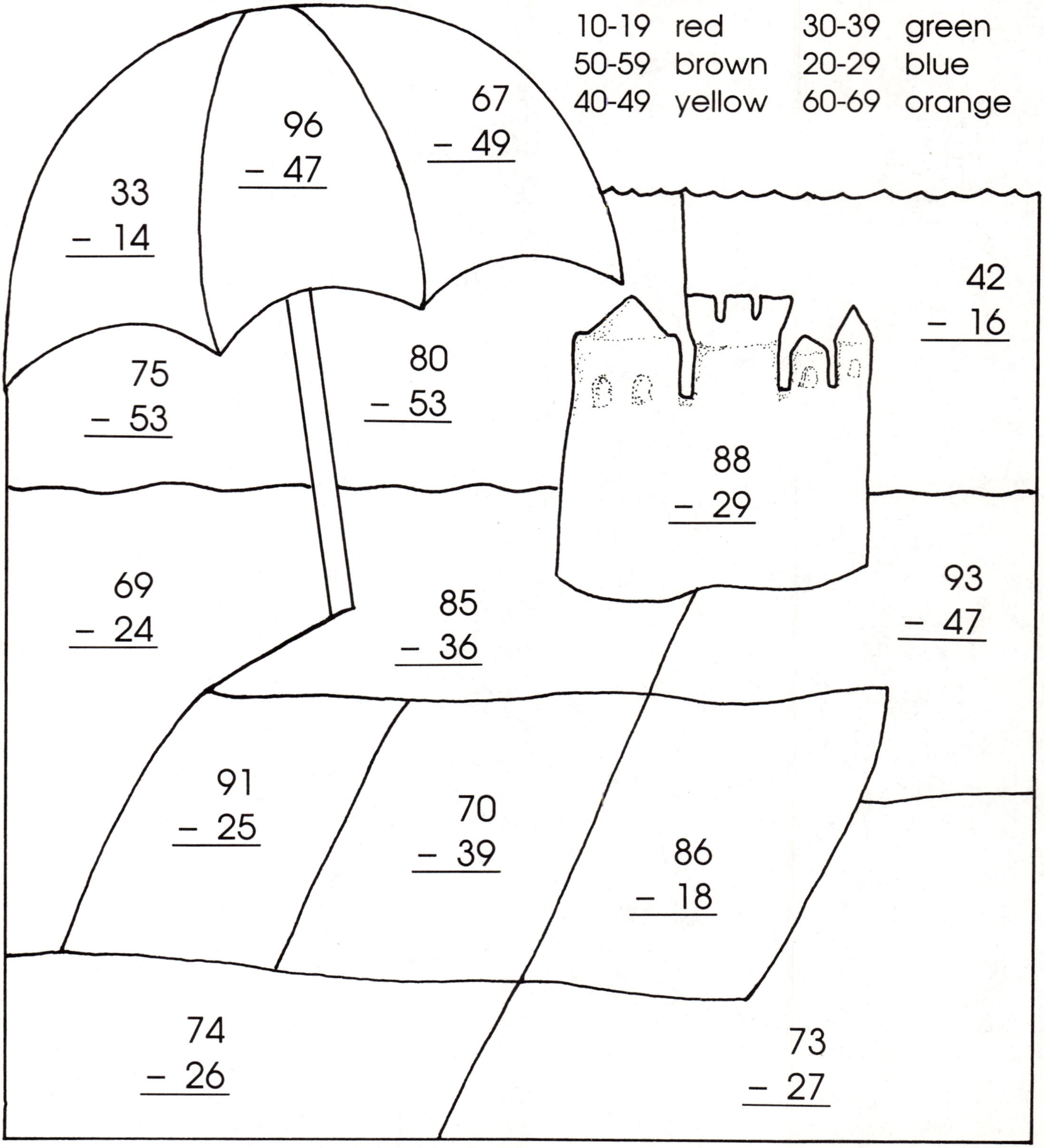
33 − 14
96 − 47
67 − 49
42 − 16
75 − 53
80 − 53
88 − 29
69 − 24
85 − 36
93 − 47
91 − 25
70 − 39
86 − 18
74 − 26
73 − 27

Name ______________________________

How's Your Pitch?

Subtract. Write each answer.

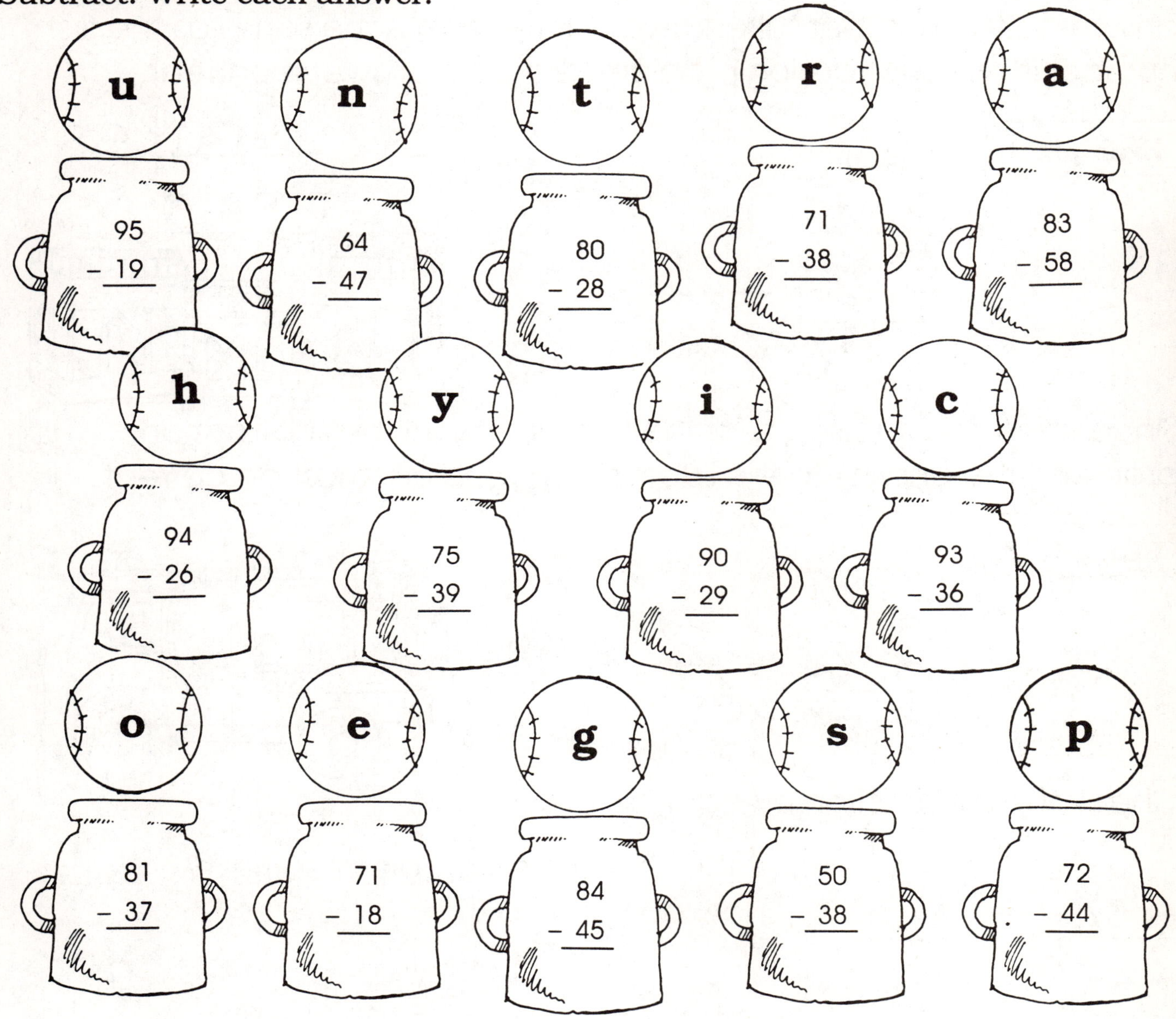

- u: 95 − 19 = ____
- n: 64 − 47 = ____
- t: 80 − 28 = ____
- r: 71 − 38 = ____
- a: 83 − 58 = ____
- h: 94 − 26 = ____
- y: 75 − 39 = ____
- i: 90 − 29 = ____
- c: 93 − 36 = ____
- o: 81 − 37 = ____
- e: 71 − 18 = ____
- g: 84 − 45 = ____
- s: 50 − 38 = ____
- p: 72 − 44 = ____

Use the answers and the letters on the baseballs to solve the code.

___ ___ ___ ___   ___ ___ ___ ___ ___   ___ ___

36 44 76 33   28 61 52 57 68   61 12

___ ___ ___ ___ ___   ___ ___   ___ ___ ___ ___ ___ ___ !

33 61 39 68 52   44 17   52 25 33 39 53 52

MATH

Name ______________________

Airport Action

To find out if the answer to a subtraction problem is correct, add the answer to the number taken away. If the sum is the same as the first number in the subtraction problem, then the answer is correct.

Example 1

$$\begin{array}{r} \overset{3\ 13}{\cancel{4}\cancel{3}} \\ -\ 27 \\ \hline 16 \end{array} \quad \longrightarrow \quad \begin{array}{r} \overset{1}{16} \\ +\ 27 \\ \hline 43 \end{array}$$

Since the sum is the same as the first number in the subtraction problem, the answer to the subtraction problem must be correct.

Example 2

$$\begin{array}{r} \overset{6\ 11}{\cancel{7}\cancel{1}} \\ -\ 28 \\ \hline 43 \end{array} \quad \longrightarrow \quad \begin{array}{r} \overset{1}{43} \\ +\ 28 \\ \hline 71 \end{array}$$

Check the subtraction by adding.

$$\begin{array}{r} 52 \\ -\ 37 \\ \hline 25 \end{array} \quad \longrightarrow \quad \begin{array}{r} \\ +\ \underline{\quad\quad} \end{array}$$

Is the subtraction problem correct? ______

How do you know?

Subtract. Then add to check.

$$\begin{array}{r} 52 \\ -\ 37 \\ \hline \end{array} \longrightarrow +\ \underline{\quad\quad} \qquad \begin{array}{r} 80 \\ -\ 26 \\ \hline \end{array} \longrightarrow +\ \underline{\quad\quad} \qquad \begin{array}{r} 64 \\ -\ 48 \\ \hline \end{array} \longrightarrow +\ \underline{\quad\quad}$$

Name ____________________

Playing in the Park

Circle **Add** or **Subtract**. Then, write a number sentence to solve each problem. Think and check to see if your answer makes sense.

1. There are 6 swings. Four children are swinging. How many swings are empty?

   Add Subtract

   ____ swings

2. The slide has 8 steps. Craig climbed 3 steps. How many more steps must he climb?

   Add Subtract

   ____ steps

3. Ellen went across the monkey bars 5 times. So did Brooke. How many times did both girls go across?

   Add Subtract

   ____ times

4. Three girls sat on one park bench. Three boys sat on another bench. How many children are sitting on both benches?

   Add Subtract

   ____ children

Name ______________________

Superstar Students

Fill in the table using the information given. Then answer the questions.

Second Grade Students at Superstar School

Class	Boys	Girls	Total
A		17	28
B	12	15	
C	9		23
Total			

1. Which class has the most students? ______
2. Which class has the least students? ______
3. How many more girls than boys are in second grade? ______
4. Which class has the most boys? ______
5. Which class has the least girls? ______
6. If each boy in class A gave his teacher an apple, how many apples would she get? ______
7. How many students are in second grade at Superstar School? ______ Outline in red the box that tells this.
8. How many more students are in class A than class C? ______
9. If each boy in class B gave a girl in class A an apple, how many girls would not get an apple? ______
10. If 9 students move away, how many students would be in second grade then? ______

0-7682-3792-0 *Skills & Practice Gr. 2*

Name ________________________

Tree Troubles

Help the squirrels get to their trees. Add or subtract in your head. Write the final answer on the tree.

3 + 4 + 5 − 3 − 2 =

5 − 2 + 6 + 3 − 4 =

9 − 3 + 5 − 4 + 2 =

6 + 6 − 5 + 3 − 2 =

8 + 4 − 6 + 5 − 3 =

MATH

Name ______________________

Roll Call

Look at the animals at the top of the page. Write the correct word to tell where each animal is standing in the line.

1. ______________________

2. ______________________

3. ______________________

4. ______________________

5. ______________________

6. ______________________

7. ______________________

8. ______________________

9. ______________________

10. ______________________

Word Bank

first
second
third
fourth
fifth
sixth
seventh
eighth
ninth
tenth

0-7682-3792-0 *Skills & Practice Gr. 2*

Name ______________________

My First Treat Will Be . . .

Circle the ordinal number word for each treat.

1. 

2. 

3. 

4. 

16. 

 third, sixteenth, fifth

5. 

 fifteenth, fourth, first

 twelfth, second, seventh

15. 

6. 

 third, eleventh, fifteenth

14. 

 eighth, first, tenth

7. 

 sixteenth, thirteenth, third

13. 

 ninth, second, thirteenth

8. 

 sixth, seventh, ninth,

12. 

11. 

10. 

9. 

MATH

Name ______________________________

Two by Two

Finish counting.

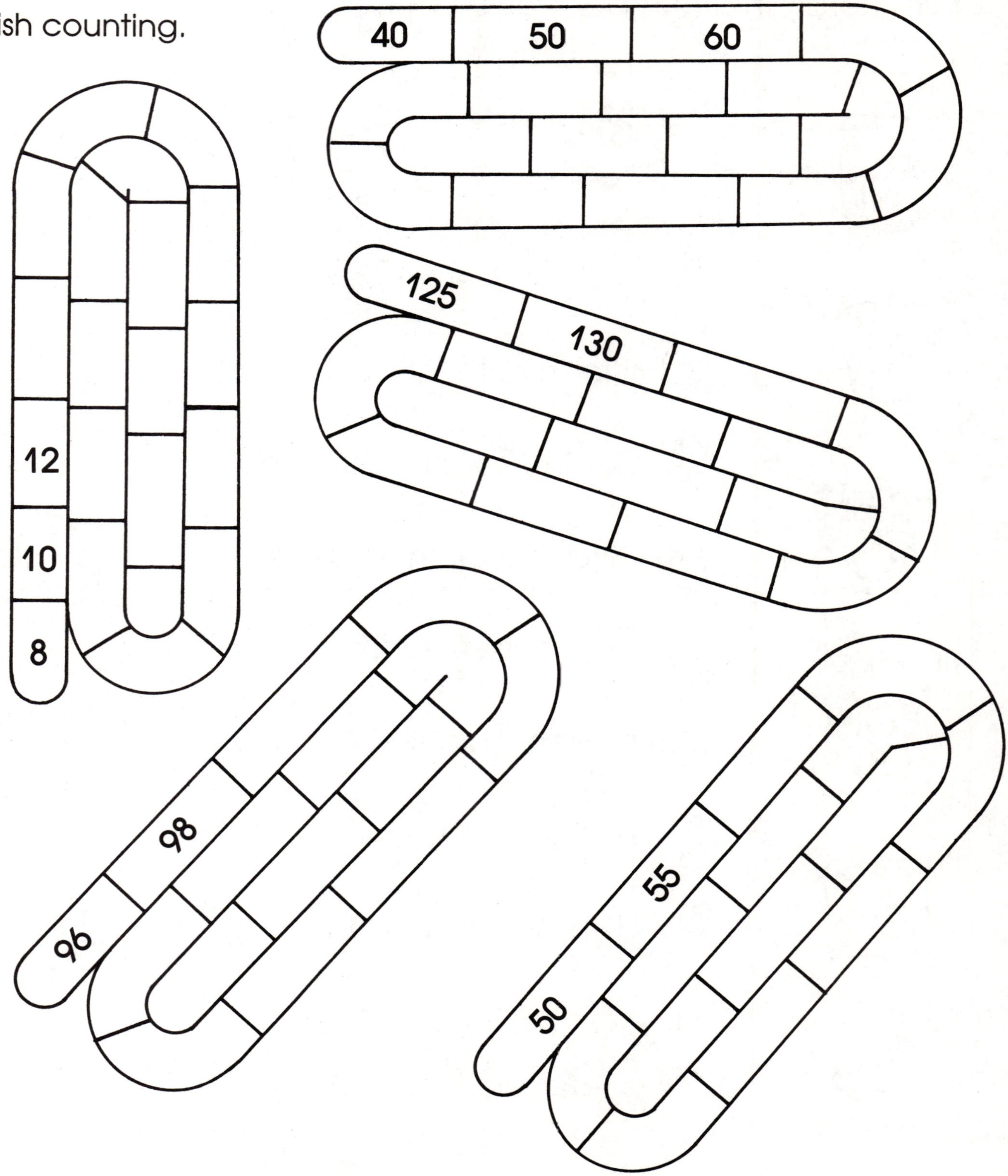
40
50
60
12
10
8
125
130
98
96
55
50

Name ______________________

Critter Count

Number of 's found.  = 5

 = 20

 = ______

 = ______

Number of 's found.  = 10

 = ______

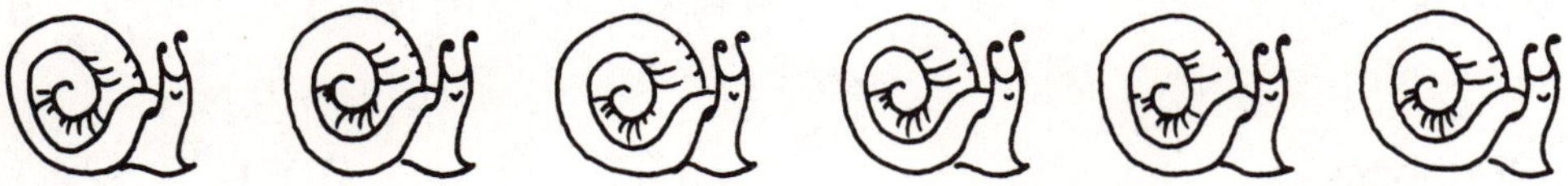 = ______

 = ______

Number of 's found.  = 2

 = ______

 = ______

 = ______

MATH

Name ____________________

Who Has the Most?

Circle the right answer.

1.

Jane has 3 's.

Bob has 4 's.

Bill has 5 's.

Who has the most 's?

Jane Bob Bill

2.

Pam has 7 's.

Joe has 5 's.

Jane has 6 's.

Who has the most 's?

Pam Joe Jane

3.

Amy has 23 's.

Sandy has 19 's.

Jack has 25 's.

Who has the most 's?

Amy Sandy Jack

4.

Ann has 19 's.

Burt has 18 's.

Brent has 17 's.

Who has the most 's?

Ann Burt Brent

5.

The boys have 14 's.

The girls have 16 's.

The teachers have 17 's.

Who has the most 's?

boys girls teachers

6.

Rose has 12 's.

Betsy has 11 's.

Ann has 13 's.

Who has the most 's?

Rose Betsy Ann

Name ______________________

Who Has the Least?

Circle the right answer.

1.
Pat had 4 's.
Charles had 3 's.
Jane had 5 's.

Who had the least number of 's?

Pat Charles Jane

2.
Jeff has 5 's.
John has 4 's.
Bill has 6 's.

Who has the least number of 's?

Jeff John Bill

3.
Jane has 7 's.
Peg has 9 's.
Fred has 8 's.

Who has the least number of 's?

Jane Peg Fred

4.
Charles bought 12 's.
Rose bought 6 's.
Mother bought 24 's.

Who bought the least number of 's?

Charles Rose Mother

5.
John had 9 's.
Jack had 8 's.
Jeff had 7 's.

Who had the least number of 's?

John Jack Jeff

6.
Alma bought 12 's.
Nina bought 16 's.
Marty bought 13 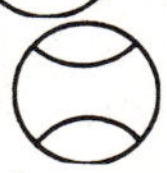's.

Who bought the least number of 's?

Alma Nina Marty

Name ______________________________

Munch a Bunch

Gertrude Goat and her friends Ginger, George, and Gus are making special popcorn balls. Each piece of popcorn has a number on it.

Read the clues to find out which pieces of popcorn each goat will use for his/her popcorn ball. Write the numbers on the popcorn.

27 40 29 10 35 2 1 4 15
32 6 3 20 12 41 17 9 43 5 34 48
16 26 44 23 49 18 45 28 19 36 31

Gertrude
odd numbers
greater than 25

Gus
even numbers
less than 25

George
even numbers
greater than 25

Ginger
odd numbers
less than 25

Name ______________________

"Mouth" Math

Write < or > in each circle. Make sure the "mouth" is open toward the greater number!

36 ○ 49	35 ○ 53
20 ○ 18	74 ○ 21
53 ○ 76	68 ○ 80
29 ○ 26	45 ○ 19
90 ○ 89	70 ○ 67

Name ______________________________

Right on Time

Cut out the time signs at the bottom of the page. Paste each sign on the engine next to the correct clock.

Cut -

12:00	1:00	2:00	3:00	4:00	5:00
6:00	7:00	8:00	9:00	10:00	11:00

Name ______________________

Space Time

What time is it?

0-7682-3792-0 *Skills & Practice Gr. 2*

Name ______________________

Turtle Time

What time is it?

0-7682-3792-0 *Skills & Practice Gr. 2*

Name ________________________

My Family Time Tree

Write the time.
Draw the hands on each clock.

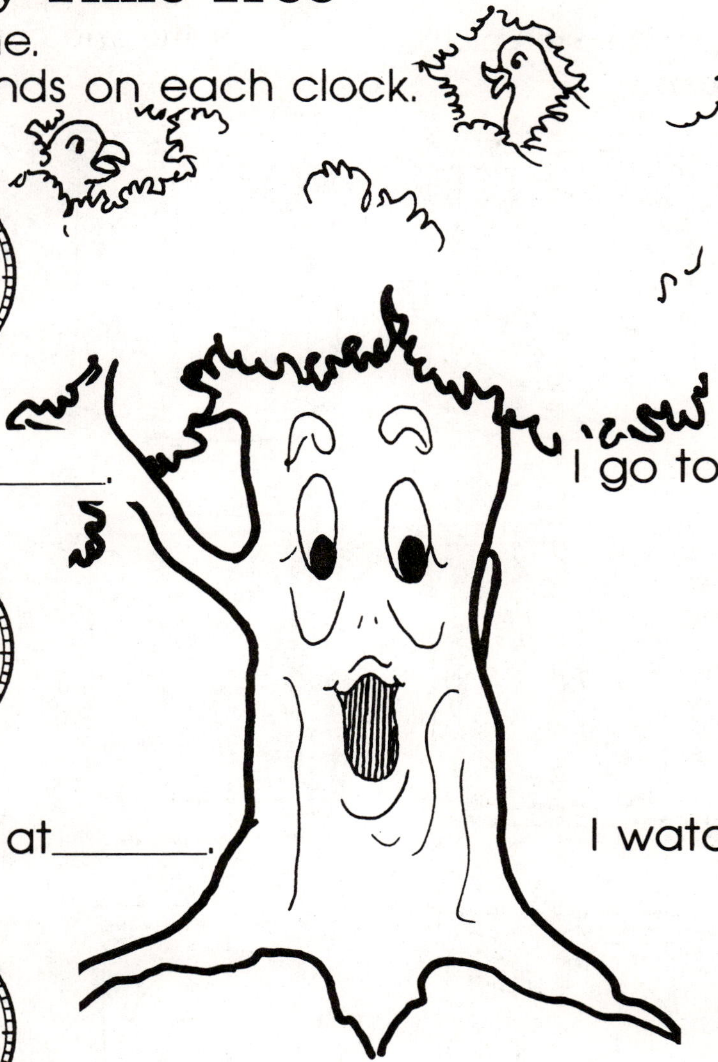

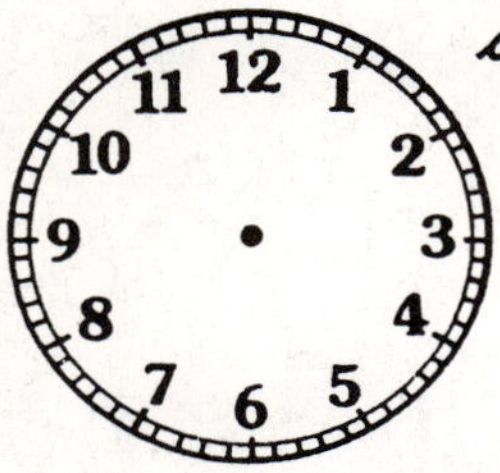

I get up at______. I go to bed at______.

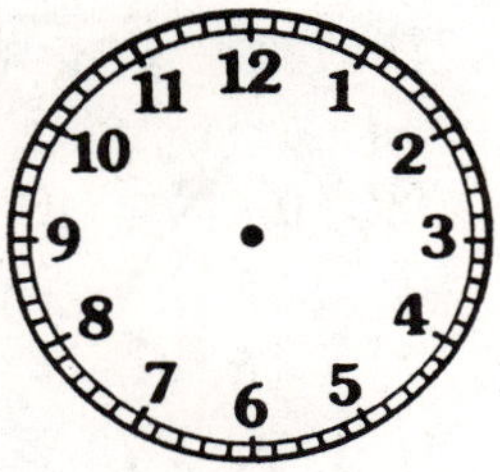

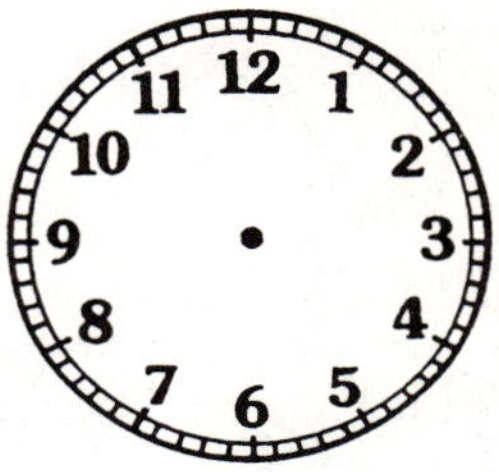

School starts at______. I watch TV at______.

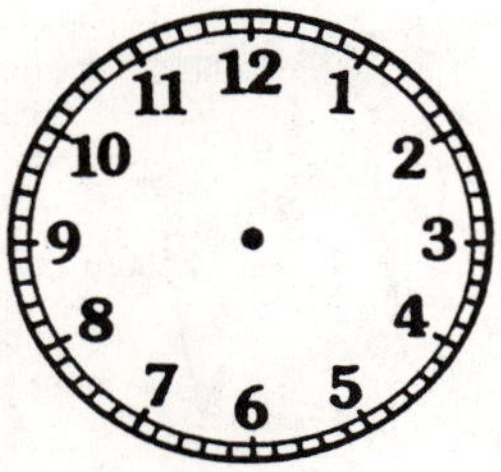

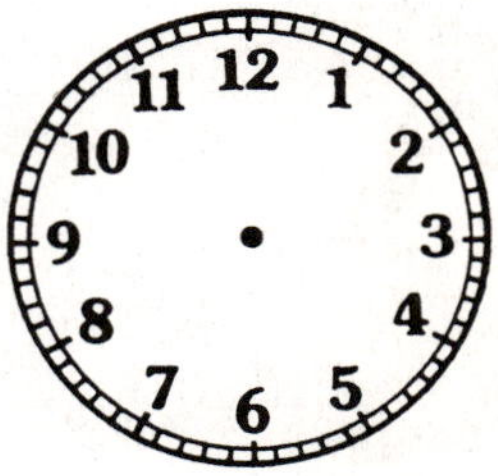

Lunch is at______. Dinner is at______.

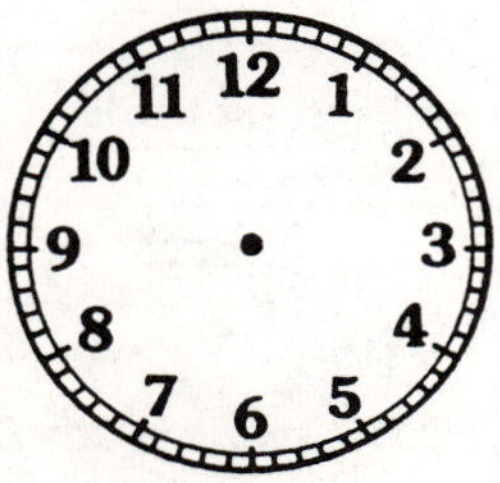

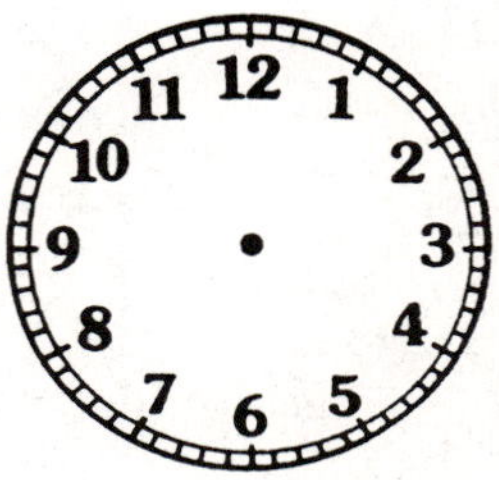

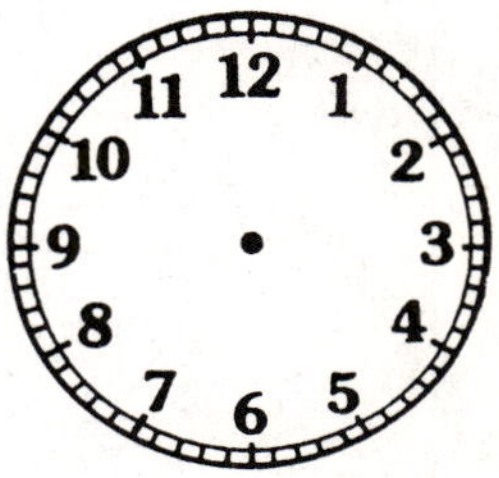

Recess is at______. School ends at______. I play at______.

MATH

Name ______________________

Time to Clean Up

Match the digital time with each clock face by cutting and pasting each lid on the correct trash can.

Cut

12:25
1:30
2:55
3:10
4:15
5:40
6:45
7:35
8:00
9:05
10:50
11:20

Name ________________________

It's About Time!

Trace each with red if it has a time word.

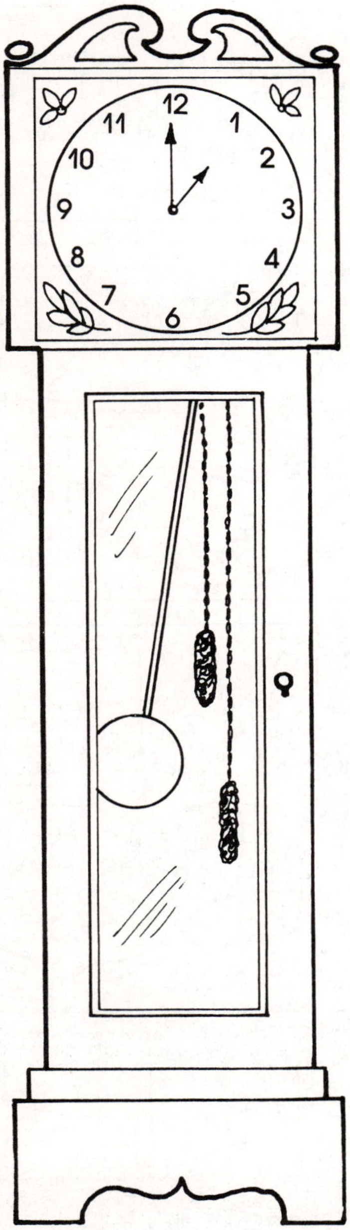
12
1
2
3
4
5
6
7
8
9
10
11

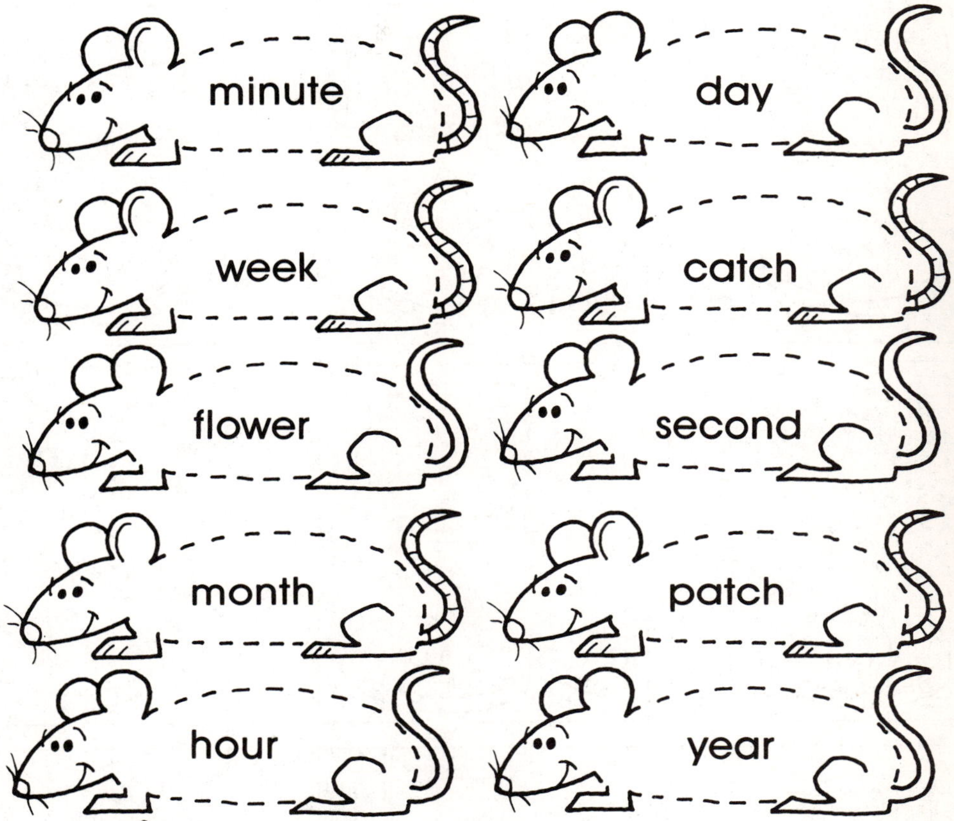
minute
day
week
catch
flower
second
month
patch
hour
year

a circle around the correct answer.

1. There are sixty seconds in a minute. / year.
2. There are sixty minutes in an second. / hour.
3. There are 24 hours in a minute. / day.
4. There are 365 days in a year. / week.
5. There are seven days in a week. / hour.
6. There are twelve months in a year. / week.

Name ____________________

Postage Stamp, Please

Add up the coins on each envelope. Write the total on the stamp.

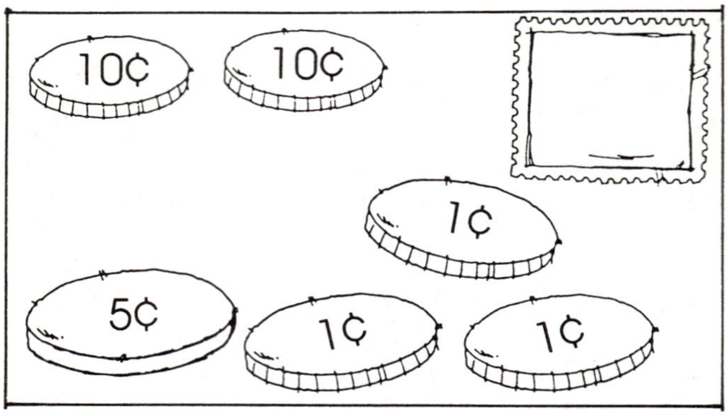

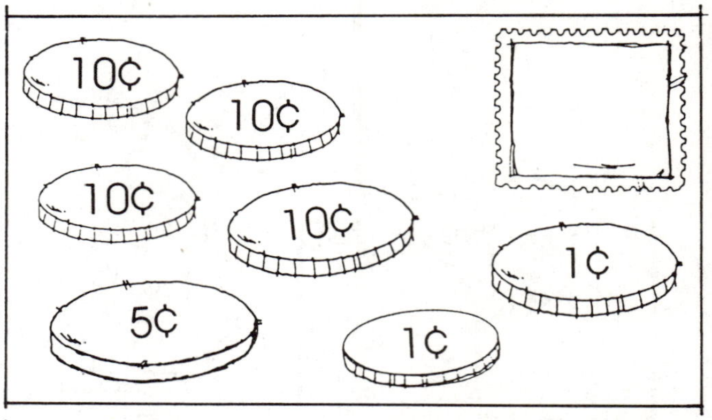

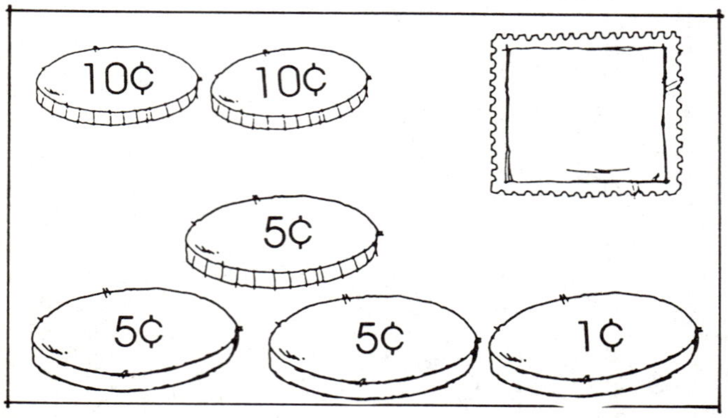

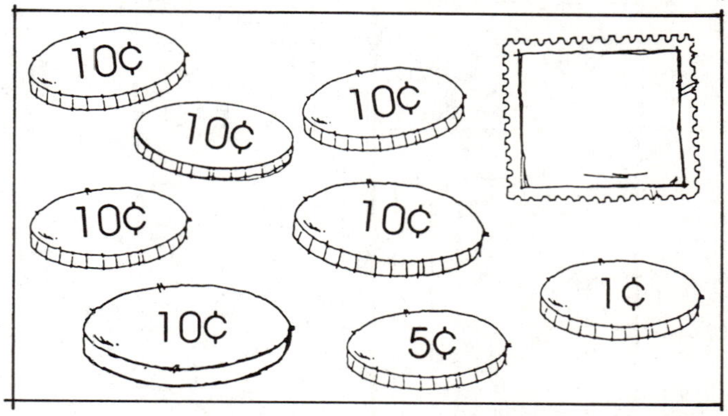

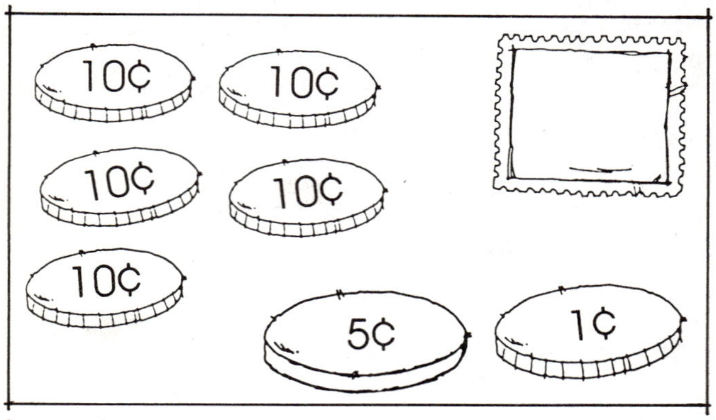

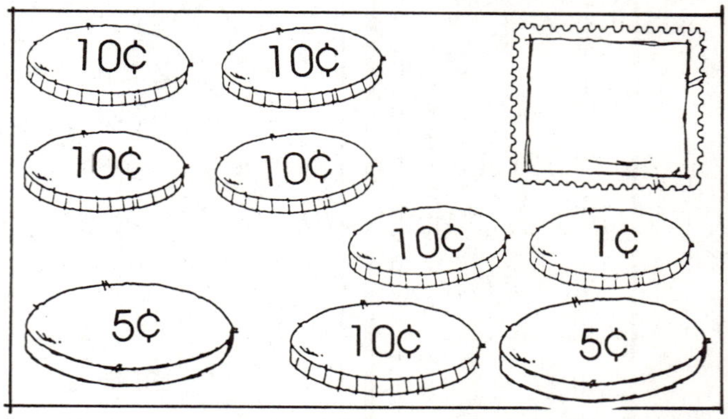

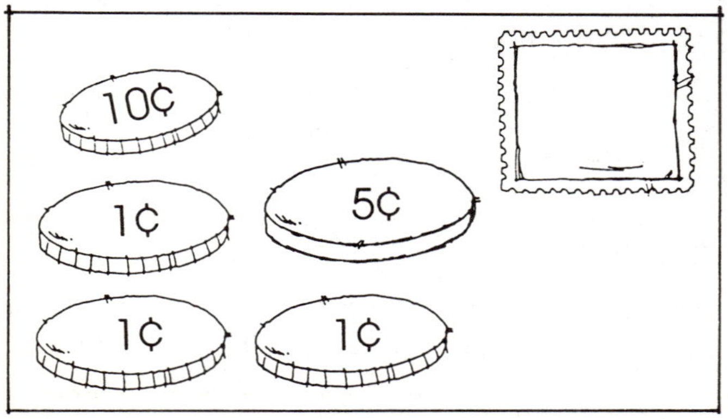

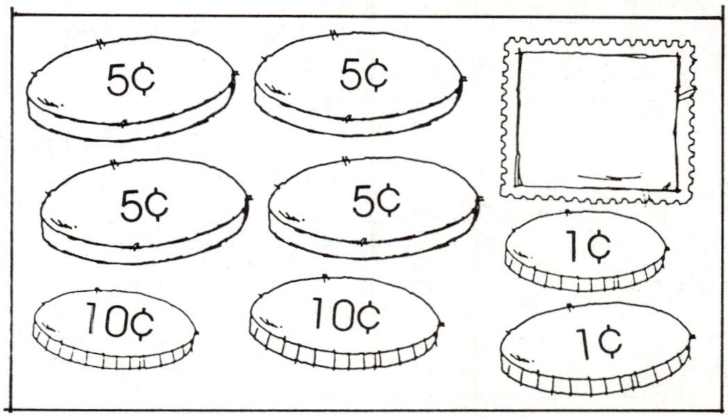

Name ______________________________

Pencil Topper Purchases

Peggy wants to buy three different pencil toppers. Look at the cost of each topper.

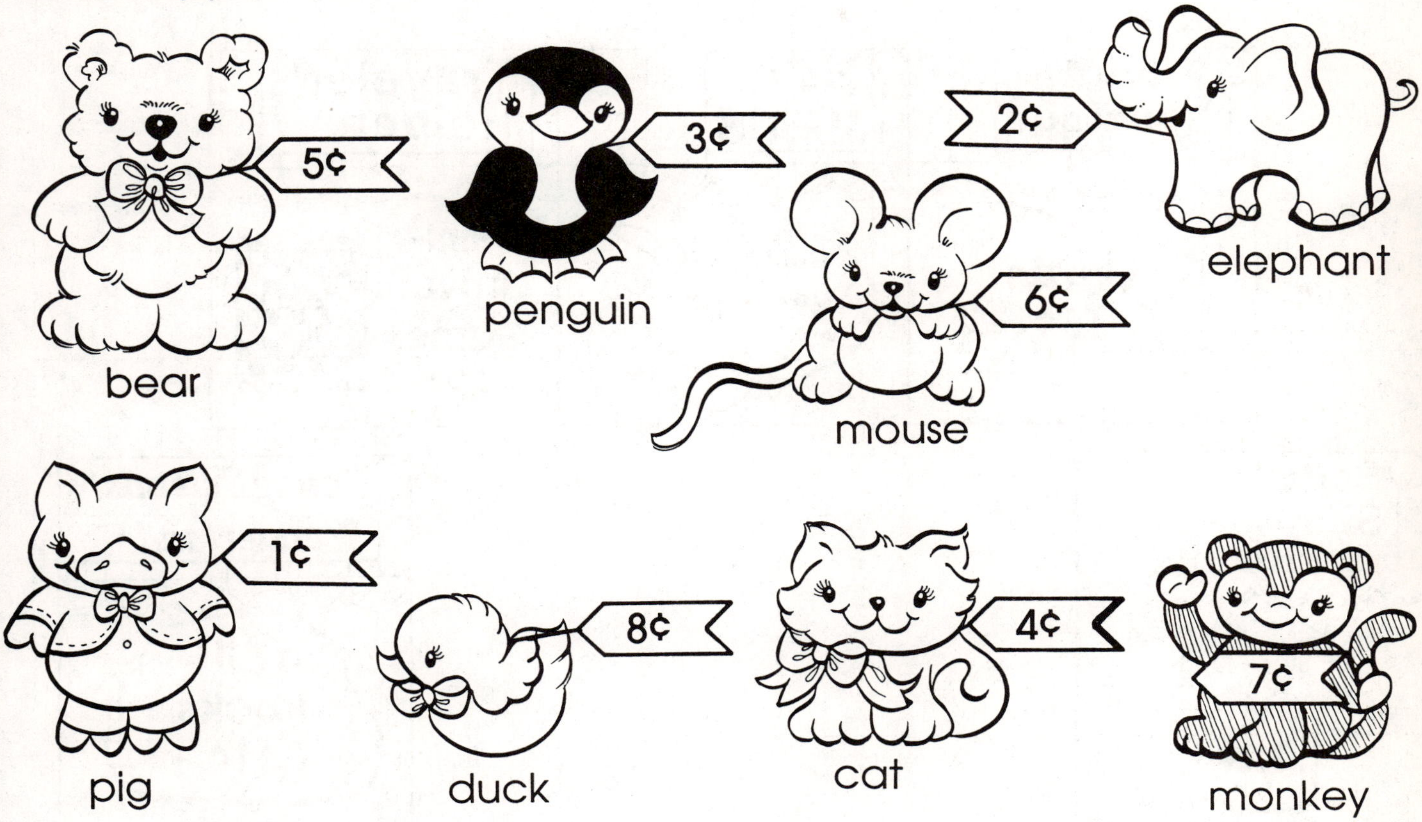
5¢
bear
3¢
penguin
2¢
elephant
6¢
mouse
1¢
pig
8¢
duck
4¢
cat
7¢
monkey

Peggy has 12¢ to spend. Write the names of the different pencil topper combinations she might pick.

1. ______________	1. ______________	1. ______________
2. ______________	2. ______________	2. ______________
3. ______________	3. ______________	3. ______________
1. ______________	1. ______________	1. ______________
2. ______________	2. ______________	2. ______________
3. ______________	3. ______________	3. ______________

  0-7682-3792-0 *Skills & Practice Gr. 2*

Name ______________________

Mall Mania

Count the coins in each purse. Then draw a line from each coin purse to the store where that amount is given.

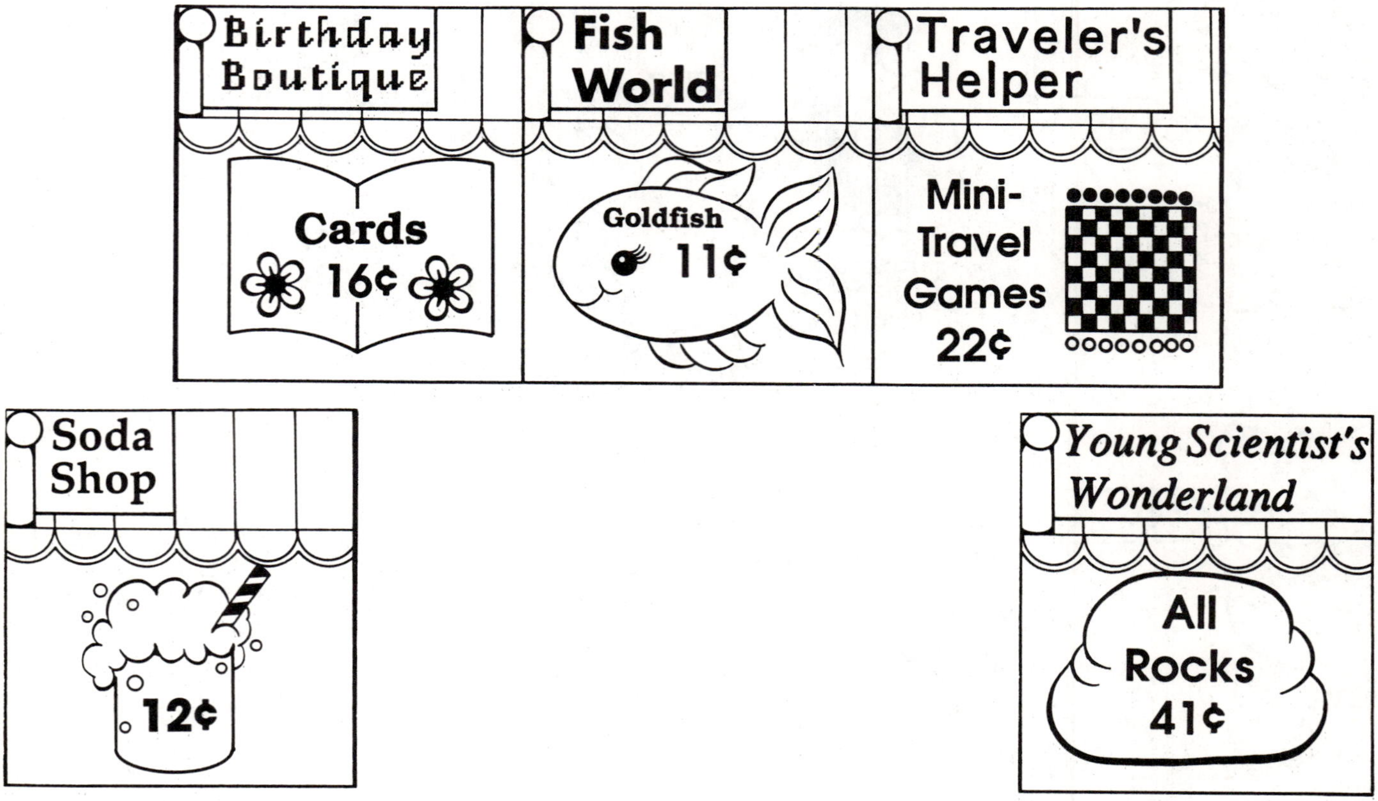
Birthday Boutique
Cards 16¢
Fish World
Goldfish 11¢
Traveler's Helper
Mini-Travel Games 22¢
Soda Shop
12¢
Young Scientist's Wonderland
All Rocks 41¢

5¢ 5¢ 1¢ 1¢
25¢ 10¢ 5¢ 1¢
10¢ 1¢ 1¢ 10¢
10¢ 1¢ 5¢

In which store did you not spend any money? ______________________

Name ______________________

MATH

So Many Choices!

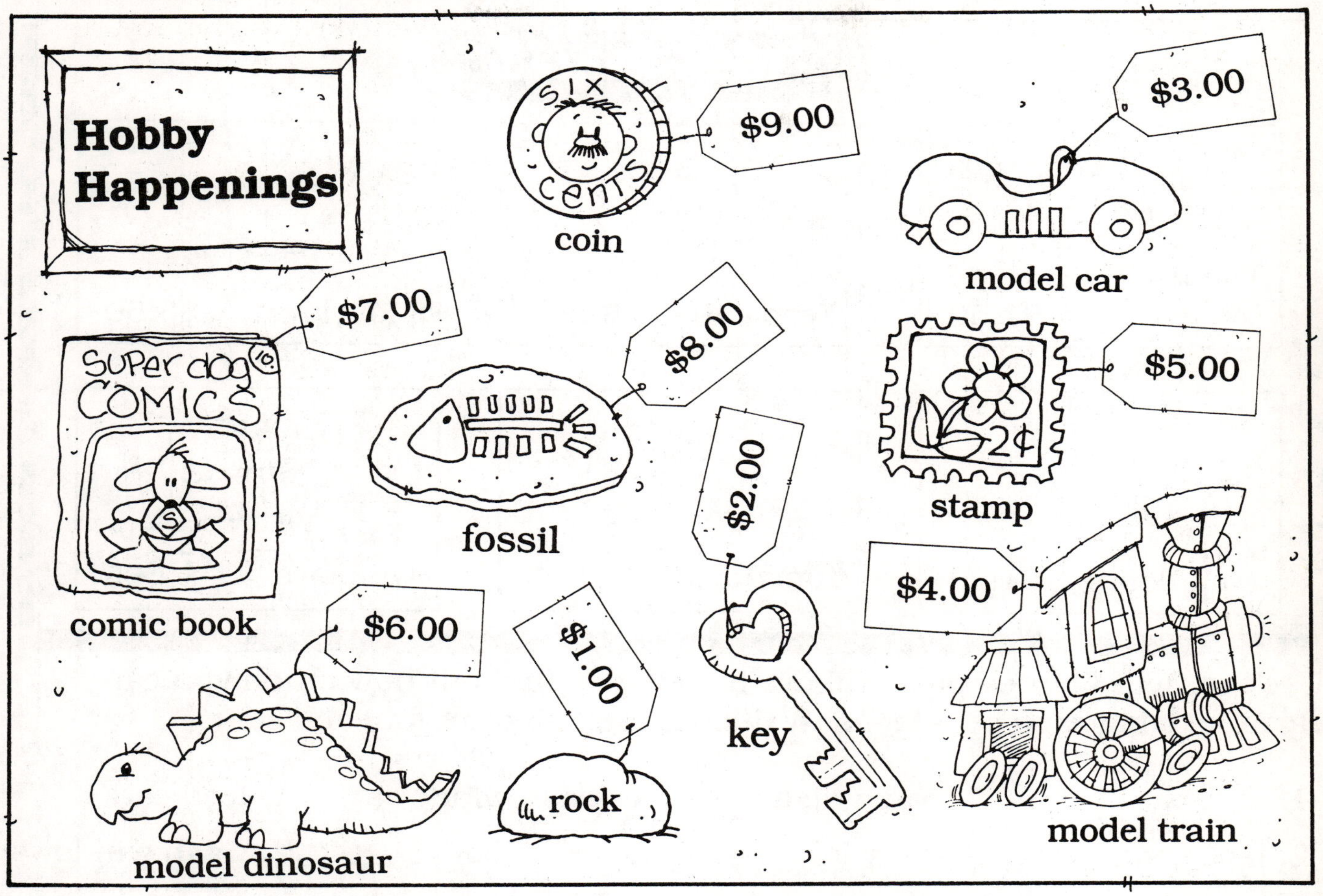
Hobby Happenings
SIX CENTS
$9.00
coin
$3.00
model car
$7.00
Super dog COMICS
comic book
$8.00
fossil
$5.00
2¢
stamp
$2.00
$4.00
model train
$6.00
model dinosaur
$1.00
rock
key

You want to buy 3 **different** items in the hobby store. You have $16.00. Write all the different combinations of items you can buy using the entire $16.00.

1. ________	1. ________	1. ________	1. ________
2. ________	2. ________	2. ________	2. ________
3. ________	3. ________	3. ________	3. ________

1. ________	1. ________	1. ________	1. ________
2. ________	2. ________	2. ________	2. ________
3. ________	3. ________	3. ________	3. ________

Name ____________________

Earnings Add Up!

Help Wanted

Wash dishes $1.50

KITTY
Feed cat $.95

Mow lawn $3.50

Mop floors $1.25

Pick tomatoes $2.75

Wash windows $2.85

Use the Help Wanted poster above to help you find out how much you can earn by doing each set of jobs. Write the total amount for each set.

1. feed cat
2. pick tomatoes
3. wash dishes

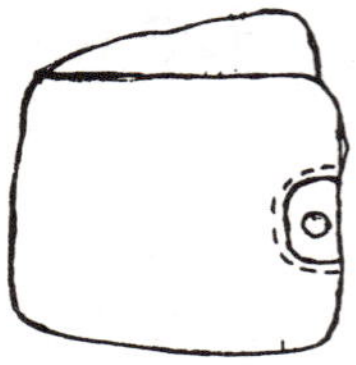

1. wash dishes
2. mow lawn
3. wash windows

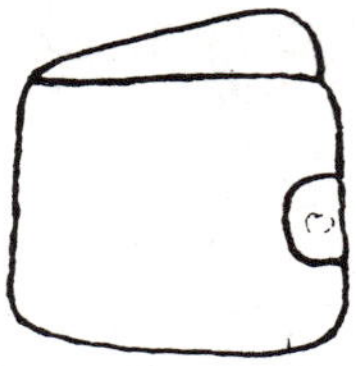

1. wash windows
2. mop floors
3. mow lawn

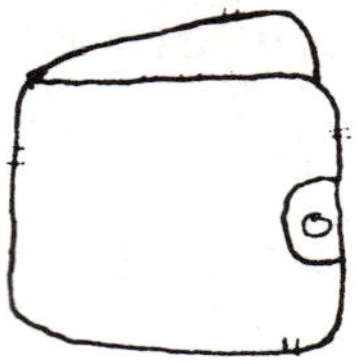

1. feed cat
2. wash windows
3. mop floors

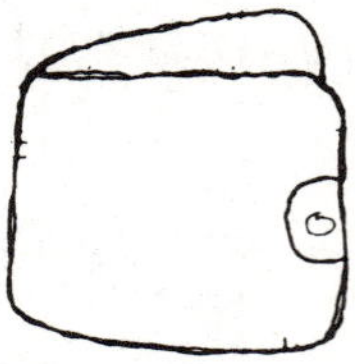

1. pick tomatoes
2. wash windows
3. feed cat

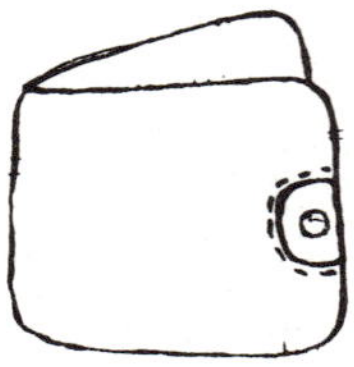

1. feed cat
2. wash dishes
3. mop floors

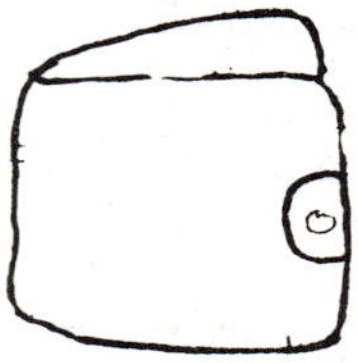

1. pick tomatoes
2. wash windows
3. mow lawn

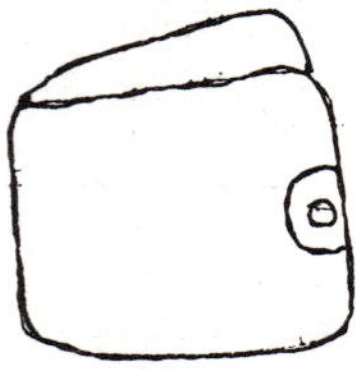

1. mop floors
2. pick tomatoes
3. wash windows

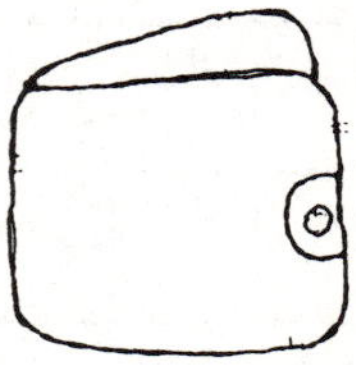

  0-7682-3792-0 *Skills & Practice Gr. 2*

Name ______________________

Here's Your Order

Count the money on each tray. Write the name of the food that costs that amount.

hamburger .. $2.45	milk .... $.64	cake $2.85
hot dog $1.77	soda pop $1.26	pie $2.25
sandwich $1.55	milkshake ... $1.89	sundae ...... $.95

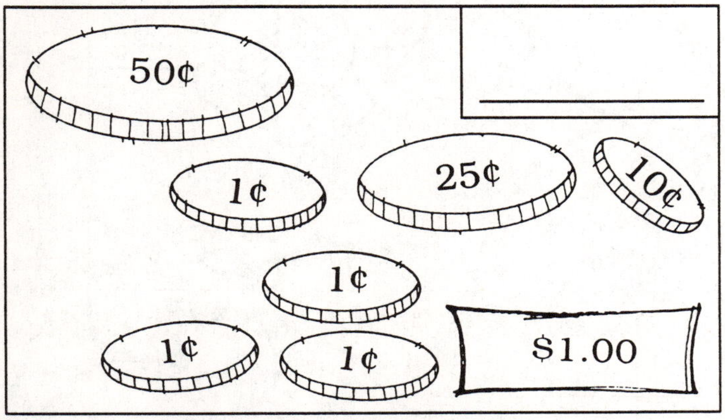

____

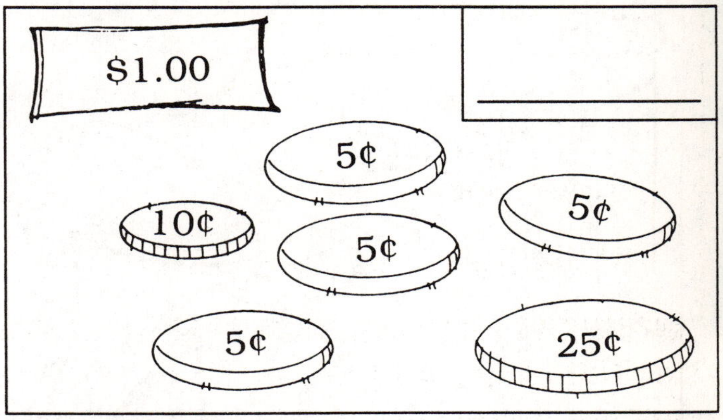

____

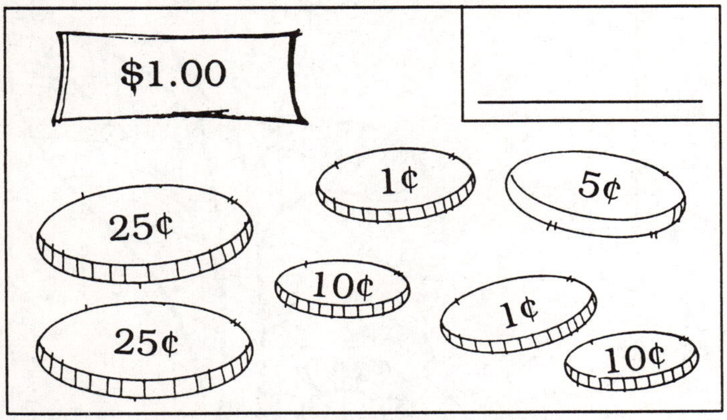

____

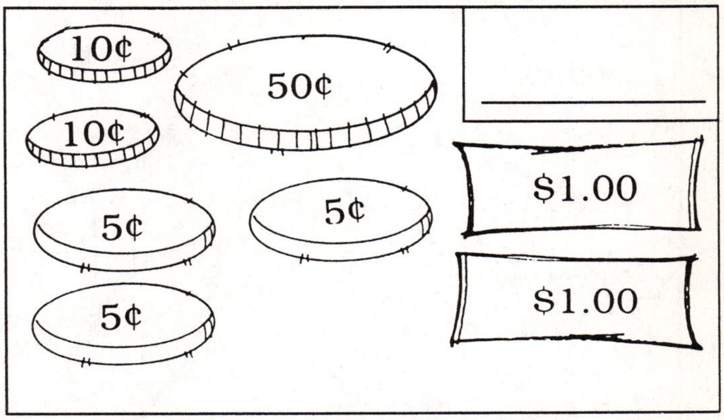

____

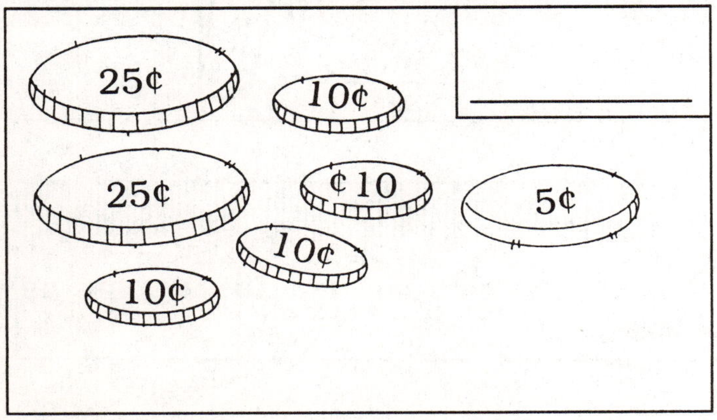

____

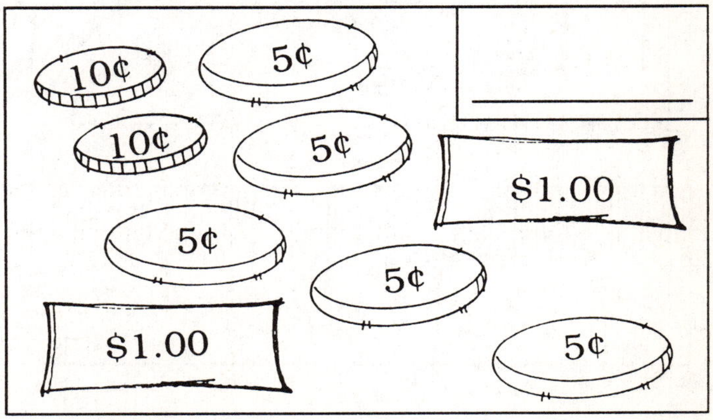

____

Name ______________________________

Flowers That "Measure" Up

Cut out the centimeter ruler at the bottom of the page. Use the ruler to measure how tall each flower is from the bottom of the stem to the top of the flower. Write the answer below the bee.

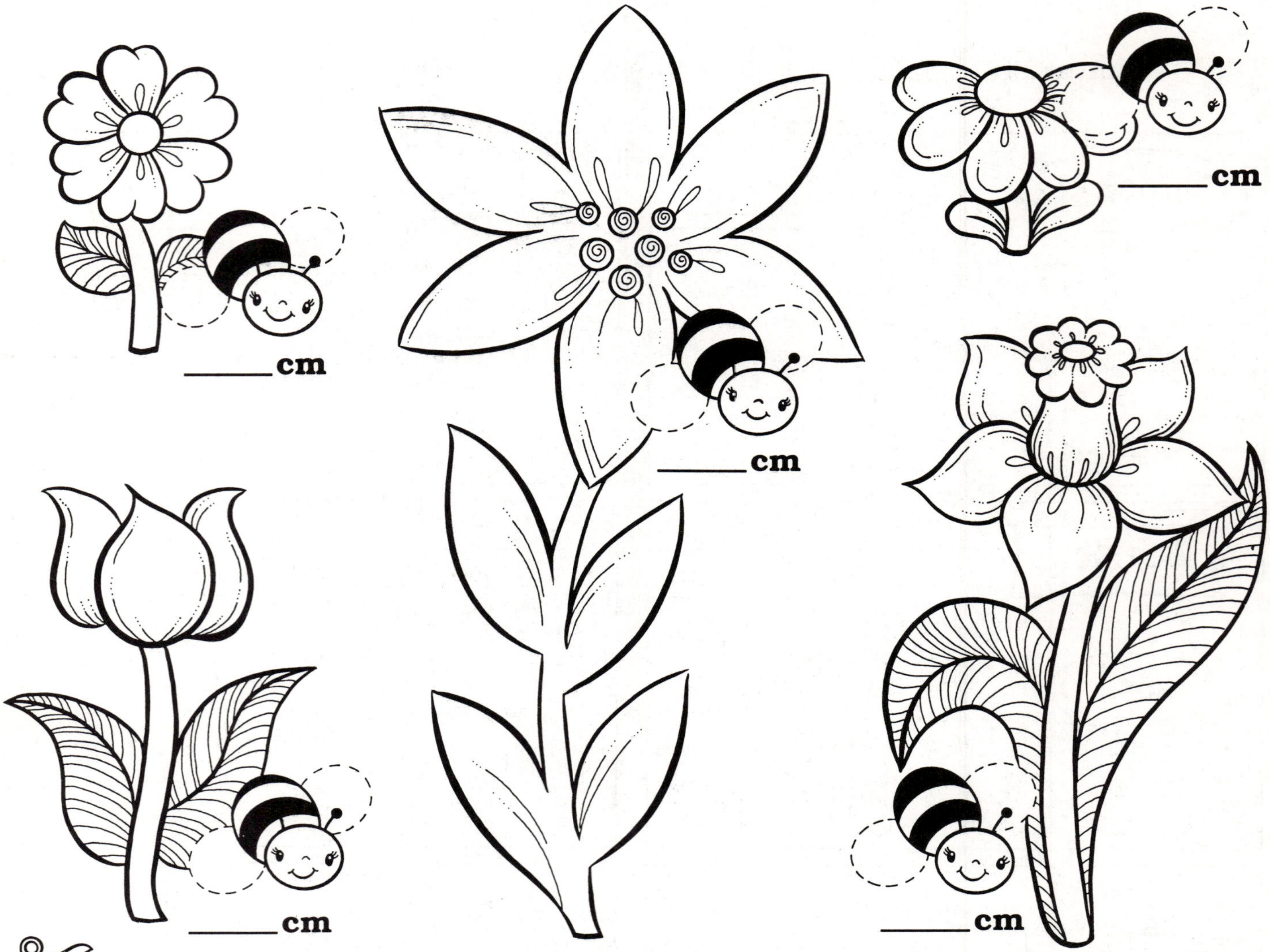
_____cm
_____cm
_____cm
_____cm
_____cm
_____cm

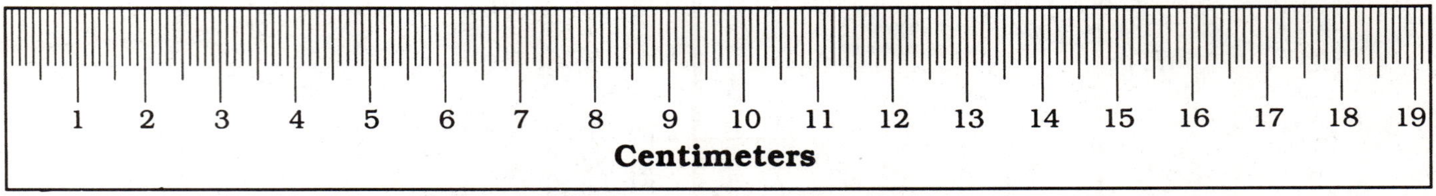
1 2 3 4 5 6 7 8 9 10 11 12 13 14 15 16 17 18 19
Centimeters

Name ______________________________

Brush Up on Measuring!

Use your centimeter ruler to measure these brushes to the nearest centimeter.

about ____ centimeters

about ____ centimeters

about ____ centimeters

about ____ centimeters

about ____ centimeters

about ____ centimeters

about ____ centimeters

about ____ centimeters

about ____ centimeters

about ____ centimeters

Name ______________________

Jungle Journey

Use a centimeter ruler to measure the line segments. Write the total length on each hut.

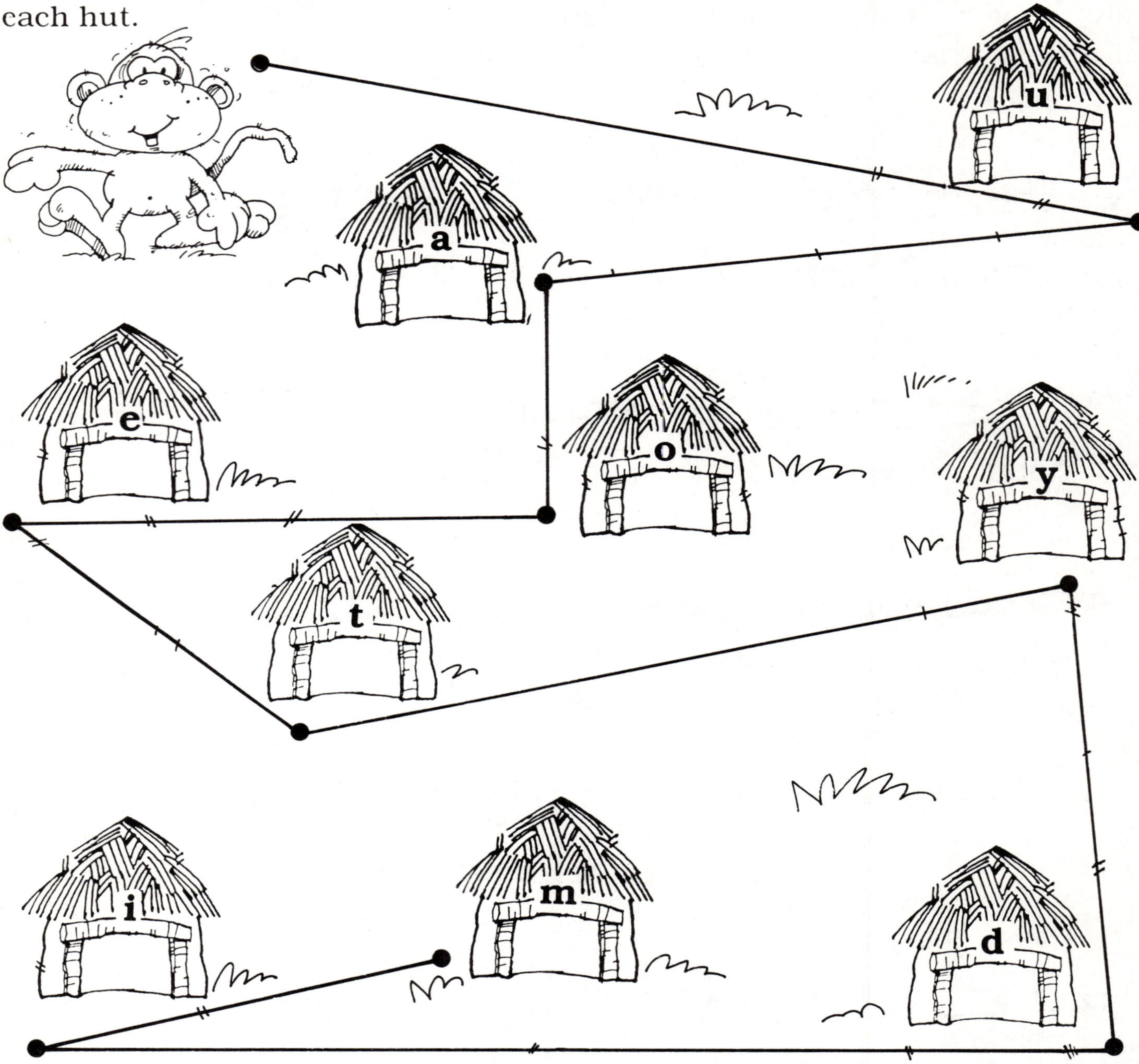

Use the numbers and the letters on the huts to solve the code.

___	___	___		___	___	___	___		___	___ !
13	4	15		7	10	8	9		18	6

Name ______________________________

Jumping Jellybeans

Use an inch ruler to measure the line segments. Write the total length on each candy jar.

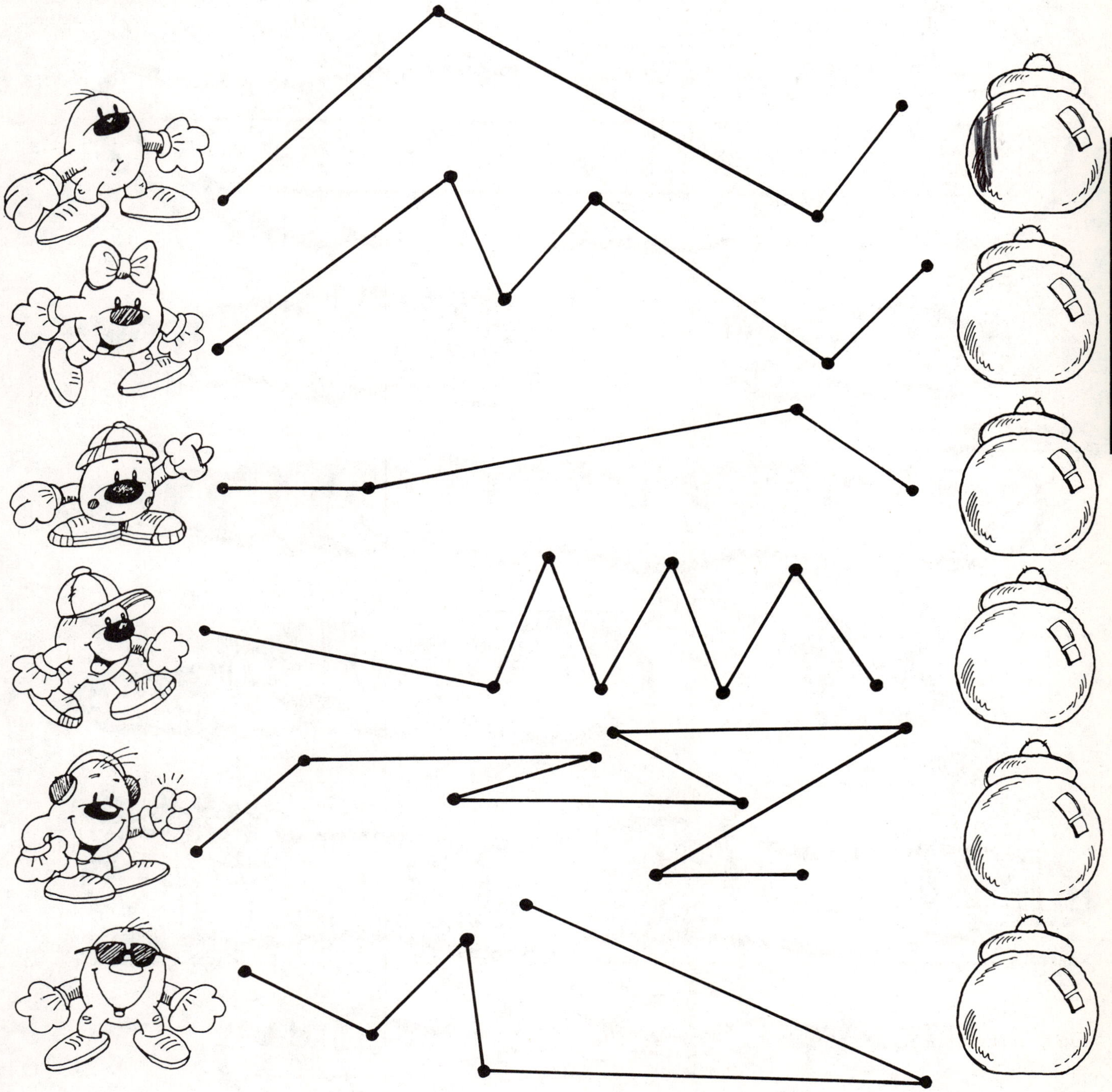

MATH

Name ____________________

The Inch Worm

Measure these worms to the nearest inch.

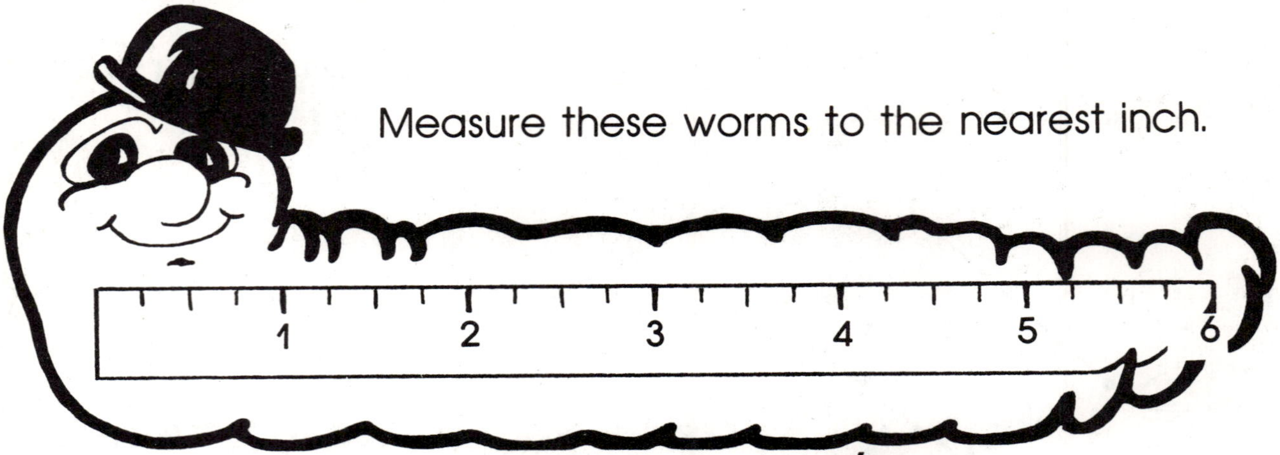

1. ______________

2. ______________

3. ______________

4. ______________

5. ______________

6. ______________

7. ______________

Name ____________________

How Big Are You?

You are getting so big! Every day, you grow a little more. Estimate how long some of your body parts are. Then, using a ruler, work with a friend to find the actual measurements.

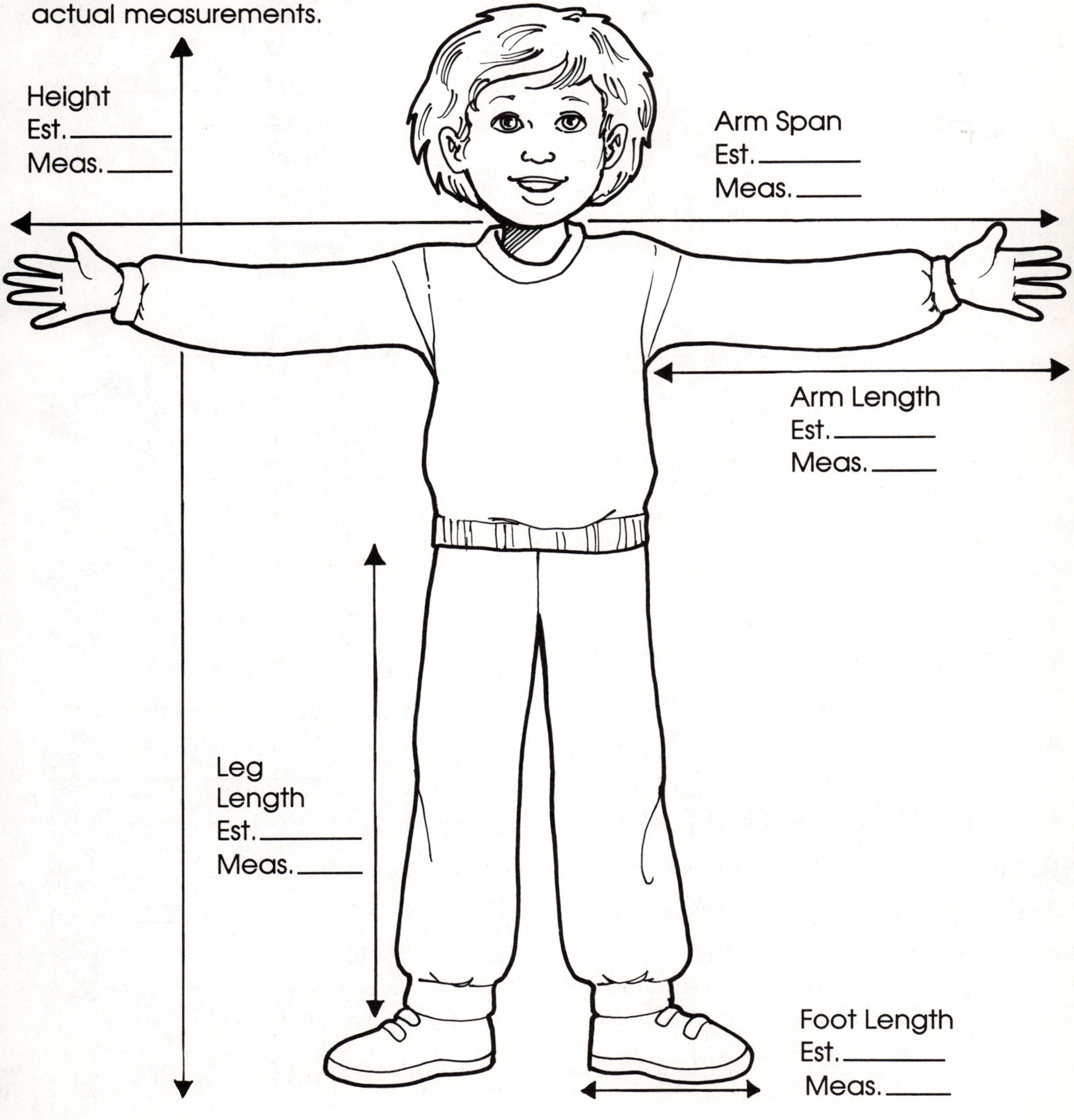
Height
Est. ________
Meas. ______
Arm Span
Est. ________
Meas. ______
Arm Length
Est. ________
Meas. ______
Leg
Length
Est. ________
Meas. ______
Foot Length
Est. ________
Meas. ______

Name ______________________

How Far Is It?

Use your ruler to measure each distance on the map. Then use the letters on the tires and your answers to solve the message at the bottom of the page.

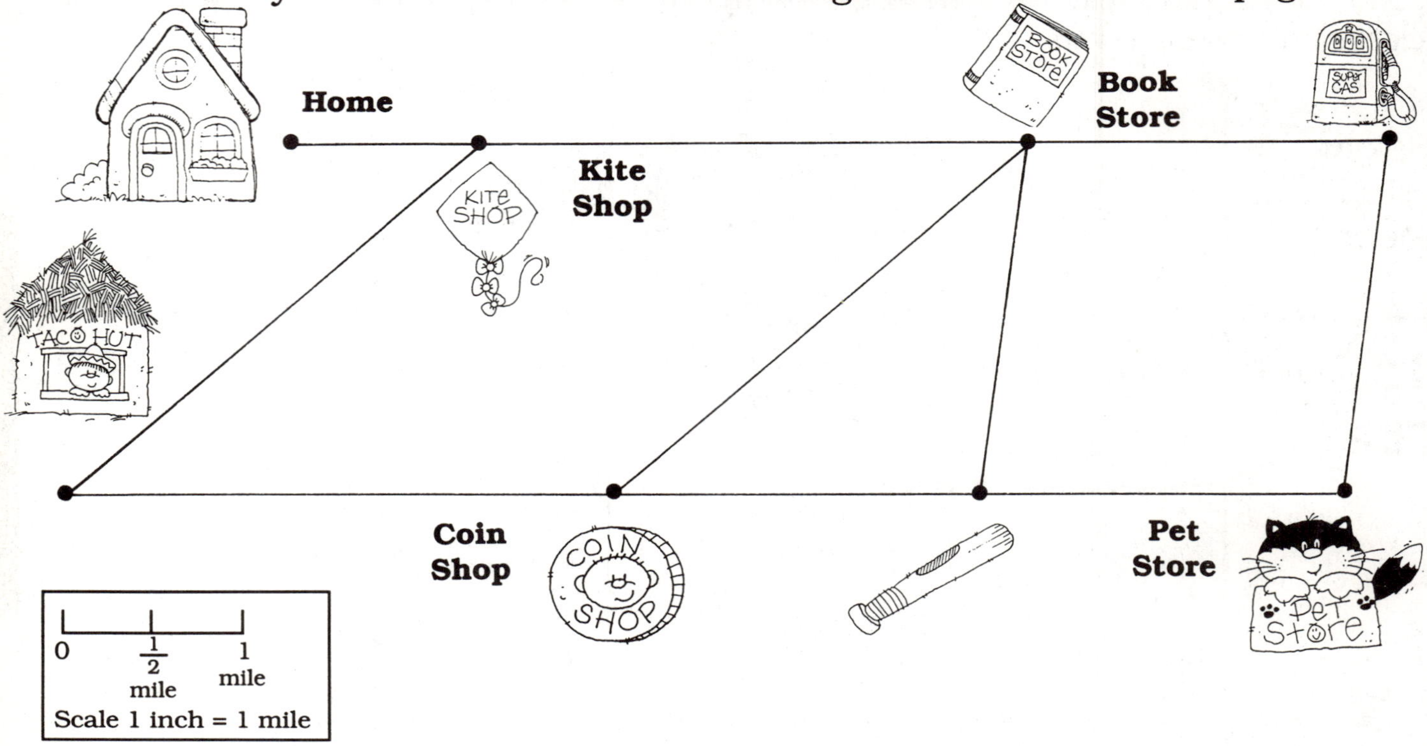

How far is it from . . .

1. home to the Kite Shop? __________ (s)
2. home to the Book Store to the Gas Station? __________ (e)
3. home to the Kite Shop to the Taco Hut? __________ (p)
4. the Taco Hut to the Coin Shop to the Book Store to the Gas Station? __________ (a)
5. the Taco Hut to the Coin Shop? __________ (u)
6. the Baseball Field to the Book Store to the Kite Shop? __________ (d)
7. the Pet Store to the Gas Station? __________ (r)
8. the Gas Station to the Pet Store to the Baseball Field to the Coin Shop to the Taco Hut? __________ (m)

You ___ ___ ___ ___ ___ ___ ___ ___   ___ ___ !
9 6 8 1 3 2 6 5   3 4

Name ______________________

Liquid Limits

Draw a line from the containers on the left to the containers on the right that will hold the same amount of liquid. **Hint:** 2 pints = 1 quart.

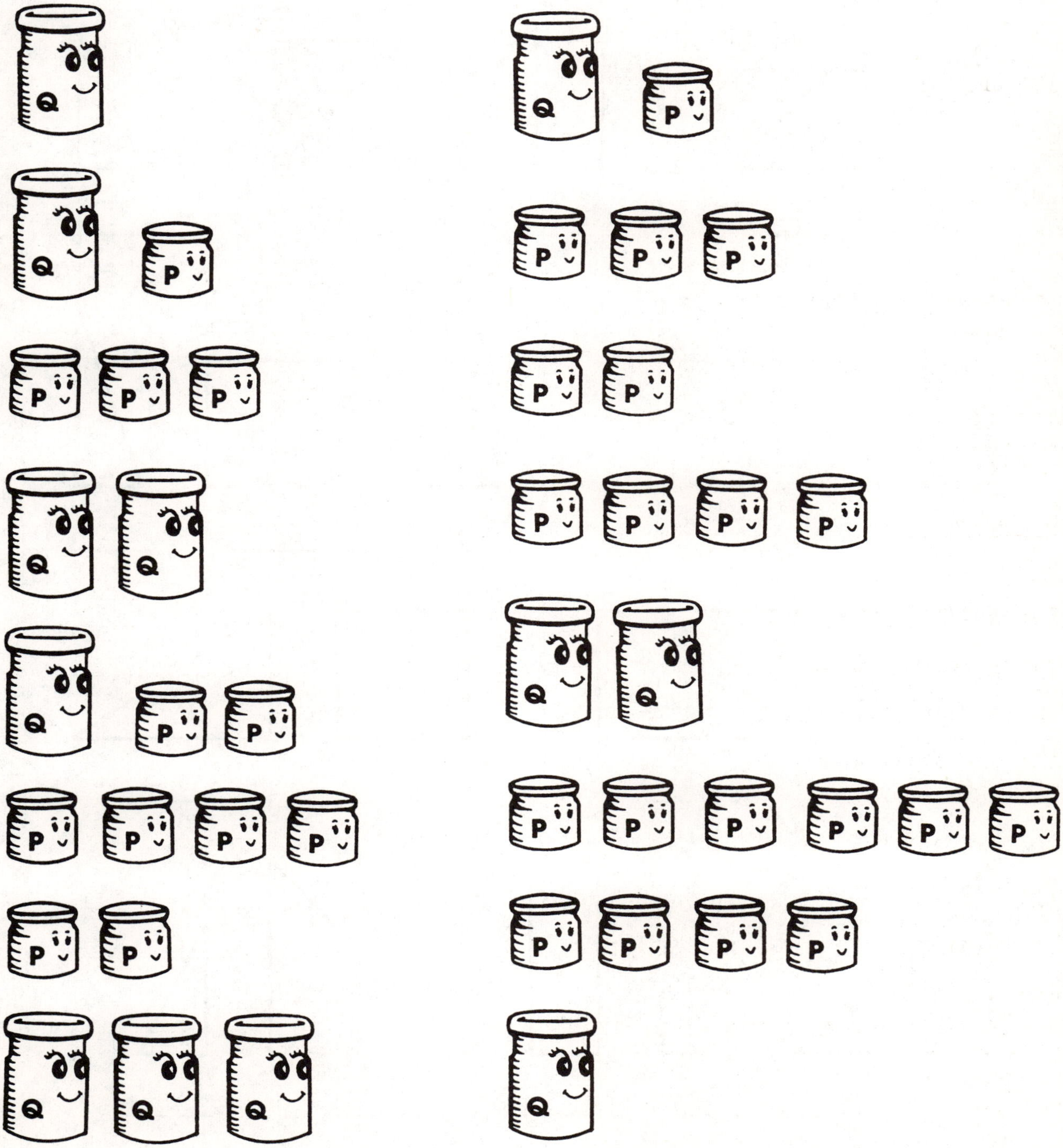

0-7682-3792-0 *Skills & Practice Gr. 2*

Name ______________________

Shape Sort

Color the ones in each row that are the same size and shape. Write **T** for triangle, **R** for rectangle and **S** for square.

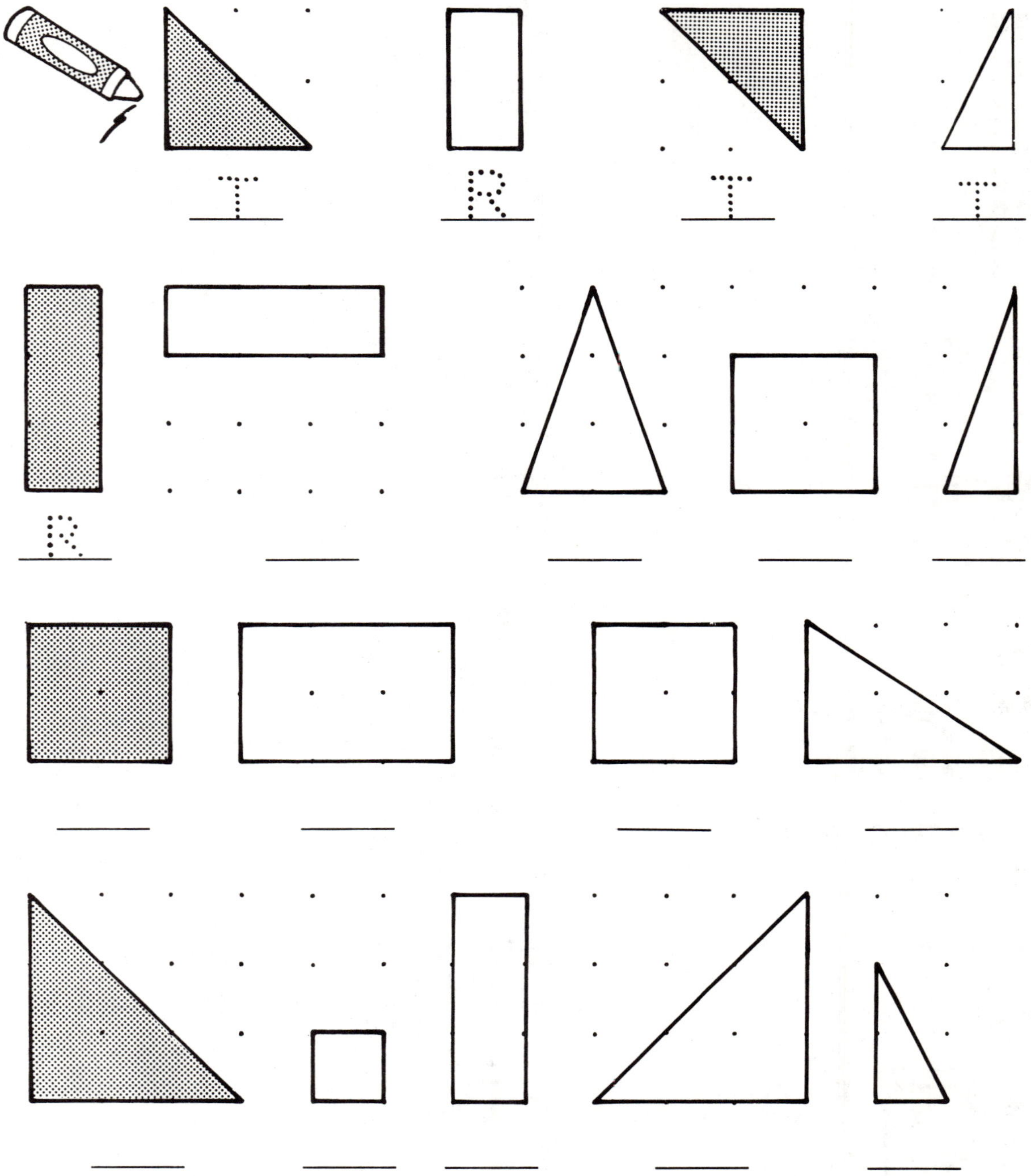

Name ________________________

Sea Shapes

Find the shapes and color them using the code.

△ red ○ blue ◇ yellow

⬭ green □ orange ▭ black

MATH

Name ______________________

Equal and Unequal Parts

Cut out each shape below along the solid lines. Then fold the shape on the dotted lines. Do you get equal or unequal parts? Sort the shapes into two piles: those with equal parts and those with unequal parts.

Name ____________________

Mean Monster's Diet

Mean Monster has to go on a diet. He is so fat he popped all the buttons off his shirt. Help him choose the right piece of food.

1. Mean Monster may have 1/4 of this chocolate pie. Color in 1/4 of the pie.

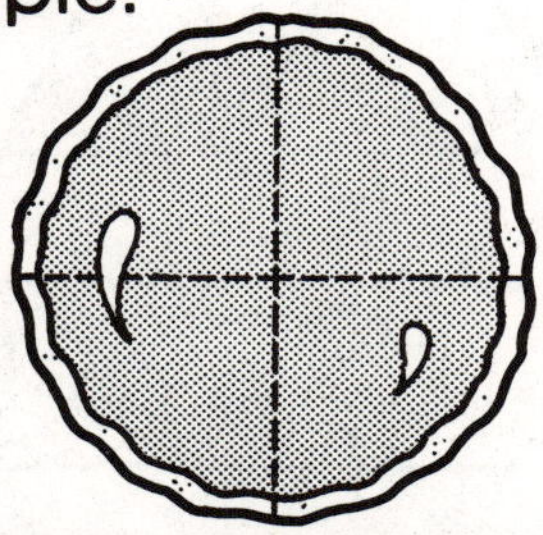

2. Mean Monster may eat 1/3 of this pizza. Color in 1/3 of the pizza.

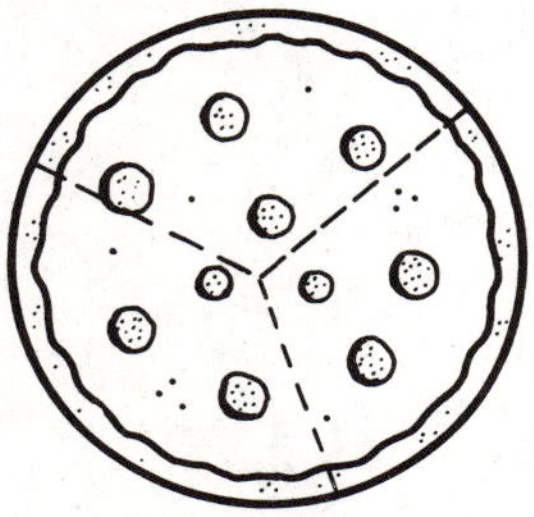

3. For a snack, he wants 1/3 of this chocolate cake. Color in 1/3 of the cake.

4. For lunch, Mean Monster gets 1/2 of the sandwich. Color in 1/2 of the sandwich.

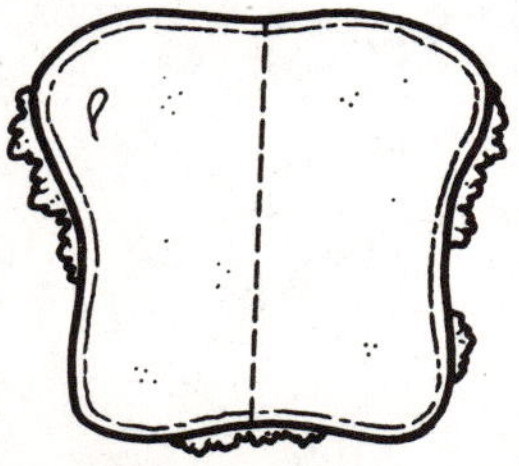

5. For an evening snack, he can have 1/4 of the candy bar. Color in 1/4 of the candy bar.

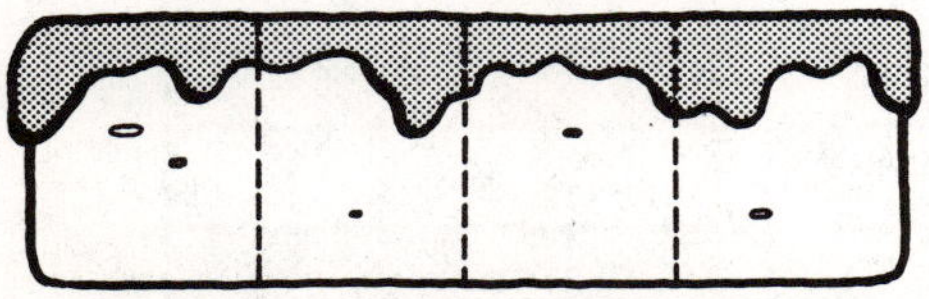

6. He ate 1/2 of the apple for lunch. Color in 1/2 of the apple.

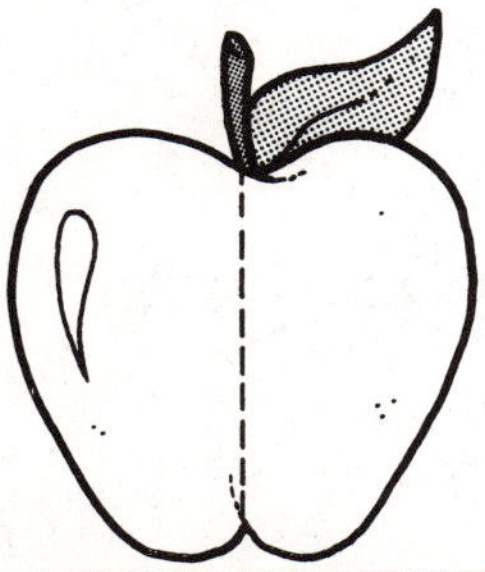

Name ______________________

Shaded Shapes

Draw line from fraction to correct shape.

$\frac{1}{3}$ shaded

$\frac{2}{4}$ shaded

$\frac{1}{4}$ shaded

$\frac{1}{2}$ shaded

$\frac{3}{4}$ shaded

$\frac{2}{3}$ shaded

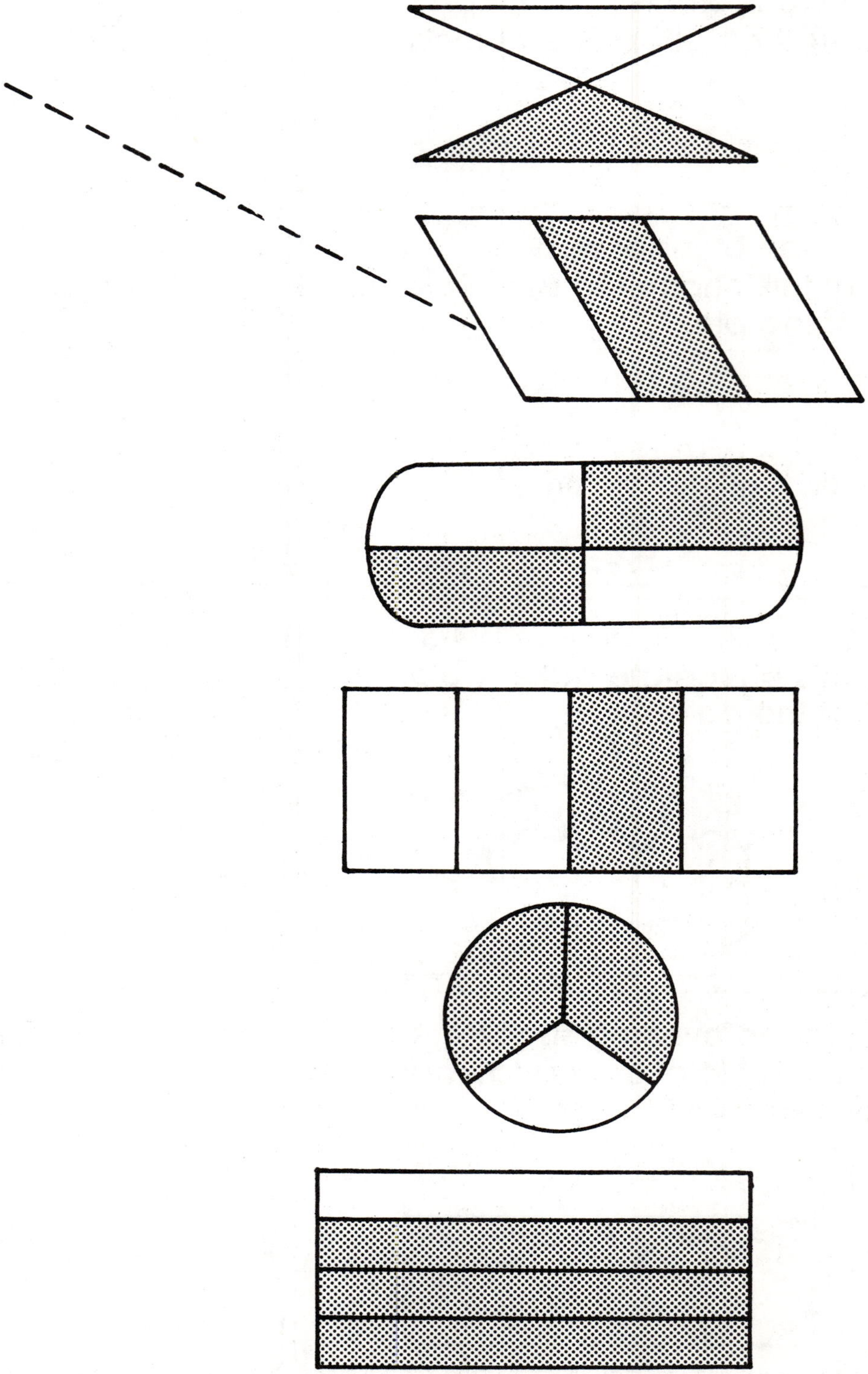

Name ______________________________

Fraction Food

Count the equal parts. Circle the fraction that names one of the parts.

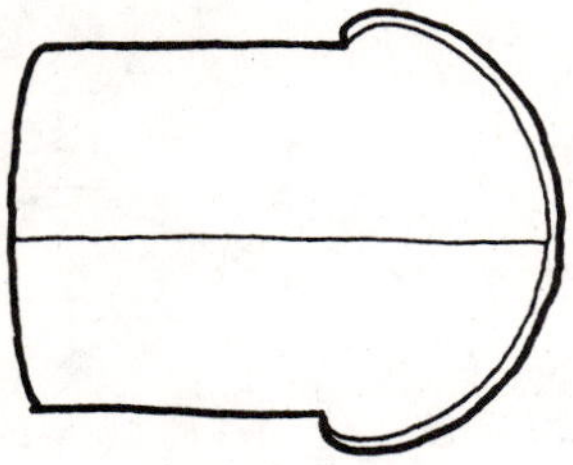

$\frac{1}{2}$ $\frac{1}{3}$ $\frac{1}{4}$

$\frac{1}{2}$ $\frac{1}{3}$ $\frac{1}{4}$

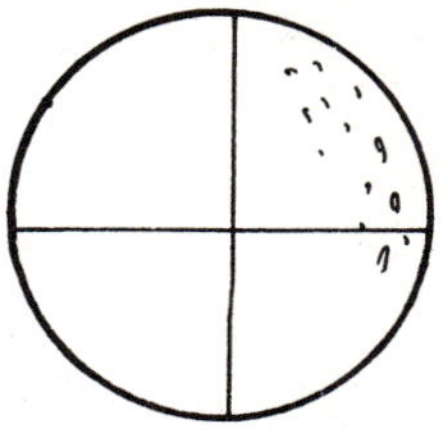

$\frac{1}{2}$ $\frac{1}{3}$ $\frac{1}{4}$

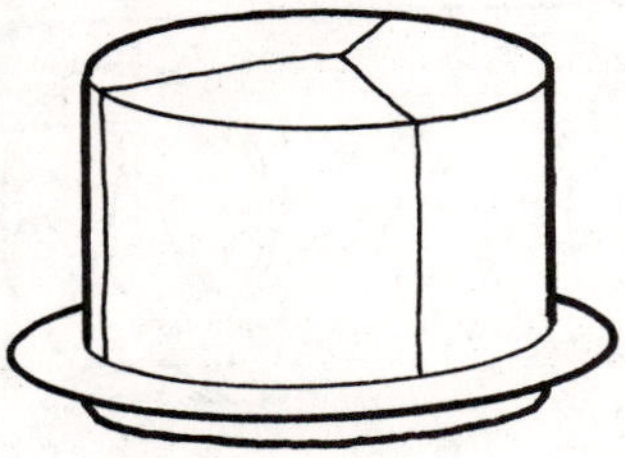

$\frac{1}{2}$ $\frac{1}{3}$ $\frac{1}{4}$

$\frac{1}{2}$ $\frac{1}{3}$ $\frac{1}{4}$

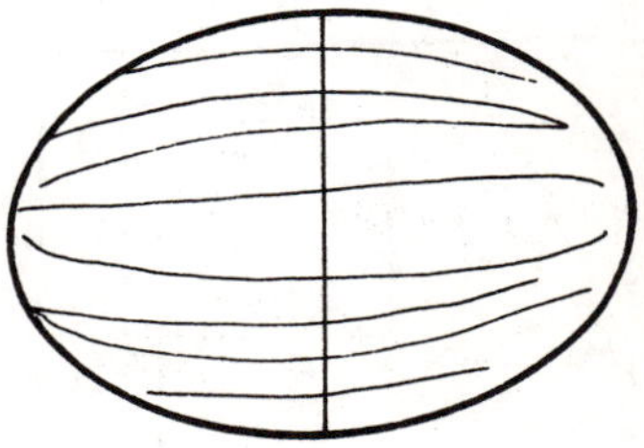

$\frac{1}{2}$ $\frac{1}{3}$ $\frac{1}{4}$

$\frac{1}{2}$ $\frac{1}{3}$ $\frac{1}{4}$

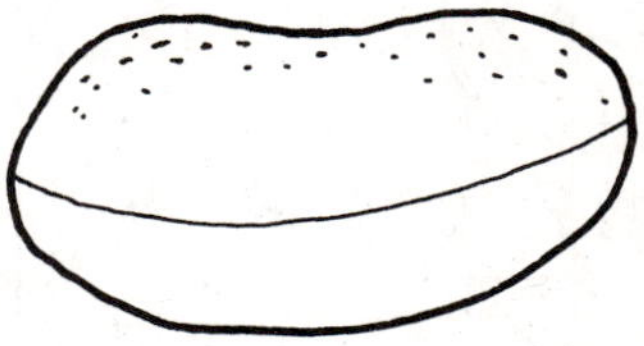

$\frac{1}{2}$ $\frac{1}{3}$ $\frac{1}{4}$

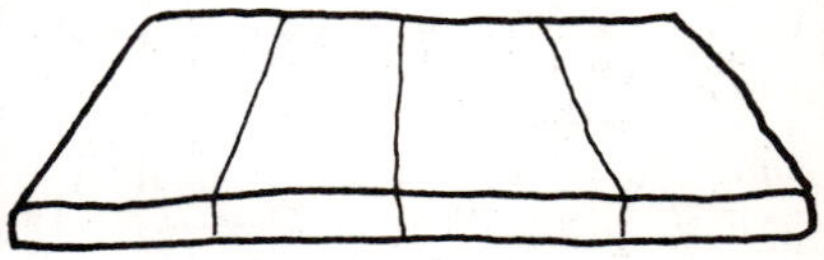

$\frac{1}{2}$ $\frac{1}{3}$ $\frac{1}{4}$

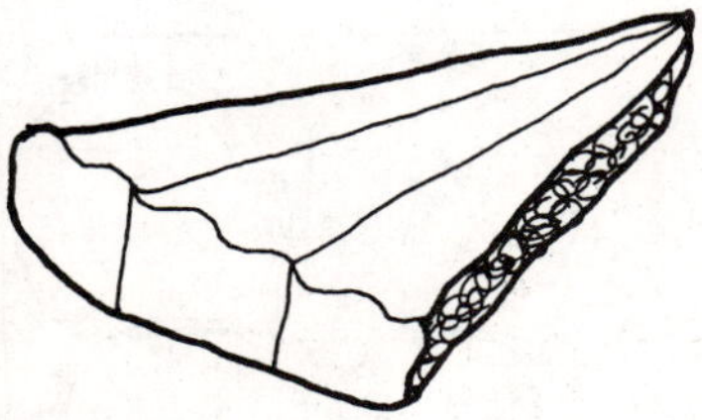

$\frac{1}{2}$ $\frac{1}{3}$ $\frac{1}{4}$

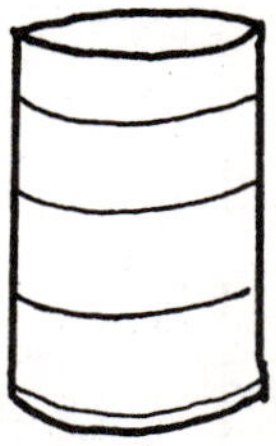

$\frac{1}{2}$ $\frac{1}{3}$ $\frac{1}{4}$

$\frac{1}{2}$ $\frac{1}{3}$ $\frac{1}{4}$

Name ____________________

Fortunate Fractions

Read the fraction on each tray. Color the correct number of fortune cookies to show each fraction.

1/2
1/3
4/6
2/6
5/6
3/8
3/4
5/8

Name ______________________

Turtle Spots

Count the spots on the turtles.
Color the boxes to show how many spots.

1	2	3	4	5	6	7	8

Name ______________________

Wormy Apples

Color the boxes to show how many worms.
Answer the questions.

1	2	3	4	5	6

How many worms in apple 1?____ 2?____ 3?____ 4?____

In apples 1 and 3? ____ In apples 2 and 4? ____

How many more worms in apple 4 than in apple 2? ____

How many more worms in apple 3 than in apple 1? ____

0-7682-3792-0 *Skills & Practice Gr. 2*

Name ______________________________

Pat's Fish

This picture graph shows how many fish Pat caught.

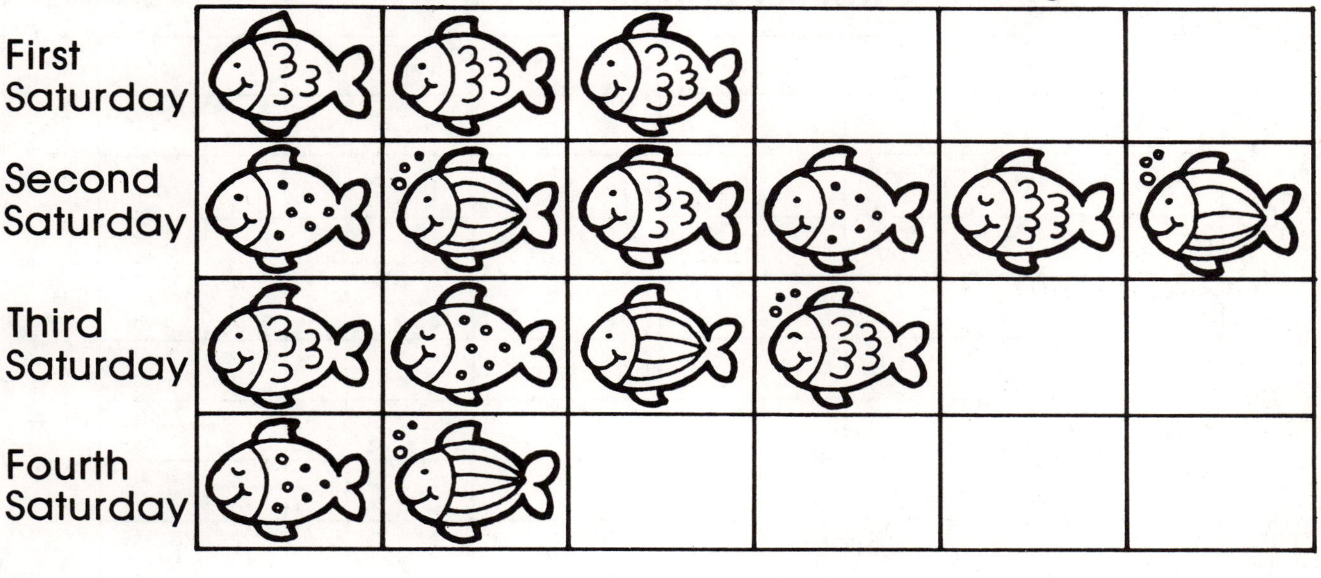

Color the fish Pat caught on the third Saturday red.
Color the fish he caught on the first Saturday blue, the second Saturday yellow, and the fourth Saturday green.
How many fish did he catch on the first Saturday? ____
second Saturday? ____ third Saturday? ____ fourth Saturday? ____

Name ______________________

Honey Bear's Bakery

Look at the picture of the bakery. Fill in the graph to show how many of each treat are in the picture.

Number of Bakery Treats

Name ______________________

Treasure Quest

Read the directions. Draw the pictures where they belong on the grid.

Start at 0 and go . . .

over 2, up 5. Draw a 

over 9, up 3. Draw a 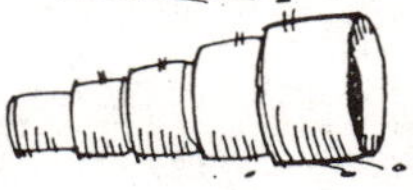

over 8, up 6. Draw a 

over 5, up 2. Draw a 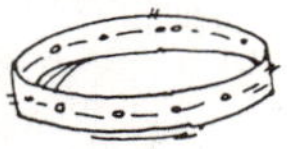

over 1, up 7. Draw a 

over 7, up 1. Draw a .

over 6, up 4. Draw a 

over 2, up 3. Draw a 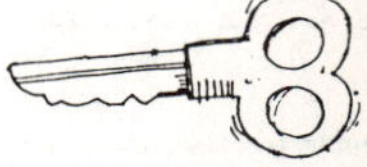

over 3, up 1. Draw a 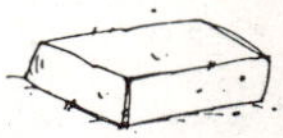.

over 4, up 6. Draw a 

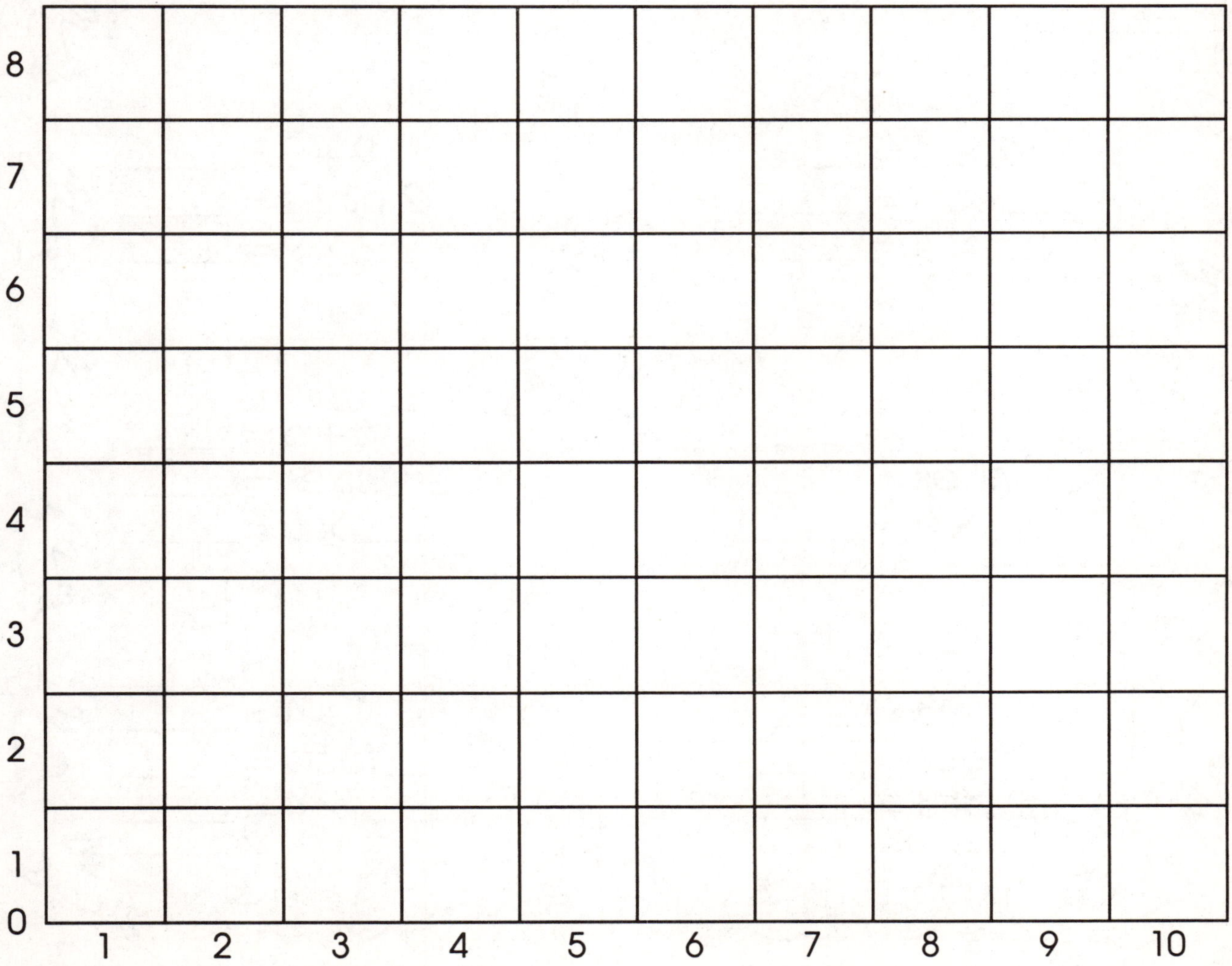

Name ____________________

Multiplying Rabbits

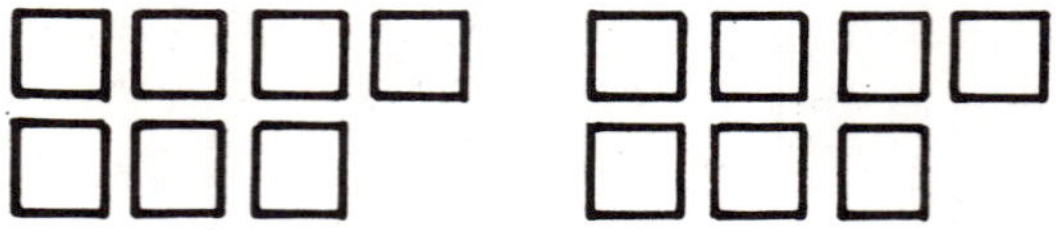

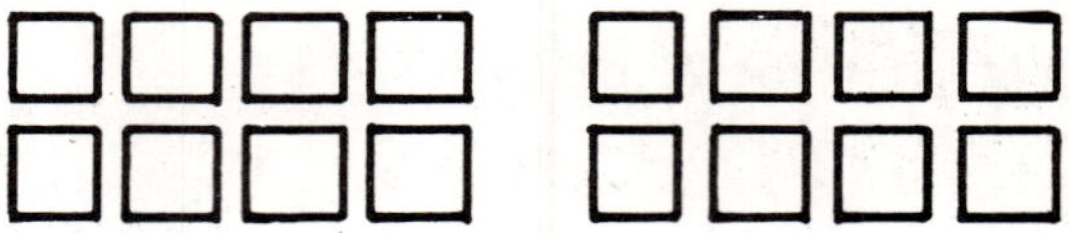

7 + 7 = 14
2 sevens = ____
2 × 7 = ____

8 + 8 = 16
2 eights = ____
2 × 8 = ____

2 + 2 + 2 + 2 = ____
____ twos = ____
____ × 2 = ____

3 + 3 + 3 + 3 + 3 = ____
____ threes = ____
____ × 3 = ____

4 + 4 + 4 = ____
____ fours = ____
____ × 4 = ____

9 + 9 = ____
2 nines = ____
____ × 9 = ____

5 + 5 + 5 = ____
____ fives = ____
____ × 5 = ____

6 + 6 = ____
____ sixes = ____
____ × 6 = ____

3 + 3 + 3 + 3 = ____
____ threes = ____
____ × 3 = ____

4 + 4 = ____
____ fours = ____
____ × 4 = ____

Name ____________________

Mr. X and His Cookies

Draw a line from each picture to its matching problem.

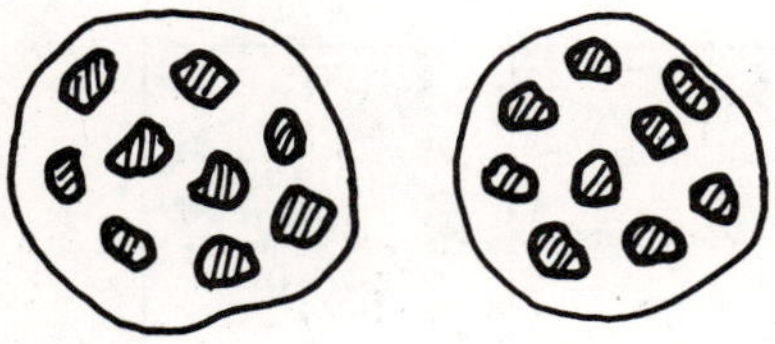

$4 \times 3 = 12$

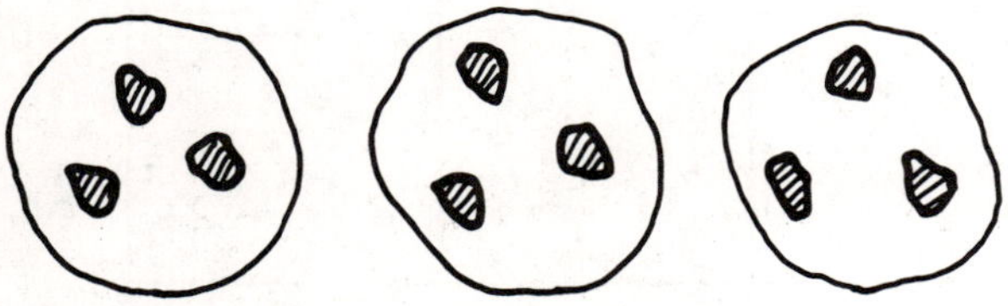

$3 \times 3 = 9$

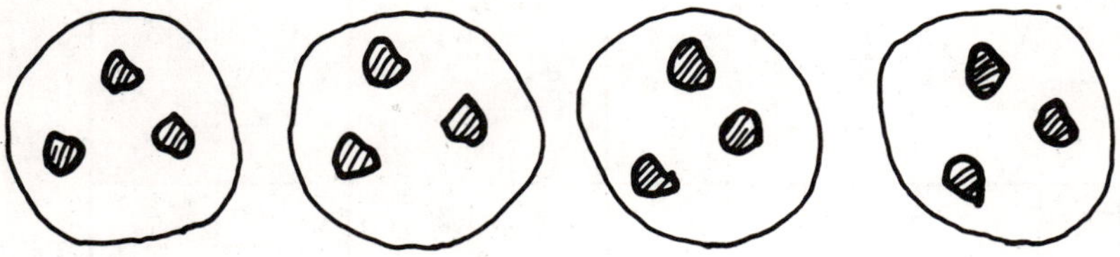

$2 \times 9 = 18$

$4 \times 4 = 16$

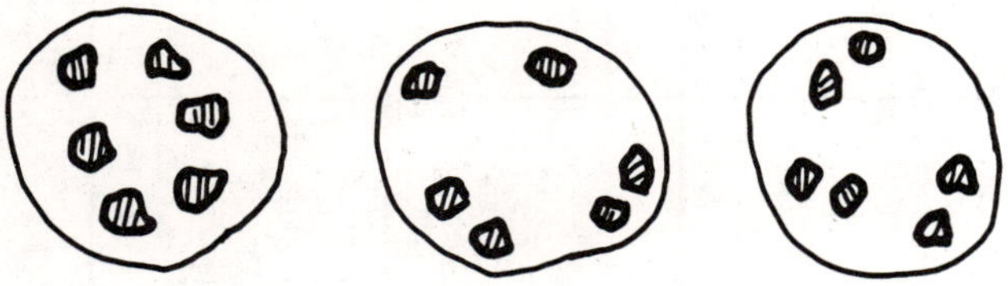

$3 \times 6 = 18$

$3 \times 5 = 15$

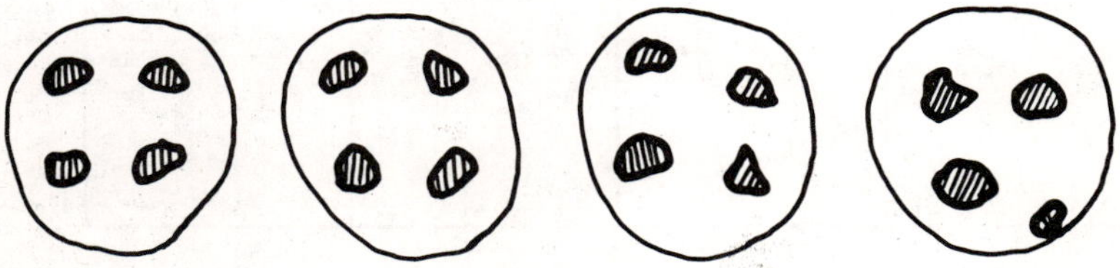

$5 \times 2 = 10$

Name ______________________________

Move That Body

Read a task on the chart. Color the spaces on the chart which show the parts of the body that would be used for the task.

Tasks	 head	 arm	 hand	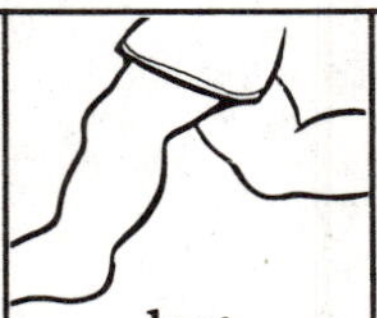 leg	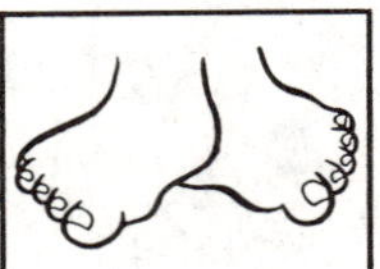 feet
 **wash dishes**					
 **pull weeds**					
 **play soccer**					
 **play on a slide**					
 **use a skateboard**					
1 + 1 = 2 **do homework**					
 **play catch**					

0-7682-3792-0 *Skills & Practice Gr. 2*

Name ___________________________

Body Works

Read the clues. Write the words in the puzzle.

Across:

2. You use these to breathe.
4. You need to do this when you're tired.
5. This breaks down food.
7. This tells your body what to do.
9. A gas you breathe.
10. It pumps blood.

Down:

1. It carries oxygen to your body.
3. Microscopic living things that can make you sick.
6. This helps when you are sick.
8. These support and shape your body.

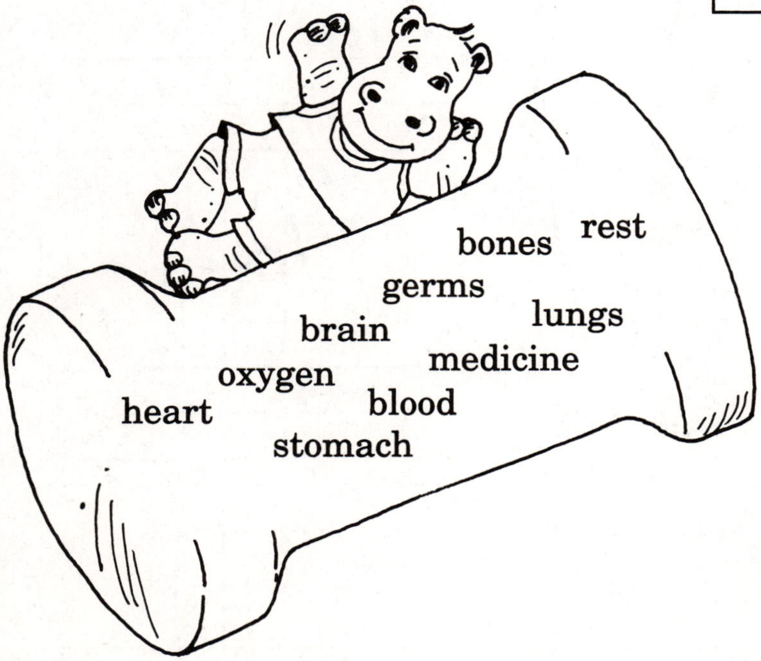
bones
rest
germs
lungs
brain
medicine
oxygen
heart
blood
stomach

Name ______________________________

My Bones

Bones give your body shape. They let you stand up tall. You cannot see your bones. But you can feel many of your bones under your skin.

Draw a line from each bone to the part of the body where it is found. Write the name of the bone(s).

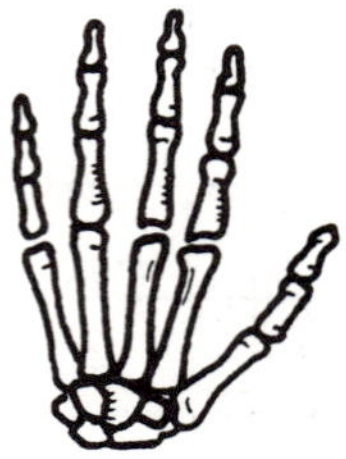

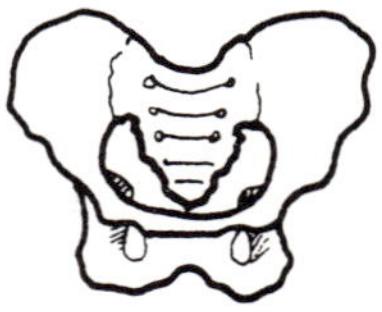

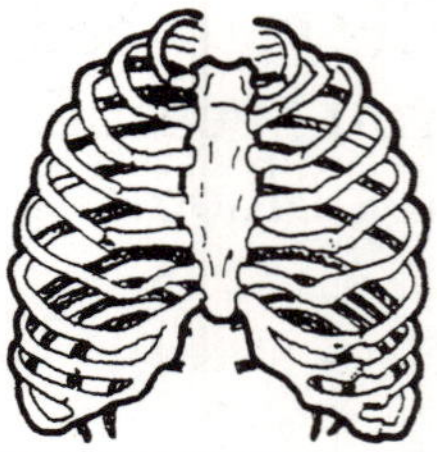

Word Bank

skull	ribs	foot
hand	knee	hips

Name ____________________

Name That Bone

Name these bones of your skeleton.

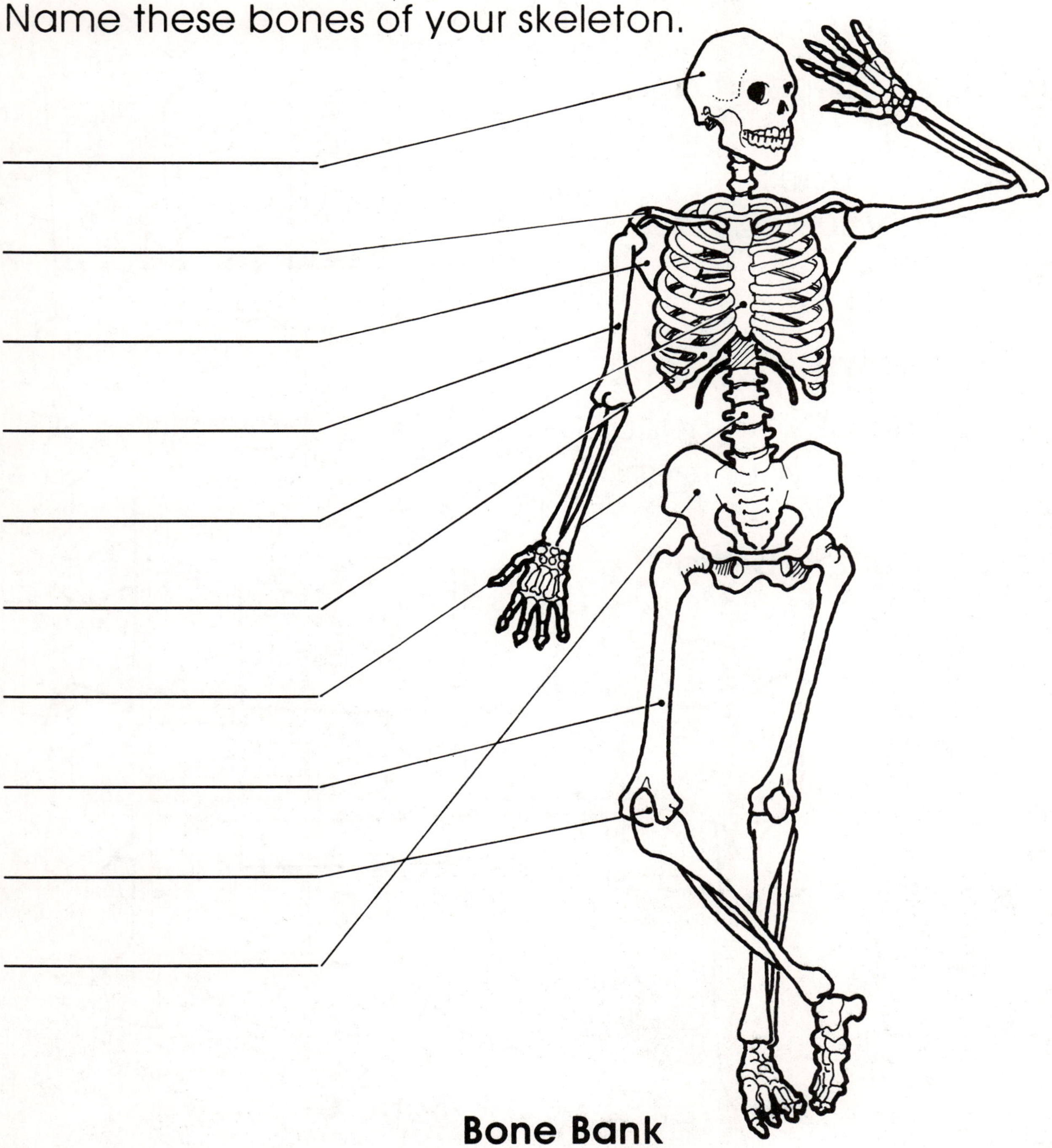

Bone Bank

hipbone	arm bone	backbone	rib
collarbone	breastbone	leg bone	skull
knee bone	shoulder blade		

SCIENCE

Name ______________________________

Crossbones

Across

3. protects your heart and lungs
6. all of your bones
7. connects your leg and foot

Down

1. on the end of your hands
2. on the end of your feet
4. spine
5. makes your leg bend
6. protects your brain

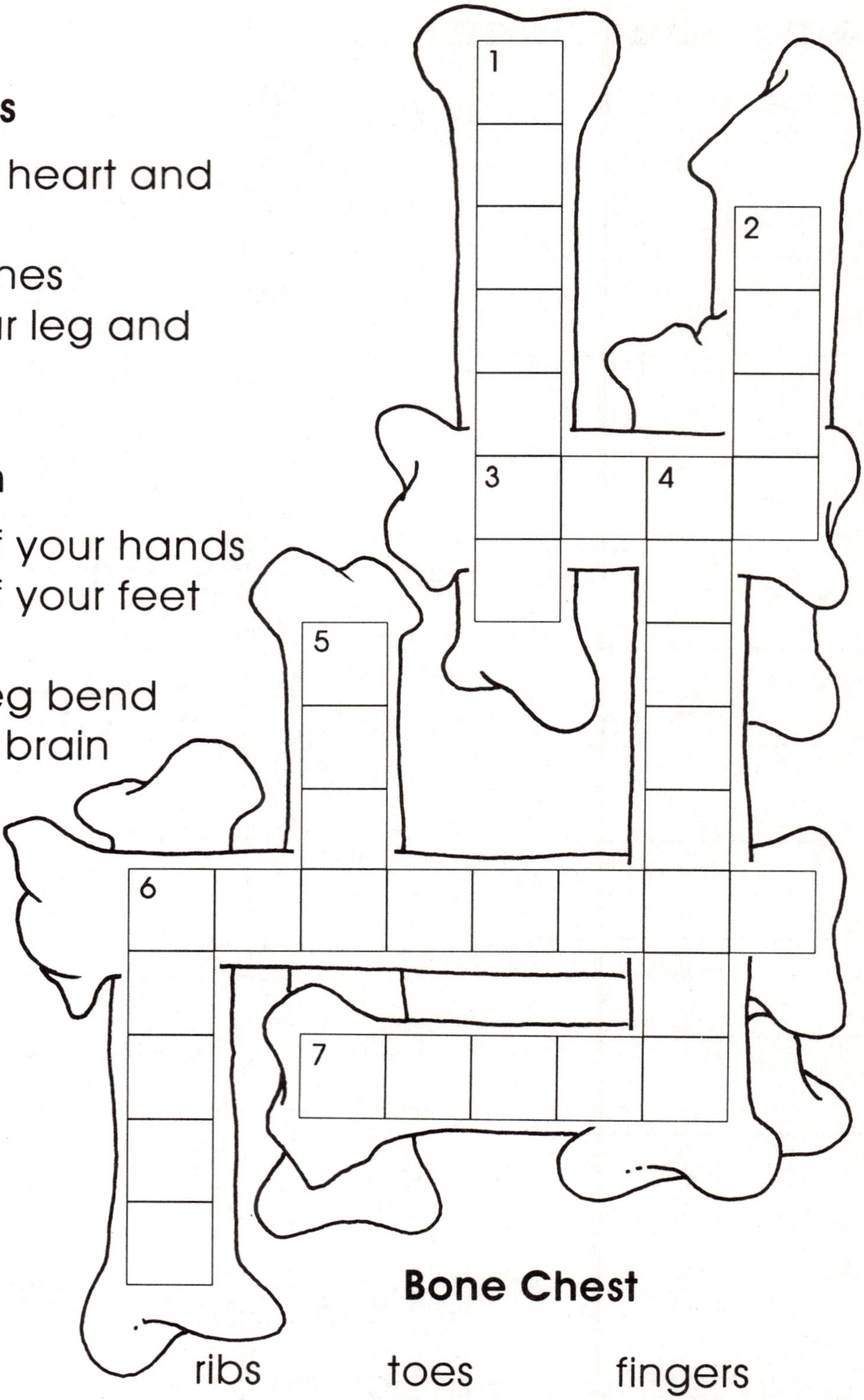

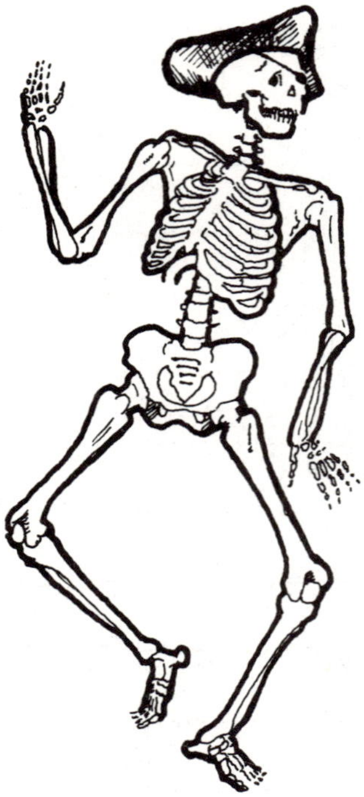

Bone Chest

ribs
knee
ankle
toes
skull
skeleton
fingers
backbone

Name ______________________________

Outfitted for Health

Read the phrases in the Word Bank. Write only the **good** health habits on the lines.

Word Bank			
	Take a bath.	Eat a lot of sweets	Stay up all night.
	Drink water.	Get plenty of sleep.	Keep cuts clean.
	Sit all day.	Never wash your hands.	Brush your teeth.
	Exercise.	Eat healthy foods.	

1. ______________________________

2. ______________________________

3. ______________________________

4. ______________________________

5. ______________________________

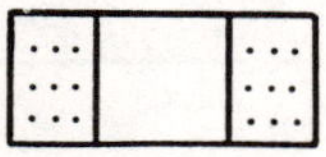

6. ______________________________

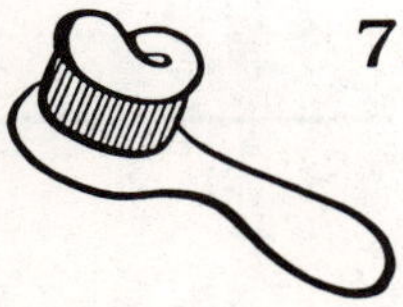

7. ______________________________

SCIENCE

0-7682-3792-0 *Skills & Practice Gr. 2*

Name ______________________________

A Delicious Dinner

Pretend that you get to plan a healthful dinner for your family. Write the menu, choosing items from the lists.

Meats	**Vegetables**	**Side Dishes**
barbecue chicken	steamed broccoli	brown rice
hamburgers	creamed corn	mashed potatoes
grilled pork chops	buttered peas	baked beans

Name ______________________

A "Sense"-ible Arrangement

Cut out the flowers at the bottom of the page. Pick one flower and look at the object and word on it. Paste the flower on the vase that tells which sense you would mainly use with the object on that flower.

taste
hear
smell
see
feel

wind
cake
bell
ammonia
cloud
star
knock
perfume
raindrops
watermelon

0-7682-3792-0 *Skills & Practice Gr. 2*

Name ______________________________

Identifying Prints

Cut out the fingerprints at the bottom of the page. Use a magnifying glass to match the cut-out fingerprints to those on the page. Paste each fingerprint next to the one it matches.

Paste Exhibit Here
Paste Exhibit Here
Paste Exhibit Here
Paste Exhibit Here
Paste Exhibit Here
Paste Exhibit Here

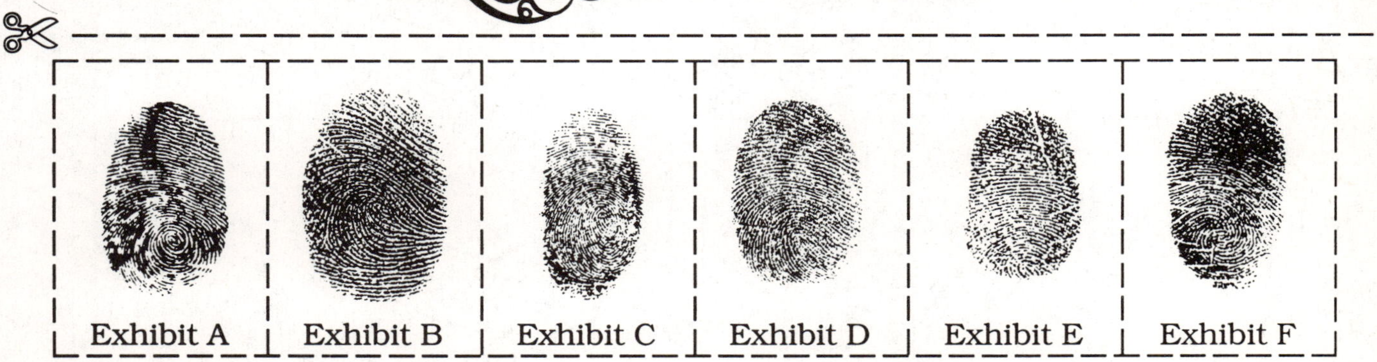
Exhibit A
Exhibit B
Exhibit C
Exhibit D
Exhibit E
Exhibit F

Name ________________________

Interesting Invertebrates

Invertebrates are animals that have no backbone or inside skeleton. Some have soft bodies protected by shells. Others have soft bodies that are not protected. Some invertebrates are so small that they can only be seen with a microscope.

Below are some examples of invertebrates. Use the clues to name each one.

_ _ _ _ I P E D E

S _ _ _ F _ _ _

E _ _ _ _ W _ _ _

J _ _ _ _

F _ _ _

S _ _ _

D _ _ _ _ _

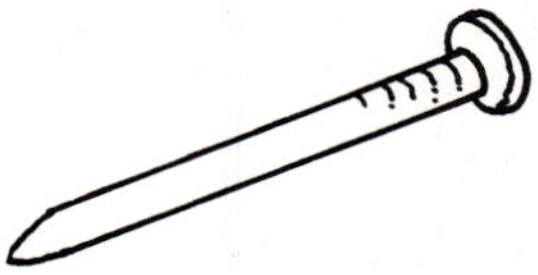

S _ _ _ _

S _ _ C _ _ _ _ _ _ _

Name ____________________________

A "Class"-y Group

Read a word. If it names a mammal, write **M** above the word. If it names a reptile, write **R** above the word. If it names an amphibian, write **A** above the word. If it names an insect, write **I** above the word. If it names a bird, write **B** above the word. If it names a fish, write **F** above the word. Then draw a line to show where three of these letters are the same in a row.

eel	dragonfly	penguin
turtle	frog	snake
camel	moose	hippopotamus

moth	panda	goldfish
woodpecker	beetle	pig
seagull	ape	fly

Name ______________________

From the Inside Out

Animals whose skeletons have backbones are called **vertebrates**. The backbone, or spine, is made up of bones called **vertebrae**.

Look at the skeletons below. Use the riddle and the Word Bank to write the name of each vertebrate.

1. 

I stand tall and proud. So please don't ask me to eat from the ground.

I am a ______________.

2. 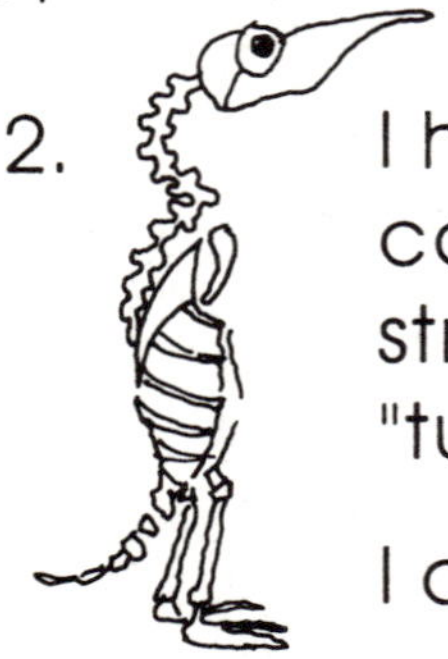

I have wings, but I cannot fly. I love to strut around in my "tuxedo."

I am a ______________.

3. 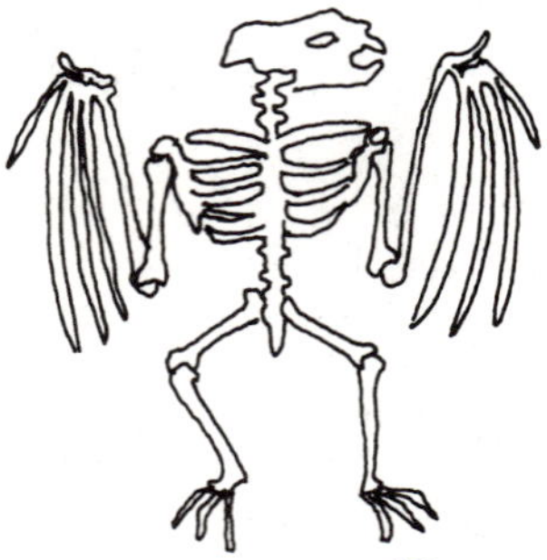

I am not a bird, but I can fly. Bruce Wayne used me as a model for his costume.

I am a ______________.

4. 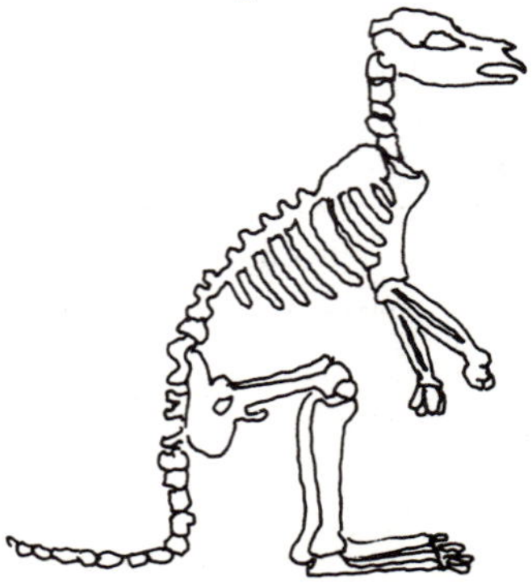

My legs and tail are very strong. I even come with a pocket.

I am a ______________.

5. 

I am thankful to be alive at holidays. People might "gobble me up!"

I am a ______________.

6. 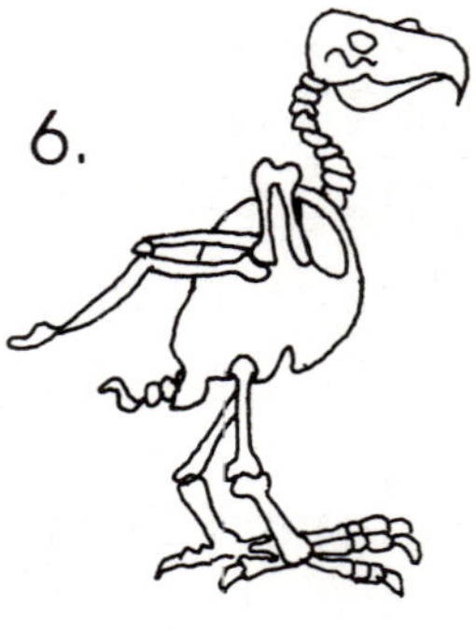

They say I have no hair, and they're right. I represent a great country.

I am a ______________.

Word Bank
bald eagle
kangaroo
turkey
penguin
giraffe
bat

Name ______________________

Fine, Feathered Friends

Do the puzzle about birds.

Color only the birds.

Down

1. ______________ keep a bird's body warm and dry.
4. A bird uses its ________ to pick up food.

Across

2. A bird is a ________ -blooded animal.
3. Baby birds are hatched from ________.
5. Birds breathe with their ________.

Word Bank				
feathers	bill	lungs	eggs	warm

Name ___________________________

Birds of a Feather

Birds are the only animals that have feathers. All birds have wings, but not all can fly. They all hatch from eggs, have backbones, and are warm-blooded.

The eggs in the nest contain names of different birds. When filling in the puzzle, the last letter of one name becomes the first letter of the next name. Write the names of the birds in the puzzle in the correct order. Start at the outside edge and spiral in toward the center. The first three names are written for you.

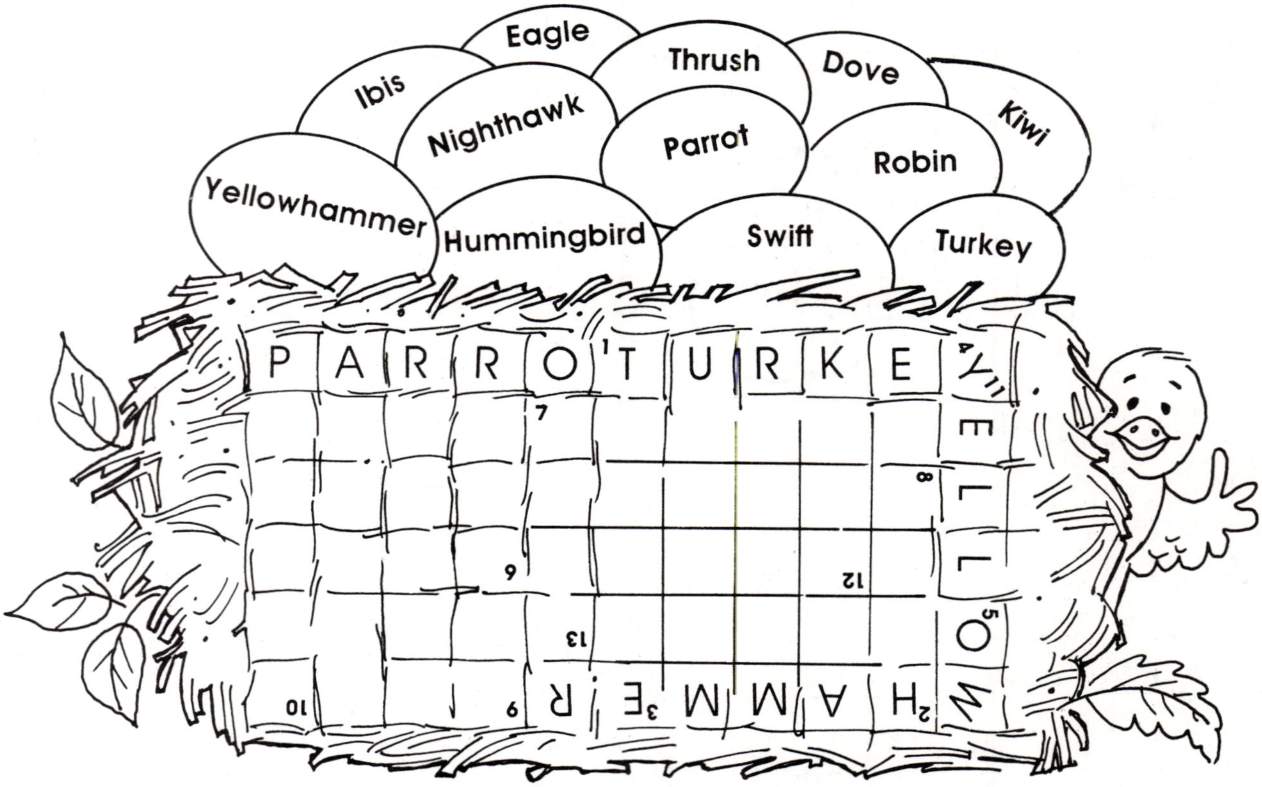

Complete this story. Write the letters from the sections with numbers in the blanks.

A sly and hungry fox quietly crept into the hen house one night. Carefully, he took a basket and began filling it with eggs. As he turned to leave, he tripped on a rake and went tumbling down, eggs and all. The hens awoke, laughed loudly, and said,

"___ ___ ___   ___ ___ ___ ___'___   ___ ___   ___ ___ ___!"

 1 2 3   4 5 6 7 8   9 10   11 12 13

0-7682-3792-0 *Skills & Practice Gr. 2*

Name ______________________

A Fish Story

Fish live almost anywhere there is water. Although fish come in many different shapes, colors, and sizes, they are alike in many ways.

- All fish have backbones.
- Fish breathe with gills.
- Most fish are cold-blooded.
- Most fish have fins.
- Many fish have scales and fairly tough skin.

Professor Fish teaches a *school* of fish in the ocean. He decided that he would make name tags for everyone. But, he decided to have some fun, and he jumbled the fish' names on their name tags.

Use the clues to unscramble the fish names. Write each name correctly at the top of the name tag. Then use your imagination to draw each fish.

______ rparto fish (a talking bird)	______ oinlfish (king of the beasts)	______ gknifish (opposite of queen)
______ tbturelfy fish (an insect with colorful wings)	______ ogatfish (a nanny – or a billy –)	______ opprucneifish (animal with quills)

Name ______________________________

A Mixture of Mammals

Mammals live in many different places. They are a special group because they . . .

- can give milk to their babies.
- protect and guide their young.
- are warm-blooded.
- have hair at some time during their lives.
- have a large, well-developed brain.

Below are some silly pictures made from two mammals put together. Write the names of the two real mammals on the lines. The last letter(s) in the name of the first animal is the first letter(s) in the name of the second animal. The first one is done for you.

1.  → **whale** **leopard**

2.  → ______________ ______________

3.  → ______________ ______________

4.  → ______________ ______________

5.  → ______________ ______________

6.  → ______________ ______________

7.  → ______________ ______________

8.  → ______________ ______________

Name ____________________

The Reptile House

There are about 6,000 different kinds of reptiles. They come in all sorts of shapes and colors. Their sizes in length range from 2 inches to almost 30 feet. Reptiles can be found on every continent except Antarctica. Even though reptiles can seem quite different, they all . . .

- breathe with lungs.
- are cold-blooded.
- have dry, scaly skin.
- have a backbone.

In the Reptile House at the zoo, each animal needs to be placed in the correct area. Read the information about each reptile. Then use the clues and the pictures to write the name of each reptile in its area.

Giant Tortoise can live over 100 years. It can hide under its shell for protection.

Reticulated Python is the longest snake. One was almost 33 feet long.

Saltwater Crocodile is one of the largest reptiles. It can weigh 1,000 lbs.

Komodo Dragon is a dragon-like reptile. It is the largest living lizard.

Tuatara is closely related to the extinct dinosaur.

Clues:
- The snake is between the largest lizard and the largest member of the turtle family.
- A relative of the alligator is on the far right side.
- The reptile who carries its "house" is in the middle.

Name ______________________

Amazing Amphibians

Amphibians are cold-blooded vertebrates (animals with backbones). They have no scales on their skin. Most amphibians hatch from eggs laid in water or on damp ground. Many amphibians grow legs as they develop into adults. Some live on land and have both lungs and gills for breathing. Frogs and toads are examples of amphibians.

Santjie, a South African sharp-nosed frog, holds the record for the longest triple jump. He jumped a total of more than 33 feet!

The frogs below won 1st, 2nd, and 3rd place in a recent triple-jump contest. Each jump after each frog's first jump was two feet shorter than the jump before. How many total feet did each frog jump? Fill in the answers on the trophies.

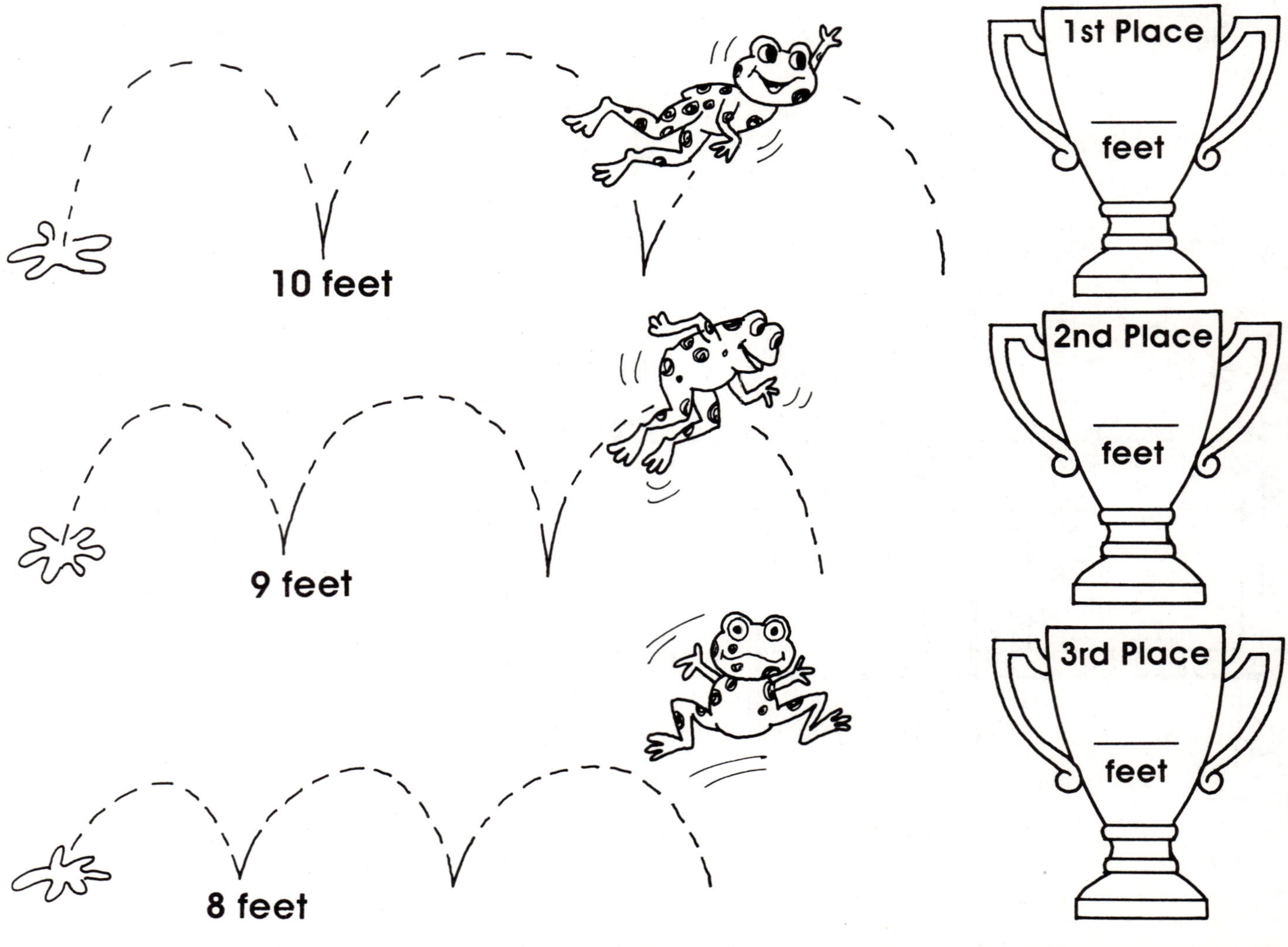

10 feet
9 feet
8 feet
1st Place
____ feet
2nd Place
____ feet
3rd Place
____ feet

Name ______________________

Plotting Plants

Follow Rupert Rabbit as he learns about plants. Use the words in the Word Bank to help you.

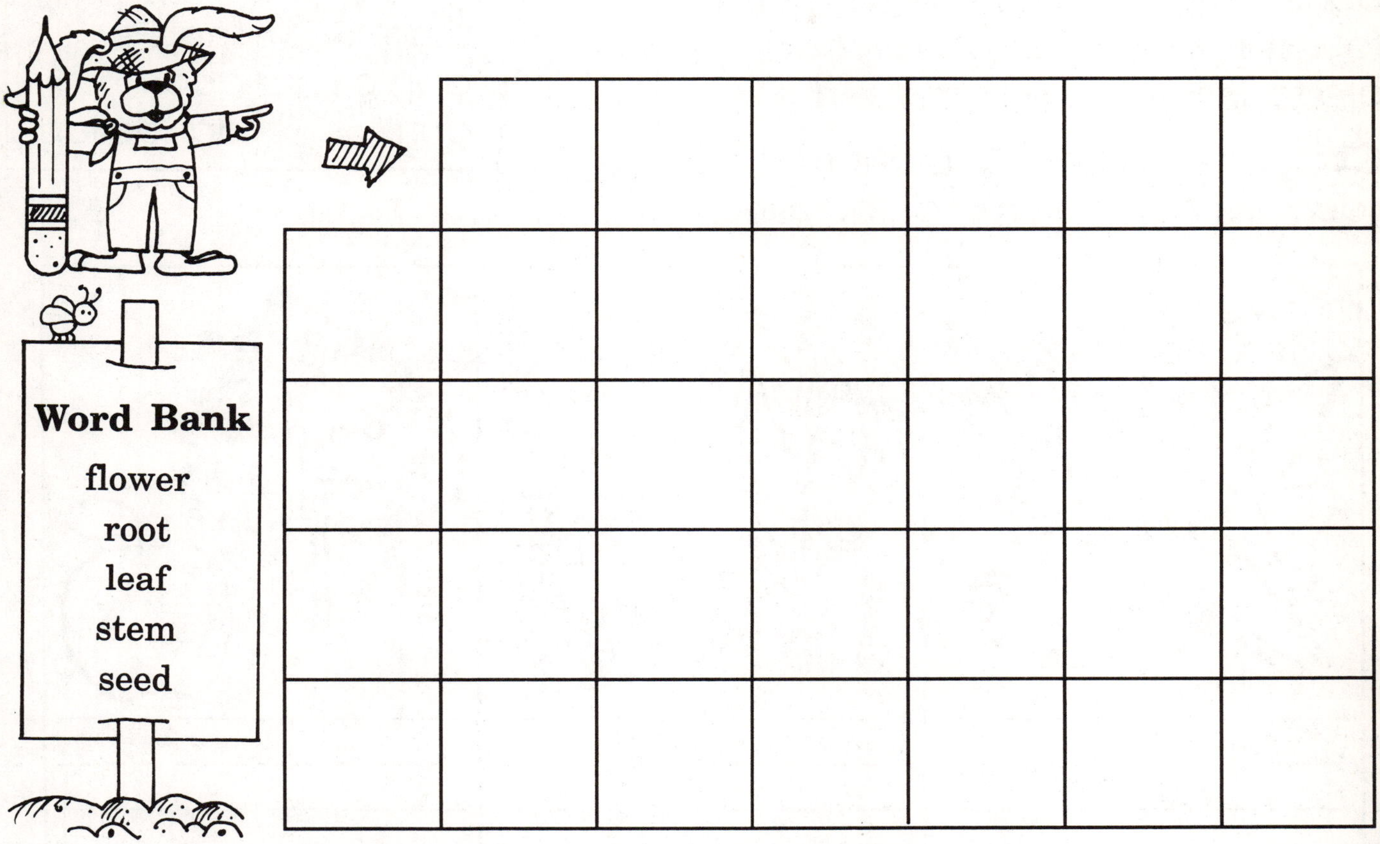
Word Bank
flower
root
leaf
stem
seed

Read and follow the directions. Start at Rupert Rabbit.

1. Go right 5 spaces. Then go down 3 spaces and left 5 spaces. Write the word that names what grows into a new plant here.
2. Now go up 2 spaces. Then go right 6 spaces and down 3 spaces. Write the word that names the part of the plant that is underground here.
3. Now go up 3 spaces. Then go left 3 spaces and down 1 space. Write the word that names the part of the plant that makes the food here.
4. Now go right 2 spaces. Then go up 1 space and left 4 spaces. Write the word that names the part of the plant that carries food and water to the rest of the plant here.
5. Now go down 2 spaces. Then go right 5 spaces and up 3 spaces. Write the word that names the part of the plant that makes the seeds here.

Name ______________________

Those Nutty Seeds

Seeds are found in different parts of the plant. Some seeds are found in the flower. Some seeds are found in the fruit or the nut.

Word Bank

pine	maple
apple	acorn
corn	dandelion

Circle the part of the plant that has the seed. Write the name of the seed.

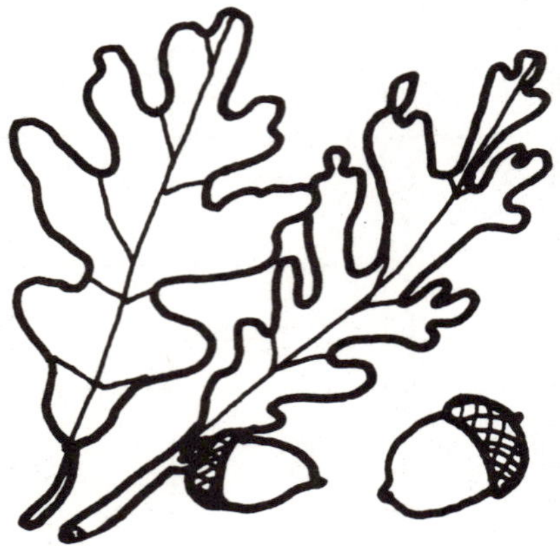

____

____

____

____

____

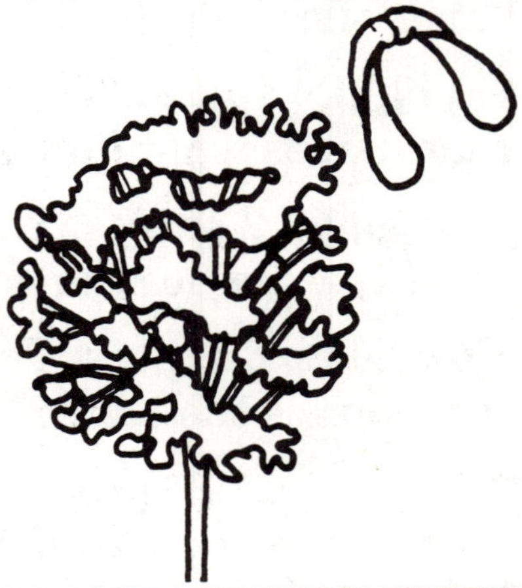

____

Name ______________________

Traveling Seeds

Seeds travel from one place to another. Sometimes people move the seeds. Sometimes they are moved in other ways.

Finish the sentences to tell how seeds travel.

Word Bank
people
animals
animals
wind
water

Seeds travel with ______________________.

Seeds travel in ______________________.

Seeds travel on ______________________.

Seeds travel in ______________________.

Seeds travel in the ______________________.

Name ____________________

Eyes in the Dark

What has eyes, but cannot see? A potato! The little white bumps that grow on a potato's skin are called "eyes." An eye can grow into a new potato plant.

You will need:
potato
potting soil
flowerpot or plastic glass

1. Put the potato in a dark cupboard or closet. Check it daily for small bumps called "eyes."

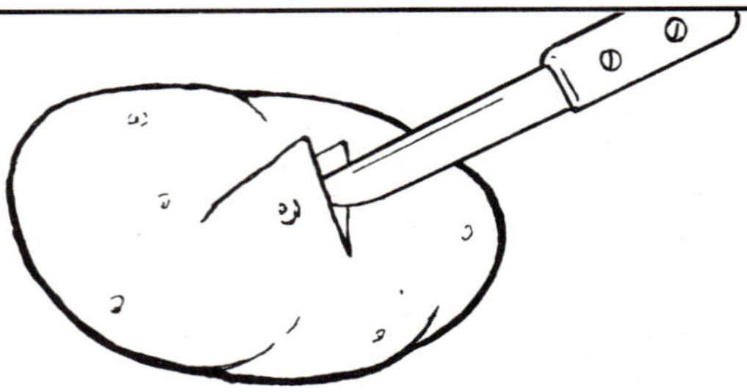

2. When the eyes appear ask an adult to cut them off the potato.

3. Fill a flowerpot half full of potting soil and lay the piece of potato on it with the "eyes" facing up.

4. Cover the "eyes" with 1 inch of soil. Water. Keep moist–but not wet. Watch closely for about two weeks.

Record what happened after . . .

1 week

2 weeks

What happened?

A potato is a tuber. A tuber is a fat underground stem with little buds that can grow into new plants. The "eye" that you planted was really a potato bud that grew into a new plant.

Name ____________________

Dynamic Dinosaurs

Dinosaurs were reptiles that lived millions of years ago. Some of them were the biggest animals to ever live on land. Some were as small as chickens. Some dinosaurs ate plants, while others were meat-eaters.

Scientists have given names to the dinosaurs that often describe their special bodies, sizes, and habits.

Look at the object(s) placed in the picture with each dinosaur. Use the objects as clues to fill in the blanks and finish each dinosaur's name.

T R I C E R A ___ ___ ___ ___

___ ___ ___ ___ ___ **E O S A U R U S**

___ ___ ___ ___ ___ **T R O D O N**

___ ___ ___ ___ ___ **A S A U R U S**

___ ___ ___ ___ ___ ___ ___ **O S A U R U S**

SCIENCE

Name ______________________________

Dial a Dinosaur

Danny loves dinosaurs. In fact, he loves them so much that everyone calls him Dinosaur Danny! Find out what Dinosaur Danny's favorite dinosaur is by decoding the message below. To do this, use the numbers on the telephone and the directional markers.

For example: \3 points to the letter D.

___ ___   ___ ___ ___ ___ ___ ___ ___ ___

\6 /9   /3 \2 /8 /6 |7 /4 \8 |3

___ ___ ___ ___ ___ ___ ___ ___   ___ ___

\3 /4 |6 /6 /7 \2 |8 |7   /4 /7

___ ___ ___ ___ ___ ___ ___ ___ ___ ___ ___

/7 \8 |3 \4 /6 /7 \2 |8 |7 |8 /7

Write your own message and share it with a classmate.

Name ______________________

Magic Square Mania

Did you know that the word dinosaur comes from two Greek words meaning terrible lizard? Dinosaurs were not lizards at all! To further improve your dinosaur vocabulary, read Column A. Choose an answer from Column B. Write the number of the answer in the Magic Square. The first one has been done for you.

Column A

A. Person who studies fossils
B. Petrified remains of animals and plants
C. Meat-eating dinosaurs
D. Plant-eating dinosaurs
E. Movement of animals over long distances
F. Large bony plates on dinosaur's neck
G. Bones on the top of a dinosaur's head
H. The Age of Dinosaurs
I. Large groups of animals that live together

Column B

1. skeleton
2. Mesozoic Age
3. carnivores
4. herbivores
5. paleontologist
6. migration
7. herds
8. frills
9. crest
10. fossils

A 5	**B** ____	**C** ____
D ____	**E** ____	**F** ____
G ____	**H** ____	**I** ____

Add the numbers across, down and diagonally. What answer do you get? ____

Why do you think this is called a magic square? ______________________

Name ____________________

Weather Watch

Weather is the condition of the air around the earth for a period of time. The weatherman's job is to predict the weather.

There were some very unusual weather patterns recorded for a recent month. Use the key to draw the correct weather symbols for each day.

- Every Monday and Tuesday it rained. Then it was sunny for the following three days.
- On the first and third weekends, the first day was cloudy, and the second day was snowy.
- On the second and fourth weekends, it was just the opposite.

Sun.	Mon.	Tues.	Wed.	Thurs.	Fri.	Sat.
		1	2	3	4	5
6	7	8	9	10	11	12
13	14	15	16	17	18	19
20	21	22	23	24	25	26
27	28	29	30	31		

Key

sunny

cloudy

rainy

snowy

Write the word that tells about the weather on these dates:

- 6th day of the month ____________
- 13th day of the month ____________
- last day of the month ____________

0-7682-3792-0 *Skills & Practice Gr. 2*

Name ______________________

Gauging the Weather

Cut out the centimeter ruler at the bottom of the page. Use the ruler to measure the amount of rainfall from the bottom of the gauge to the top of the water. Write the measurement on the raindrop.

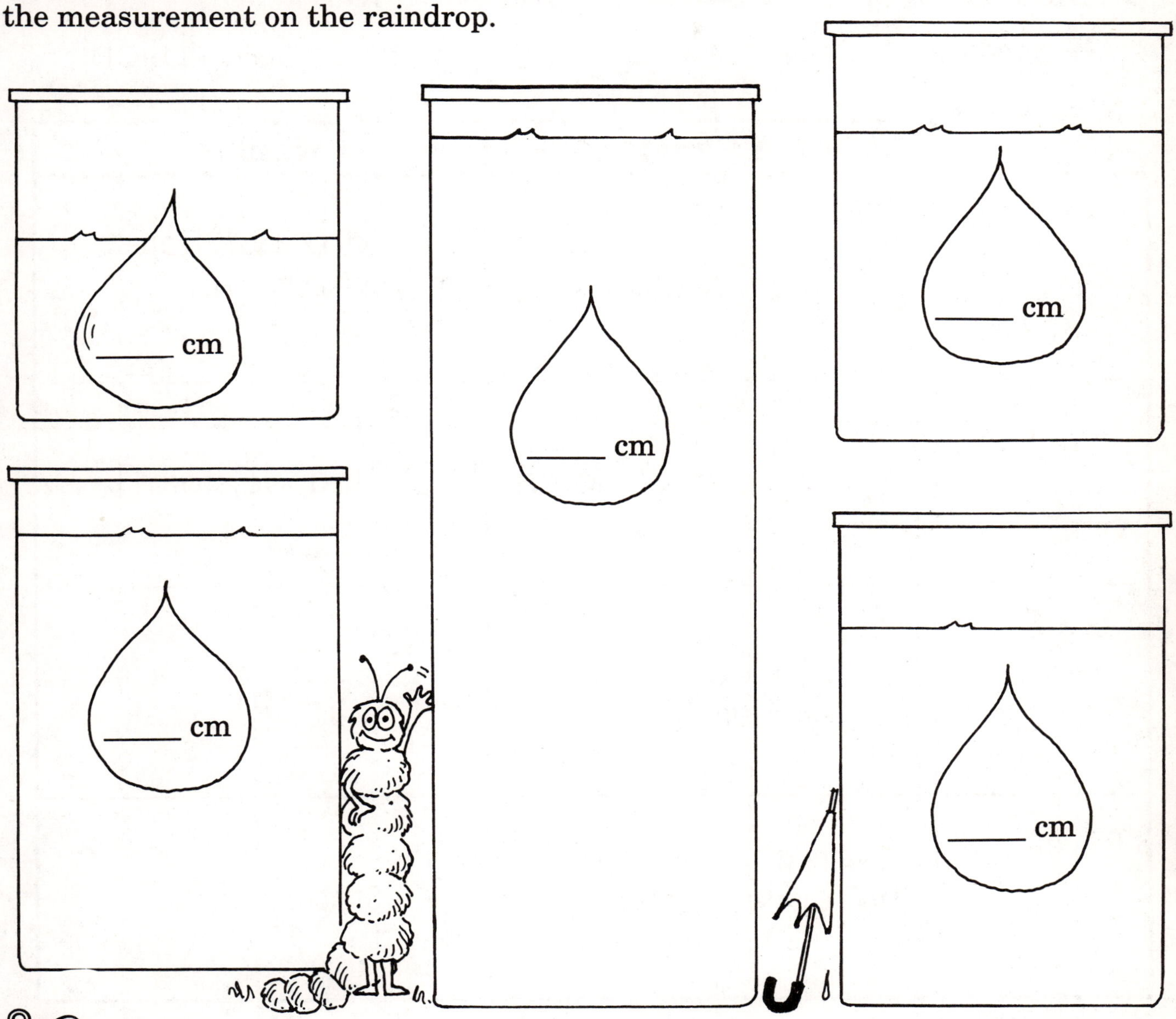

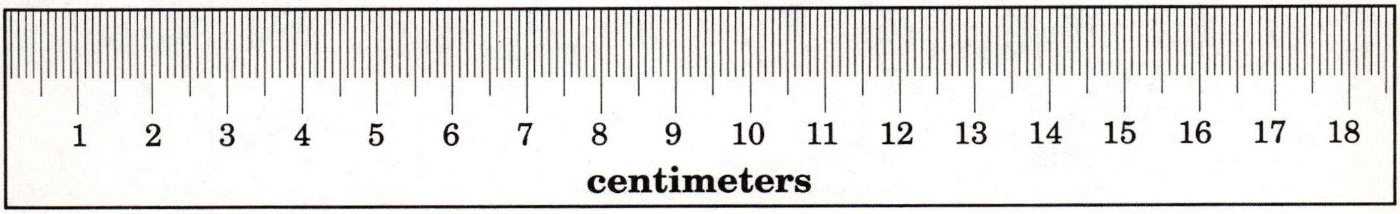

Name ______________________

A Cloudy Day

Clouds bring us many kinds of weather. Some clouds give us fair weather. Other clouds bring rain.

Paste the picture of the cloud next to its description.

	How the Clouds Look	Weather
	Big, puffy clouds	Nice day, but there might be a small shower.
	Tall, dark, piles of clouds.	Thunderstorm
	Whispy clouds that look like feathers.	Fair
	Layers of gray clouds that cover the whole sky.	Steady drizzle.

Stratus
Cumulus
Cumulo-
nimbus
Cirrus

Name ______________________

Lacy Patterns

Kim likes to look at the lacy patterns of snowflakes with her magnifying glass. Most of them have six sides or six points. But she has never seen two snowflakes that are alike. Kim catches them on small pieces of dark paper so that she can see them better. Some of the snowflakes are broken because they bump into each other as they fall from the clouds.

Color.

What does Kim use to make the snowflakes look bigger?

   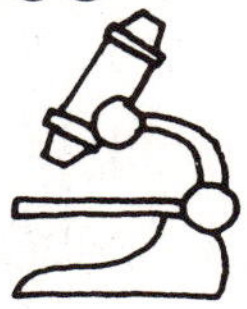

Check.

Most snowflakes have ☐ seven ☐ six ☐ five sides or points.

Kim looks at them on dark pieces of paper so that she can…

☐ take them to school. ☐ make a picture. ☐ see them better.

Write.

Why are some of the snowflakes broken?

____

____

• Finish the snowflake.

Name ______________________

Sink or Float?

Why do some objects float? Why do other objects sink? Is it because of their shape? Is it because of their color? Let's find out!

You will need:
large bowl of water
test objects such as –
apple, nail, orange,
eraser, wood, stone, egg,
penny, crayon

Sinker or Floater?

1. List your objects.
2. Make guesses. Will they sink or float?
3. Test your objects to find the actual results.

Object	Guess	Actual Results

What happened?

If an object is heavy for its size, it will sink. If it is light for its size, it will float. A brick is heavy for its size so it will sink. A piece of wood the same size will float.

Names ____________________

Salty Water Evaporation

1. With a partner, decide which of you will be responsible for each job below.

   Experimenter—responsible for following the given directions, gathering materials, and cleaning up.
   Recorder—responsible for reading the directions and questions out loud and for recording the answers.

2. Gather the following materials:
   spoon
   salt
   paper cup
   1/4 cup water
3. Stir the salt into the water.
4. Put the cup in a warm place.
5. Use what you already know about science to predict:

   What do you think will happen to the water? ____________________

   ____

   What do you think will happen to the salt? ____________________

   ____

6. Check the cup in a few days and record:

   What has happened to the water? ____________________

   ____

   What has happened to the salt? ____________________

   ____

   What do you think happens to ocean water when it is exposed to the sun?

   ____

   ____

   What do you think happens to the ocean salt when the water evaporates?

   ____

   ____

Name ______________________

Anti-Freeze

Water turns into a solid at a temperature of 32°F. This is called the freezing point. Does all water freeze at 32°F? Let's find out!

You will need:
- 2 small paper cups
- 4 teaspoons of salt
- water
- marking pen
- freezer

1. Fill both cups with water.

2. Mix 4 teaspoons of salt in one of the cups. Write "salt" on that cup.

3. Put both cups in the freezer. Check on them every hour for four hours.

I found out . . .

the cup of plain water ______________________

____

the cup of salt water ______________________

____

What happened?

When the temperature of water gets very cold, the particles of water hook together to make ice crystals. Salt gets in the way of this process, and an even lower temperature is needed before ice crystals will form.

Names ______________________

Layers of the Ocean Floor

Have you ever wondered what is under the sand on a beach? Some beaches are really layers of rock, pebbles, shells, and sand. Work in a group of four students and choose one of these materials to bring to school for your group. Write your name next to the material that you will bring:

sand ______________________ shells ______________________

rock ______________________ pebbles ______________________

Your teacher will provide a glass jar and water.

1. Gather the materials and take turns adding them to the jar. Add the same amount of each material.
2 Fill the jar to the top with water.
3. Close the lid tightly!
4. Take turns shaking the jar 10 times each.
5. Set the jar aside for one day.
6. Each student should draw and label one layer of the jar on the worksheet. Then put your names on the paper.
7. For follow-up, draw a picture of the layers of the ocean floor. Think about the layers you saw in your jar.

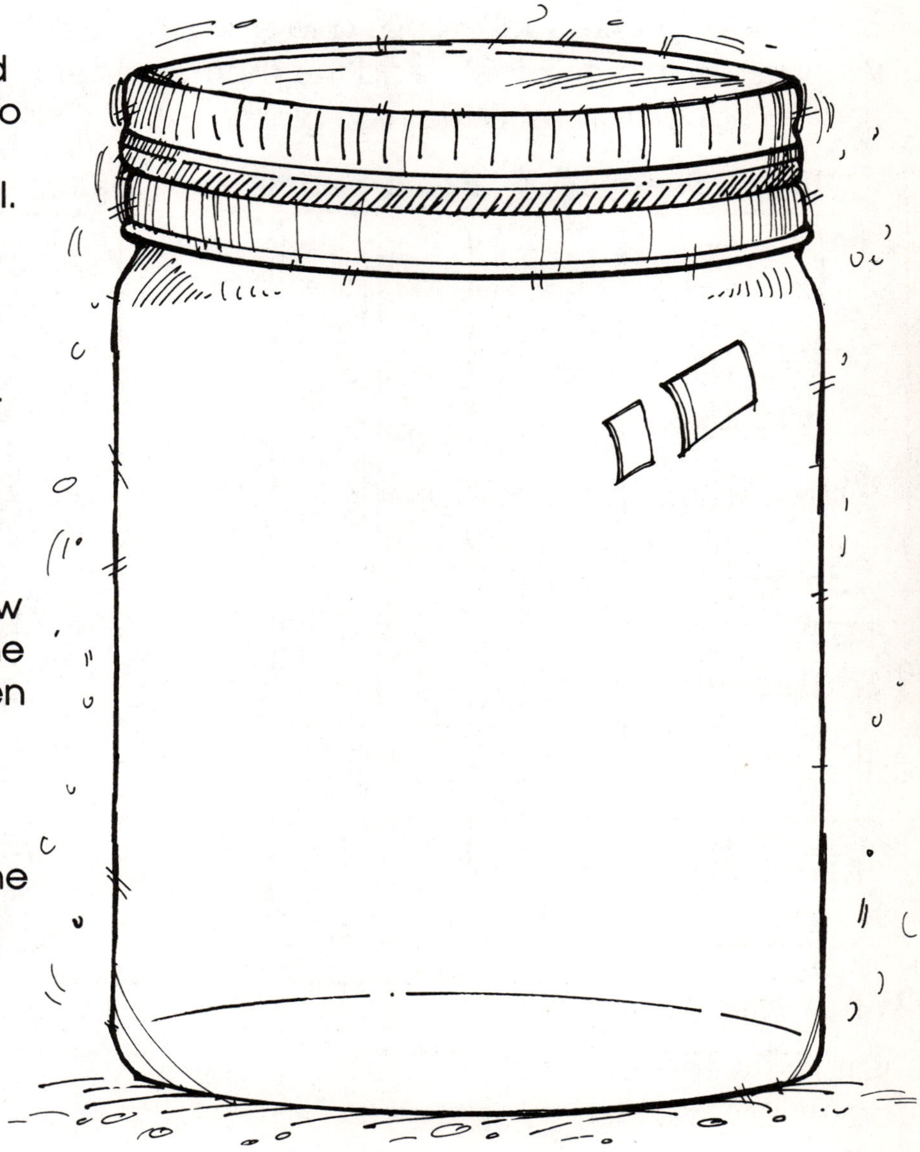

SCIENCE

Name ______________________________

Ocean Temperatures

Where do you think the ocean temperatures are the warmest? Do you think the salt makes the ocean warmer or cooler? Do you think the sun makes the ocean warmer or cooler? Try this experiment to find out!

1. Get 4 clear glasses of water.
2. Add salt to 2 of the glasses and stir well.
3. Set one freshwater glass and one saltwater glass in the shade outside.
4. Set the other 2 glasses in the sun outside.
5. Set thermometers in each of the 4 glasses.
6. Divide into 4 equal groups and start at a different glass.
7. Wait 15 minutes, then read the thermometer and record below.
8. On signal, rotate to the next glass.

Fresh/Shady

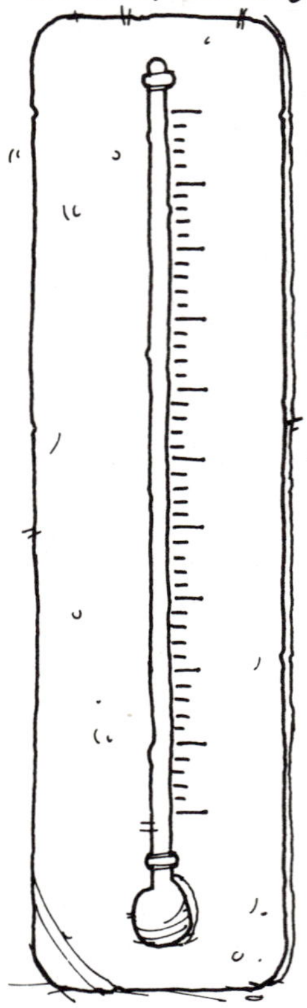

__________ °C

Fresh/Sunny

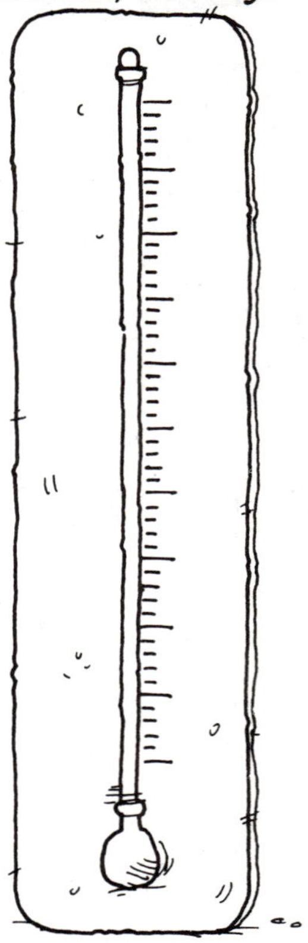

__________ °C

Salty/Shady

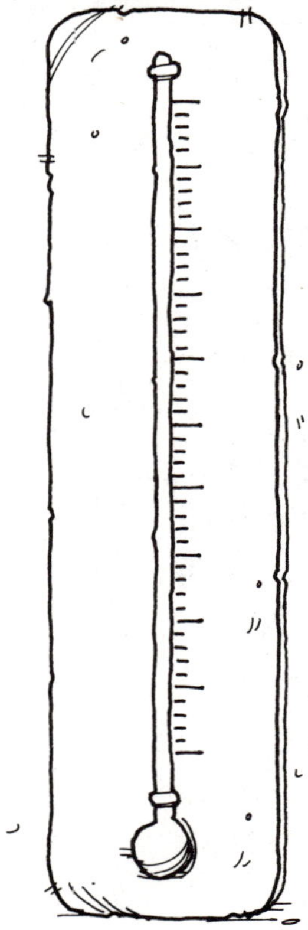

__________ °C

Salty/Sunny

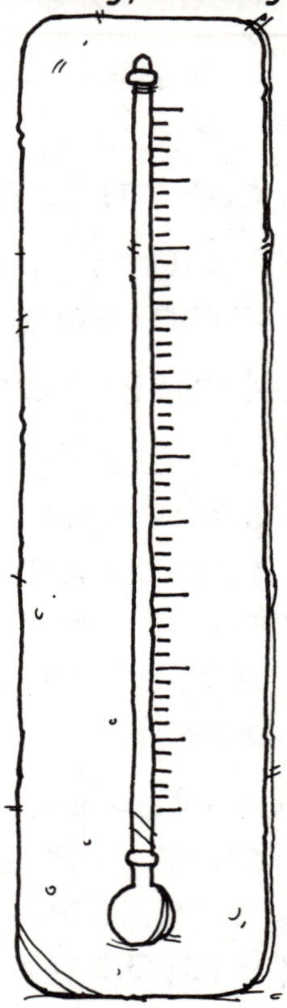

__________ °C

Name ____________________

The Dancing Coin

You can make a coin dance on the top of a bottle as if a ghost were pushing on it. Let's try!

You will need:
glass soft-drink bottle
coin

1. Wet the rim of an empty bottle and one side of the coin.

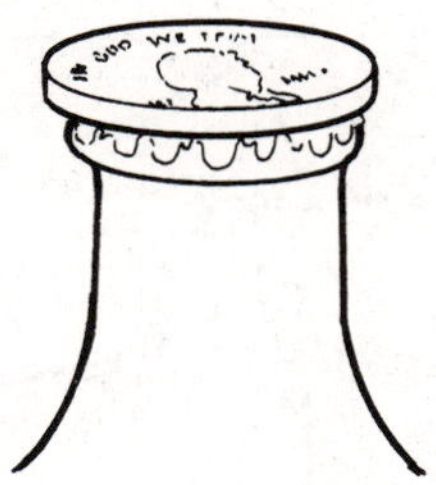

2. Place the wet side of the coin on rim of the bottle.

3. Hold the bottle with your warm hands. Watch closely!

What happened to the coin? ____________________

____

What happened to the temperature of the air in the bottle when you put your hands around the bottle? ____________________

____

What happened?

Your warm hands heated the cool air in the bottle. The air expanded and tried to escape. It pushed on the coin and made it dance.

Name ____________________

The Crusher

I'll bet you can crush a plastic soft-drink bottle without even touching it. Of course there is a little trick. Let's try it!

You will need:
- plastic soft-drink bottle
- hot water
- cold water

1. Fill the bottle with hot water from the faucet. Be careful. Let the bottle stand for a minute.

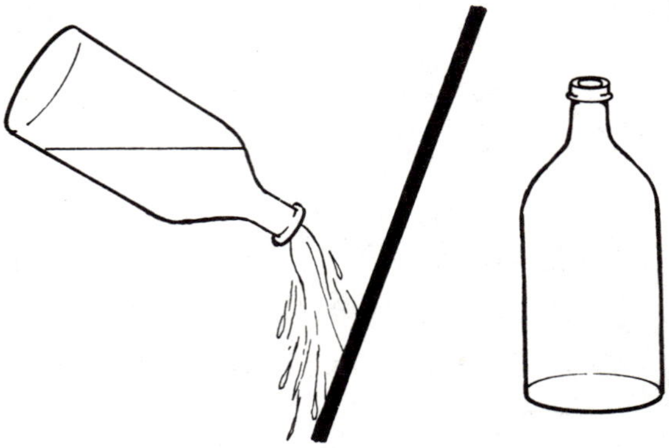

2. Pour out the hot water. Quickly screw on the cap. Make sure the cap is on tight.

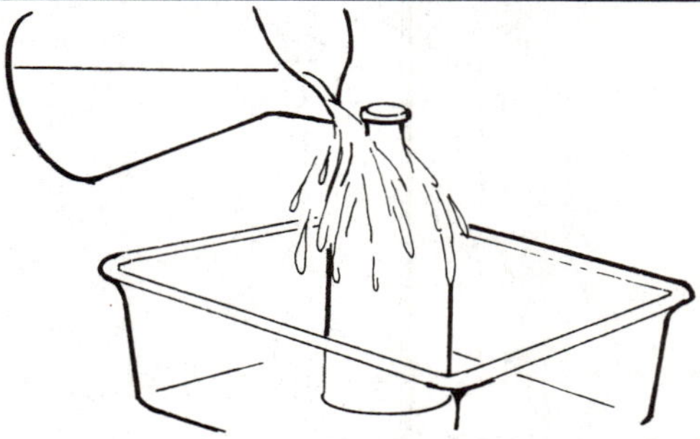

3. Pour a pitcher of very cold water over the bottle or hold the bottle under the cold water faucet. Watch what happens!

What happened?

The hot water made the air in the bottle very warm. The bottle cap captured the warm air in the bottle. The cold water made the warm air become cold. Cold air takes less space and the air pressure outside the bottle pushed in the sides of the bottle.

0-7682-3792-0 *Skills & Practice Gr. 2*

Name ____________________

Powerful Push-Up

Can air hold up water? It can with a little help from you. Let's find out how!

You will need:
- drinking glass
- card the size of a postcard
- water

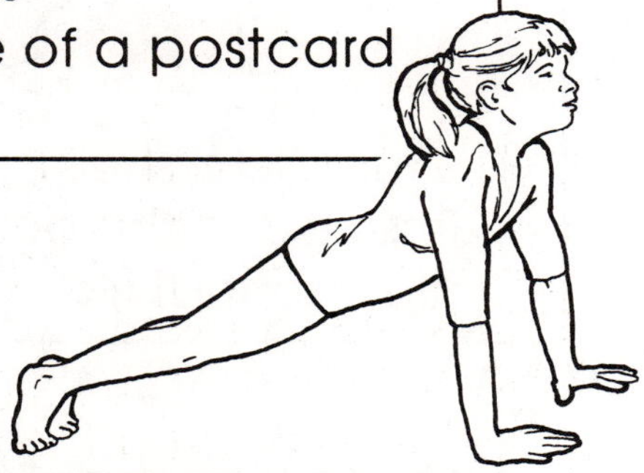

1. Fill the glass to overflowing.

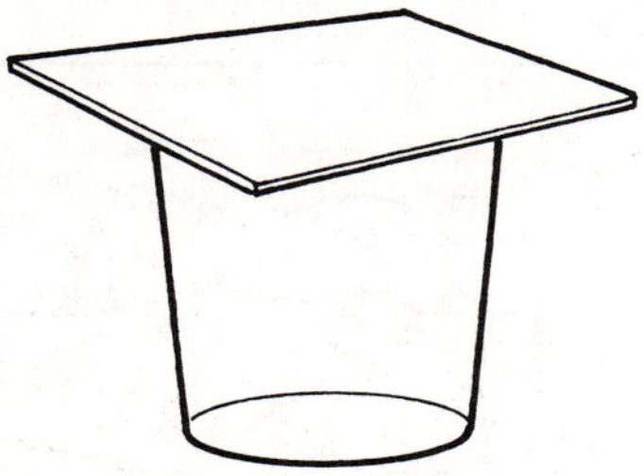

2. Lay the card on top of the glass.

3. Hold the card down with one hand. Turn the glass over. Remove your hand. Wow!

What happened to the water in the glass? ____________________

____

What happens if you tilt the glass? ____________________

____

What happened?

Air pushes in all directions. The air pressure pushing up under the card is greater than the pressure of the water pushing down. The card stays in place.

Name ______________________________

High and Dry

Can you put a piece of paper under water without getting it wet? You can do it with a little help from air pressure. Let's try!

You will need:
drinking glass
sheet of paper
sink full of water

1. Crumple a sheet of paper. Push it into the bottom of a glass so that it stays in place.

2. Hold the glass upside down.

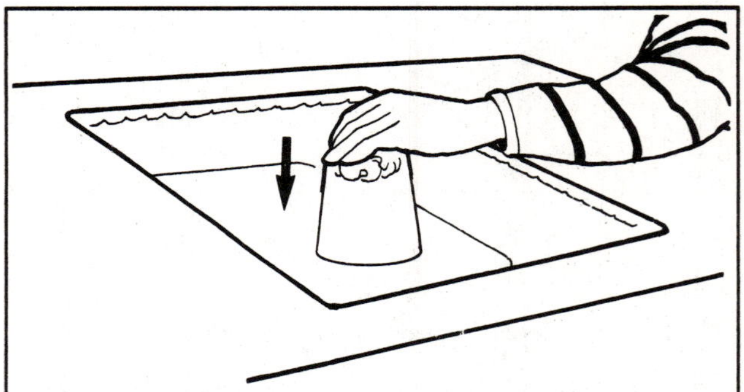

3. Push it straight down into the water.

What happens to the paper if you pull the glass straight up? ____________________

____

What happens if you tilt the glass when putting it in the water? ____________________

____

What happened?

The glass is full of air. The air cannot come out because it is lighter than the water. If you tilt the glass, the air escapes and water enters.

0-7682-3792-0 *Skills & Practice Gr. 2*

Name ______________________

The Last Straw

Sodas, milkshakes and root beer are all fun to sip through a straw. It would be fun to sip them through two straws. Could you sip liquid through three straws? four straws? What is the most you could use? Let's find out!

You will need:
- plastic straws
- clear tape
- plastic pop bottle
- water

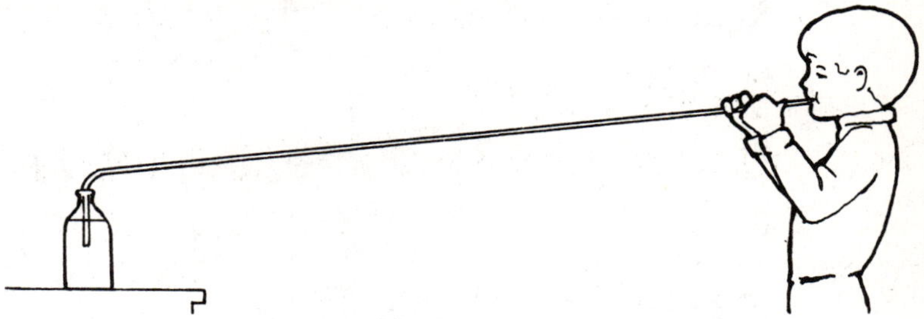

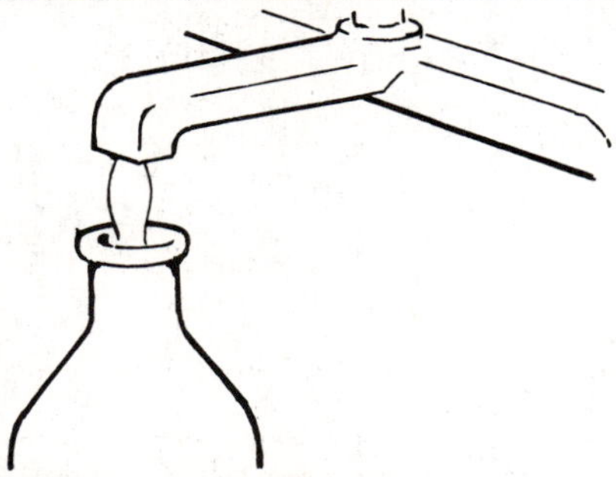

1. Fill the bottle with water.

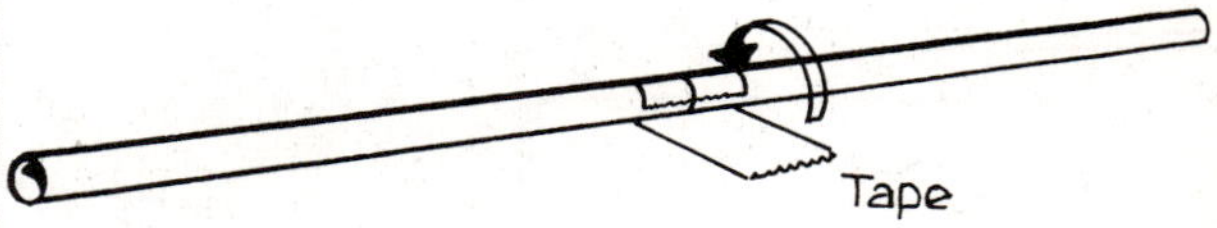

2. Tape two straws together.

3. Now try to drink through the two straws. Was it hard?

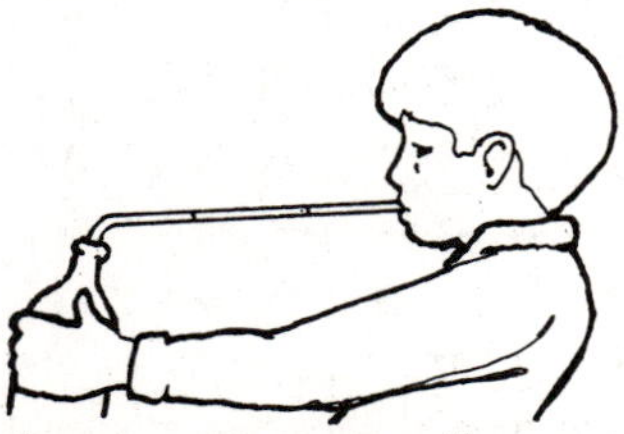

4. Add one more straw. Suck hard! Did it work? Try adding more!

How many straws can you tape together and still drink through? ________

What happened?

Air pressure pushes down on the water in the bottle and also down on the water in the straw. When you suck the air out of the straw there will be no air pressure pushing down on the water in the straw, only air pressure pushing on the rest of the water in the bottle. The air pressure in the bottle pushes the water up the straw.

Name ____________________

What's the Matter?

All things are made of **matter**. Matter takes up space. It can take three forms – solid, liquid or gas.

Solids have shape and volume. They do not change shape easily.

Liquids have volume, but they have no shape of their own. They take the shape of the container they are in.

Gases have no shape or volume. Most gases are invisible.

Find and circle the words in each wordsearch that are examples of each kind of matter. Then write the words on the lines.

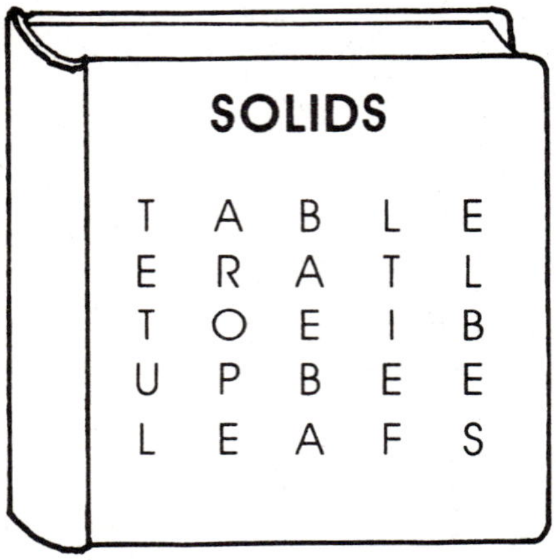
SOLIDS
T A B L E
E R A T L
T O E I B
U P B E E
L E A F S

LIQUIDS
A P O P K
B C O L A
J U I C E
A M L I T
W A T E R

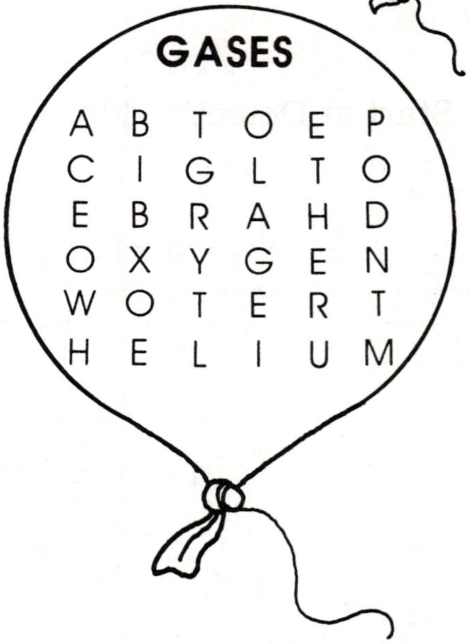
GASES
A B T O E P
C I G L T O
E B R A H D
O X Y G E N
W O T E R T
H E L I U M

Name ______________________

"Shadowing" Shadows

Cut out the pictures at the bottom of the page. Read the directions and paste the objects where they belong.

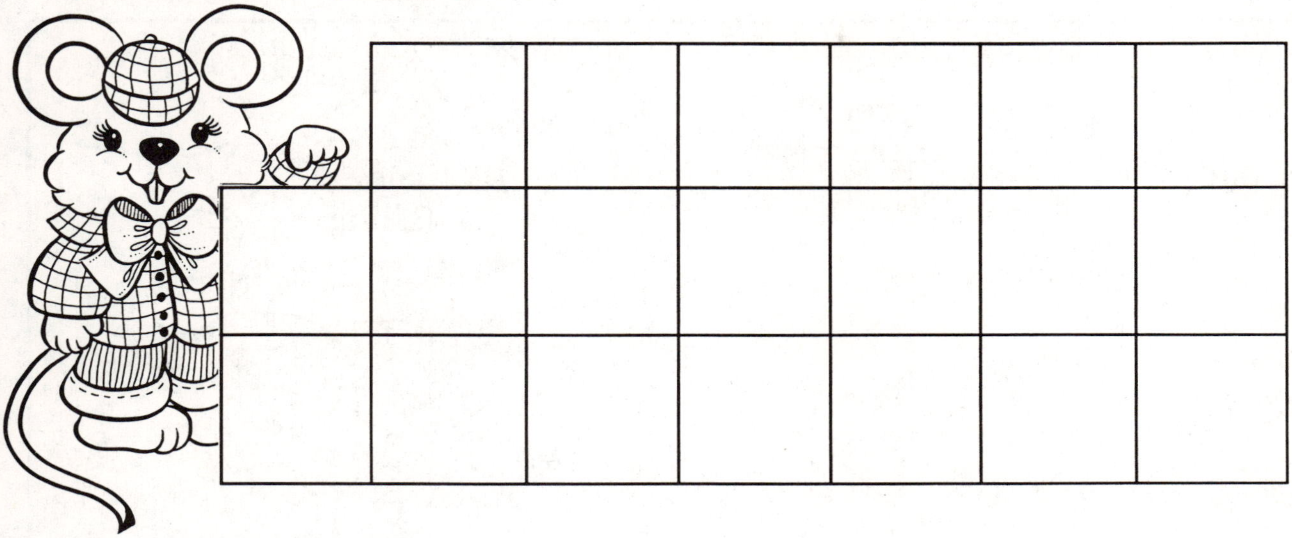

Start at Detective Mouse.

1. Go down 1 space and right 4 spaces. Paste the picture here of what would make this shadow. 
2. Now go left 3 spaces and down 1 space. Paste the picture here of what would make this shadow. 
3. Then go right 5 spaces and up 1 space. Paste the picture here of what would make this shadow. 
4. Go up 1 space and left 4 spaces. Paste the picture here of what would make this shadow. 
5. Go down 1 space and left 2 spaces. Paste the picture here of what would make this shadow. 

notebook
clothesline
lollipop
peanut
telephone pole
mouse
telephone

Name ______________________

Volume Control

If the words name something that makes a loud sound, color the space **gray**.
If the words name something that makes a soft sound, color the space **red**.

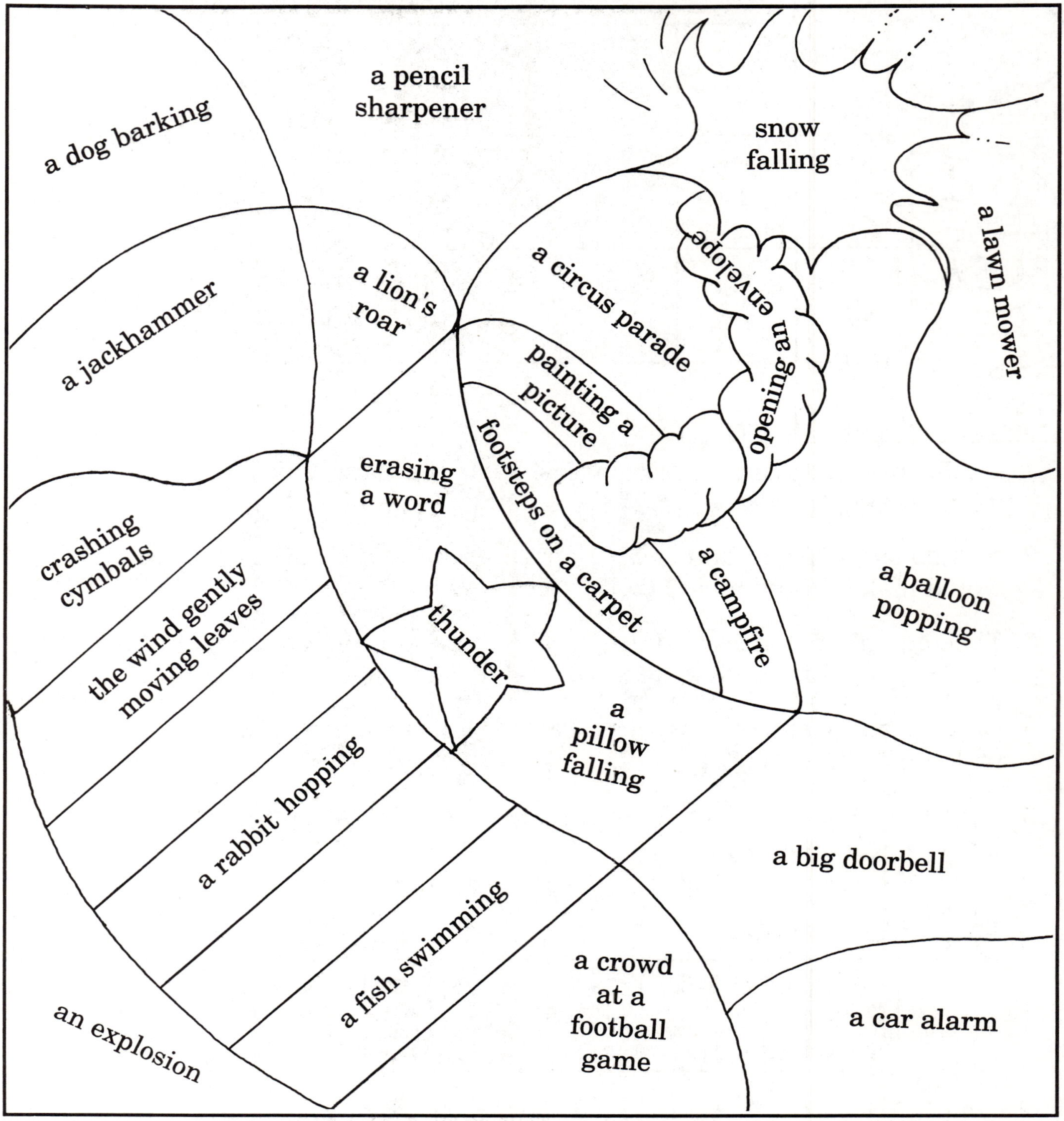
a dog barking
a pencil sharpener
snow falling
a lawn mower
a jackhammer
a lion's roar
a circus parade
opening an envelope
painting a picture
footsteps on a carpet
erasing a word
crashing cymbals
the wind gently moving leaves
thunder
a campfire
a balloon popping
a pillow falling
a rabbit hopping
a big doorbell
a fish swimming
a crowd at a football game
a car alarm
an explosion

0-7682-3792-0 *Skills & Practice Gr. 2*

Name ____________________

Gravity: The Force Is with You

Before you drop the pairs of objects, predict which of each pair will reach the ground first. Drop the two objects at the same time from a height of 5 feet (1.5 m). Record the result after each drop.

Objects	Prediction	Result
pencil and piece of chalk		
piece of chalk and chalkboard eraser		
pencil and empty cup		
tissue box and textbook		
textbook and basketball		
encyclopedia and thick rubberband		

Name ______________________________

Keep It Clean!

Have you ever cleaned a penny? Let's try it!

Materials:

4 dirty pennies
salt
vinegar
soap
water
taco sauce
window cleaner
steel wool pad
paper towels

Directions:

1. In the "I predict . . . " section on the chart, explain what you think each penny will look like after you clean it with one of the materials.
2. Your teacher will place a small amount of each material in the center of each table.
3. Try cleaning one penny using window cleaner. Explain what it looks like in the "I observed . . . " section.
4. Now try cleaning another penny using soap, water, and the steel wool pad. Explain what it looks like.
5. Clean a different penny in salt and vinegar. Explain what it looks like.
6. Now clean the last penny in taco sauce. Explain what it looks like.

Materials	I predict . . .	I observed . . .
window cleaner		
soap, water, and steel wool pad		
salt and vinegar		
taco sauce		

Name ______________________________

Magnetic Attraction

The word **magnet** begins with the same three letters as the word magic, and sometimes magnets do seem a little magical.

Every magnet has two poles — north and south. The north pole of one magnet attracts and pulls toward the south pole of another magnet. Two poles that are the same (two north poles or two south poles) do **not** attract each other. Instead, they push away from each other.

Using the information above, continue labeling the horseshoe and bar magnets below with **N** (for north) and **S** (for south).

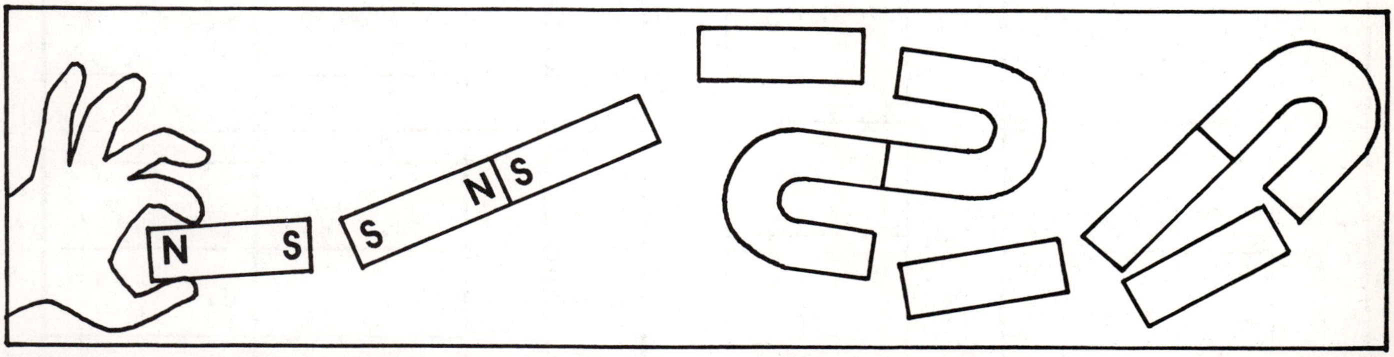

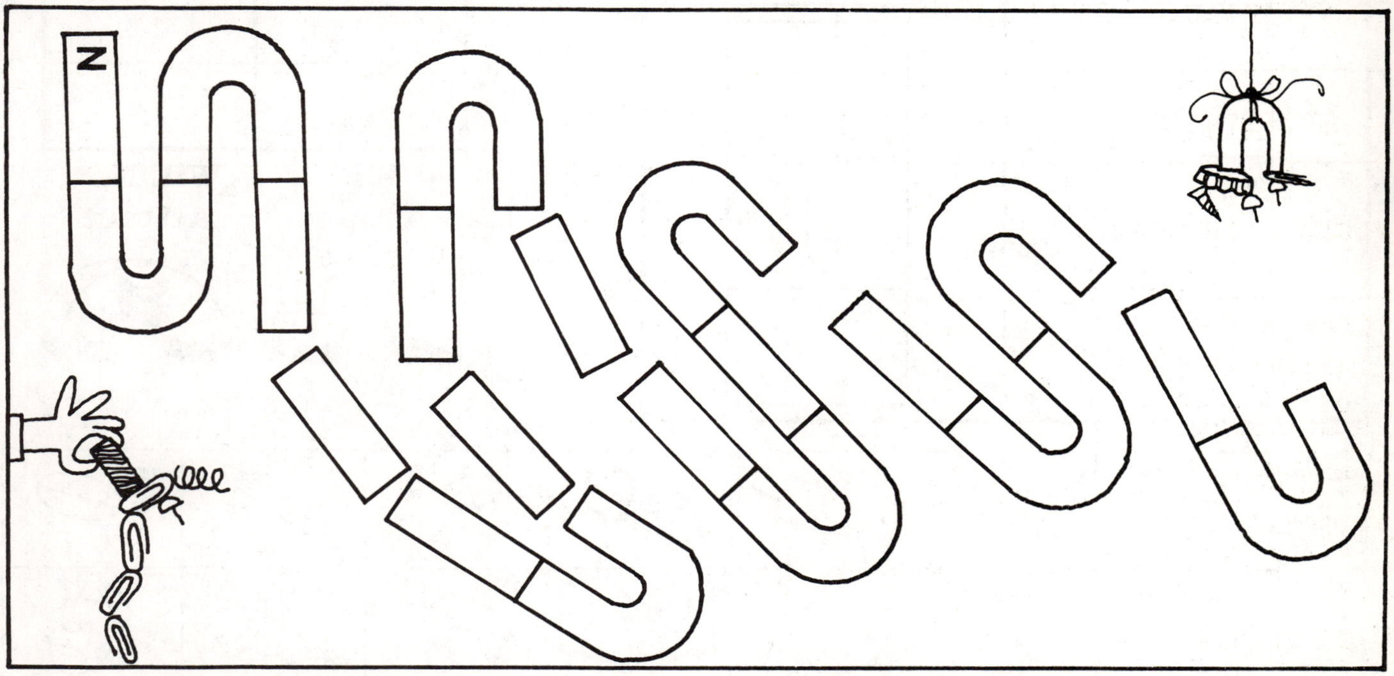

Name ______________________________

"Attractive" Magnets

Cut out each object and paste it on the chart where it belongs. Use a crayon to graph the results.

Will Attract
Will Not Attract

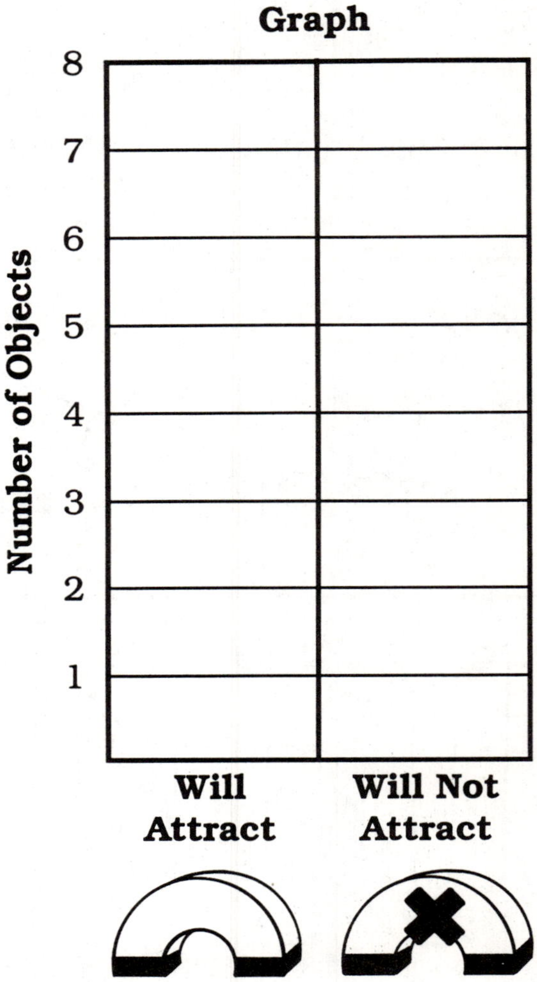
Graph
8
7
6
5
4
3
2
1
Number of Objects
Will Attract
Will Not Attract

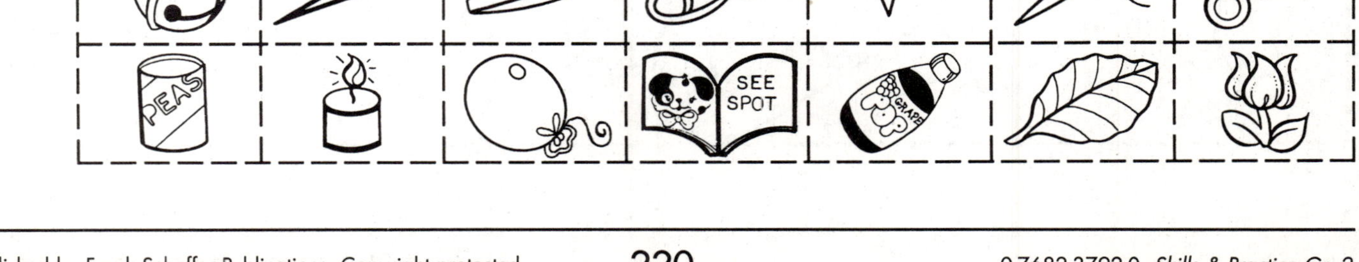
PEAS
SEE SPOT

Name ____________________

Lifting with Levers

A lever is a simple machine used to lift or move things. It has two parts. The **arm** is the part that moves. The **fulcrum** supports the arm and does not move.

Name the parts of this lever.

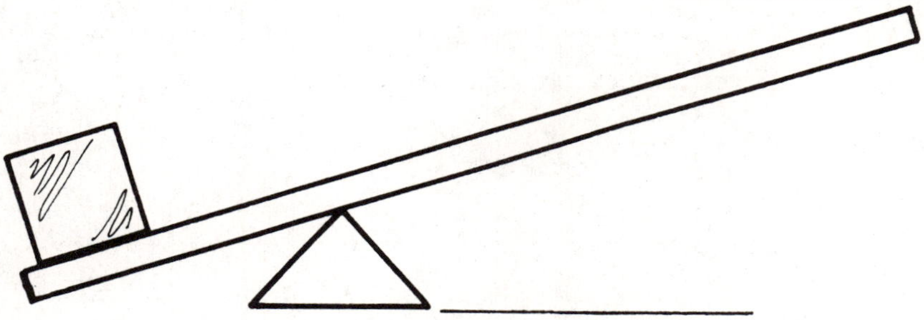

Unscramble the names of these levers.

velosh

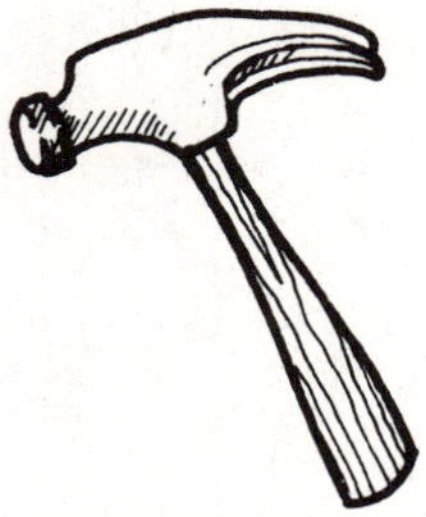

mrahem

moorb

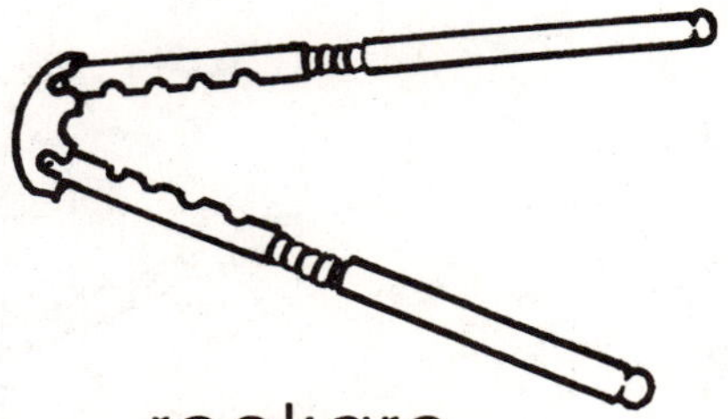

tun reckarc

Name ______________________

Levers at Work

Levers help make our work easier. Circle all the levers. Then find their names in the wordsearch.

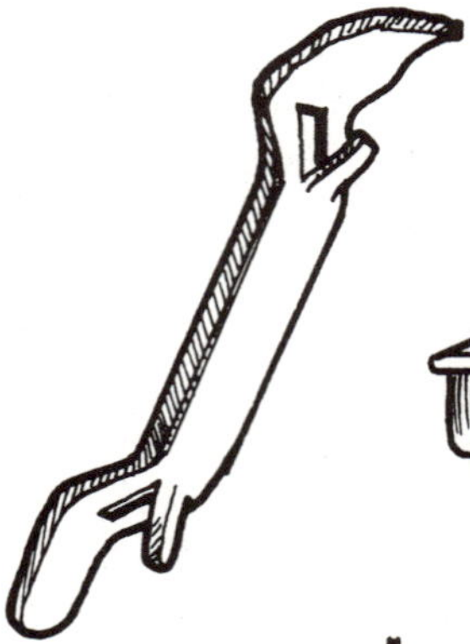

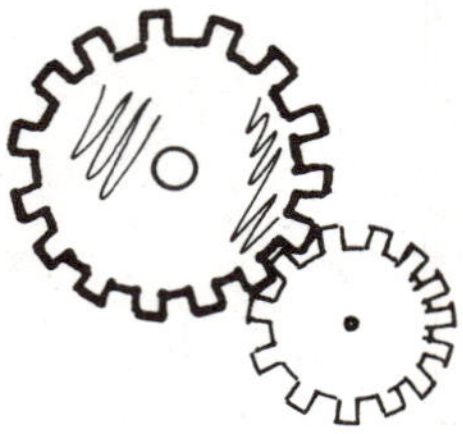

c	a	n	o	p	e	n	e	r	d
r	s	d	d	l	j	k	l	m	n
o	h	s	c	i	s	s	o	r	s
w	v	h	b	e	z	x	c	a	w
b	t	o	b	r	o	o	m	k	l
a	d	v	n	s	u	k	f	s	w
r	u	e	h	a	m	m	e	r	g
w	f	l	h	g	f	a	d	s	v

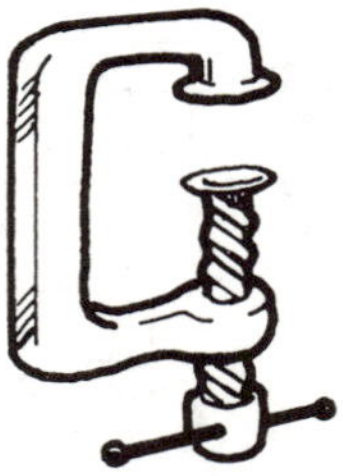

0-7682-3792-0 *Skills & Practice Gr. 2*

Name ______________________________

The Right Tool for the Job

Mother gave Tyrone and Kim a list of jobs. Help them pick the right tool for each job. Draw a line from the job to the tool.

What will help Kim raise the flag up the flagpole?

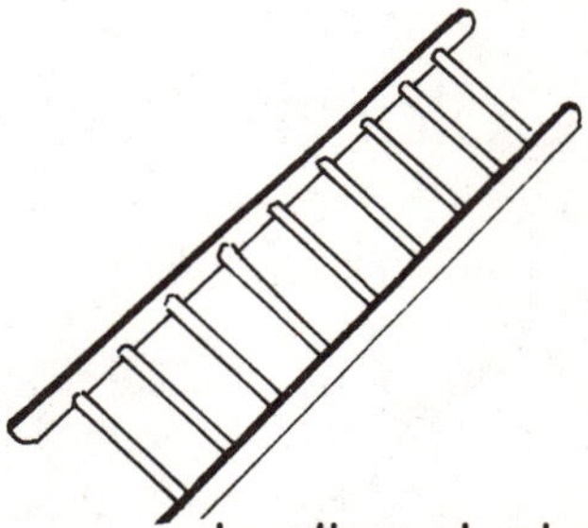

inclined plane

What will Tyrone use to help him get the cat out of the tree?

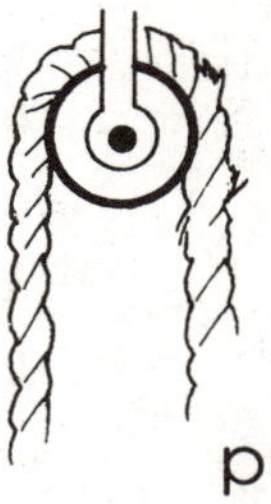

pulley

What will Kim use to carry sand to her new sandbox?

lever

What will Tyrone use to get the nail out of the board?

screw

What will Kim use to hang the mirror on her bedroom door?

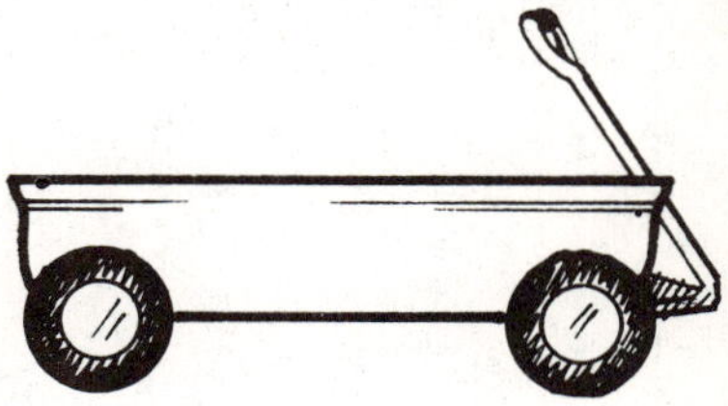

wheel and axle

What will Tyrone use to slice the turkey?

wedge

SCIENCE

Name ______________________________

Slanted Machines

An inclined plane has a slanted surface. It is used to move things from a low place to a high place. Some inclined planes are smooth. Others have steps.

Color the inclined planes in the picture.

Name ____________________

The Wedge

A wedge is a type of inclined plane. It is made up of two inclined planes joined together to make a sharp edge. A wedge can be used to cut things. Some wedges are pointed.

Color only the pictures of wedges.

Name ____________________

Ready for Work!

Read the names of the objects in the Word Bank. Write the objects under the correct kind of simple machine.

Inclined Plane

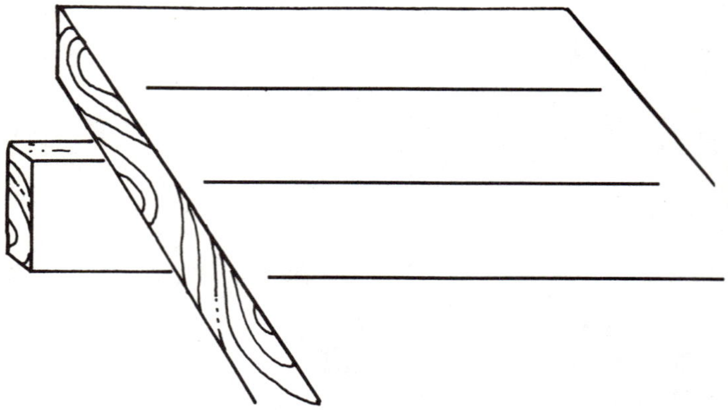

Wheel and Axle

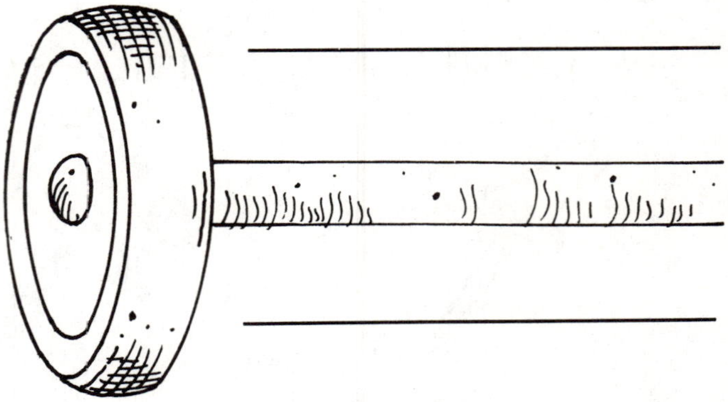

Wedge

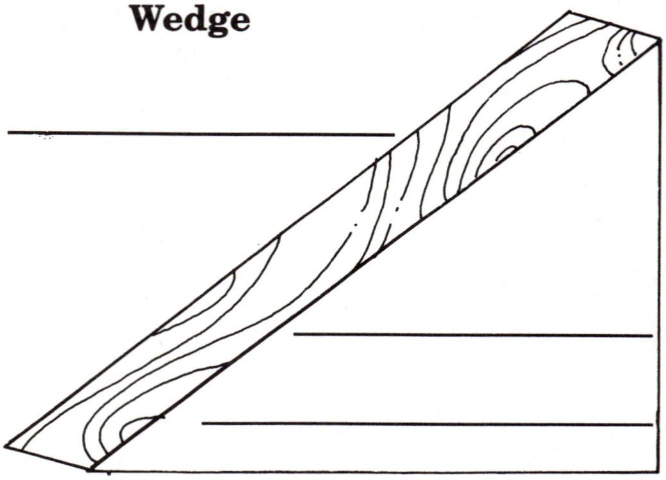

Lever

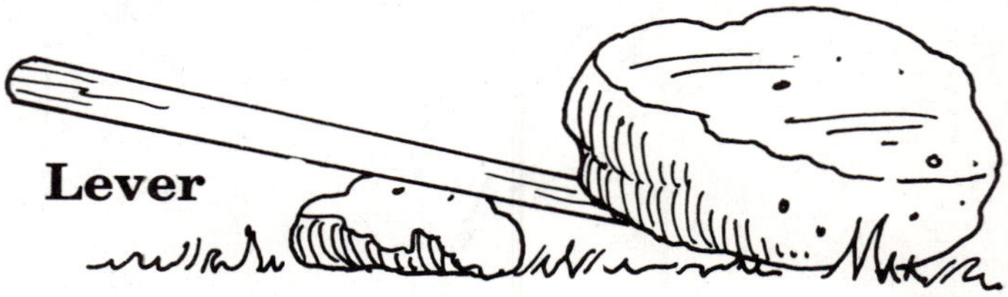

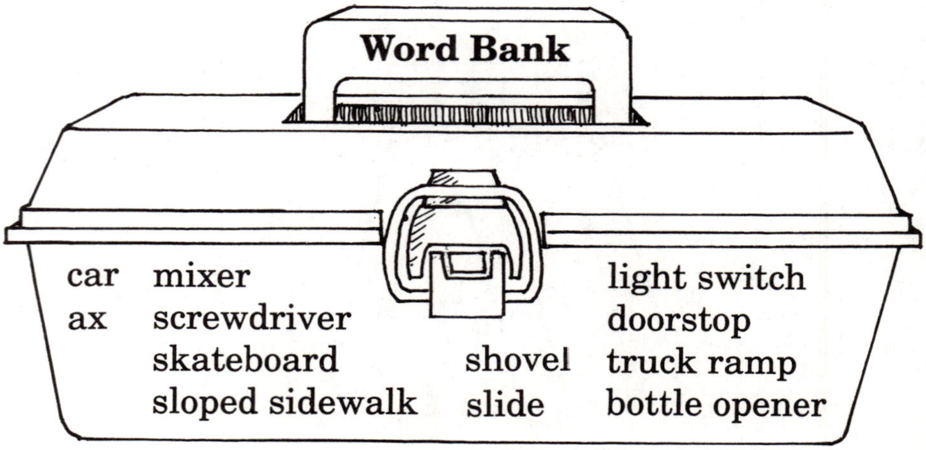
Word Bank
car
ax
mixer
screwdriver
skateboard
sloped sidewalk
shovel
slide
light switch
doorstop
truck ramp
bottle opener

Name ____________________

Faraway and Close Up

Kim's favorite subject is science. She has a telescope and a microscope in her bedroom. At night, she looks through her telescope. Things that are far away, like the moon, stars and planets, look bigger. When she looks through her microscope, she can see tiny things close up, like a drop of water or a bit of salt.

Unscramble and write.

Kim's favorite subject is ____________________.
niecsec

Circle.

She has a bicycle / telescope and a microscope / planet in her bedroom.

Color.

What faraway things look bigger with a telescope?

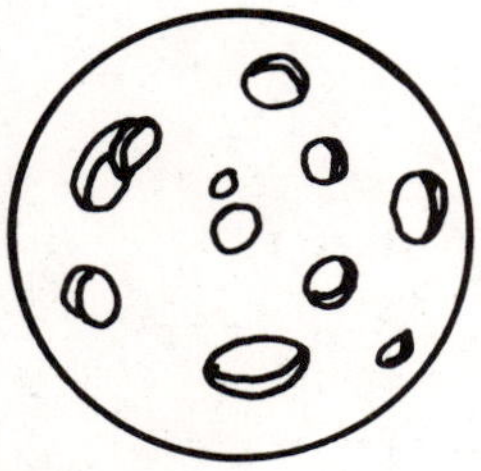

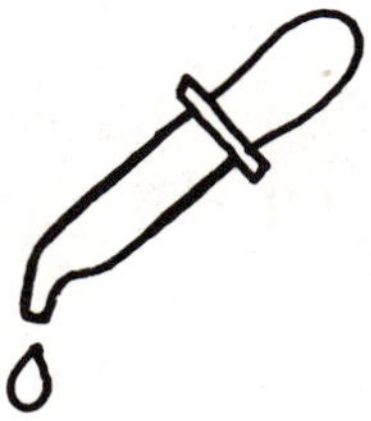

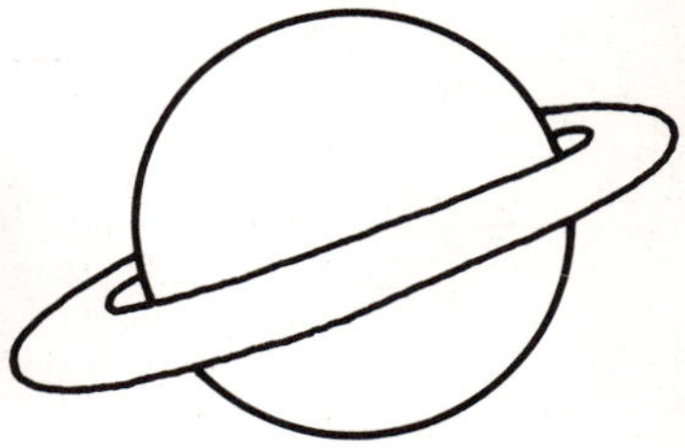

Check.

When Kim looks through her microscope, she can see ...

☐ tiny things close up. ☐ big things far away.

•SOMETHING EXTRA•

What is your favorite subject? Why?

Name ______________________

Planets

There are eight planets that move around the sun. Our planet is Earth. Earth is closest to Mars and Venus. Jupiter is the largest planet. It is many times larger than Earth. Saturn is the planet with seven rings around it. The smallest planet is called Mercury!

Circle.

How many planets are there? three nine eight

Mercury	Earth	Jupiter	Mars	Venus	Saturn

Write.

______________ I am your planet.

____
______________ } We are closest to Earth.

______________ I am the largest planet.

______________ I am the planet with seven rings.

______________ I am the smallest planet.

Color.

Draw three red rings around Saturn.

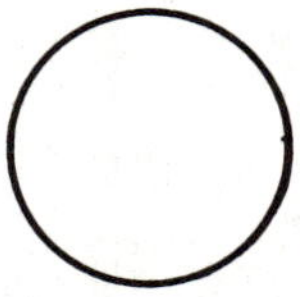

- Draw what you think you would find on the planet Mercury.

Name ____________________

Position the Planets

Write the names of the planets on the lines according to their distance from the sun. Use the Word Bank to help you spell the words correctly.

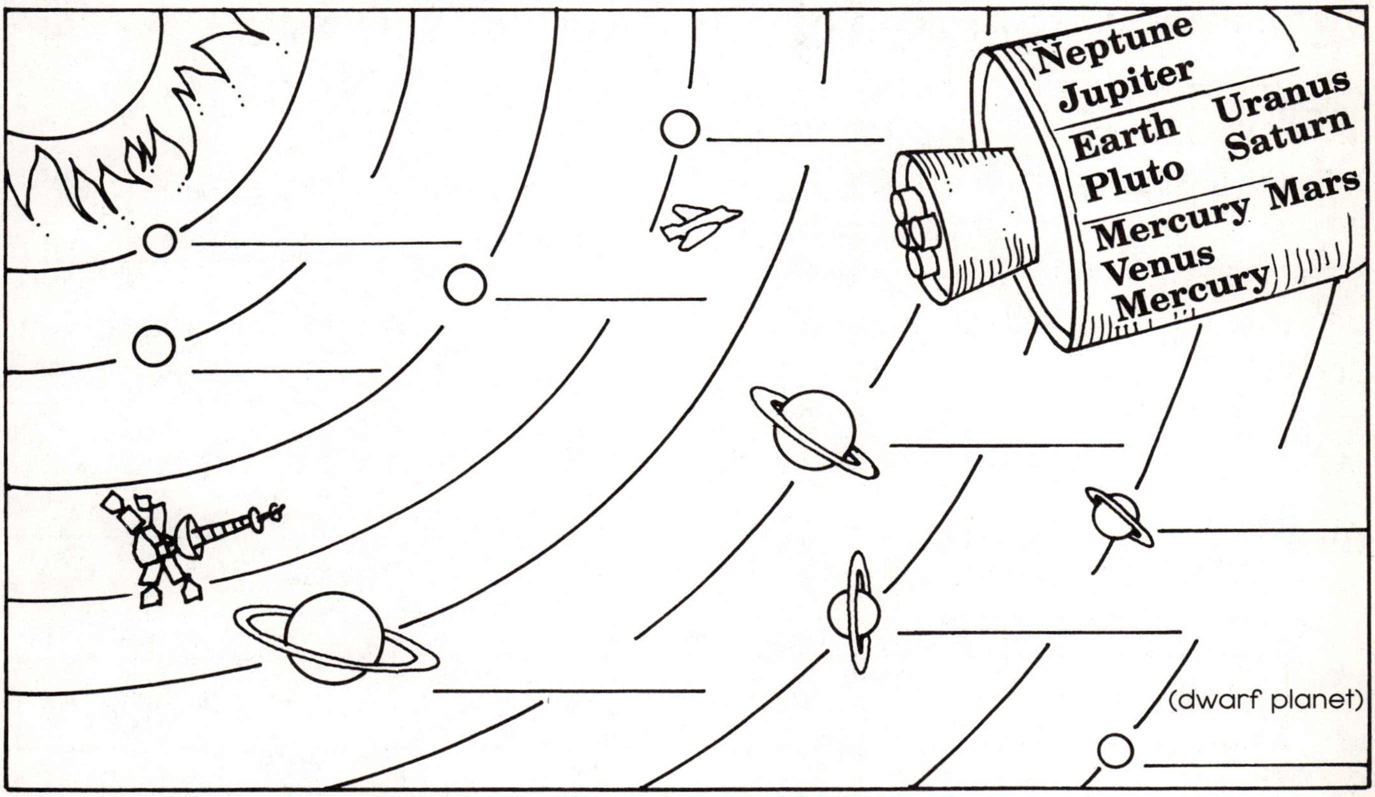
Neptune
Jupiter
Uranus
Earth
Saturn
Pluto
Mercury
Mars
Venus
Mercury
(dwarf planet)

Read the sentences. Record the information on the chart.

1. *Viking 2* took close-up pictures of Mars on September 3, 1976, but scientists still are not sure if there is life on the planet.
2. Two of Saturn's outer rings were very clear in pictures taken by *Pioneer-Saturn* on September 1, 1979.
3. In March of 1979, the probe *Voyager 1* discovered that Jupiter has a thin ring around it.

Name of Probe	Planet Destination	Date	Results or Discoveries

SCIENCE

Name ____________________

Spacing Out

Read a clue. Find the matching word in the puzzle and write it on the line. Then connect the puzzle dots in the same order as your answers.

Clues

1. The planet we live on __________
2. The closest star __________
3. They shine in the sky at night __________
4. Earth is a __________ .
5. Planets, stars, and moons are in __________ .
6. Time when the sun shines __________
7. A group of stars __________
8. A person who travels in space __________
9. The path a planet follows to travel around the sun __________
10. It gives us light at night __________
11. People who study the stars __________
12. You use this to see the stars close up __________
13. Time when the sun does not shine __________
14. We feel this from the sun __________

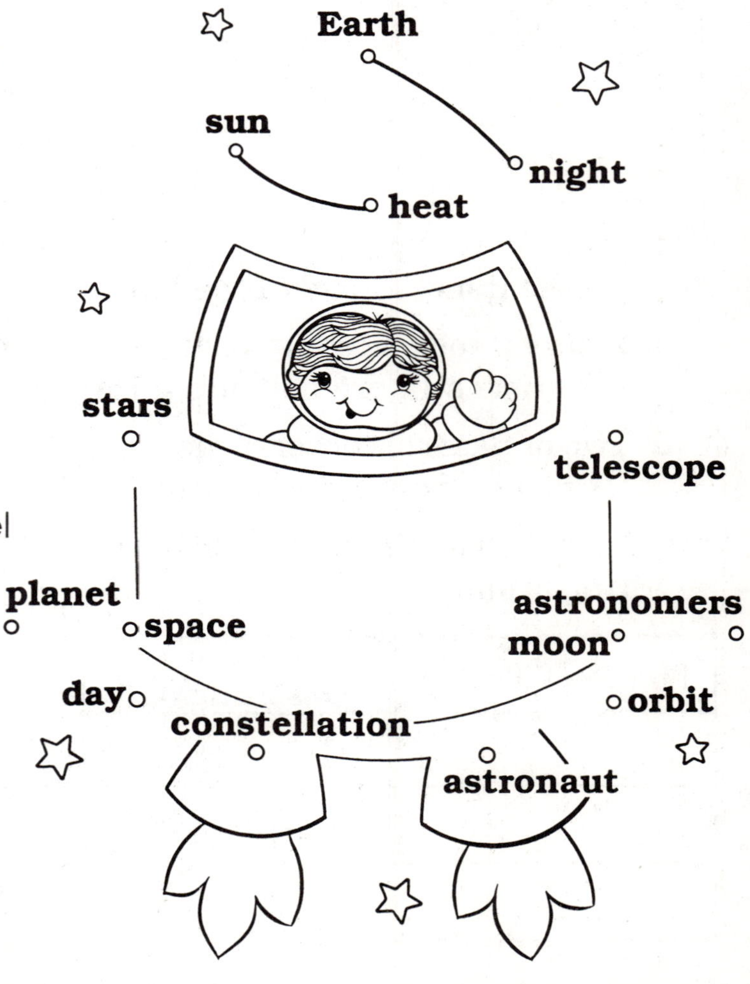

Name ______________________

Birthday Surprise!

1. Complete sentences 1 and 2.
2. Connect the numbers in the dot-to-dot.
3. Color 2 presents red and 3 presents blue.
4. Draw candles on the dot-to-dot picture to show how old you are.
5. Color the dot-to-dot.

1. My birthdate is ______________ (month) ________ (date) __________ (year).

2. I am __________ years old.

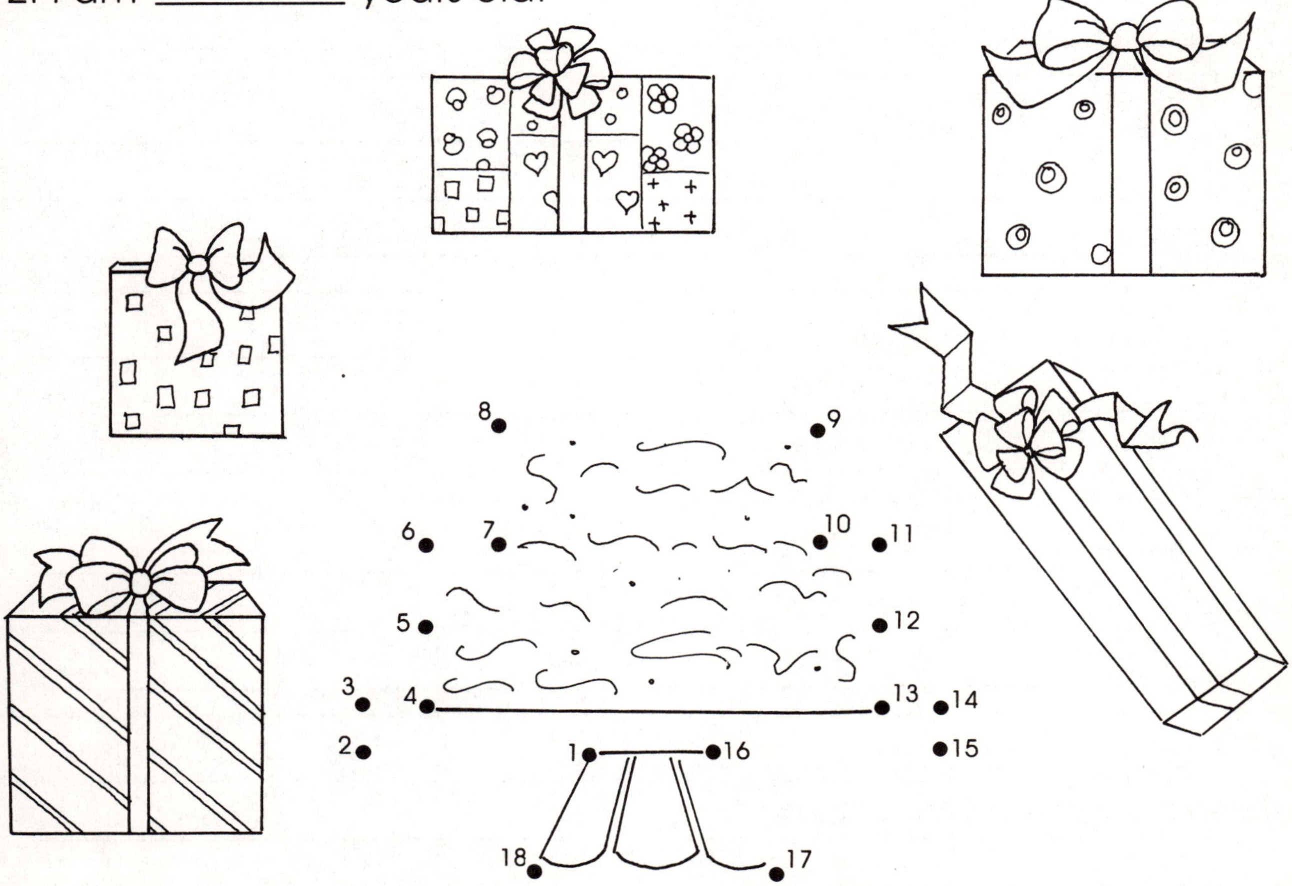

Name ______________________

I Like Me!

Complete the sentences below to tell about you.

Most people like the way I ______________________
____
______________________________.

I feel happy when ______________________
____
______________________________.

The thing I like best about me is
____
______________________________.

I feel sad when ______________________
____
______________________________.

I feel special when ______________________
____
______________________________.

At home I ______________________
____
______________________________.

At school I ______________________
____
______________________________.

0-7682-3792-0 *Skills & Practice Gr. 2*

Name ___________________________

Featuring the One and Only Me

In each box write about a different event in your life. Draw a picture to go with each event.

I was born.		

Name ______________________

My Body Homework

You know how special your body is! To keep your body working and looking its best, you should start developing good habits now and keep them as you grow older. Use this check list to keep yourself on track for the next week. Keep it on your bathroom mirror or next to your bed where it will remind you to do your "homework!"

	Sun.	Mon.	Tues.	Wed.	Thurs.	Fri.	Sat.
I slept at least 8 hours.							
I ate a healthy breakfast.							
I brushed my teeth this morning.							
I ate a healthy lunch.							
I washed my hands after using the bathroom.							
I exercised at least 30 minutes today.							
I drank at least 6 glasses of water.							
I stood and sat up straight.							
I ate a healthy dinner.							
I bathed.							
I brushed my teeth this evening.							

Name ______________________

People Scavenger Hunt

Get to know the kids in your class. Find someone to fit each description. Try not to use the same name twice!

How We Look

1. ________________ has freckles on his/her arms.
2. ________________ is wearing a watch, ring or necklace.
3. ________________ has red on his/her socks.
4. ________________ has 3 buttons on his/her shirt.
5. ________________ is missing 3 baby teeth.

How We Feel

1. ________________ likes green beans.
2. ________________ wants a baby brother or sister.
3. ________________ is scared during thunderstorms.
4. ________________ would like a snake as a pet.
5. ________________ would like his/her room painted blue.

What We Do

1. ________________ ate cereal for breakfast.
2. ________________ played a sport last weekend.
3. ________________ can dive into a swimming pool.
4. ________________ made his/her bed today.
5. ________________ is taking lessons to learn how to do something.

Name ______________________

Shooting for My Goals

What is something new you want to do? Maybe you want to improve at something you already do. Fill in the sentences below.

There are two goals I have for the rest of the school year.

One is ____

____

____

Two is ____

____

____

I will do this by

day ____________________

month ____________________

year ____________________

____

signed

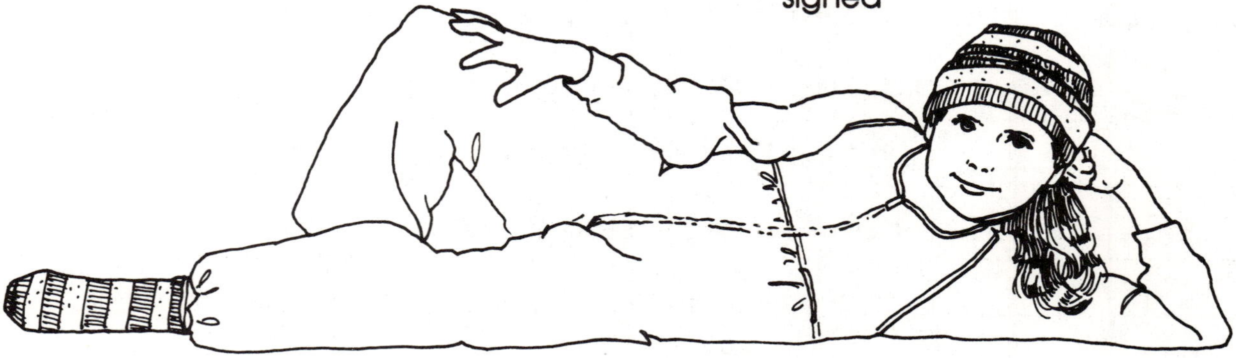

Name ______________________

My Personal Shield

Let your friends learn more about how special you are. Complete each sentence and draw a picture to go with it.

My proudest moment is ________
____
____

I am good at ______________
____
____

I helped ________________
____
____

I try very hard at __________
____
____

Name ______________________________

Interview a Friend

Interview your friend and then fill out the information below.

My friend is ________________ .

Favorite Colors

____

____

____

Favorite Book

____

____

____

Favorite Activities

____

____

____

Favorite Foods

____

____

____

0-7682-3792-0 *Skills & Practice Gr. 2*

Name ____________________

Create a Comrade!

Imagine that you could create a perfect friend. Describe your "creation" on the lines below.

Name ____________

Age ____________

Favorite Pastime ______

____

Personal Qualities

____

____

____

____

Special Interests/Hobbies

____

____

____

____

Talents

____

____

____

____

What we could do together

____

____

____

____

SOCIAL STUDIES

0-7682-3792-0 *Skills & Practice Gr. 2*

Name ______________________

Friendly Favorites

Think of the names of favorite animals, food and places that begin with the letters in the word FRIENDS. Write the names in the correct boxes below. One word in each column has already been done for you. For extra fun, play with a friend. The one who can think of the most names is the winner.

	Animal	Food	Place
F			
R			
I		ice cream	
E			
N			New York
D	dog		
S			

Name ______________________

Buddy's Lists

Buddy likes to make lists. Yesterday, he wrote a list of his favorite things to do with friends. Today, he wants to divide this list into three more lists. Help Buddy by filling in these three lists with one-syllable, two-syllable and three-syllable words from his word list. The first word has been done for you.

One-syllable words

1. golf
2. ______________
3. ______________
4. ______________
5. ______________

Buddy's Word List
Things to Do with Friends

golf	basketball
Ping-Pong™	camp
swim	snorkeling
backpacking	biking
volleyball	skate
baseball	canoeing
fishing	soccer
swing	

Two-syllable words

1. ______________
2. ______________
3. ______________
4. ______________
5. ______________

Three-syllable words

1. ______________
2. ______________
3. ______________
4. ______________
5. ______________

Name ______________________

Cars and Colors

What is the color of your family car? ______________________

If you have more than one car, what are the other colors? ______________________

____

Record the colors of all the cars in your class on the bar graph below. If a color is not shown, include it in "Other."

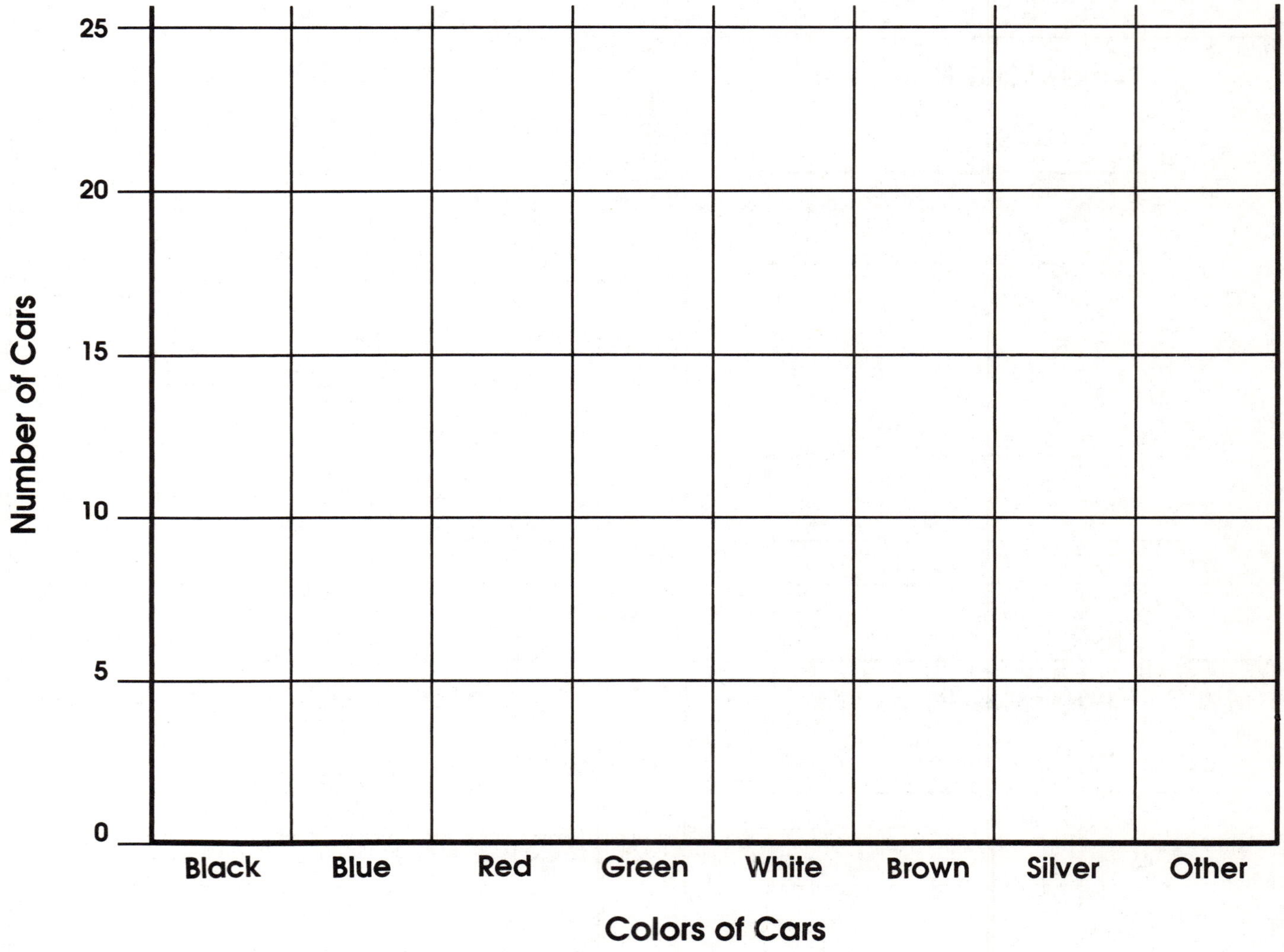
Number of Cars
25
20
15
10
5
0
Black
Blue
Red
Green
White
Brown
Silver
Other
Colors of Cars

1. What is the most popular color of car? ______________________
2. What is the least popular color of car? ______________________
3. What is the total number of cars that were counted? ______________________
4. Were there any colors that were equally popular? ______________________

0-7682-3792-0 *Skills & Practice Gr. 2*

Name ____________________

Comparing a Car and a Truck

In some ways, cars and trucks are alike. In other ways, they are different. On the car, write words and phrases that are true about it but are not true about the truck. Do the same with the truck. Where the car and the truck overlap, write words and phrases that are common to both of them.

Name ______________________________

Sightseeing by Train

Follow the train as it travels through the countryside.
Identify by number the places where the train:

goes through a forest _____
comes to a stop _____
crosses a high bridge _____
passes a water tower _____
exits a tunnel _____
crosses a low bridge _____
passes a school _____
enters a tunnel _____

goes through a covered bridge _____
passes through a plowed field _____
comes down the mountain _____
passes a volcano _____
goes through rocks _____
crosses a lake _____
goes by a small town _____
passes cows _____

Name ______________________

Sights and Sounds of Travel

Look at the numbered pictures below. Write the numbers of the pictures by each question.

What can carry more than one person? ______________

What moves on wheels? ______________

What moves on just two wheels? ______________

What makes a very loud noise? ______________

What moves through water? ______________

What has a motor to make it run? ______________

What can hold large, heavy objects? ______________

What can travel very fast? ______________

What has to be pushed or pulled? ______________

 1	 2	 3
 4	 5	 6
 7	 8	 9
 10	 11	 12

Name ____________________________

Transportation Sort

Study the examples of transportation below. Sort the objects into three groups. Think how each type travels.

Draw a ○ around objects in group one.

Draw a △ around objects in group two.

Draw a □ around objects in group three.

Name ______________________________

How Many Wheels?

Cut out the pictures of the vehicles at the bottom of the page.

Paste the vehicles with no wheels in section 1.
Paste the vehicles with two wheels in section 2.
Paste the vehicles with three wheels in section 3.
Paste the vehicles with four wheels in section 4.
Paste the vehicles with more than four wheels in section 5.

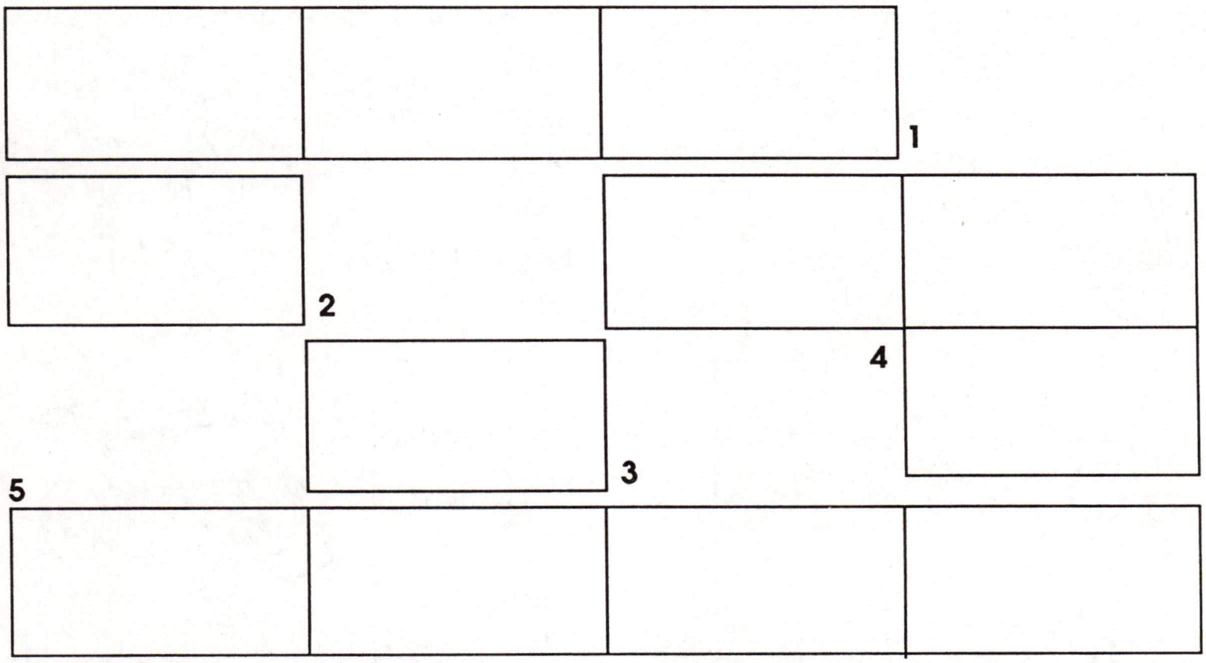

Name ____________________

Transportation Magic Square

1. Read Column A. Choose an answer from Column B. Write the number of the answer in the correct square. The first one has been done for you.

Column A

A. Filled with helium
B. Runs on gasoline
C. Powered by wind
D. Burns coal or wood
E. Runs on nuclear energy
F. Moves on snow or ice
G. Moves by pedals
H. Powered by oars
I. Pulled by horses or oxen

Column B

1. jet plane
2. rowboat
3. sailboat
4. steam locomotive
5. blimp
6. submarine
7. wagon
8. sled
9. bicycle
10. car

A 5	B ____	C ____
D ____	E ____	F ____
G ____	H ____	I ____

2. Add the numbers across, down, and diagonally. What answer do you get? ______

   Why do you think this is called a magic square? ____________________

   ____

Name ____________________

Traveling to a Large City

1. Circle the correct answer. Then follow the directions.
   A large truck used for moving furniture is called a:
   a. dump truck - Mark out all letter M's below.
   b. van - Mark out all letter C's below.
   c. pickup truck - Mark out all letter I's below.

   A large vehicle for transporting children to school is called a:
   a. bus - Mark out all letter B's below.
   b. yacht - Mark out all letter A's below.
   c. jet - Mark out all letter F's below.

   A vehicle pulled by horses or oxen is called a:
   a. hot air balloon - Mark out all letter D's below.
   b. tricycle - Mark out all letter O's below.
   c. wagon - Mark out all letter P's below.

   A long line of boxcars that runs on a track is called a:
   a. submarine - Mark out all letter L's below.
   b. train - Mark out all letter N's below.
   c. bicycle - Mark out all letter R's below.

   A vehicle that sails through water is called a:
   a. ship - Mark out all letter E's below.
   b. tank - Mark out all letter M's below.
   c. sled - Mark out all letter A's below.

C	M	B	N	I	P	E	C
A	P	C	M	B	N	E	I
B	F	N	C	P	E	B	N
P	C	L	B	N	P	E	C
B	E	C	P	B	O	E	N
R	B	N	C	I	P	B	E
C	D	B	P	N	B	A	C

2. Start at the top. Write the name of the remaining letters in the spaces below.
   I will travel to what city? __ __ __ __ __ __ , __ __ __ __ __ __ __ __

SOCIAL STUDIES

Name ________________________

By Land, by Sea, and by Air

Write the first letter of the names of the objects below.
The letters form words.
Underline the word in red if it travels "By Land."
Underline the word in green if it travels "By Sea."
Underline the word in orange if it travels "By Air."

______ ______ ______ ______ ______ ______

______ ______ ______ ______ ______ ______ ______

______ ______ ______ ______

______ ______ ______ ______ ______ ______

Name ______________________

Follow That Sign!

Look at the road sign symbols below. Each sign is matched to a letter. Use the road sign code to find the names of four vehicles that travel on roads.

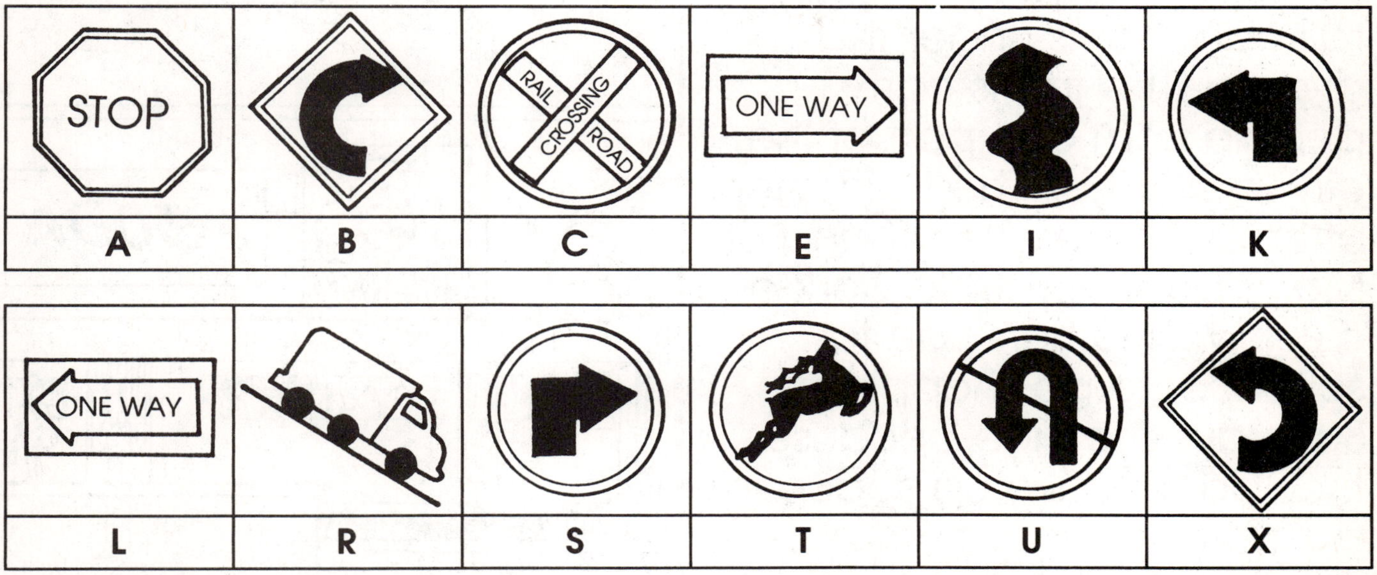
STOP
A
B
RAIL CROSSING ROAD
C
ONE WAY
E
I
K
ONE WAY
L
R
S
T
U
X

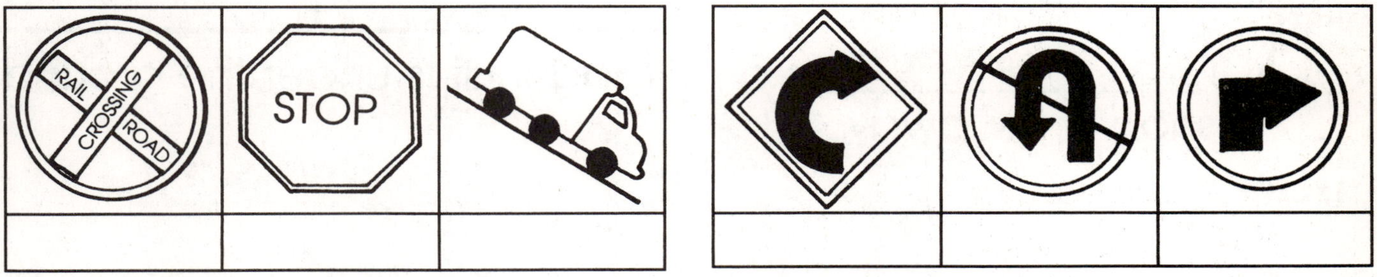
RAIL CROSSING ROAD
STOP

RAIL CROSSING ROAD

STOP

SOCIAL STUDIES

Name ______________________

The Subway

Some big cities have a subway. A subway is a railroad that is under the ground. The trains carry people from one part of the city to another. The trains stop often to let people off and on. Many people ride to work on a subway. Others ride to school or to go shopping. Subways are nice because they do not take up space in a city.

Write.

A ________________ is a railroad that is under the ground.

shop subway

Circle.

Yes or No

The subway takes people to parts of the city.	**Yes**	**No**
The subway stops only one time each day.	**Yes**	**No**
The subway stops to let people off and on.	**Yes**	**No**

Circle.

Where are some people on the subway going?

work

sleep

school

shopping

Color the subway train red.

- Draw where **you** would go on the subway.

Name ____________________

A Helicopter

Would you like to ride in a helicopter? A helicopter flies in the air. It can fly **up** and **down**. It can fly **forward** and **backward**. It can fly **sideways**. A helicopter can even stay in one spot in the air! Helicopters can be many sizes. Some helicopters carry just one person. Some carry 30 people. Helicopters can be used for many jobs.

Write.

A ____________________ flies in the air.

trailer helicopter

Write.

Which way can a helicopter fly? (Look at story.)

4→u _ **3→d** _ _ _ **5→f** _ _ _ _ _ _

2→b _ _ _ _ _ _ _ **1→s** _ _ _ _ _ _ _

Write the answers in the puzzle above.

Circle.

Yes or No

A helicopter can stay in one spot in the air.	Yes	No
Helicopters come in many sizes.	Yes	No
All helicopters can carry 10 people.	Yes	No

• Draw a big green helicopter.

Name ____________________

Hot Air Balloons

Would you like to fly in a hot air balloon? A hot air balloon can fly when it is filled with hot air or a gas, called helium. Most hot air balloons use helium to fly. People can ride in a basket that is tied to the balloon. The wind moves the balloon in the sky. To come down, the people must let some of the air or gas out of the balloon.

Circle.

What does a hot air balloon need to fly?

hot air   music   gas

Write.

Most hot air balloons use ____________________ to fly.

helmets   helium

Circle.

What do people ride in?

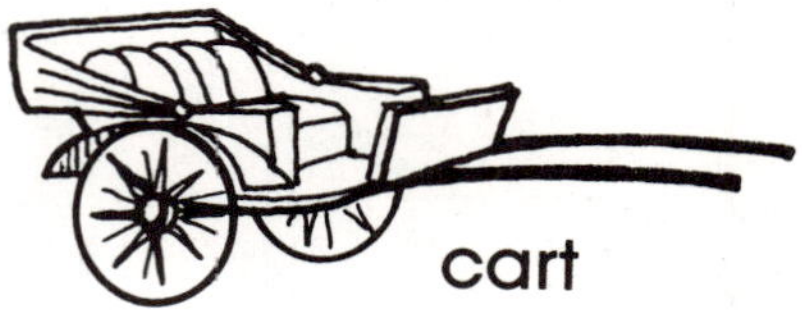

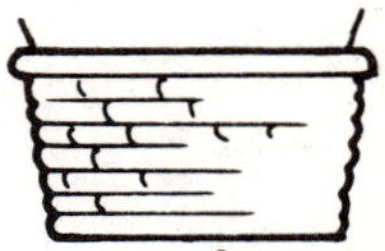

Circle.

The moon / wind moves the balloon in the sky.

Color.

1 - red   **2** - purple   **3** - green

- Draw a hot air balloon with two people in the basket.

Name ____________________

What's New?

Inventions help to make life easier. Various inventors from all around the world try to come up with ways to improve upon things presently used.

Below are pictures of inventions that have changed as inventors improved them. Number them in the correct order each version appeared by writing 1, 2, and 3 in the boxes.

Automobile

☐  ☐  ☐ 

Bicycle

☐  ☐  ☐ 

Airplane

☐ 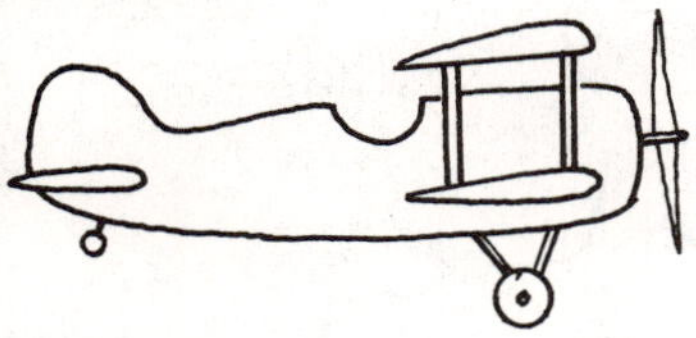 ☐  ☐ 

Telephone

☐  ☐ 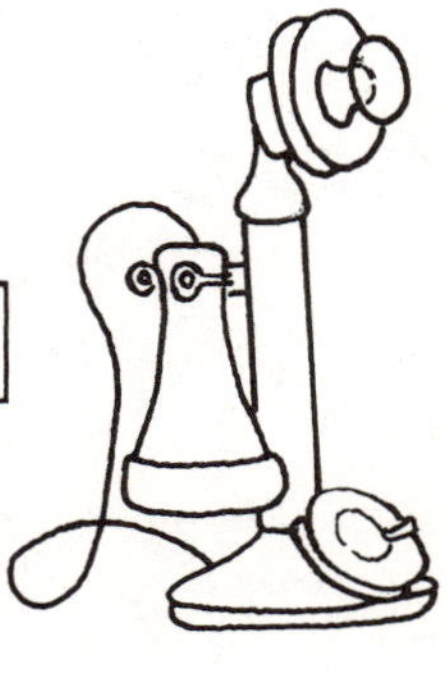 ☐ 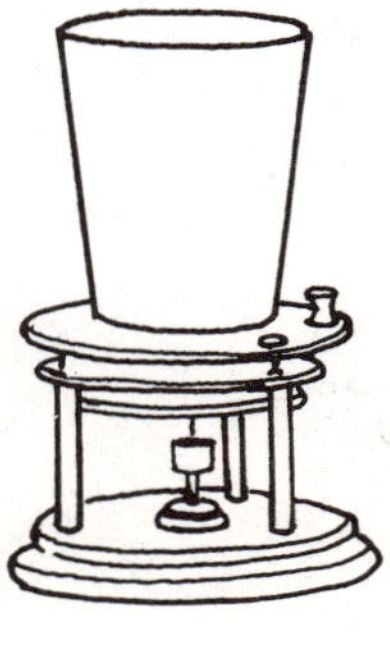

Name ______________________

Selecting Supplies

Read each word in the Word Bank. If a word names a **need**, write it on the sack of flour. If a word names a **want**, write it on the pickle barrel.

Word Bank
videotape milk bracelet
kite soda pop bed candy bar
soccer ball home backpack
vegetables balloon fruit
bread coat hat

Want

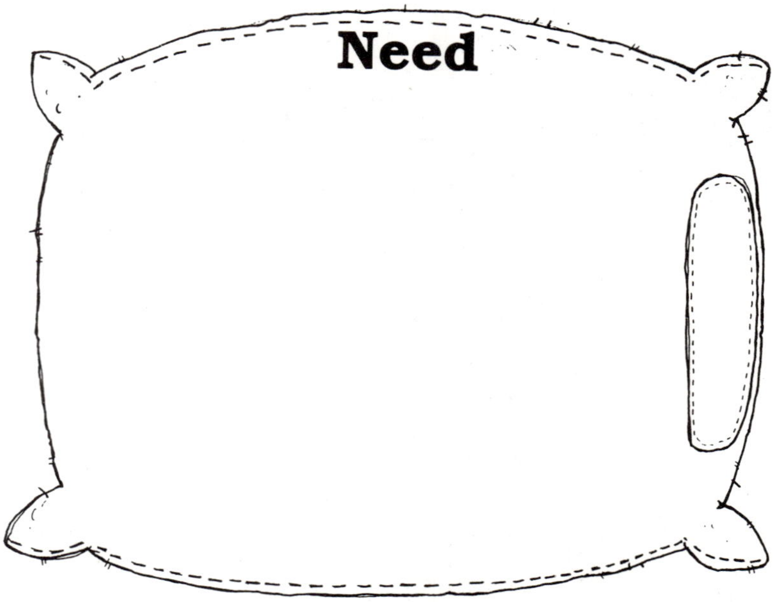
Need

Name ____________________

"Good Service" Delivery

Read each word. If it names an occupation that provides goods, mark **G** on the word. If it names an occupation that provides a service, mark **S** on the word. Then draw a line to show where three answers are the same in a row.

television salesperson	veterinarian	zookeeper
receptionist	pizza parlor owner	lawyer
crossing guard	school bus driver	kite manufacturer

actor	plumber	toy maker
firefighter	music store owner	principal
shoe salesperson	cook	babysitter

Name ____________________

Brought to You from . . .

Look at each picture. If the picture shows something that comes from a farm, mark **X** on the picture. If it shows something that comes from a factory, mark **O** on the picture. Then draw a line to show where three answers are the same in a row.

 chair	 SEE SPOT book	 carrot
 bow	 strawberry	 football
 potato	 glass	 pencil

Made in the U.S.A.
U.S.A.

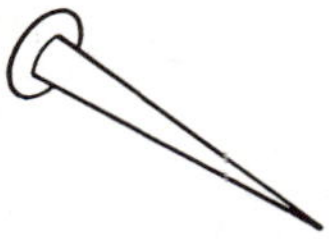 nail	 backpack	 peanuts
 lettuce	 swimsuit	 apple
 radish	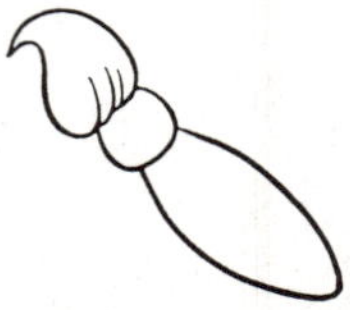 paintbrush	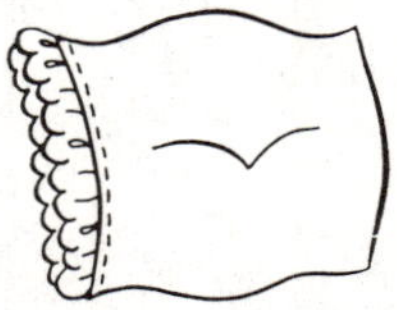 pillow

0-7682-3792-0 *Skills & Practice Gr. 2*

Name ______________________________

My Community

Finish the sentences. Draw a picture to match.

The name of my community

is ______________________________

One place I like to visit is

____

Here is a picture of the place.
MAIL
DAIRY PRODUCTS

Name ______________________

About My Community

Write about your community.

I live in

____

______________________.

It is in the state of

____

______________________.

In winter the weather is

____

______________________.

In summer the weather is

____

______________________.

I live in or near a

____

______________________.

suburb	city	farm	town

My community is in or near

- ☐ mountains.
- ☐ a desert.
- ☐ a plain.
- ☐ a valley.
- ☐ hills.

This is a picture that shows me shopping at the market.

The water nearest my community is

- ☐ an ocean.
- ☐ a river.
- ☐ a lake.
- ☐ a swamp.

0-7682-3792-0 *Skills & Practice Gr. 2*

Name ______________________________

Build a Community

Cut out the pictures at the bottom of this page. Read the directions. Paste the pictures where they belong.

1. Place the school **west** of the house and **east** of the row of trees.
2. Place the train at the **southwest** edge of the railroad tracks.
3. Place the Police Station **west** of the Train Station and **east** of the train.
4. Place the Grocery Store **east** of the house and **south** of the rising sun.
5. Place the Bank **north** of the train.
6. Place the Firehouse **south** of the Grocery Store and **east** of the Train Station.

Cut

Name ______________________________

Just Being Neighborly

Go along with Percival Porcupine as he delivers the Welcome basket.

Follow the directions. Trace a path from one place to the next.

1. Start at Percival and go east 3 spaces. Write **library.**
2. Then go south 4 spaces. Write **market**.
3. Next go west 2 spaces. Write **gas station**.
4. Now go north 3 spaces. Write **school**.
5. Go west 2 spaces. Write **fire station**.
6. Go south 2 spaces. Write **park**.
7. Go east 6 spaces. Write **welcome**.

Name ____________________

Find the Ring

Look at the map. Read each clue and write the correct word on the line. Then draw a line from one place to the next to show where each clue takes you.

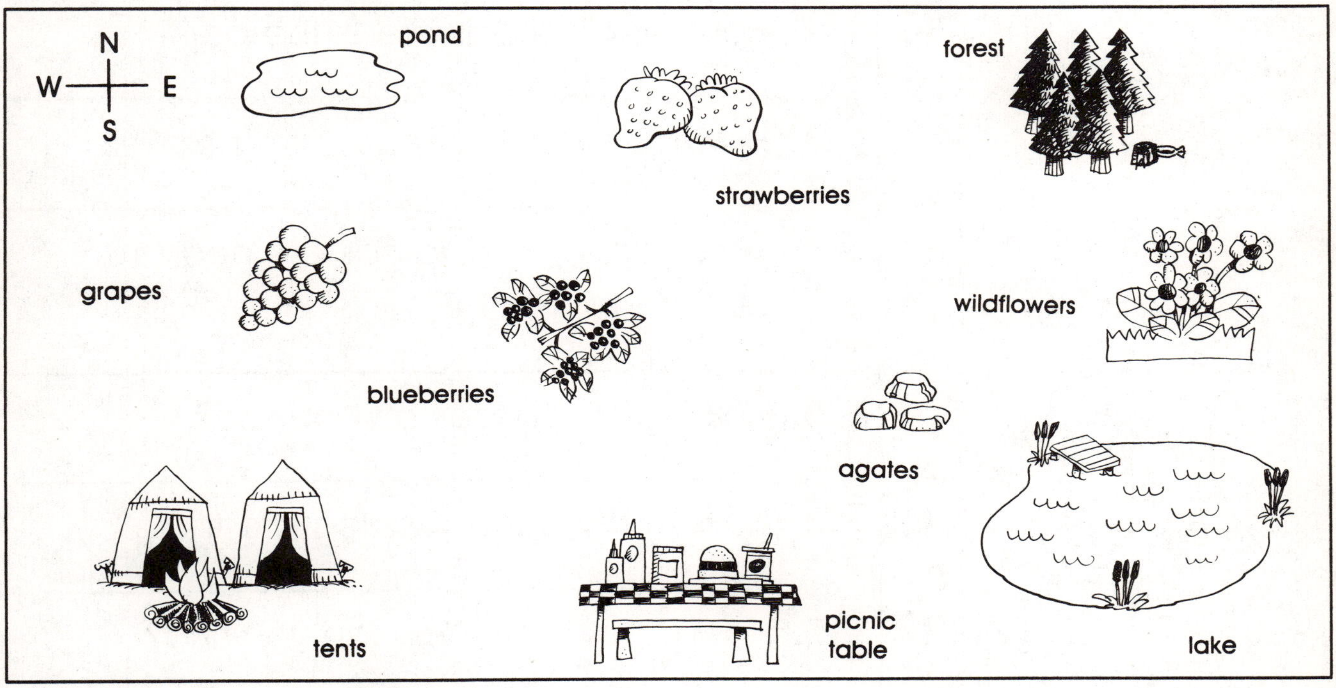

1. Begin where campers sleep. ____________________
2. Go north to a fruit that makes a purple-colored juice. ____________________
3. Go southeast to a place where you can sit and eat. ____________________
4. Then go east where you can row a boat. ____________________
5. Turn north to the small plants with colored petals. ____________________
6. Go southwest to find some special rocks. ____________________
7. Now go northwest to pick some sweet, red berries. ____________________
8. Go west to a place where you can swim. ____________________
9. Then go southeast and pick some round, blue-colored fruit. ____________________
10. At last, go northeast to a place where there are many trees. ____________________
11. Look closely to find the missing ring. Draw a circle around it.

SOCIAL STUDIES

Name ______________________

Follow the Map

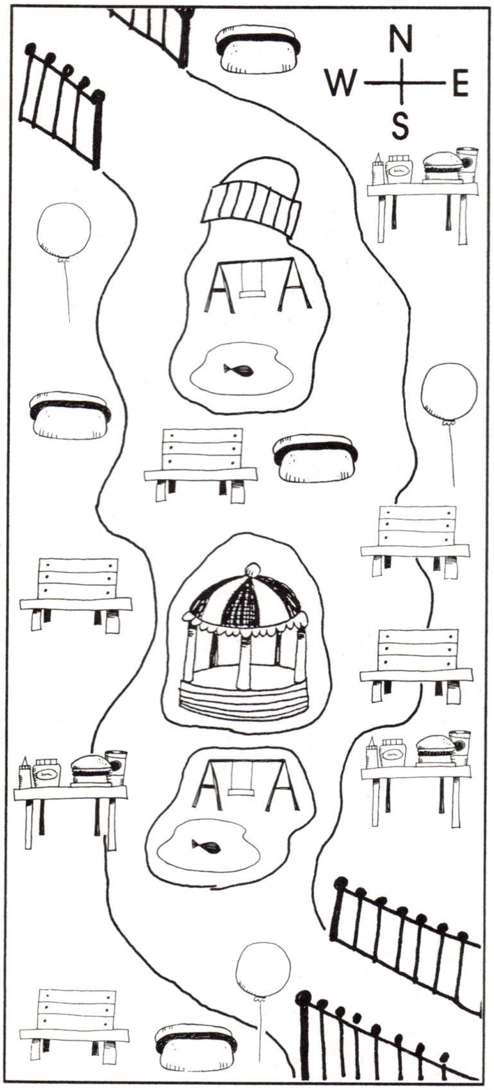

Use the map to answer the questions.

1. How many entrances do you see?
   ____
2. How many ponds are in the park?
   ____
3. How many picnic areas are there?
   ____
4. How many picnic areas are near a playground?
   ____
5. How many bridges do you see?
   ____
6. How many balloon sellers are there?
   ____
7. How many benches can you find?
   ____
8. How many places are there to buy food?
   ____
9. How many carousels are there?
   ____

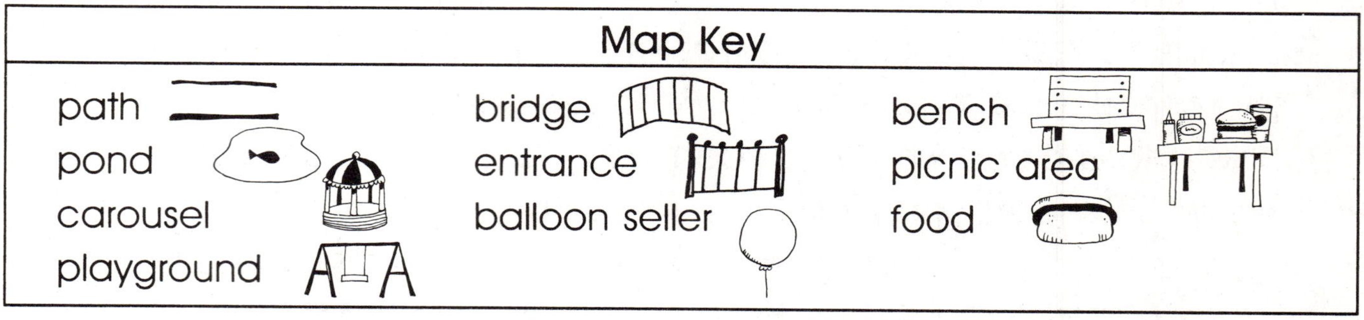

0-7682-3792-0 *Skills & Practice Gr. 2*

Name ________________

The Adventure Begins

One rainy Saturday morning, Patrick, Brenda, and Jamie decided they needed something new and exciting to do that morning. They took out the telephone book and turned to the yellow pages. In it they found these advertisements for special places to visit.

Aquarium

Open weekdays from
10:00 a.m. to 6:00 p.m.
Closed weekends

Call 123 - Fish

Museum of American History

Open Monday – Saturday
from 9:00 a.m. to 5:00 p.m.
Closed Sundays

Call HIS-TORY

Planetarium

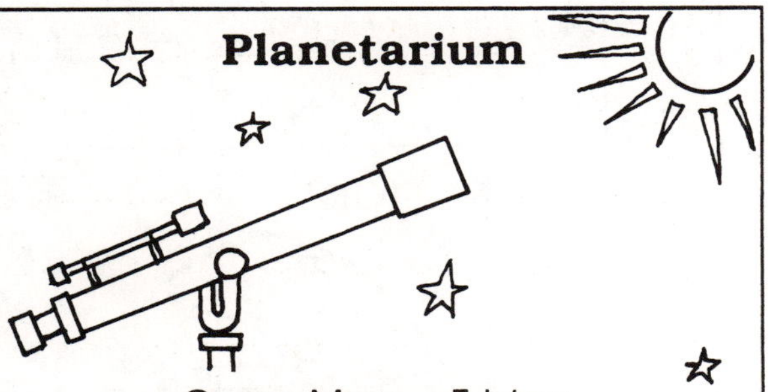

Open Mon. – Friday
12:00 noon to 6:00 p.m.
Saturday 3:00 p.m. to 9:00 p.m.

Call 83S - TARS

Zoo

Open daily from
9:00 a.m. to 5:00 p.m.
Weather Permitting

Call ANI - MALS

The children looked carefully at the ads. Which place did they choose to visit and why?

They chose to go to the ________________________________

because ________________________________

SOCIAL STUDIES

0-7682-3792-0 *Skills & Practice Gr. 2*

Name ____________________

Home Sweet Home

At the Museum of American History, Patrick, Brenda, and Jamie saw large exhibits of Native Americans and their homes.

Use the rebuses below to discover the different types of houses various nations of Native Americans lived in. Your answers will sound right, but the spellings won't be right. Get the the correct spellings from the Word Box.

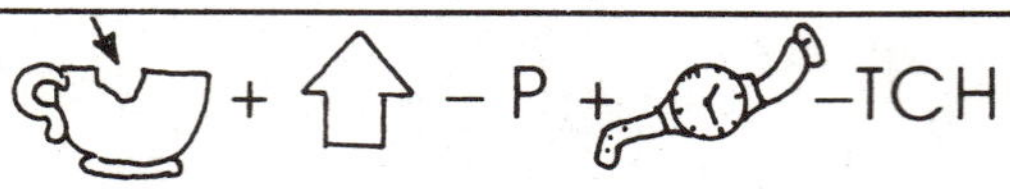

The ____________________ Indians lived in domed bark lodges.

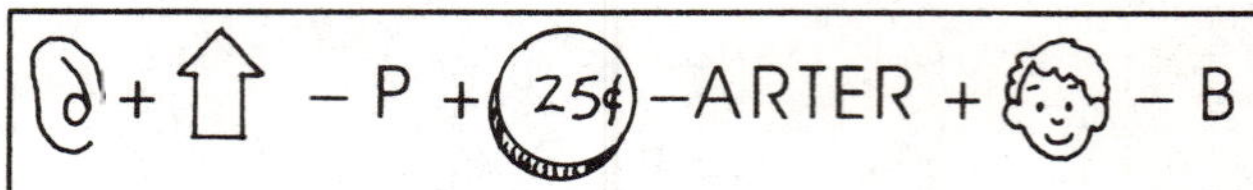

The ____________________ Indians lived in long houses.

The ____________________ Indians lived in buffalo-hide tepees.

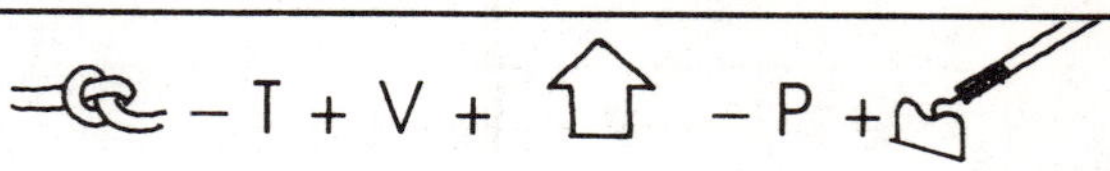

The ____________________ Indians lived in hogans.

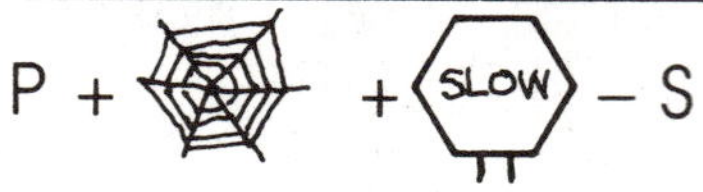

The ____________________ Indians lived in adobes.

Word Box

Pueblo	Iroquois	Sioux
Navajo	Chippewa	

0-7682-3792-0 *Skills & Practice Gr. 2*

Name ______________________________

Whose House?

Use the pictures of the Native American houses to answer the riddles.

Eastern woodland tribes

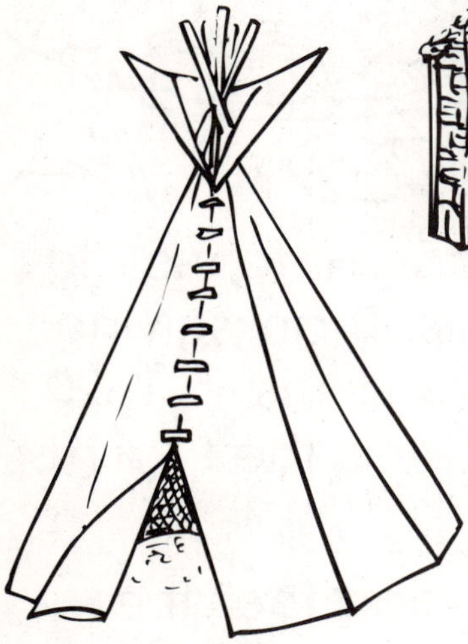

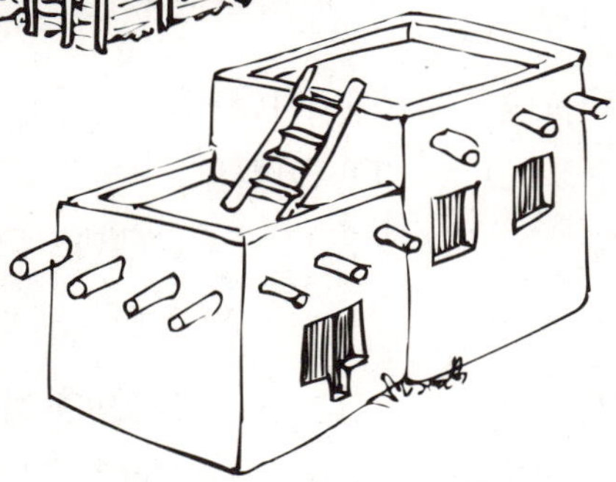

Northwest coastal tribes

Plains tribes

Southwest tribes

This house has no beds. Many families live in it. It is made of adobe brick. It has no doors, only windows. Whose house is it? ______________________________	This is called a plank house. Many families live in it. It is made of large beams and trees. It has a totem pole in front. Whose house is it? ______________________________
This is called a long house. It has bunk beds. It is made of branches and bark. Fire burns in the center of it. Whose house is it? ______________________________	This house can be set up in 10 minutes. One family lives in it. It is made of poles and animal skins. A fire burns inside. Whose house is it? ______________________________

Name ______________________________

A Family of Friends

There was a great exhibit at the Museum of American History of figures of Native Americans and Pilgrims sharing the first Thanksgiving feast. When the Pilgrims came to Plymouth, Massachusetts, in 1620, they had a very difficult year. Native Americans helped the Pilgrims hunt and harvest food.

Read each riddle. Use the Word Box to write each food that the Native Americans helped the Pilgrims find or grow.

1. Water doesn't stick –
It rolls off my back;
And when it does,
I loudly say, "Quack, quack!"

I am ______________________ .

2. I'm not inside a whale,
But I'm found in a "wheel."
You'll also find me
In a piece of "steel."

I am ______________________ .

3. When your roof "leaks,"
You may want to cry.
You'll do the same thing
When I'm near your eye.

I am ______________________ .

4. Boil me or pop me
When I am ripe.
Cook me in bread
Or use my cob as a pipe.

I am ______________________

5. I like to "honk,"
And I can fly.
Ask the lady who rode me,
Reciting rhymes in the sky.

I am ______________________ .

Word Box		
a goose	a leek	a duck
corn	an eel	

Name ____________________

Then and Now

The museum had great examples of things the colonists used. Although their lives were different than ours today, many of their needs were the same.

Unscramble the names of objects we use today. (The first letter is underlined.) Then write the correct letter to match similar objects of the past and present.

Present | **Past**

cetelrci nkablte

a. ____________ ____________

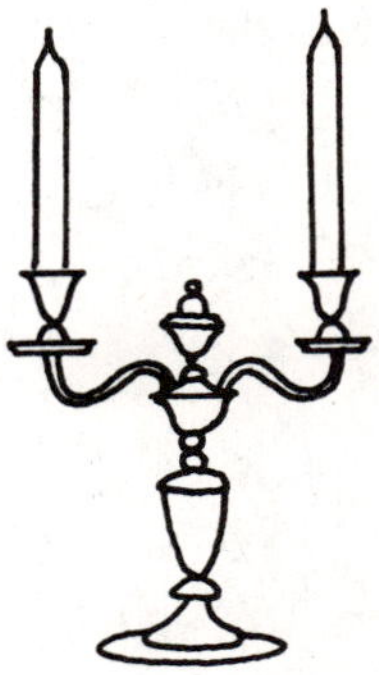

____ candles

mapl

b. ____________

____ bed warmer

satemhc

c. ____________

____ quill and ink well

tlpea

d. ____________

____ wooden trencher

epn

e. ____________

____ tinder box

SOCIAL STUDIES

Name ______________________________

Down on the Farm

At the museum the children learned that though the colonists worked very hard, they also took time for some fun. One favorite form of fun was corn-husking competitions.

In the cornfield below, Thomas picked and husked corn from the cornstalks that have circles around the numbers.

Jonathon picked and husked corn from the cornstalks that have squares around the numbers.

James did the same with the cornstalks that have triangles around the numbers.

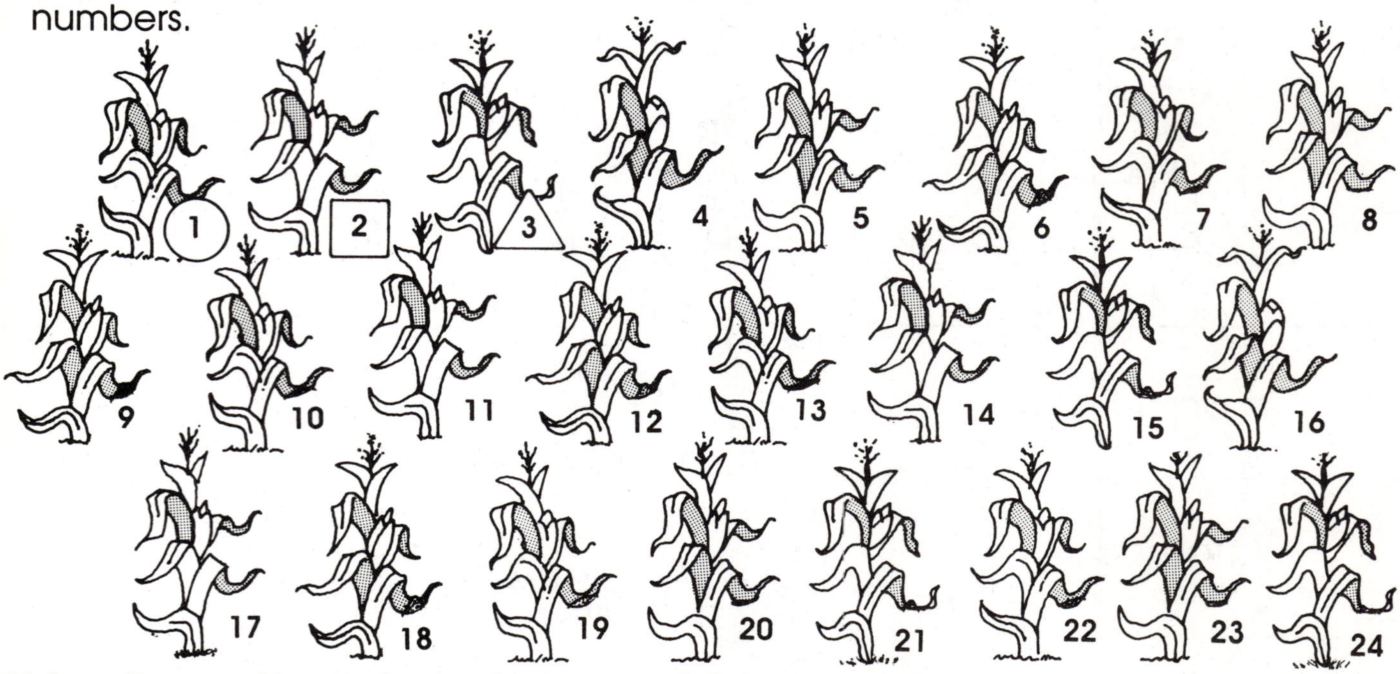

Using the pattern started above, finish drawing the circles, squares, and triangles. Then answer these questions.

1. Who picked and husked corn from cornstalk #20? ______________

2. Who picked and husked corn from cornstalk #22? ______________

3. If all of the even-numbered cornstalks had two ears of corn, and all of the odd-numbered cornstalks had one ear of corn, how many ears of corn did each boy husk?

   Thomas ______ Jonathon ______ James ______

Name ______________________

Sew What?

A favorite activity of colonial women and girls was getting together for a quilting bee. The quilts, made from scraps of linen, wool, and cotton, were frequently sewn together in a pattern.

Look carefully at the pattern in the unfinished quilt below. Then continue the pattern by drawing pictures in the blank sections to complete the quilt.

Name ______________________________

Go West, Young Man!

From about 1760 to 1850, pioneers moved westward across the United States. They traveled in big covered wagons called **Conestoga** wagons.

Some of the trails that the pioneers took in their Conestoga wagons are marked on the map below.

Look closely at the trails. Then answer the questions.

1. If the pioneers started at Nauvoo and traveled **west**, how many different trails could they take? ________
2. If the pioneers began at Independence and traveled **west**, how many choices of trails would they have? ________

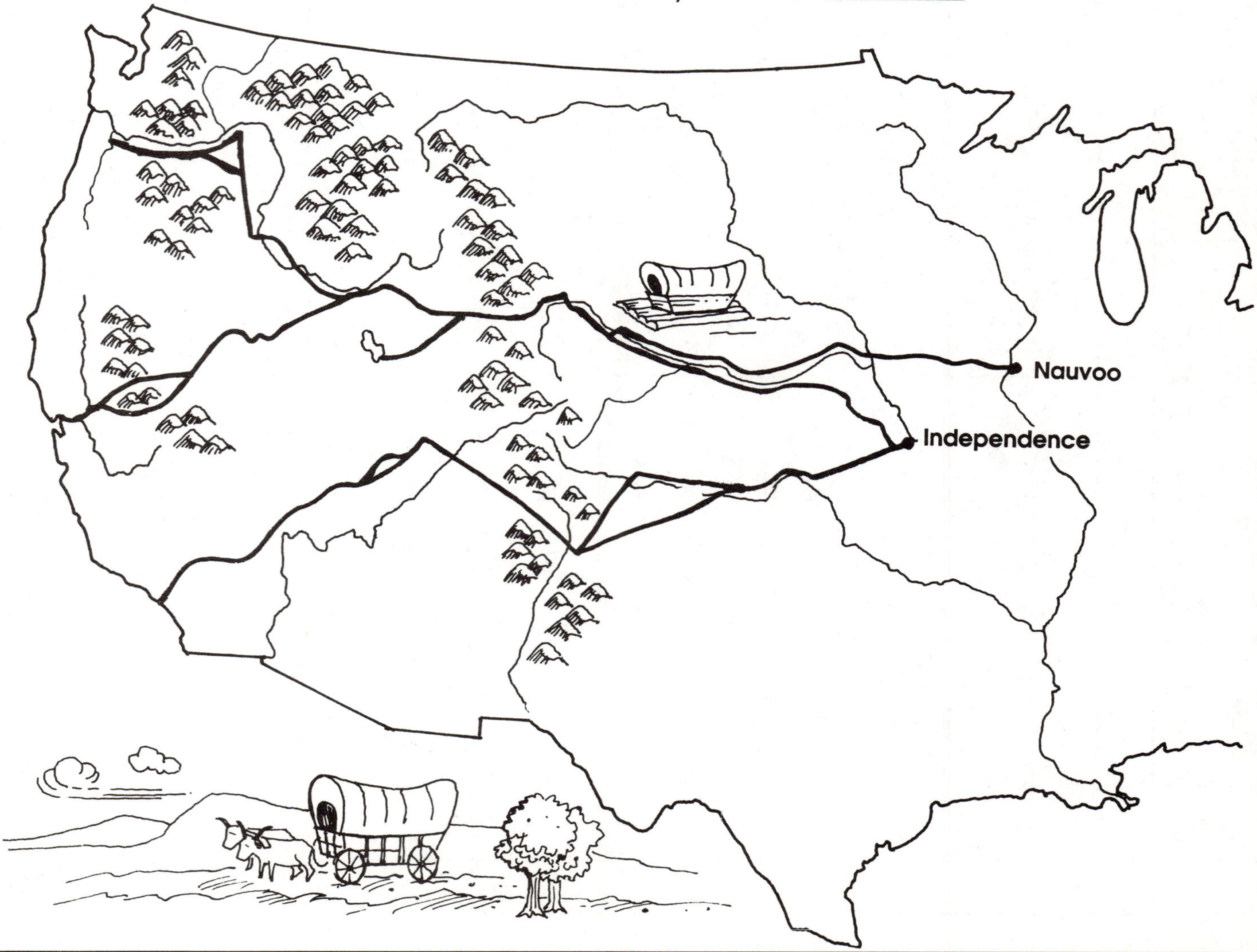

Name ______________________

A Man of Peace

A large picture of the Lincoln Memorial was on display at the museum. Abraham Lincoln was our 16th president. Shortly after he became President in 1861, America's Civil War began between the people living in the South and the people living in the North.

Abraham Lincoln made a famous speech in which he said that all people are created equal. He wanted all people in our country to live together in peace.

Look carefully at the tall columns around the outside of the building. If you walked around the whole building, how many columns would you pass? _____

SOCIAL STUDIES

Name ______________________________

What's Your Brand?

The Museum of American History had a great display on cowboys who lived from the 1860's to the 1880's. These cowboys went on cattle drives for two to three months at a time and sometimes traveled 1,000 miles! They were often in danger from rattlesnakes, quicksand, cattle stampedes, and wild horses.

During cattle roundups in the spring and fall, cowboys branded the newborn calves to show what ranch they belonged to.

Look at the brands below. Use the Word Box to write what each brand meant.

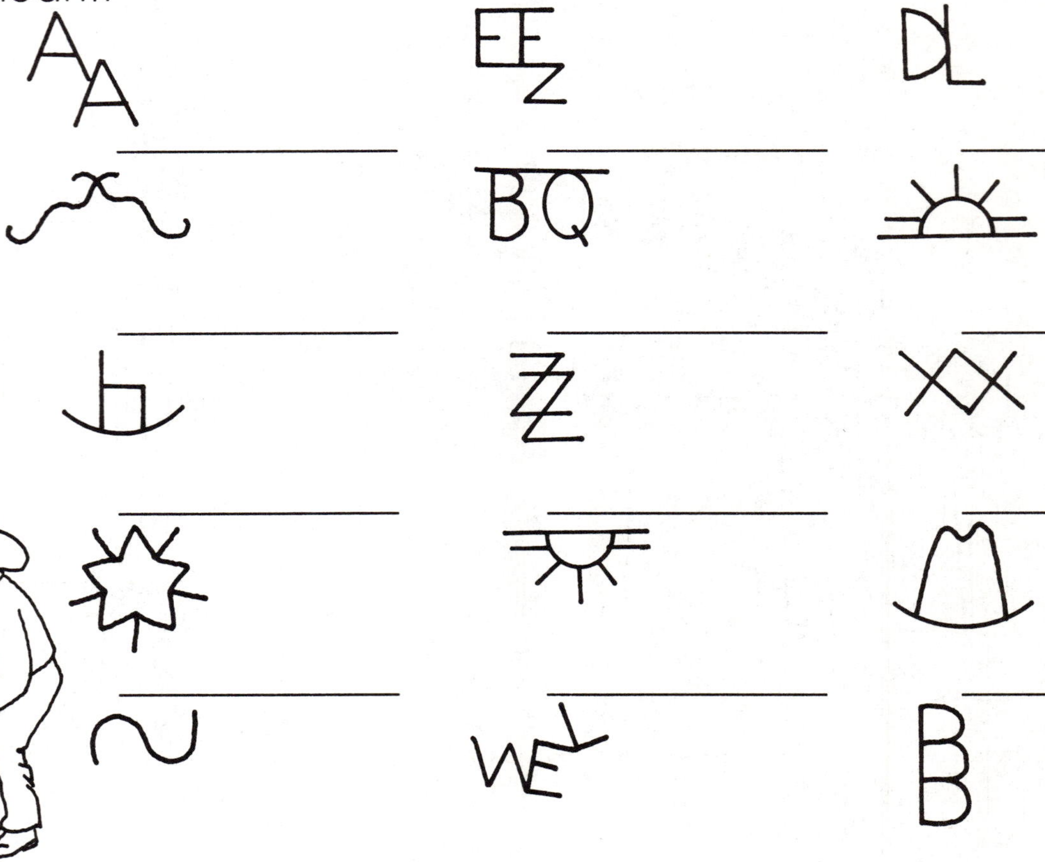

Word Box

Twin Snakes	Double Z	Pair of Aces	Sunrise	Too Easy
Rocking Chair	Extra X	Big Deal	Sunset	Barbecue
Broken Wheel	Lazy S	Starlight	Tall Hat	Two Bees

Name ______________________

News Flash!

One large room in the museum had pages from calendars on its walls, listing events from America's past. Pretend that you were a newspaper reporter in the year 1888. You wrote a story about each event on the day it happened, as shown on the calendar below.

October – 1888

Sunday	Monday	Tuesday	Wednesday	Thursday	Friday	Saturday
	1	2	3	4	5	6
7	8	9 National Monument to George Washington opened	10	11	12	13
14	15	16	17	18 First school for agriculture set up in Minnesota	19	20 American baseball teams go on world tour
21	22	23	24	25 Double-decker ferry-boat launched in New York	26	27
28	29	30 J.J. Loud develops ball-point pen in Plymouth, Mass.	31 			

Here are headlines for your newspaper stories. Write the date each story was written.

"Piggyback Ride Across River" ______________________

"A Hit 'Round The World" ______________________

"First President Honored" ______________________

"New Invention Makes Mark" ______________________

"Learning to Farm Is Fun" ______________________

Name ______________________

Help Wanted

America has often been called a "Land of Opportunity." Its people may choose from many types of careers.

Use the Word Box to write two different careers that have the following characteristics in common.

1. Place importance on books ____________ ____________
2. Consider water an important tool ____________ ____________
3. Work with needle and thread ____________ ____________
4. Work with food ____________ ____________
5. Make sure people follow rules ____________ ____________
6. Deliver mail and packages ____________ ____________
7. Takes care of medical needs ____________ ____________
8. Work with animals ____________ ____________
9. Use numbers quite often ____________ ____________
10. Provide entertainment ____________ ____________

Word Box

mathematician	veterinarian	teacher	chef
actor	police officer	nurse	doctor
accountant	mail carrier	seamstress	gardener
musician	fireman	librarian	tailor
delivery person	farmer	umpire	zookeeper

0-7682-3792-0 *Skills & Practice Gr. 2*

Name ____________________

Geography Magic Square

Read column A and choose an answer from column B. Write the number of the answer in the correct magic square. The first one has been done for you.

Column A

A. Large areas of water
B. A flat area of land that is higher than the land around it
C. One of the seven areas of land on Earth
D. A hot, wetland area of thick trees, plants and animals
E. A sun-dried clay brick used for building
F. A piece of land with water on three sides
G. A cone-shaped mountain made of ash and melted rock
H. A hot, dry area of land covered with sand
I. A group of mountains

Column B

1. peninsula
2. volcano
3. plateau
4. desert
5. continent
6. rain forest
7. ocean
8. adobe
9. range

A 7	B ____	C ____
D ____	E ____	F ____
G ____	H ____	I ____

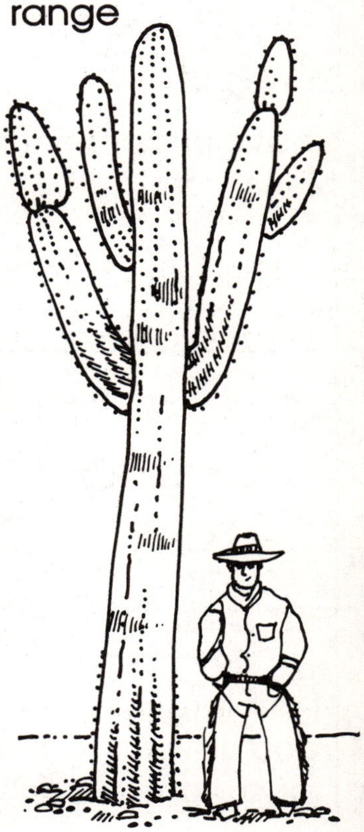

Add the numbers across and down. What answer do you get? ________

SOCIAL STUDIES

Name ______________________

Landform Riddles

Use the Word Bank to solve the riddles. Then color the pictures.

Word Bank

lake island plain river mountain peninsula

I have water on three sides. I am a

_ _ _ _ _ _ _ _ _

I have water all around me. I am an

_ _ _ _ _ _

I am wet and have land all around me. I am a

_ _ _ _

I am long and narrow and flow through the land. I am a

_ _ _ _ _

I am raised land, larger than a hill. I am a

_ _ _ _ _ _ _ _

I am low and flat. I am a

_ _ _ _ _

Name ____________________

Seeking the Sights

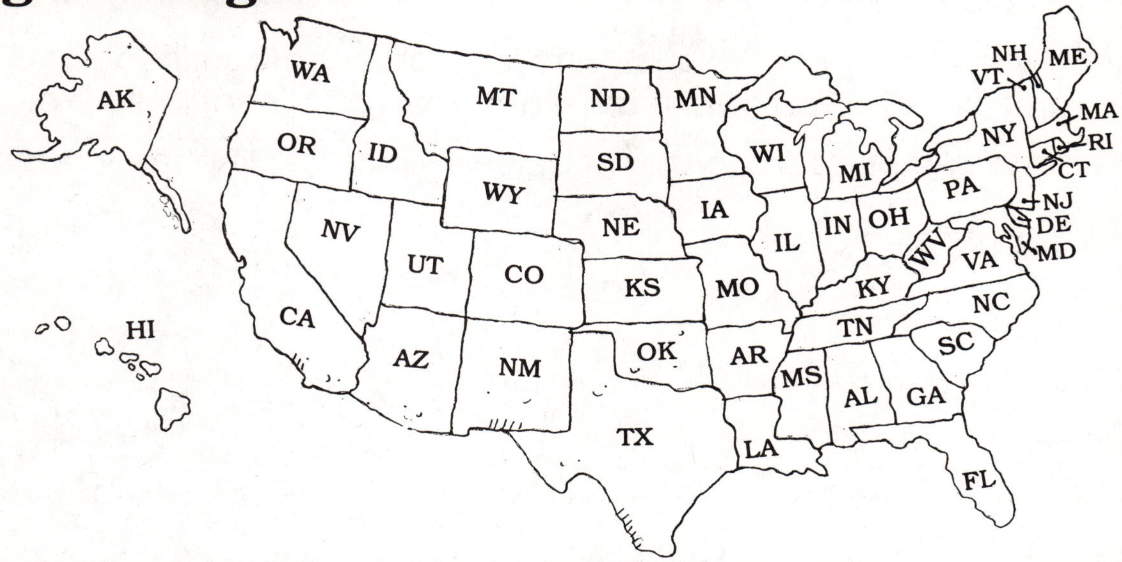

Read each clue. Use the map to locate the matching state. Write the abbreviation on the line.

1. The Space and Rocket Center is in the state south of Tennessee, **east** of Mississippi and **west** of Georgia. ____________________
2. Buffalo Bill's home is in the state **west** of Iowa and **south** of South Dakota. ____________________
3. Elephant Rock is in the state **southeast** of Oregon and **west** of Utah. ____________________
4. Casey Jones Railroad Museum is in the state **north** of Alabama and **south** of Kentucky. ____________________
5. Fossil National Monument is in the state **east** of Idaho and **south** of Montana. ____________________
6. The Corn Palace is in the state **southeast** of Montana and **northwest** of Iowa. ____________________
7. A life-size model of one of Columbus' ships, the *Santa Maria*, is in the state **west** of Pennsylvania and **east** of Indiana. ____________________
8. Gillette Castle is in the state **east** of New York and **south** of Massachusetts. ____________________

SOCIAL STUDIES

Name ____________________________

The Seven Continents

Pretend you are a pilot. Your job is to land on each continent for a top-secret mission. You must learn what each continent looks like.

Write the name of each continent below its picture. Use the word bank below.

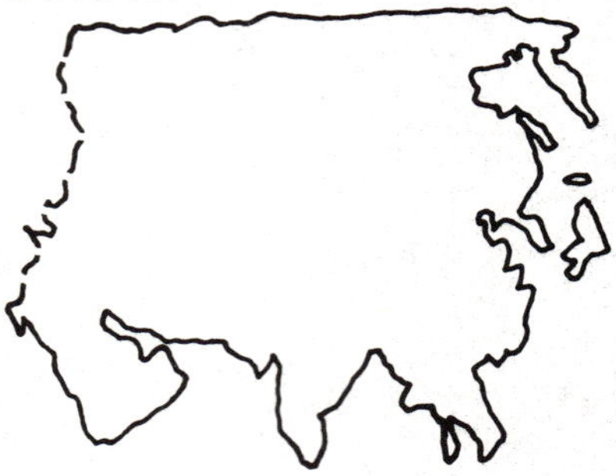

1. ____________________

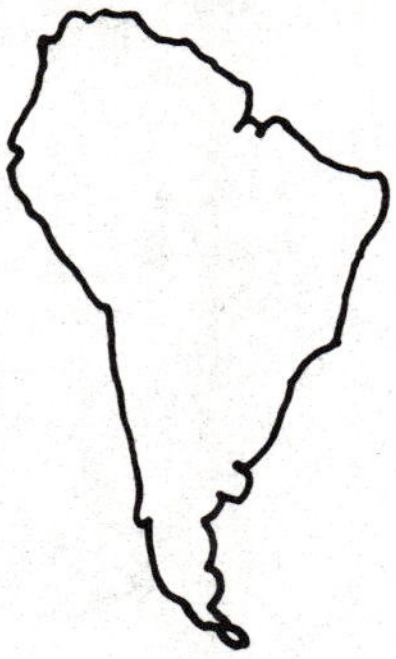

2. ____________________

3. ____________________

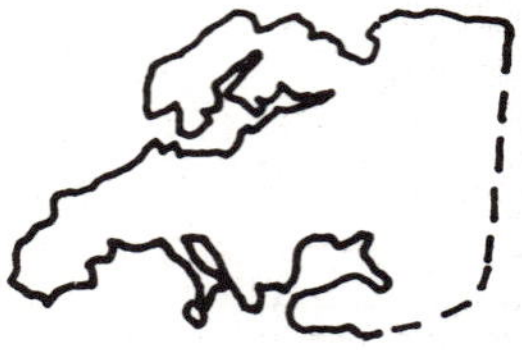

4. ____________________

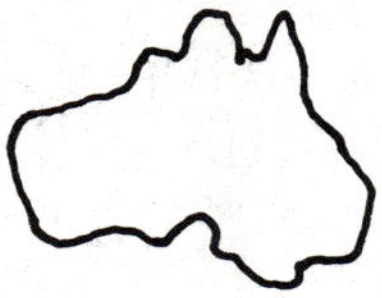

5. ____________________

6. ____________________

7. ____________________

Africa	Asia	Europe	South America
Antarctica	Australia	North America	

Name ______________________________

Animals Around the World

Color the animals and the continents.

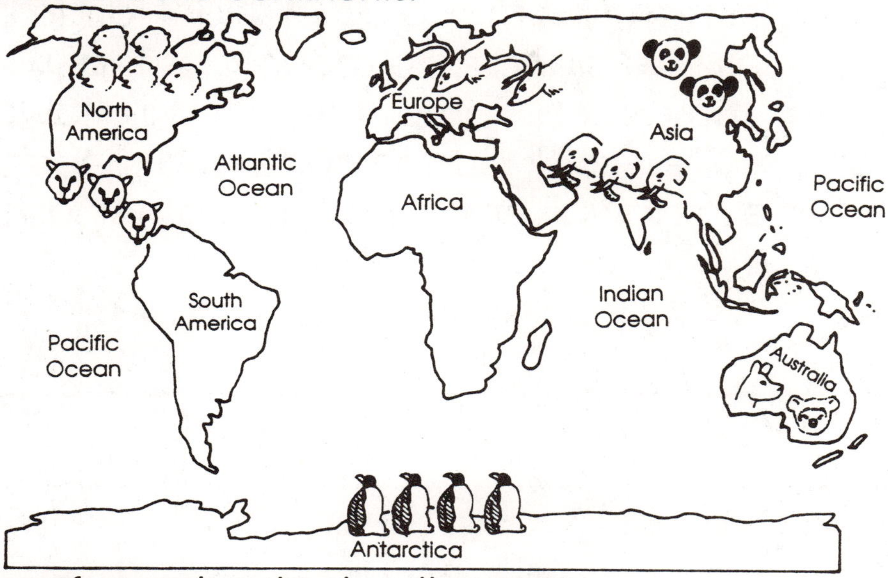

Color one square for each animal on the map.
Use a different color for each animal.

kangaroo					
elephant					
panda					
koala					
polar bear					
reindeer					
penguin					
jaguar					
	1	2	3	4	5

Name ______________________________

Hawaii

Hawaii was the last state to become part of the United States. It is the 50th state. Hawaii is made up of eight large islands and many small islands. The islands are mountains that were made long ago under the ocean. Some mountains in Hawaii still shoot out steam and melted rock. Sugar cane and pineapples grow in Hawaii. People in Hawaii enjoy warm weather and colorful flowers.

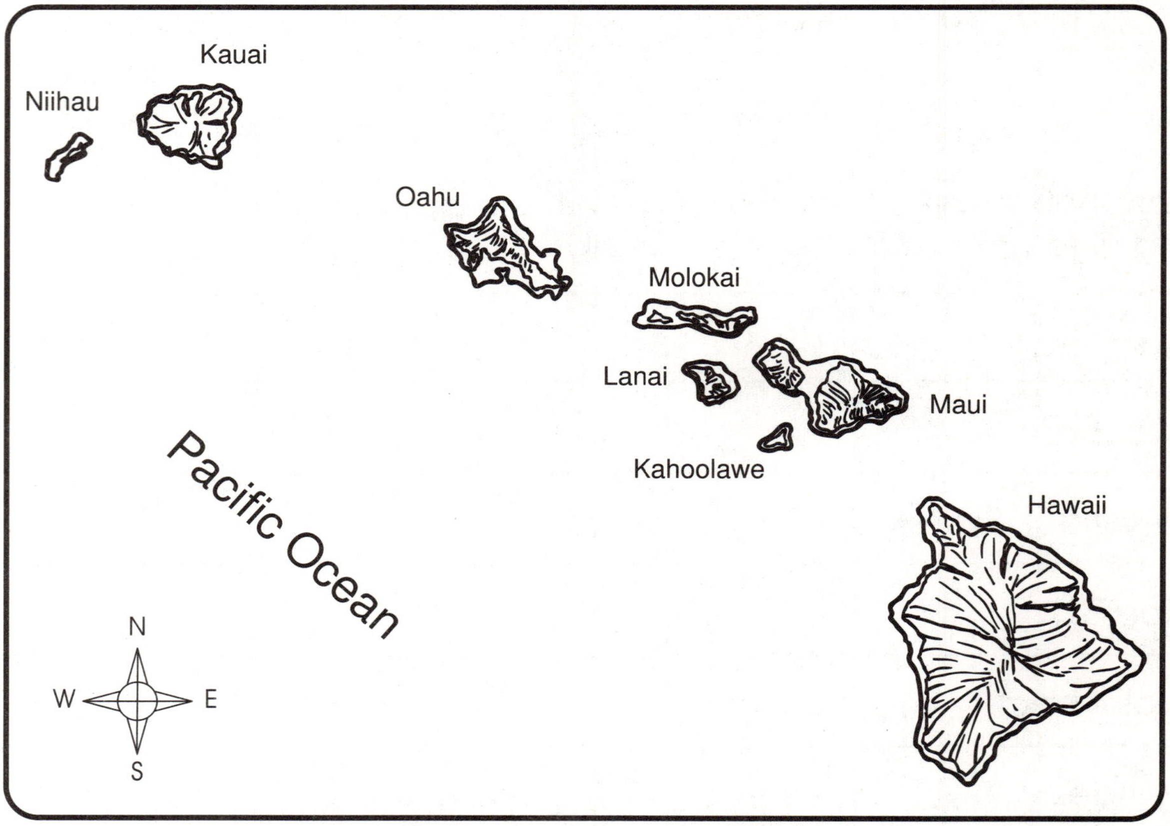

Name ____________________

Hawaii

Use facts from the story to fill in the crossword puzzle. The Word Bank will help you.

Word Bank

Hawaii
mountains
islands
sugar
pineapple
flowers
eight

Across

2. Colorful _______ grow in Hawaii.
4. The 50th state
6. _______ cane grows on the islands.
7. Hawaii has _______ large islands.

Down

1. The islands are _________.
3. _______ grows in Hawaii.
5. Hawaii is made up of many _______.

0-7682-3792-0 *Skills & Practice Gr. 2*

Name ____________________

Speaking Strine

Australians, like Americans, have their own "language" called Strine. An Aussie might say something like this, "I'm going to take my swag and tucker down to the billabong while my jumbucks are resting." That sounds like a foreign language!

In the box to the left below is a Strine dictionary so you can translate what the "bloke" said. ____________________

____

Using the dictionary, write and illustrate two sentences of your own.

How to Speak Strine

billabong - water hole
billy - container for boiling tea
bloke - man
bonzer - great, terrific
bush - country away from the city
chook - chicken
dingo - Australian wild dog
dinkum, fair dinkum - honest, genuine
dinki-di - the real thing
fossick - to prospect for gold or gems
grazier - ranch
jumbuck - sheep
make a good fist - do a good job
ocker - basic down-to-earth Aussie
outback - remote bush
pom - English person
roo - a kangaroo
shout - buy a round of drinks
station - sheep or cattle ranch
Strine - what Aussies speak
swag - bedroll and belongings
tucker - food
ute - utlity or pickup truck
waltz matilda - carry a swag

Name ______________________________

Happy New Year!

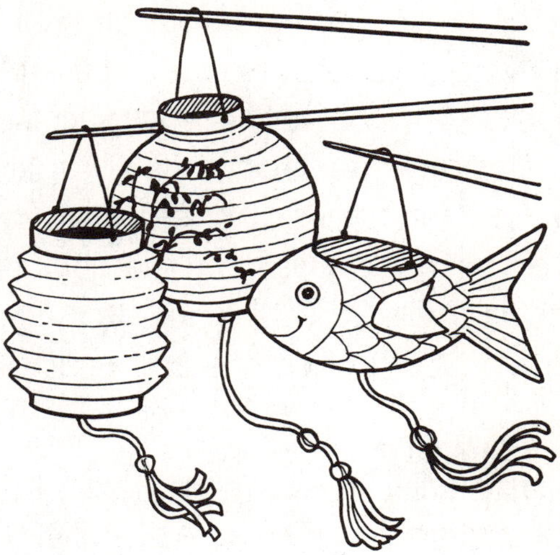

In China, the most celebrated holiday is the New Year. The Lantern Festival is part of the celebration. That is when Chinese people welcome the first full moon of the year. The Chinese New Year is fixed according to the lunar calendar. It occurs somewhere between January 30 and February 20. Each Chinese year is represented by one of 12 animals.

Look at the chart below to see what animal represents the year you were born.

RAT	OX	TIGER	HARE (RABBIT)	DRAGON	SNAKE	HORSE	RAM	MONKEY	ROOSTER	DOG	PIG
1900	1901	1902	1903	1904	1905	1906	1907	1908	1909	1910	1911
1912	1913	1914	1915	1916	1917	1918	1919	1920	1921	1922	1923
1924	1925	1926	1927	1928	1929	1930	1931	1932	1933	1934	1935
1936	1937	1938	1939	1940	1941	1942	1943	1944	1945	1946	1947
1948	1949	1950	1951	1952	1953	1954	1955	1956	1957	1958	1959
1960	1961	1962	1963	1964	1965	1966	1967	1968	1969	1970	1971
1972	1973	1974	1975	1976	1977	1978	1979	1980	1981	1982	1983
1984	1985	1986	1987	1988	1989	1990	1991	1992	1993	1994	1995
1996	1997	1998	1999	2000	2001	2002	2003	2004	2005	2006	2007
2008	2009	2010	2011	2012	2013	2014	2015	2016	2017	2018	2019

The Festival of the Lanterns is celebrated on the third day of the New Year. Make a colorful lantern to hang in your classroom.

1. Fold a bright-colored piece of construction paper vertically.
2. Cut strips from the folded side stopping 2" from the open edge.

3. Open, bend in circle, and staple.

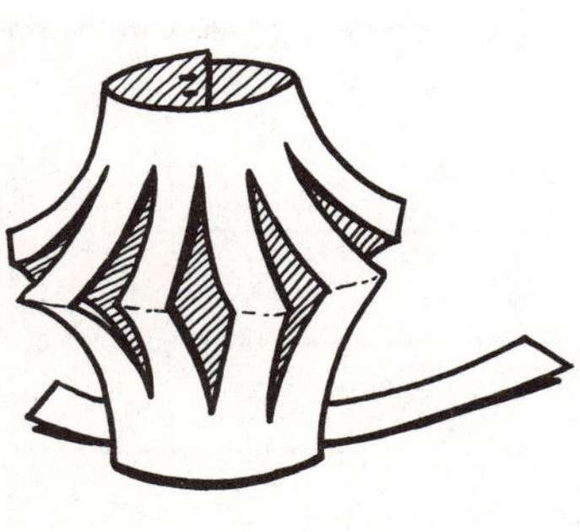

4. Cut out a long paper strip and staple to make a handle.

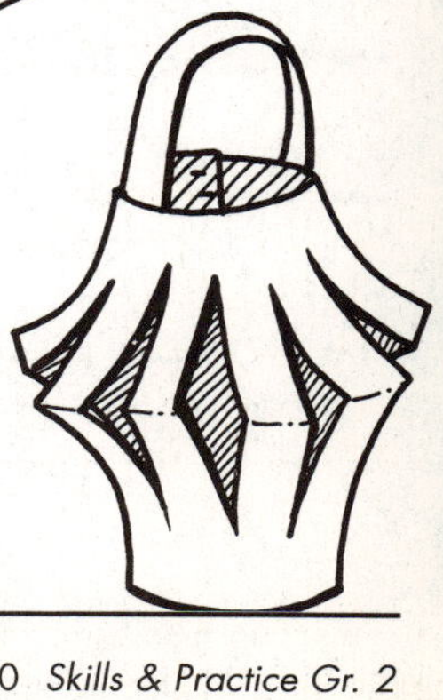

0-7682-3792-0 *Skills & Practice Gr. 2*

Name ______________________________

The "Boot"

From America, Italy is across the Atlantic Ocean. It is part of a continent called Europe. Most of Italy is shaped like a boot. It also has two islands named Sicily and Sardinia. Its "boot," or mainland, extends into the Mediterranean Sea. The shape of the mainland is called a peninsula because it has water around three of its sides. Rome is Italy's capital and largest city. It has been an important city for more than 2,500 years. Italy got its name from the Romans who called its southern part Italia, meaning "land of oxen" or "grazing land."

Color Italy green.
Color the Mediterranean Sea blue.
Use the map to unscramble the names of some Italian cities below it.

ALSNEP ______________ ENCLEOFR ______________ MERO ______________

LMNIA ______________ AENOG ______________ NCVEIE ______________

OGBNLOA ______________

Name ______________________

The American Alphabet

The United States attracts people from all over the world. We are sometimes called a nation of immigrants.

Write the alphabet in order in the boxes. Then use the Word Box and the letter in each box to write the name of each country where it belongs.

1. _ _ _ _ ☐
2. _ _ _ _ _ ☐ _ _ _ _ _
3. ☐ _ _ _ _
4. _ _ _ _ _ _ ☐
5. _ _ _ _ _ ☐
6. _ ☐ _ _ _ _ _ _ _ _ _
7. _ ☐ _ _ _
8. _ _ _ ☐ _ _ _ _ _ _ _ _
9. ☐ _ _ _ _ _
10. ☐ _ _ _ _
11. ☐ _ _ _ _
12. _ _ _ ☐ _ _ _ _ _ _ _ _
13. _ _ _ ☐ _ _ _ _
14. _ _ ☐ _ _ _ _
15. _ ☐ _ _ _ _
16. ☐ _ _ _ _ _   _ _ _ _
17. _ _ _ ☐
18. _ ☐ _ _ _ _
19. _ _ ☐ _ _ _ _ _ _
20. _ ☐ _ _ _
21. _ ☐ _ _
22. ☐ _ _ _ _ _ _
23. _ _ _ ☐ _ _
24. _ _ ☐ _ _ _
25. _ _ _ ☐ _
26. _ _ _ _ ☐ _ _ _ _

Word Box

Afghanistan
Australia
Canada
China
Cuba
Egypt
France
Germany
Greece
India
Iraq
Ireland
Israel
Italy
Japan
Kenya
Korea
Mexico
Mozambique
Netherlands
Norway
Philippines
Poland
Puerto Rico
Venezuela
Vietnam

SOCIAL STUDIES

Name ______________________________

A Capital Idea

This is what Tommy's suitcase might have looked like after visiting the eight countries on his adventure. Color and cut out the travel stickers below. Paste them on the suitcase so each capital matches its country.

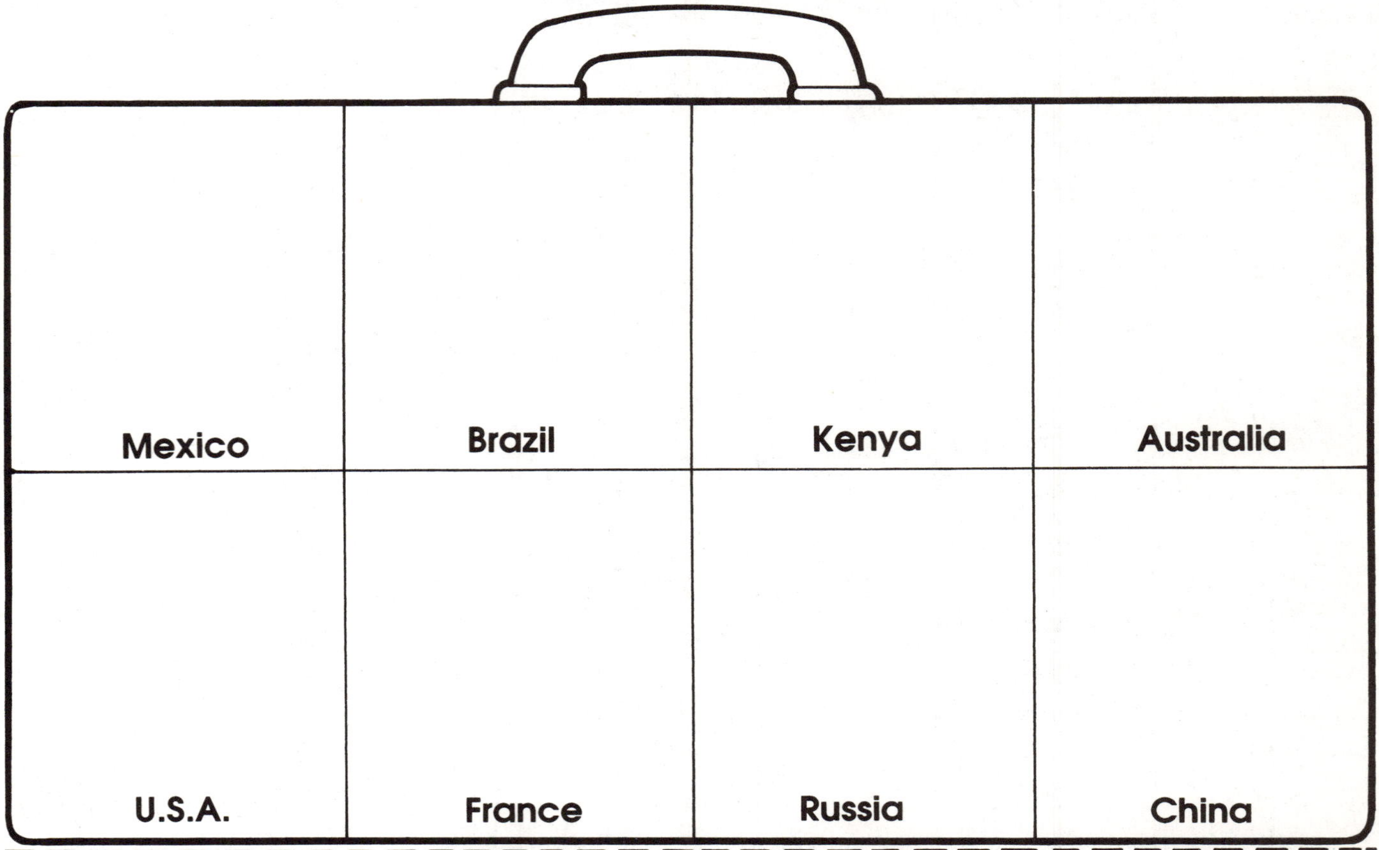
Mexico
Brazil
Kenya
Australia
U.S.A.
France
Russia
China

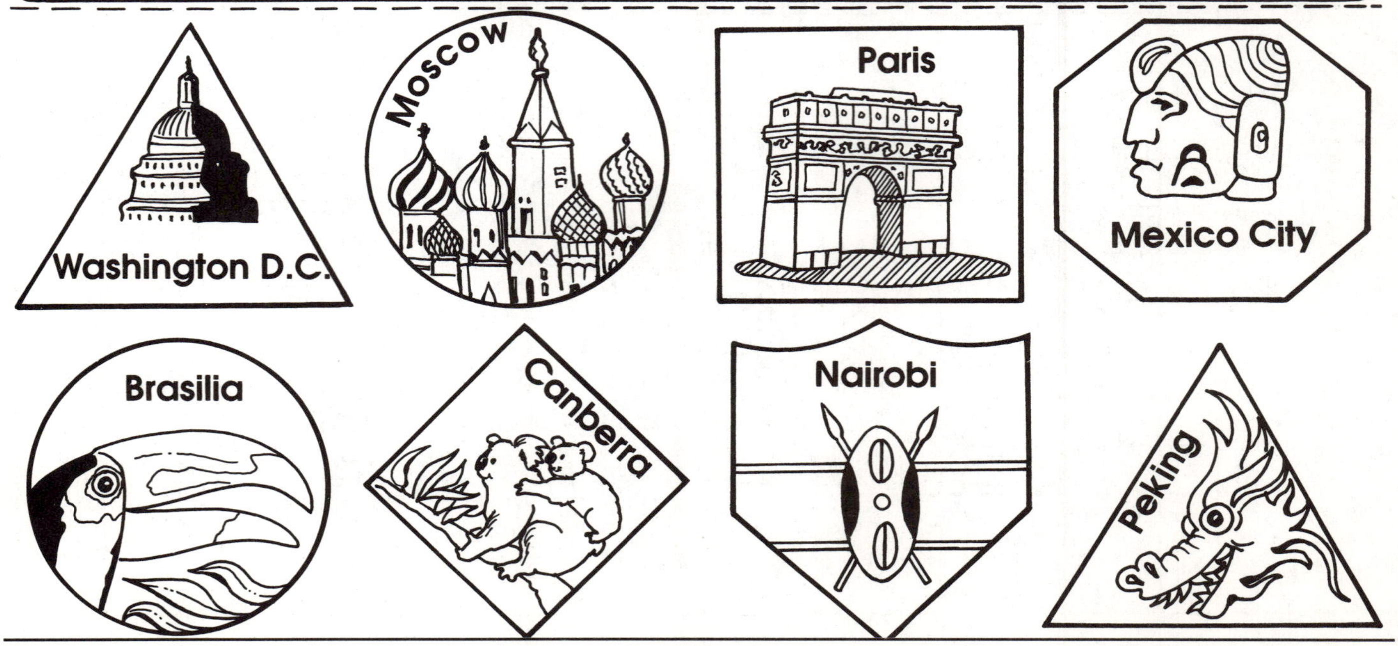
Washington D.C.
Moscow
Paris
Mexico City
Brasilia
Canberra
Nairobi
Peking

Answer Key

Food for Gregory

Print Gregory's food in ABC order. Then draw each meal on the plate.

Breakfast

tin can juice
eggs ham

eggs
ham
juice
tin can

Lunch

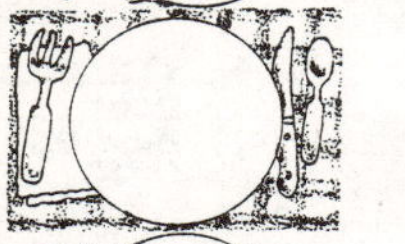

milk rubber boot
hot dog apple

apple
hot dog
milk
rubber boot

Dinner

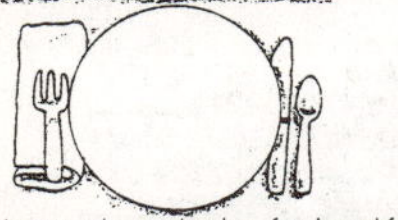

shoe fish
carrots bread

bread
carrots
fish
shoe

Draw what you ate yesterday for breakfast, lunch and dinner on these plates. Pictures will vary.

Breakfast Lunch Dinner

Page 1

Which Part Shall I Play?

Grace loves to act out stories. Read the list of characters. Then write them in alphabetical order.

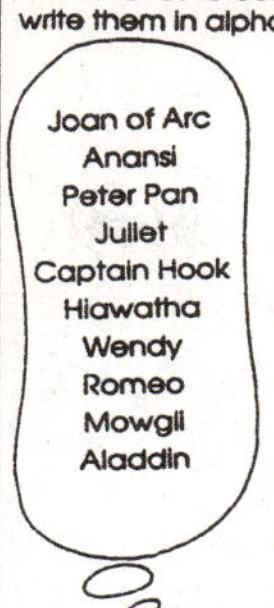

1. Aladdin
2. Anansi
3. Captain Hook
4. Hiawatha
5. Joan of Arc
6. Juliet
7. Mowgli
8. Peter Pan
9. Romeo
10. Wendy

Page 2

Which Way?

Read the words in the Word Bank. Write them in alphabetical order on the lines.

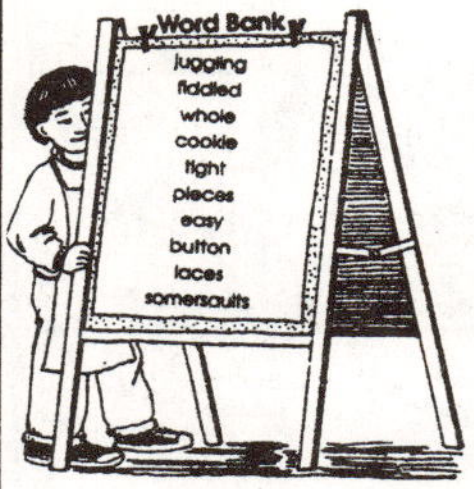

1. button
2. cookie
3. easy
4. fiddled
5. juggling
6. laces
7. pieces
8. somersaults
9. tight
10. whole

Write the missing lowercase letters in alphabetical order.

a b c d e f g h i j k l m
n o p q r s t u v w x y z

Page 3

ABC Potion

Write the words in alphabetical order.

1. always
2. baron
3. control
4. drink
5. flashed
6. hard
7. ketchup
8. lightning
9. monster
10. overhead
11. point
12. rumbled
13. scientist
14. thunder
15. world

Page 4

Crazy Creatures

Draw a line to each letter in ABC order to finish this dot-to-dot picture.

Now color and add details to the picture. Then write all the consonants in order on these lines.

1. b	5. g	9. l	13. q	17. v	21. z
2. c	6. h	10. m	14. r	18. w	
3. d	7. j	11. n	15. s	19. x	
4. f	8. k	12. p	16. t	20. y	

Page 5

Alphabet Soup

Nan Cook has a special way of making alphabet soup. She mixes two boxes of soup together. Then she adds two secret ingredients — mystery and fun. After the soup is cooked, a strange thing happens. All the vowels rise to the top of the pot.

Write the consonant that can be used in both the front and back of each vowel or pair of vowels to make a word. One is done for you.

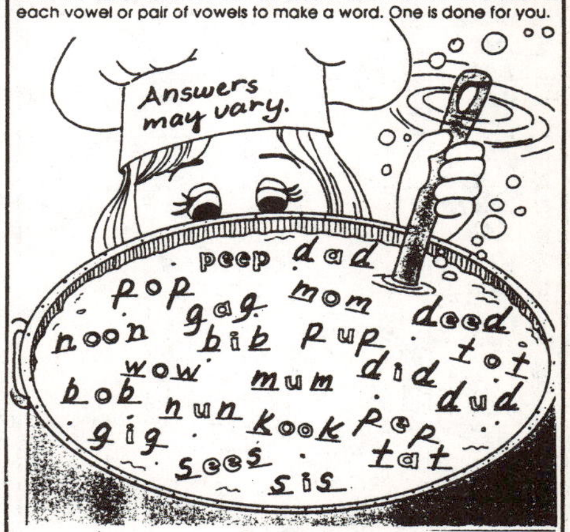

Page 6

Stretch and Grow

Goofy Gladys got new glasses. The glasses had springs on them which stretched words out and then added another vowel to each one.

Add a vowel to each word below to see what words Gladys saw through her glasses.

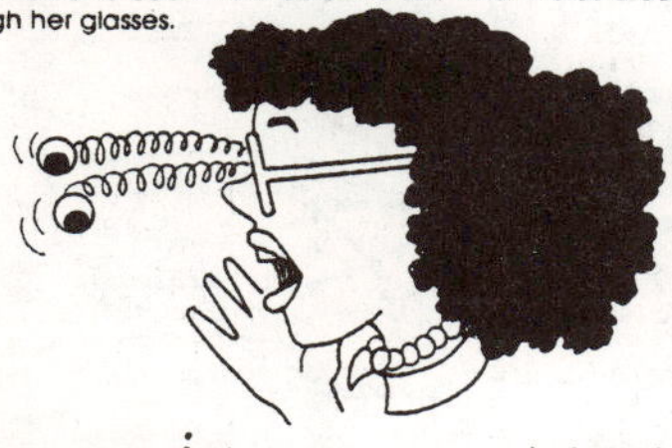

1. pal pail	9. lid laid
2. fed feed or feud	10. hat heat
3. chin chain	11. bad bead
4. ran rain	12. flat float
5. cat coat	13. bit bait
6. Jon join	14. pin pain
7. shut shout	15. men mean
8. bran brain	

Page 7

Motorcycle Maze

Help Ralph move through the maze to the Mountain View Inn by tracing over the path in which all of the words have two syllables.

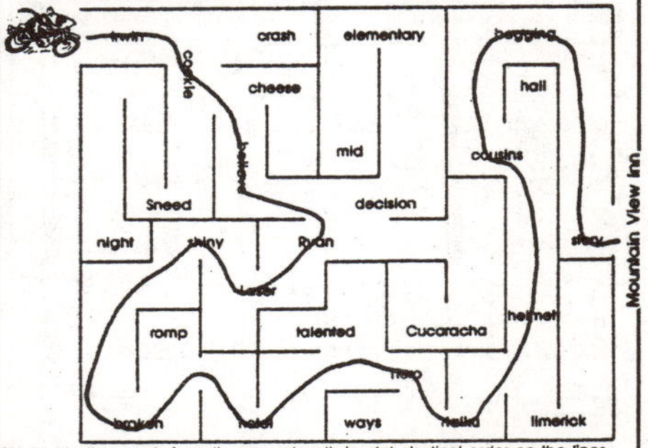

Now write the words from the correct path in alphabetical order on the lines below.

1. begging
2. believe
3. broken
4. cookie
5. cousins
6. Haiku
7. helmet
8. hero
9. hotel
10. Irwin
11. Laser
12. Ryan
13. shiny
14. story

Page 8

Trick or Treat Syllables

Think about how many syllables are in each word in the Word Bank. Then write each word on the correct jack-o'-lantern.

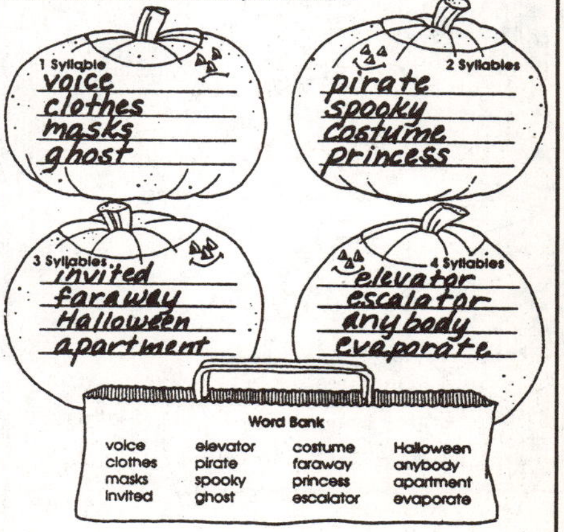

Word Bank

voice	elevator	costume	Halloween
clothes	pirate	faraway	anybody
masks	spooky	princess	apartment
invited	ghost	escalator	evaporate

Page 9

All Together Now

Match a word in the Word Bank with a word on a feather to make a compound word. Then write it on the line.

space *man* · cup *cakes* · out *fit*

Thanks *giving* · with *out* · on *stage*

news *paper* · your *self* · some *thing*

Word Bank

back	out	paper	thing
fit	self	yard	cakes
man	giving	stage	school

Page 10

Word Magic

Maggie Magician announced, "One plus one equals one!" The audience giggled. So Maggie put two words into a hat and waved her magic wand. When she reached into the hat, Maggie pulled out a word and a picture. "See," said Maggie, "I was right!"

Look at each picture below. Use the Word Bank to help write a compound word for each.

shoelace · *cupcake* · *doorbell*

basketball · *mailbox* · *footstool*

rainbow · *shirttail* · *starfish*

sunlight · *bookworm*

earphone

Word Bank

ball	door	rain
basket	ear	shirt
bell	fish	shoe
book	foot	star
bow	lace	stool
box	light	sun
cake	mail	tail
cup	phone	worm

Page 11

Compound Your Effort

Is BUZZARDLIPS A COMPOUND WORD?

Read each word. Find the word in the Word Bank that goes with it to make a compound word. Cross it out. Then write the compound word on the line.

1. coat *room*
2. snow *ball*
3. home *work*
4. waste *basket*
5. tip *toe*
6. chalk *board*
7. note *book*
8. grass *hopper*
9. school *bag*
10. with *out*

Look at the words in the Word Bank you did not use. Use those words to make your own compound words.

Answers may vary.

1. *handwriting*
2. *something, anything*
3. *classroom, classmate*
4. *outside, inside*
5. *somewhere, anywhere*

Word Bank

~~board~~	~~room~~	thing	side
writing	~~book~~	~~hopper~~	~~toe~~
~~bag~~	~~ball~~	class	where
~~work~~	~~out~~	~~basket~~	

Page 12

Mystery Word Mix-Up

Put on your detective hat! How many words can you make using only the letters in the words:

Nate the Great

1. *neat*
2. *net*
3. *eat*
4. *ate*
5. *gate*
6. *get*
7. *treat*
8. *teeth*
9. *tea*
10. *green*
11. *ten*
12. *tan*
13. *teen*
14. *hear*
15. *heart*
16. *ear*
17. *gear*
18. *near*
19. *tear*
20. *greet*
21. *nag*
22. *tag*

Others possible.

Page 13

Flower Fun

Find words in the Word Bank that are synonyms for the words in the leaves. Write them on the leaves.

yell *scream* · begin *start* · scared *afraid*

drop *fall* · nice *kind*

sleepy *tired* · soil *dirt* · near *close*

place *put* · difficult *easy*

Word Bank

pick	start	easy	sky
kind	rain	afraid	fall
close	hard	scream	awake
put	whisper	dirt	tired

Page 14

Where?

Read each word on the left. Find its synonym in the Word Bank and write it on the line.

1. below *beneath*
2. drummed *tapped*
3. hear *listen*
4. scrambled *hurried*
5. over *above*
6. close *shut*
7. slipped *slid*
8. woods *forest*
9. spring *leap*
10. cleaned *washed*
11. sturdy *strong*
12. paths *trails*
13. perhaps *maybe*
14. house *home*
15. evening *sunset*

Word Bank

above, listen, shut, maybe, beneath, forest, leap, tapped, home, hurried, strong, sunset, trails, washed, slid

Page 15

Who's Afraid?

Help Frog and Toad escape from the snake. Read the two words in each space. If the words are antonyms, color the space green. Do not color the other spaces.

go stop *green* · large small *green* · wide narrow *green* · dinner supper · scared afraid · brave afraid *green* · shut close · happy sad *gr.* · fall rise *gr.* · outside inside *gr.* · higher lower *gr.* · leap jump · dark light *gr.* · tremble shake · fast quick · happy glad · look see · none all *gr.* · top bottom *green* · stones rocks · covers blankets · friend pal · down up *green* · shout whisper *green* · loud soft *green* · under over *green*

Toad's House

Page 16

Should We Wake Them?

Read the words on each of the pillows. Find a word in the Word Bank that means the opposite and write it on the line.

sold *bought* · off *on* · first *last*

hated *loved* · warm *cool* · front *back*

remembered *forgotten* · small *big* · to *from*

yours *mine* · everybody *nobody* · early *late*

Word Bank

bought	on	all	tiny
nobody	big	last	late
ahead	mine	from	cool
forgotten	loved	back	

Page 17

Flying Free Like an Eagle

Read the beginning of each sentence. Draw a line to the words on the feather that best complete each sentence.

1. The strong stallion fought like...
2. The bolt of lightning lit the sky like...
3. The wild horses roamed the hills as free as...
4. The thunder roared like...
5. The running herd crossed the land like...
6. The stallion's eyes were as cold as...
7. The hills were as dark as...
8. The rising sun was like...

- the wind.
- a wave rolling to shore.
- a match being lit on a dark night.
- a panther's coat.
- a mighty warrior.
- an arching rainbow.
- an ice-covered pond.
- an angry lion.

Page 18

Rain, Rain Go Away!

Read the naming parts in the tent.
(pencil) one of the naming parts to begin each sentence.

Rain
Black clouds
A big wind
The campfire
Todd and Clint
The old green tent

1. Todd and Clint went camping.
2. The old green tent was hard to set up.
3. A big wind blew the trees.
4. Black clouds filled the sky.
5. Rain ran off the tent.
6. The campfire went out.

Page 19

It Takes Many Colors

Read the words in the Word Bank. If the word means one, write it on the paint jar. If the word means more than one, write it on the paintbrushes.

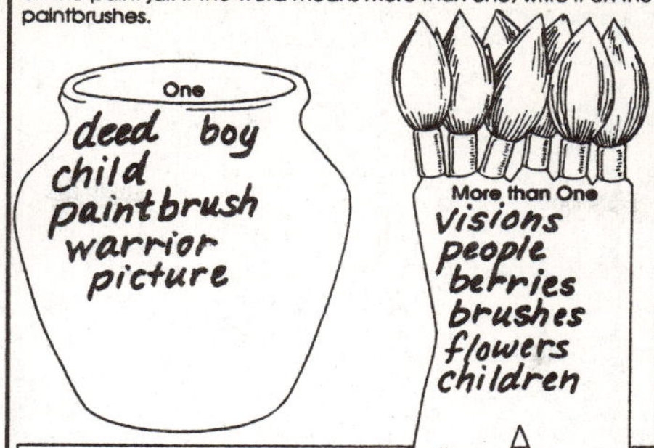

One
deed boy
child
paintbrush
warrior
picture
More than One
visions
people
berries
brushes
flowers
children

Word Bank
deed people berries child brushes
visions paintbrush boy flowers
children warrior picture

Page 20

Fun Around the Campfire

Word Bank
beat sang told
danced sat wore

(pencil) a verb in each sentence below. Use the word bank to help you.

1. The boys and girls danced around the campfire.
2. They sang songs.
3. Brian beat a drum.
4. Jerry and Helen wore costumes.
5. They sat around the campfire.
6. The teacher told stories.

Page 21

It's Time

(pencil) these verbs in the correct Time Machine.

play pull barked jumped danced
looked laugh walk listen lived

Now
In the Past
play
pull
laugh
walk
listen
barked
jumped
danced
looked
lived

Page 22

I Was. Were You?

Use "was" and "were" to tell about something that happened in the past. Use "was" to tell about one person or thing. Use "were" to tell about more than one person or thing. Always use "were" with the word "you."

(pencil) "was" or "were" in each sentence below.

1. Lois was in the second grade last year.
2. She was eight years old.
3. Carmen and Judy were friends.
4. They were on the same soccer team.
5. I was on the team, too.
6. You were too young to play.

Page 23

Playing in the Summer Sun

Look at the picture. Read the sentence. Circle the missing word. Then write it on the line.

It is raining
rain (raining)

He can row the boat.
(row) rowing

The kite is flying
fly (flying)

He is swinging
swing (swinging)

He is picking
pick (picking)

Page 24

An Owlish Activity

Write the words where they belong.

Word Bank
bite school children skip donkey house
jump lunchbox kitten write hop run

Who?
Did What?
Nouns
Verbs

Nouns	Verbs
school	bite
children	skip
donkey	jump
house	write
lunchbox	hop
kitten	run

Flip Fun! Draw a picture of one of the nouns.

Page 25

Tic-Tac-Toe

Circle all of the naming words (nouns).
Put an X on all of the doing words (verbs).
Under each game, write the X words that scored a tic-tac-toe.

boy	well	fell
mother	wished	ladder
ran	man	cake

ran
wished
fell

fished	water	book
told	stone	lamp
pumped	people	shoe

fished
told
pumped

child	sent	house
tree	ate	China
Chang	raced	body

sent
ate
raced

paper	bear	bridge
Tikki	table	flower
read	yelled	jump

read
yelled
jump

Page 26

Picking Pronouns

The words *he, she, it,* and *they* can be used in place of a noun.

Read the sentence pairs. Write the correct pronoun in each blank.

1. John won first place.
He got a blue ribbon.

2. Janet and Gail rode on a bus.
They went to visit their grandmother.

3. Sarah had a birthday party.
She invited six friends to the party.

4. The kitten likes to play.
It likes to tug on shoelaces.

5. Ed is seven years old.
He is in the second grade.

Page 27

Marvelous Me!

You know that you are a very special person for many reasons. Some of these reasons include your body!

Draw hair and eyes on the body below to make it look like you. Then, use the describing words listed in the box with the names of your beautiful body parts to label yourself. Be sure both words start with the same sound. Write a story about your body and how each part is special!

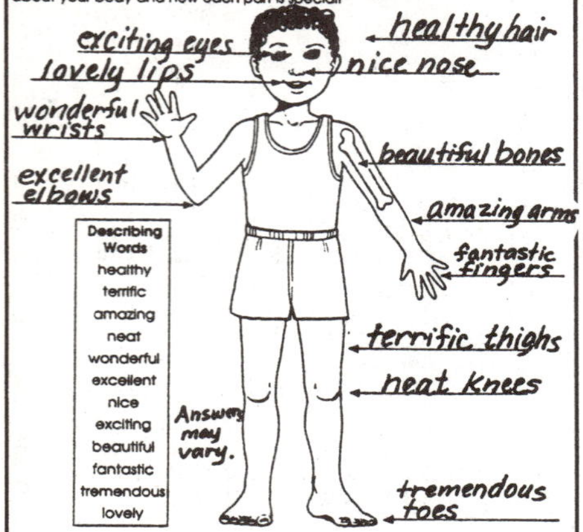

exciting eyes
healthy hair
lovely lips
nice nose
wonderful wrists
beautiful bones
excellent elbows
amazing arms
fantastic fingers
terrific thighs
neat knees
Answers may vary.
tremendous toes

Describing Words
- healthy
- terrific
- amazing
- neat
- wonderful
- excellent
- nice
- exciting
- beautiful
- fantastic
- tremendous
- lovely

Page 28

Add the Adjectives

Read each sentence. Write a describing word on each line. Draw a picture to match each sentence.

Answers will vary.

High Mountain

The __________ flag waved over the __________ building.

A __________ lion searched for food in the __________ jungle.

We saw __________ fish in the __________ aquarium.

Her __________ car was parked by the __________ van.

The __________ dog barked and chased the __________ truck.

The __________ building was filled with __________ packages.

Page 29

Wordy Treats

Write the word from the Word Bank on the correct trick or treat bag. If the word **names** a person, place or thing, write it on the bag marked **Nouns**. If the word **describes** something, write it on the bag marked **Adjectives**.

Nouns
1. costumes
2. ghosts
3. party
4. elevator
5. wings
6. pirate
7. robot
8. stairs
9. crown

Adjectives
1. special
2. spooky
3. squeaky
4. heavy
5. scary
6. high
7. silly
8. fifth
9. bossy

Word Bank

costumes	elevator	pirate	fifth
ghosts	spooky	robot	bossy
party	squeaky	scary	stairs
special	wings	high	crown
	heavy	silly	

Page 30

Summer Camp

A telling sentence begins with a capital letter and ends with a period. Write each telling sentence correctly on the lines.

Camp
Camp Rules

1. everyone goes to breakfast at 6:30 each morning
   Everyone goes to breakfast at 6:30 each morning.
2. only three people can ride in one canoe
   Only three people can ride in one canoe.
3. each person must help clean the cabins
   Each person must help clean the cabins.
4. older campers should help younger campers
   Older campers should help younger campers.
5. all lights are out by 9:00 each night
   All lights are out by 9:00 each night.
6. everyone should write home at least once a week
   Everyone should write home at least once a week.

Page 31

Tell-a-vision

Look at each TV picture. Write a telling sentence about each program. *Answers will vary.*

Page 32

Telephone Talk

An asking sentence is called a question. A question begins with a capital letter and ends with a question mark.

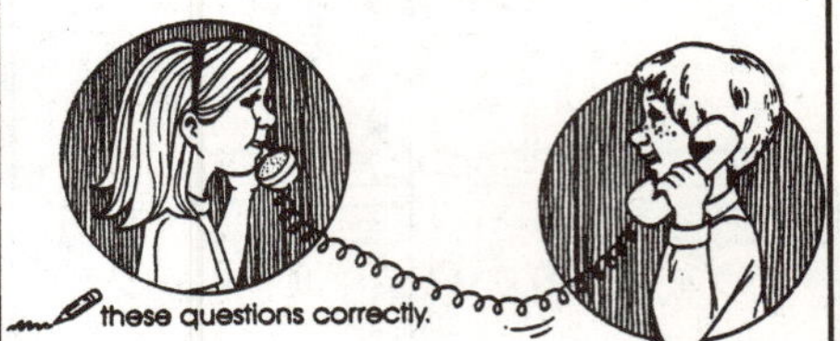

... these questions correctly.

1. how old are you
   How old are you?
2. are you in second grade
   Are you in second grade?
3. who is your teacher
   Who is your teacher?
4. did you read that book
   Did you read that book?
5. where do you live
   Where do you live?

Page 33

Asking Questions

Look at the picture. Write five asking sentences about the picture.

Answers will vary.

Blue

Page 34

That Doesn't Make Sense!

A sentence must make sense. Read each sentence. Put an X on the two words which do not belong. Write the corrected sentence on the lines below.

Yard Sale

My neighbor is orange having a yard very sale.
1. *My neighbor is having a yard sale.*

She is snow selling lots of old things phone.
2. *She is selling lots of old things.*

A man until is buying five candle old books.
3. *A man is buying five old books.*

My brother is buying an salt old checkers X game.
4. *My brother is buying an old checkers game.*

Two ladies pull are buying an old touch toy chest.
5. *Two ladies are buying an old toy chest.*

Page 35

Flight to Fun

Would you like to fly away for a fun trip? Write words about a trip on the plane. Use the words to write five sentences about the trip.

TICKET

1. *Answers will vary.*
2.
3.
4.
5.

Page 36

About Me

Sentences can tell much about you. Begin at the START sign and write sentences that tell all about you– how you look, your age, things you like to do, etc. Write as many sentences as you can going around and around the circle.

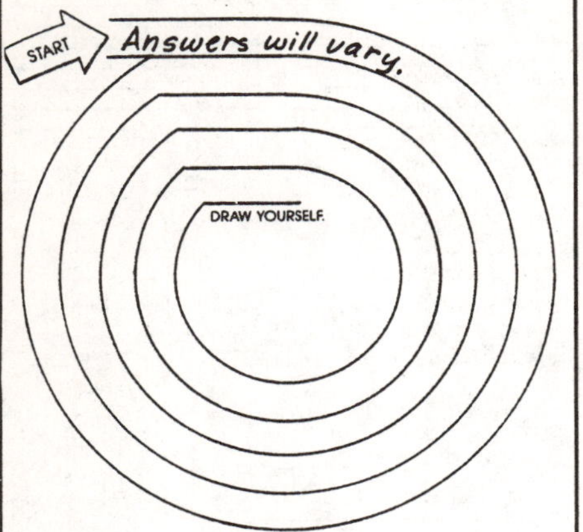

START
Answers will vary.
DRAW YOURSELF.

Page 37

A Sensational Scent

Circle the letters that should be capital letters. Then write them in the matching numbered blanks to answer the question.

1. eddie, Homer's friend, lives on elm Street.
2. Homer's aunt lives in kansas City, kansas.
3. are you sure Aunt aggie is coming?
4. did Rip Van Winkle come to town.
5. The doughnuts were made by homer Price.
6. Miss terwillinger and Uncle telly saved yarn.
7. Homer Price was written by robert McCloskey.
8. Uncle ulysses owned a lunch room.
9. The super – Duper was a comic book hero.
10. Doc kelly lived in Homer's town.
11. money was stolen by the robbers.
12. now you have the answer to the question.

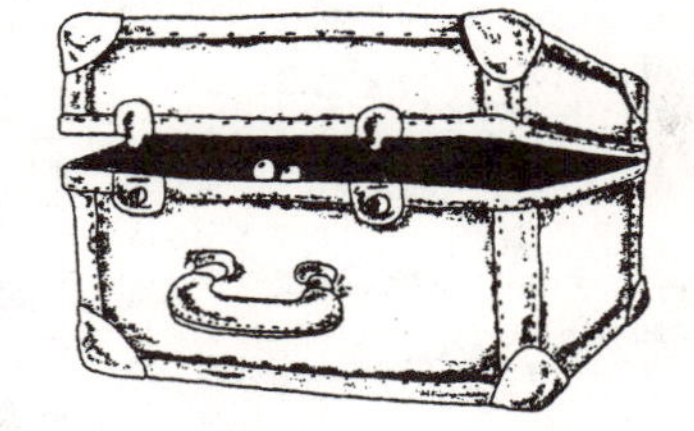

Who is hiding in the suitcase?

A r o m a   t h e   p e t   s k u n k
3 7 4 11 3   6 5 1   10 1 6   9 2 8 12 2

Page 38

Now, How Does That Go?

Write the sentences correctly. Be sure to put capital letters, periods and exclamation marks where they belong.

1. muffy spoke the words very quietly
   Muffy spoke the words very quietly.
2. buster said that the pilgrims sailed on a ship named the mayflower
   Buster said that the pilgrims sailed on a ship named the Mayflower.
3. francine said, "i will not play the part of a turkey "
   Francine said, "I will not play the part of a turkey!"
4. arthur thought about turkeys while he and d w did dishes
   Arthur thought about turkeys while he and D.W. did dishes.
5. arthur worried about finding a turkey
   Arthur worried about finding a turkey.
6. everyone looked at the audience and said, "happy thanksgiving "
   Everyone looked at the audience and said, "Happy Thanksgiving!"

Page 39

Punctuation Magic

POWERFUL PUNCTUATION Gives sentences PIZZAZ!

Write the sentences correctly. Be sure to put capital letters, periods and question marks where they belong.

1. mrs paris talked to richard, alex, matthew and emily about the trip to the museum
   Mrs. Paris talked to Richard, Alex, Matthew and Emily about the trip to the museum.
2. the children read a story about a king who was greedy
   The children read a story about a king who was greedy.
3. everyone but richard drew a picture about the story
   Everyone but Richard drew a picture about the story.
4. why was drake sick
   Why was Drake sick?
5. mrs gates asked matthew to take homework to drake
   Mrs. Gates asked Matthew to take homework to Drake.
6. did richard's wish make drake sick
   Did Richard's wish make Drake sick?

Page 40

An Excellent Exercise

The words *a* and *an* help point out a noun. Use *a* before a word that begins with a consonant. Use *an* before a word that begins with a vowel.

1. Our class visited a farm.
2. We could only stay an hour.
3. A man let us pick eggs out of a nest.
4. We saw an egg that was cracked.
5. We watched a lady milk a cow.
6. We got to eat an ice cream cone.

Page 41

Add an Apostrophe

Add 's to a noun to show who or what **owns** something.

(circle) the correct word under each picture.

The ___ nose is big. clown clowns (clown's)	This is ___ coat. Bettys (Betty's) Betty
I know ___ brother. (Burt's) Burt Burts	The ___ hat is pretty. girls girl (girl's)
That is the ___ ball. (kitten's) kitten kittens	My ___ shoe is missing. sisters sister (sister's)
The ___ coach is Mr. Hall. teams (team's) team	The ___ cover is torn. (book's) books book

Page 42

Fish for Plurals

Write the words on the fish in the correct tank.

kites   mitten   star   cats   chick   matches   foxes   lunch

One

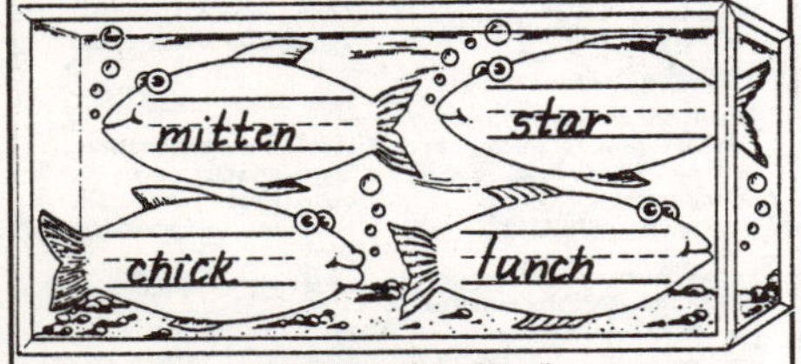

mitten
star
chick
lunch

More Than One (Plural)

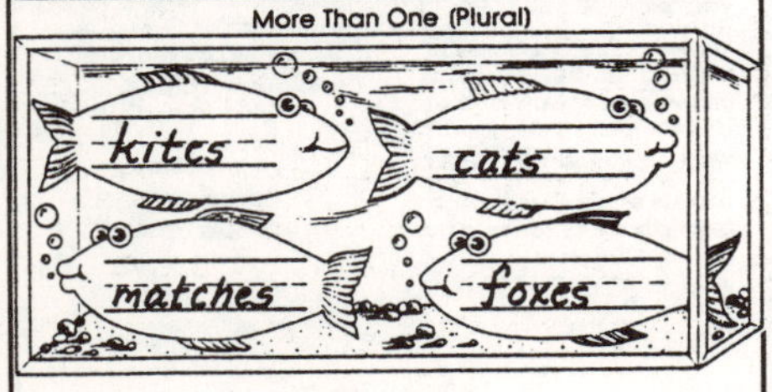

kites
cats
matches
foxes

Page 43

Who Is Hungrier?

Use the pictures to help you complete each sentence with the correct word.

Sludge   Fang   Big Hex

sleepy / sleepier / sleepiest
1. Fang is sleepier than Big Hex.
2. Big Hex is sleepy.
3. Sludge is the sleepiest of all.

Rosamond   Annie   Eric

dirty / dirtier / dirtiest
1. Rosamond's shirt is the dirtiest of all.
2. Eric's shirt is dirtier than Annie's.
3. Annie's shirt is dirty.

Marshmallow   cotton ball   pillow

soft / softer / softest
1. The pillow is soft.
2. The cotton ball is the softest.
3. The marshmallow is softer than the pillow.

Nate   Finley   Pip

hungry / hungrier / hungriest
1. Pip is hungrier than Nate.
2. Nate is hungry.
3. Finley is the hungriest.

Page 44

Is It a World Record?

Read each sentence. Choose the correct word and write it on the line.

big / bigger / biggest
1. The town made the biggest snowball on record.
2. Emmett made a big snowball.
3. Sara helped him make it even bigger.

fast / faster / fastest
1. The snowball started to roll very fast.
2. It was the fastest rolling snowball anyone had ever seen.
3. It rolled faster than they could run.

white / whiter / whitest
1. As the snowball rolled closer, Mr. Wetzel's face became even whiter.
2. After it snowed all night, the town was the whitest it had ever been.
3. Mr. Wetzel's face turned white when he saw the snowball rolling toward his candy store.

Page 45

Can I, or Can't I?

Read each sentence. Write **can** or **can't** on the line.

1. The day is warm so I *can't* wear my mittens.
2. It is snowing so I *can* wear my snowsuit.
3. My boots are too big so I *can't* wear them.
4. My hat is too little so I *can't* wear it.
5. It snowed so I *can* make a snowman.
6. The shade will not open so I *can't* see if it has snowed.

Page 46

Bunny Bunch

There are ten bunnies in this family. Each one is special.
Read the clues and fill in the blank with the word that rhymes and makes sense.

1. I like to hop and drink *pop*.
2. I can run fast, but still I am always *last*.
3. I like to run and jump, but sometimes I fall and get a *bump*.
4. I like to help Mom and Pop by scrubbing the floor with a *mop*.
5. After I feed the cat, I take out my baseball and *bat*.
6. I like to go on a hike or ride my *bike*.
7. I like to dig in the sand and play the drums in a *band*.
8. I like to play with a toy car while I eat a candy *bar*.
9. I can walk in the fog and also chop a *log*.
10. I can fly my kite but not during the *night*.

band
bar
bat
bike
bump
cast
daylight
far
fat
fog
hand
last
like
log
mop
night
pop
pump
stop
top

Page 47

Loosey Goosey

Find the names of the birds at the bottom of the page that will rhyme with the words given. For example: Loose goose

narrow	*sparrow*	bobbin	*robin*
hairy	*canary*	dark	*lark*
men	*wren*	pinch	*finch*
pork	*stork*	muffin	*puffin*
love	*dove*	beagle	*eagle*
pleasant	*pheasant*	frail	*quail*
perky	*turkey*	hull	*gull*
soon	*loon*	lay	*jay*
luck	*duck*	howl	*owl*
darling	*starling*		

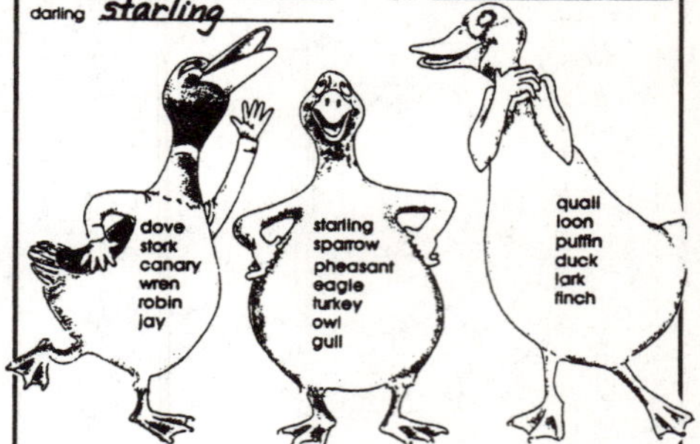

dove
stork
canary
wren
robin
jay
starling
sparrow
pheasant
eagle
turkey
owl
gull
quail
loon
puffin
duck
lark
finch

Page 48

Do You Know a Boa?

Print a rhyming word under each word on the boa's body. Slither down from the head to the tail. Sssssssssssss.

words will vary.

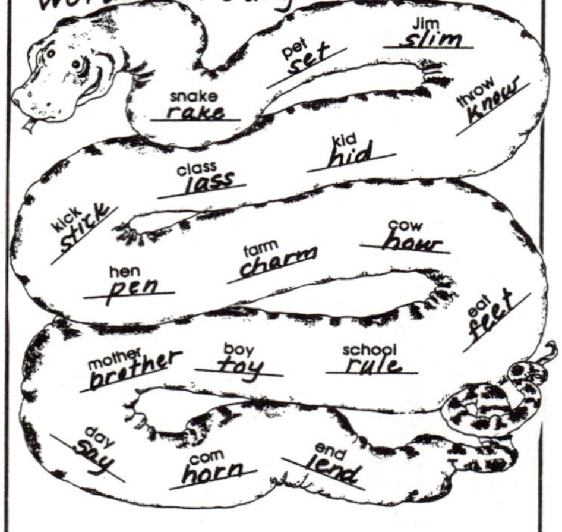

Jim *slim*
pet *set*
snake *rake*
throw *know*
kid *hid*
class *lass*
kick *stick*
farm *charm*
cow *how*
hen *pen*
eat *feet*
mother *brother*
boy *toy*
school *rule*
day *say*
corn *horn*
end *lend*

Page 49

What an Act!

Read about each act. Read the titles in the Word Bank. Write the best title for each act.

1. The lady climbed on the horse's back. The horse galloped around the ring as she stood up on its back. *Lady on a Galloping Horse*
2. Four seals stood up on their flippers. They spun and tossed a ball to each other. The biggest seal threw it to his trainer, Mac, who threw it back. *Mac and His Ball-Playing Seals*
3. The trainer led the five bears into the ring. Each bear had its own bike. They rode up and down ramps as they raced each other around the ring. *The Bike-Riding Bears*
4. The clowns tumbled as they came into the ring. They did forward rolls, backward rolls and even walked on their hands. *The Tumbling Clowns*

Word Bank

Three Brown Bears
Mac and His Ball-Playing Seals
A Horse Rider
The Tumbling Clowns
Mac and His Seals
The Bike-Riding Bears
Lady on a Galloping Horse
The Lazy Clowns

Page 50

High-Flying Acts

LA-A-A-DIES AND GENTLEMEN...

Read each sentence. Look at the underlined words. Write who, what, when, where or why to show what the underlined words tell.

1. Clifford and Emily Elizabeth spent the day at the circus. *where*
2. The biggest elephant couldn't lead the parade because he had a cold. *why*
3. The circus owner was afraid there would not be a show. *who*
4. Clifford shot a tent pole at the hot air balloon. *what*
5. Clifford caught the diver before he landed in the empty tank. *when*
6. The clowns needed help because some had quit. *why*
7. Clifford liked the cotton candy. *what*
8. The poster said there would be a circus today. *when*
9. The human cannon ball landed on top of a haystack. *where*
10. The lions and tigers didn't listen to the lion tamer. *who*

Page 51

Donuts, Anyone?

Wanna Buy a DonuT?

Write who, what, when, where or why to show what the underlined words in each sentence tell you.

1. The Pee Wee Scouts went to Mrs. Peter's house on Tuesday. *where*
2. The Scouts turned in the money they had received for selling the boxes of donuts. *who*
3. Roger and Rachel sold the most boxes of donuts. *what*
4. Sonny's mother sold many boxes at work. *where*
5. Rachel sold the donuts to her relatives. *who*
6. Rachel was angry at Molly because she was making fun of her relatives. *why*
7. Sonny and Rachel would win badges because they sold the most boxes of donuts. *why*
8. If people eat a lot of donuts, they might get fat. *what*
9. Everyone was happy that they had earned enough money to go to camp in two weeks. *when*
10. The scout meeting started after three o'clock. *when*

Page 52

It's a Surprise!

Read the clues. Find the answers in the Word Bank.

1. You need snow to do this. You can go fast or slow. You can turn corners. You need a pair of something to do this. What is it? *skiing*
2. This can be soft or hard. It can be made of paper or metal. You need it when you want to buy something. What is it? *money*
3. It is a place where you can buy sweet treats to eat. Many of the treats that can be bought there have to be baked in an oven. What is it? *bakery*
4. In larger cities these come out every day. It can have a few pages or many pages. It tells you what is happening in the world. What is it? *newspaper*
5. It can be large or small. It smells very good. It is green. It is very special and people like to decorate it at one time of the year. What is it? *Christmas tree*
6. It needs gas. It is very big. Its driver stops a lot at people's houses to pick up things. What is it? *garbage truck*

Word Bank

book	magazine	newspaper	garbage truck
coins	paper bag	holly plant	Christmas tree
money	gas station	candy store	snowballing
skiing	sledding	bakery	

Page 53

Reflect on the Riddles

Read each riddle. Find the answer in the Word Bank and write it on the line.

1. There are two of me. We can blink. We can see. We can wink. We can weep. What are we? *eyes*
2. There is one of me. I can sing. I can form words. I can eat. I can even blow a big bubble. I can eat ice cream, too. What am I? *mouth*
3. There is one of me. If I tickle, I will sneeze. I like to sniff flowers. I like the whiff of hot dogs, also. What am I? *nose*
4. We need to bend and stretch. We need rest. We need to work and we need to play. We are all different. What are we? *bodies*
5. I can be almost any color. I can be long or short. I can be curled and I can be spiked. What am I? *hair*
6. We can change. We can be happy or sad. We can be worried or excited. We can even be scared. What are we? *feelings*
7. I cover a lot. I keep muscles, bones, and blood inside your body. I let you know if it is hot or cold. I tell you if something is wet or dry. What am I? *skin*
8. We all have feelings. We all have bodies. We all like to do many of the same things. But, we also are all very different. Who are we? *people*

Word Bank

bodies	eyes
people	feelings
hair	mouth
nose	skin

Page 54

It's a Fact!

Read each sentence. If it states a fact, write the word fact on the line. If it states an opinion, write the word opinion on the line.

1. An opera is a play that is sung. *fact*
2. Many operas are terribly boring. *opinion*
3. Opera stars wear costumes on stage. *fact*
4. People who have trunks filled with jewels are robbers. *opinion*
5. In many cities people dial 911 for emergency help. *fact*
6. It is fun to check the mailbox every day. *opinion*
7. Seventy is a very old age. *opinion*
8. Second and third grade are about the same. *opinion*
9. Many operas are recorded on records. *fact*
10. It is all right to snoop in other people's things if you have a reason. *opinion*

Page 55

Is This for Real?

Read each sentence. If it tells something that could really happen, draw a pumpkin on the line.

1. Spiders spin cobwebs.
2. Robots are people.
3. Cats have nine lives.
4. Bats hang upside down.
5. Ghosts haunt houses.
6. There really are spooks.
7. A mask can hide your face.
8. Boys and girls can run in high heels.
9. Owls have wings.
10. Witches ride on brooms.
11. Some people buy costumes.
12. Pirates sail on ships.

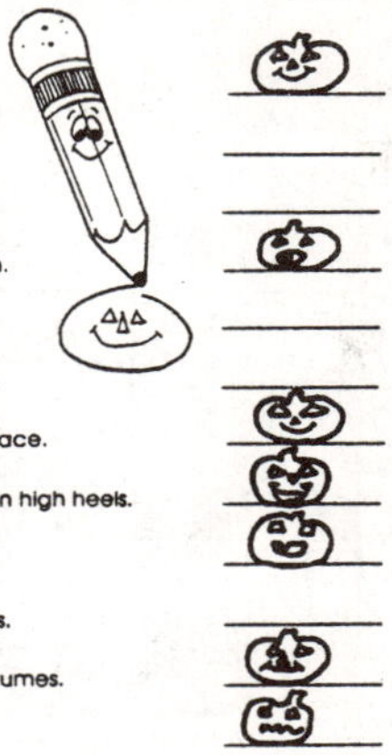

Page 56

Elephant Dressing

Mrs. Marsh's kids need your help dressing. First color all of the elephants' skin gray. Then follow the directions to color their clothes.

1. Color Robbie's pants brown and his shirt yellow. His shoes are brown.
2. Color Mollie's dress pink polka dots. Put a pink bow in her hair. Her shoes are black.
3. Color Lisa's dress blue, green and purple stripes. Her bow and shoes are purple.
4. Color Jason's jeans blue and his shirt red. His shoes are red.
5. Color Gary's pants orange. His shirt is orange and white stripes. His shoes are black.
6. Color Megan's dress red with pink flowers. Her shoes are red.

Page 57

Top or Bottom?

Read and follow the directions.

1. Paste the dog in the middle of the bottom shelf.
2. Paste the cat on the right side of the bear.
3. Paste the rabbit on the left side of the top shelf.
4. Paste the elephant on the shelf below the rabbit.
5. Paste the frog on the left side of the bottom shelf.
6. Paste the horse on the middle shelf below the cat.
7. Paste the giraffe on the middle shelf above the dog.
8. Paste the turtle on the right side of the bottom shelf.

Page 58

Where Is It?

Follow the directions. **Hint:** Read through all of the directions before starting.

Pictures will vary.

1. Draw a brown mound in the middle of the box.
2. Draw a red car on top of the mound.
3. Draw apartments behind and to the left of the mound.
4. Draw a bird nest, with four blue eggs inside, on top of the car.
5. Draw three yellow birds flying away from the nest.
6. Draw two tin cans at the bottom of the mound.
7. Put an X on one of the tin cans.
8. Draw you and your friend looking at the car.

Page 59

I'll Try Another Way

Help the little mole find his way to Percy's hut. Read and follow the directions. Write each word that tells what blocks his path as he looks for the loose floorboard. Then draw a line to show where the mole traveled.

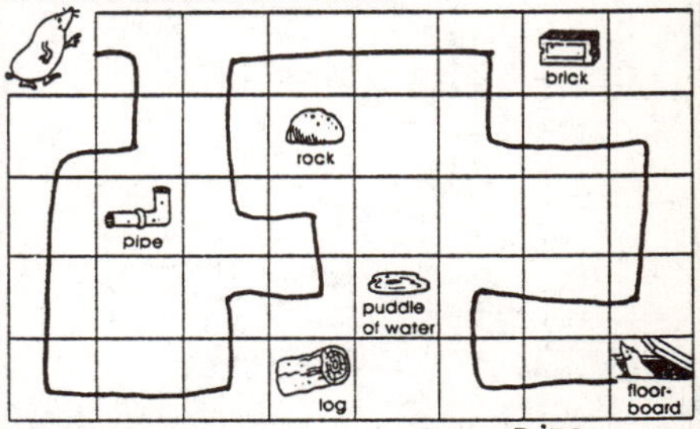

Go right 1 space, then down 1 space. There is a *pipe*.
Go left 1 space, down 3 spaces, then right 2 spaces. There is a *log*.
Go up 1 space, right 1 space, then up 1. There is a *rock*.
Go left 1 space, up 2, then right 3 spaces. There is a *brick*.
Go down 1 space, right 2 spaces, down 2, then left 2 spaces. There is a *puddle of water*.
Go down 1 space, then right 1 space. Hooray! It's the *floorboard*.

Page 60

What Did I Say?

Unscramble the words in each 💬. ✏ each sentence on the line.

I'm hiking in the woods.

Today is my friend's birthday.

I will solve this mystery.

The bee stung my finger.

I enjoy being a nurse.

Page 61

The One in the Middle

Print the words in order to make a sentence. The word in the middle is there to help you. Print the sentences.

1. good Dissel jumper Freddy a — *Freddy Dissel* was *a good jumper.*
2. was Gumber teacher Ms. — *Ms. Gumber was* Freddy's *teacher.*
3. and one sister had Freddy one — *Freddy had one* brother *and one sister.*
4. Freddy play going in was to a — *Freddy was going to* be *in a play.*
5. green They face on painted his — *They painted green* dots *on his face.*
6. break Gumber to a told leg Ms. — *Ms. Gumber told* Freddy *to break a leg.*

Now color this picture.

Page 62

What Do I Do First?

Look at the pictures. Number them in the correct order. Then read and number the sentences in the correct order.

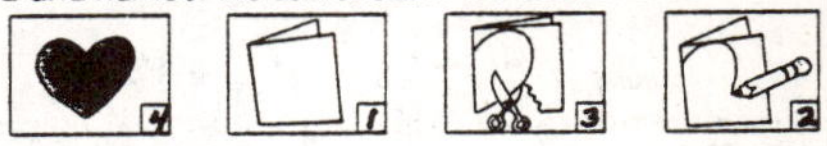

3 Cut along the line.
1 Fold a piece of paper in half.
2 Draw one half of a heart on the paper.
4 Open the heart.

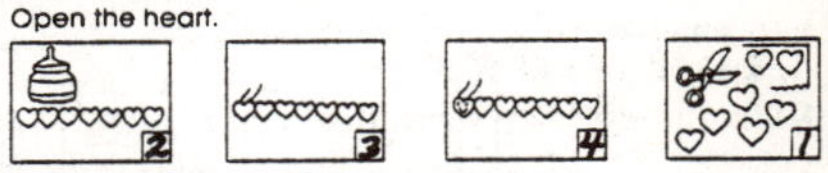

3 Draw two antennas on the first heart.
2 Paste the hearts in a line.
4 Then draw two eyes and a mouth on the first heart.
1 Cut out seven small hearts.
What did you make? *caterpillar*

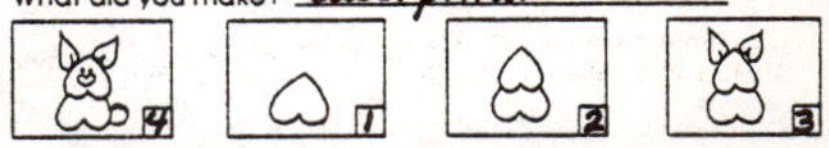

4 Draw two eyes and a nose. Paste a cotton ball on the big heart.
1 Paste a big heart upside down on a piece of paper.
2 Glue a smaller heart upside down on top of the big heart.
3 Paste two long skinny hearts upside down on the smaller heart.
What did you make? *rabbit*

Page 63

Terrific Toast

Lionel said he made the best toast in the world! Number the sentences to show the best order to make terrific toast. The first two are done. *Order may vary.*

- 13 Close the jar of jam.
- 6 Close the package of bread.
- 5 Push down on the toaster button.
- 11 Put butter on the hot toast.
- 14 Place the plate of toast on the table and enjoy.
- 2 Open the package of bread.
- 1 Plug in the toaster.
- 10 Put the toast on a plate.
- 3 Take out two slices of bread.
- 4 Place the two slices of bread in the toaster.
- 7 Open the jar of jam.
- 8 Wait for the toast to pop up.
- 12 Put jam on the toast.
- 9 Take the toast out of the toaster.

What do you like to put on your toast? ______

What is your favorite flavor of jam? ______

Page 64

What's What?

Write the words from the Word Bank in the correct category.

Living	Non-Living
1. hen	1. car
2. bird	2. nest
3. kitten	3. boat
4. cow	4. rocks
5. dog	5. plane
6. tree	6. truck

Word Bank: car, truck, hen, bird, kitten, nest, boat, rocks, cow, plane, dog, tree

Page 65

Tidying Up

Write the words from the Word Bank in the correct category.

Household Chores: wash dishes, scrub floors, dust, mop

Rooms in a House: parlor, dining room, bedroom, kitchen

Furniture: chair, table, desk, couch

Word Bank: parlor, dust, chair, mop, bedroom, couch, wash dishes, kitchen, table, scrub floors, desk, dining room

Page 66

Cookie Jar

Read the categories on the jars. Cut and paste the cookies in the correct jar.

Animals: frog, toad, bird

Things You Can Climb: tree, ladder, mountain

Things That Hold Something: jar, bag, box

Action Words: eat, climb, read

Page 67

Sense-ational!

hearing, smelling, tasting, seeing, touching

Read each sentence. Then write which sense would be used for each one. *Answers may vary.*

1. Andrew found page 64 in his reading book. *seeing*
2. Andrew heard Sharon giggling at him. *hearing*
3. Andrew poked Nicky. *touching*
4. Sharon was listening when Andrew asked Nicky about his freckles. *hearing*
5. Andrew liked to count Nicky's freckles. *seeing*
6. The number of freckles you get depends on how much of the juice you drink. *tasting*
7. The bell rang and the students lined up. *hearing*
8. Andrew couldn't find any freckles on Sharon's face. *seeing*
9. Sharon ate bugs. *tasting*
10. Miss Kelly told Andrew that it was time for his reading group. *hearing*

Page 68

What's Going On?

Look at the pictures. Find the sentence in the Word Bank that explains each one. Write it on the lines.

They won the big Thanksgiving game.

The team was treated to hot dogs after their win.

The team had lost every game.

Coach Swamp made them practice hard.

Word Bank: The team was treated to hot dogs after their win. / Coach Swamp made them practice hard. / They won the big Thanksgiving game. / The team had lost every game.

Page 69

Just Rolling Along!

Help Emmett roll the snowball down the hill. Read the clues. Then find the words in the Word Bank and write them in the correct spaces. **Hint:** The last letter of each answer is the first letter of the next answer.

1. Boasting
2. Very, very good
3. Many moving cars and trucks
4. A little cold
5. Paid attention
6. Twice an amount
7. Comes after seventh
8. One of two equal parts
9. Very well-known
10. Not crooked

Answers on the path: *bragging, great, traffic, cool, listened, double, eighth, half, famous, straight*

Word Bank: listened, bragging, cool, famous, eighth, half, great, double, traffic, straight

Page 70

A-maze-ing

Draw a line through the maze in the order of the clues to help baby bird find his way back to his nest.

Clues

1. A very young child
2. Opposite of father
3. A large farm animal
4. A bird that lives on a farm
5. Opposite of new
6. Something that can float
7. A very large plant
8. Opposite of up
9. An animal that can fly
10. Something you can drive
11. Opposite of left
12. A bird hatches out of it
13. A sound
14. To leap
15. Your house
16. A baby cat
17. A machine that flies

Page 71

Circus Sights

Find the answers to the puzzle in the Word Bank.

Across
1. To save from danger — *rescue*
4. The last act — *finale*
6. A silly person — *clown*
8. Your mistake — *fault*
10. To give an order — *command*
11. A poster — *sign*

Down
2. A large weapon — *cannon*
3. A show with clowns and animal acts — *circus*
5. You dress up in these — *costumes*
7. Great — *grand*
9. A person who trains animals — *trainer*
11. A trick — *stunt*

Word Bank: cannon, costumes, command, trainer, grand, circus, rescue, clown, fault, stunt, sign, finale

Page 72

Hidden Mystery

Read the clues. Find the matching words in the Word Bank and write them on the lines. Then find each two-letter mystery word by circling the letters that are the same in each set of matching words. Write each mystery word on a magnifying glass.

1. Something you put on a hot dog *mustard*
2. Outside part of bread *crust*
3. Dance or sing to . . . *music*
4. Someone who might be guilty *suspect*

The hidden mystery word is *us*

1. Words you can sing *song*
2. Not weak *strong*
3. A small rock *stone*
4. A round fastener *button*

The hidden mystery word is *on*

1. A note asking you to a party *invitation*
2. Start *begin*
3. The meal you eat at night *dinner*
4. A part of a fish *fin*

The hidden mystery word is *in*

Word Bank

strong	dinner	fin	stone
invitation	begin	crust	song
button	music	mustard	suspect

Page 73

We're Just Hopping!

Find and circle the words in the puzzle.
Look → and ↓.

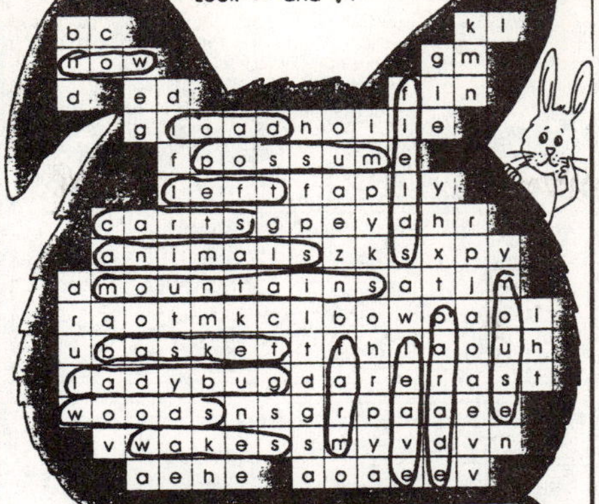

mouse	mountains	load	parade
basket	ladybug	carts	possum
leave	animals	left	wakes
farm	fields	now	woods

Page 74

Lazy One Liners

Use your laziest imagination to finish these lazy lines. An example would be, "The lion was so lazy that . . . he made his mate roar for him." Choose three of your best one liners and illustrate them on another paper.

1. The doctor was so lazy that *Answers will vary.*
2. The baker was so lazy that
3. The teacher was so lazy that
4. The fireman was so lazy that
5. The dentist was so lazy that
6. The truck driver was so lazy that
7. The vet was so lazy that
8. The plumber was so lazy that
9. The house builder was so lazy that
10. The principal was so lazy that
11. The astronaut was so lazy that
12. The football player was so lazy that
13. The zookeeper was so lazy that
14. The TV repairman was so lazy that
15. The traffic cop was so lazy that

Page 75

A Story for the People

Look carefully at the picture on the buckskin. Write a story on the lines to tell what is happening in the picture.

Stories will vary.

Page 76

Using Descriptive Language

Stories are always more exciting when you can picture them happening in your mind. Descriptive words help make the story imaginable. Use these categories to think of words that describe a walk along the beach. Pretend you are barefoot walking close to the water. With a partner, write three words in each area. Then, use all the words in a story.

What I smell: 1. 2. 3.

What I taste: 1. 2. 3.

What I hear: 1. 2. 3.

What I see: 1. 2. 3.

What I feel on my feet: 1. 2. 3.

My Walk Along the Beach

Stories will vary.

Page 77

Writing Haiku Poetry

Haiku poetry is originally from the country of Japan. It is a very simple form of poetry and does not have to rhyme.

Example	Poem Pattern
The polar bear cubs	5 syllables
learn to swim and dive for fish	7 syllables
in the cold, blue sea.	5 syllables

Write your own haiku poem by yourself or with a partner. Give it a title and illustrate it.

Poems will vary.

Title

By a Beary Special Poet ____________
Name

Page 78

Ready to Mail

Read the envelope Tilly addressed to Mr. Bunny.

tilly mole
102 garden road
forest maine 25136

LOVE

mr bunny
523 sweet potato lane
forest maine 25136

Address the envelope correctly. Be sure to use capital letters, periods and commas where they belong.

Tilly Mole
102 Garden Road
Forest, Maine 25136

Mr. Bunny
523 Sweet Potato Lane
Forest, Maine 25136

Draw and color a stamp on the envelope.

Page 79

Write, Please

Read the thank you letter Louis wrote to his Uncle McAllister.

october 5 1990

dear uncle mcallister
thank you for the tadpole I named him alphonse he likes to eat cheeseburgers this is the best gift you ever sent me
thank you again
love
louis

Write the letter correctly. Be sure to use capital letters, periods and commas where they belong.

October 5, 1990

Dear Uncle McAllister,
Thank you for the tadpole. I named him Alphonse. He likes to eat cheeseburgers. This is the best gift you ever sent me.
Thank you again.

Love,
Louis

Page 80

Which Book?

Read the questions. Write which book you would use to find the answer.

Dictionary — Encyclopedia — Telephone Book

1. What makes rain? *encyclopedia*
2. What does purify mean? *dictionary*
3. When does the waterworks plant allow visitors? *telephone book*
4. Where would you find glaciers? *encyclopedia*
5. What is a water cycle? *encyclopedia*
6. What are impurities? *dictionary encyclopedia*
7. Where is your town's waterworks located? *telephone book*
8. What chemicals are put into the water on its way to the storage tank? *encyclopedia*
9. How do you pronounce the word evaporation? *dictionary*
10. What time does the waterworks open? *telephone book*
11. How do you pronounce the word reservoir? *dictionary*
12. How are clouds formed? *encyclopedia*

Page 81

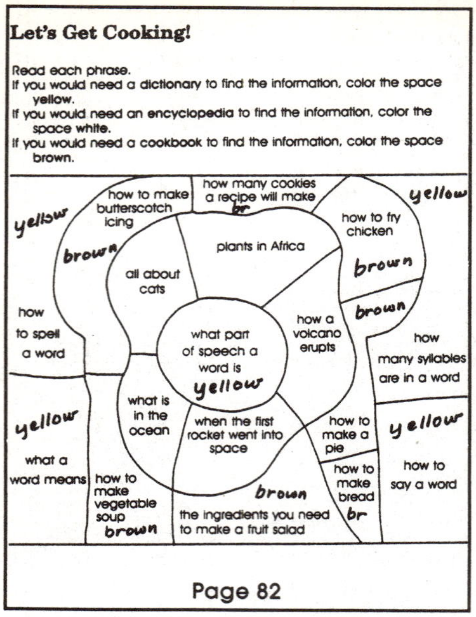

Let's Get Cooking!

Read each phrase.
If you would need a **dictionary** to find the information, color the space **yellow.**
If you would need an **encyclopedia** to find the information, color the space **white.**
If you would need a **cookbook** to find the information, color the space **brown.**

yellow
how to make butterscotch icing
brown
how many cookies a recipe will make
br
yellow
how to fry chicken
brown
plants in Africa
all about cats
how to spell a word
what part of speech a word is
yellow
how a volcano erupts
brown
how many syllables are in a word
yellow
what a word means
what is in the ocean
when the first rocket went into space
how to make a pie
yellow
how to say a word
how to make vegetable soup
brown
brown
how to make bread
br
the ingredients you need to make a fruit salad

Page 82

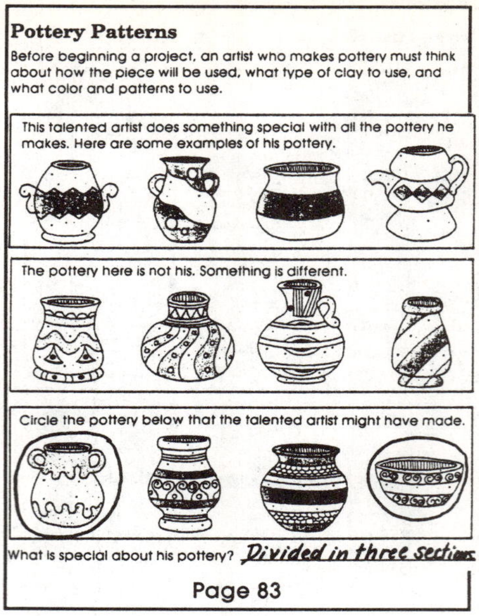

Pottery Patterns

Before beginning a project, an artist who makes pottery must think about how the piece will be used, what type of clay to use, and what color and patterns to use.

This talented artist does something special with all the pottery he makes. Here are some examples of his pottery.

The pottery here is not his. Something is different.

Circle the pottery below that the talented artist might have made.

What is special about his pottery? *Divided in three sections*

Page 83

Dressing the Part

People who act in plays are called actors and actresses. For each play, costumes are chosen that make the characters in the story seem more realistic.

Below is the inside of a costume closet.

Dragon
Mouse
Cowboy
Batman
Lion
Princess
Ghost
Gorilla
Dog
Superman

Pretend that you want to act in some silly plays. Look at the titles of each play below. Write the names of the two costumes you would combine to fit the main character of each play.

1. "The Strong, Flying Ape" *Superman* *Gorilla*
2. "The Invisible Man on His Horse" *Cowboy* *Ghost*
3. "The Cat Who Squeaked" *Mouse* *Lion*
4. "Her Royal Highness Barks up the Wrong Tree" *Princess* *Dog*
5. "Flying Animal-like Man Saves Building from Fire" *Batman* *Dragon*

Page 84

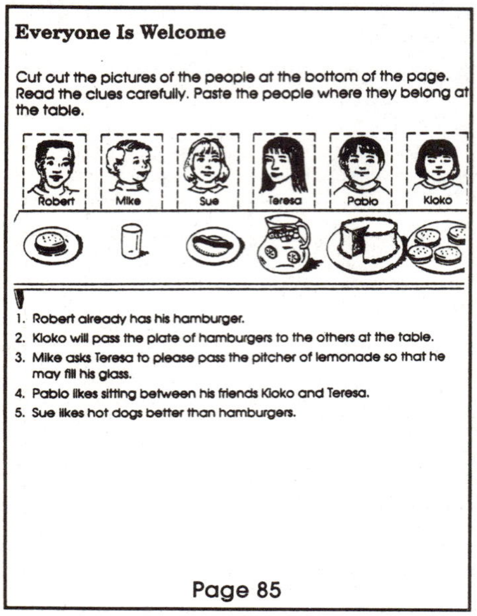

Everyone Is Welcome

Cut out the pictures of the people at the bottom of the page. Read the clues carefully. Paste the people where they belong at the table.

Robert
Mike
Sue
Teresa
Pablo
Kioko

1. Robert already has his hamburger.
2. Kioko will pass the plate of hamburgers to the others at the table.
3. Mike asks Teresa to please pass the pitcher of lemonade so that he may fill his glass.
4. Pablo likes sitting between his friends Kioko and Teresa.
5. Sue likes hot dogs better than hamburgers.

Page 85

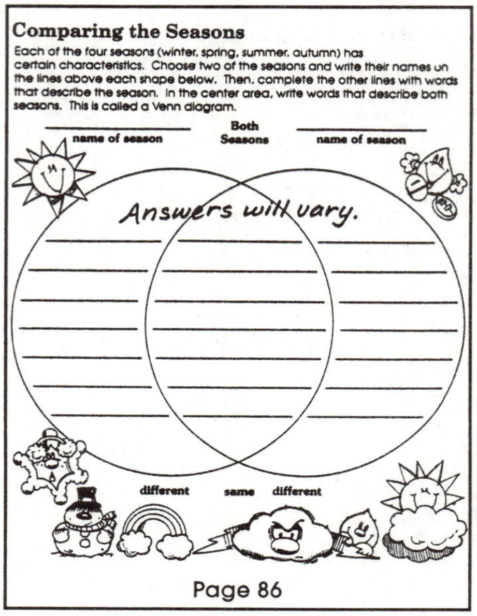

Comparing the Seasons

Each of the four seasons (winter, spring, summer, autumn) has certain characteristics. Choose two of the seasons and write their names on the lines above each shape below. Then, complete the other lines with words that describe the season. In the center area, write words that describe both seasons. This is called a Venn diagram.

name of season
Both Seasons
name of season
Answers will vary.
different
same
different

Page 86

Just Napping

Count. Write the correct number of cats in the box on each cat bed.

5
3
9
12
6
10
4
2
11
8
1
7

Page 87

Plump Piglets

Pigs like to eat corn. These little pigs just ate lunch.
Read the clues to find out how many ears of corn each pig ate. Write the number on the line below each pig.

I ate the number that comes before 26.
I ate the number that comes between 87 and 89.
I ate the number that comes after 92.
Patsy
Horace
Portly
25
88
93
I ate the number that comes before 57.
I ate the number that comes between 39 and 41.
Hilda
Pesky
56
40

Who ate the most and was really piggy? *Portly*
Who ate the least? *Patsy*

Page 88

Unpack the Teddy Bears

Cut out the bears at the bottom of the page. Paste them where they belong in numbered order.

39 40 41
29 30 31
10 11 12
78 79 80
84 85 86
64 65 66

Page 89

Air Bear Addition

Help Buddy off the ground. Solve the problems. Then color the clouds with sums of 9 to find the right path.

5 +5 10
3 +7 10
7 +4 11
4 +4 8
8 +1 9
6 +3 9
6 +4 10
2 +7 9
2 +5 7
10 +1 11
5 +4 9
6 +5 11
3 +4 7
3 +2 5
2 +5 7
4 +5 9
0 +9 9
9 +0 9
8 +2 10
2 +6 8
3 +6 9

Page 90

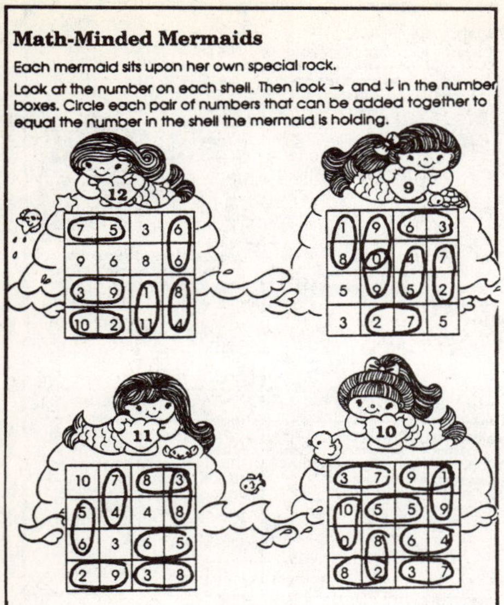

Math-Minded Mermaids

Each mermaid sits upon her own special rock.

Look at the number on each shell. Then look → and ↓ in the number boxes. Circle each pair of numbers that can be added together to equal the number in the shell the mermaid is holding.

12

7	5	3	6
9	6	8	6
3	9	1	8
10	2	11	4

9

1	9	6	3
8	0	4	7
5	9	5	2
3	2	7	5

11

10	7	8	3
5	4	4	8
6	3	6	5
2	9	3	8

10

3	7	9	1
10	5	5	9
0	8	6	4
8	2	3	7

Page 91

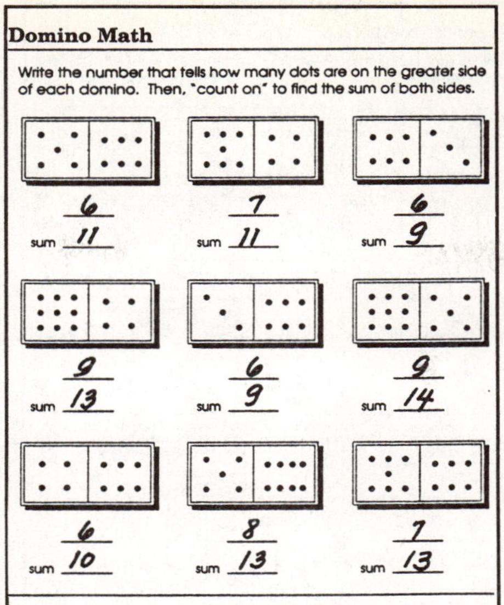

Domino Math

Write the number that tells how many dots are on the greater side of each domino. Then, "count on" to find the sum of both sides.

6 sum 11 | 7 sum 11 | 6 sum 9

9 sum 13 | 6 sum 9 | 9 sum 14

6 sum 10 | 8 sum 13 | 7 sum 13

Page 92

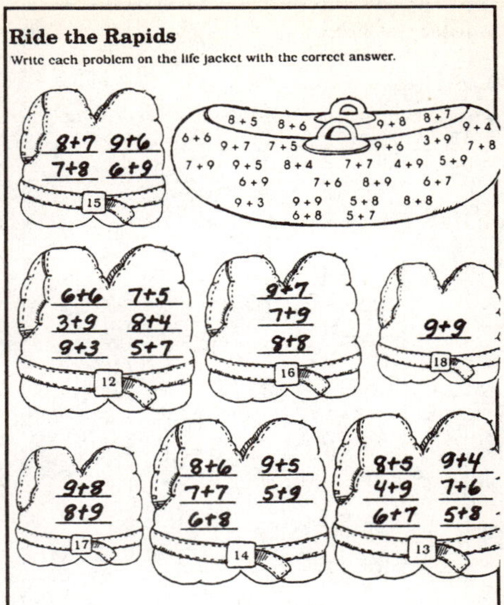

Ride the Rapids

Write each problem on the life jacket with the correct answer.

Page 93

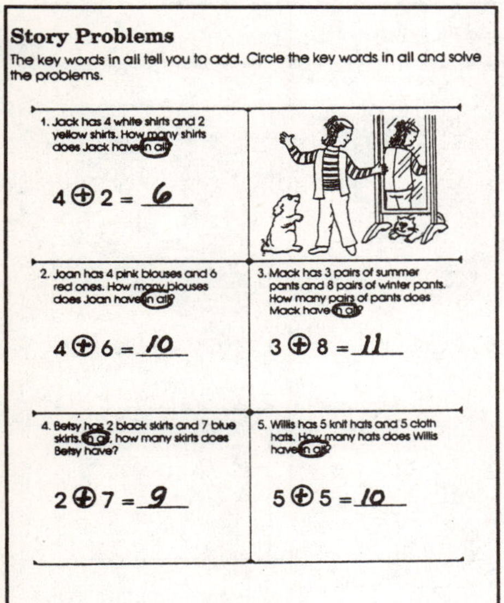

Story Problems

The key words in all tell you to add. Circle the key words in all and solve the problems.

1. Jack has 4 white shirts and 2 yellow shirts. How many shirts does Jack have in all?
   4 ⊕ 2 = 6
2. Joan has 4 pink blouses and 6 red ones. How many blouses does Joan have in all?
   4 ⊕ 6 = 10
3. Mack has 3 pairs of summer pants and 8 pairs of winter pants. How many pairs of pants does Mack have in all?
   3 ⊕ 8 = 11
4. Betsy has 2 black skirts and 7 blue skirts. In all, how many skirts does Betsy have?
   2 ⊕ 7 = 9
5. Willis has 5 knit hats and 5 cloth hats. How many hats does Willis have in all?
   5 ⊕ 5 = 10

Page 94

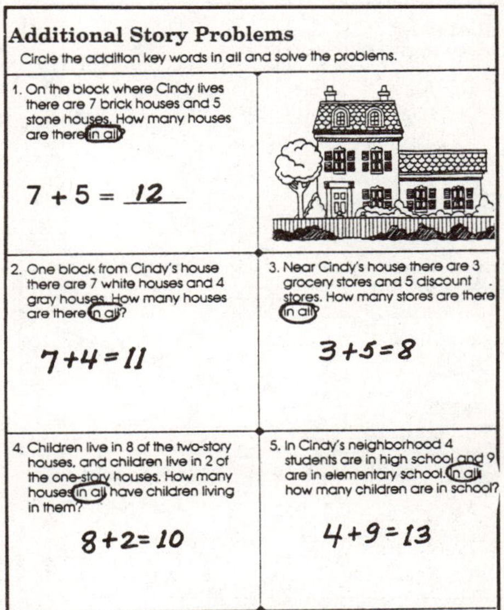

Additional Story Problems

Circle the addition key words in all and solve the problems.

1. On the block where Cindy lives there are 7 brick houses and 5 stone houses. How many houses are there in all?
   7 + 5 = 12
2. One block from Cindy's house there are 7 white houses and 4 gray houses. How many houses are there in all?
   7+4=11
3. Near Cindy's house there are 3 grocery stores and 5 discount stores. How many stores are there in all?
   3+5=8
4. Children live in 8 of the two-story houses, and children live in 2 of the one-story houses. How many houses in all have children living in them?
   8+2=10
5. In Cindy's neighborhood 4 students are in high school and 9 are in elementary school. In all, how many children are in school?
   4+9=13

Page 95

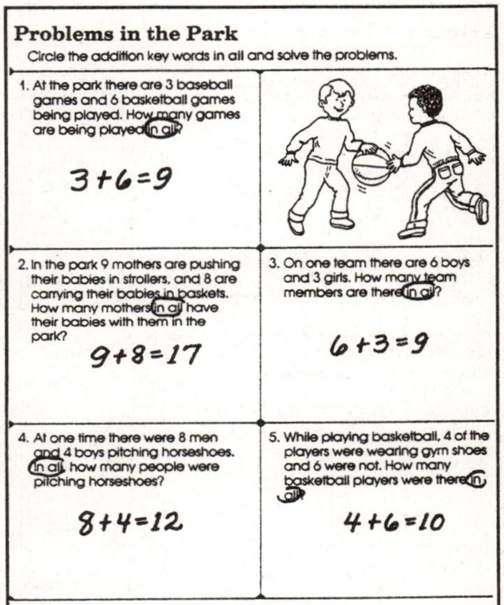

Problems in the Park

Circle the addition key words in all and solve the problems.

1. At the park there are 3 baseball games and 6 basketball games being played. How many games are being played in all?
   3+6=9
2. In the park 9 mothers are pushing their babies in strollers, and 8 are carrying their babies in baskets. How many mothers in all have their babies with them in the park?
   9+8=17
3. On one team there are 6 boys and 3 girls. How many team members are there in all?
   6+3=9
4. At one time there were 8 men and 4 boys pitching horseshoes. In all, how many people were pitching horseshoes?
   8+4=12
5. While playing basketball, 4 of the players were wearing gym shoes and 6 were not. How many basketball players were there in all?
   4+6=10

Page 96

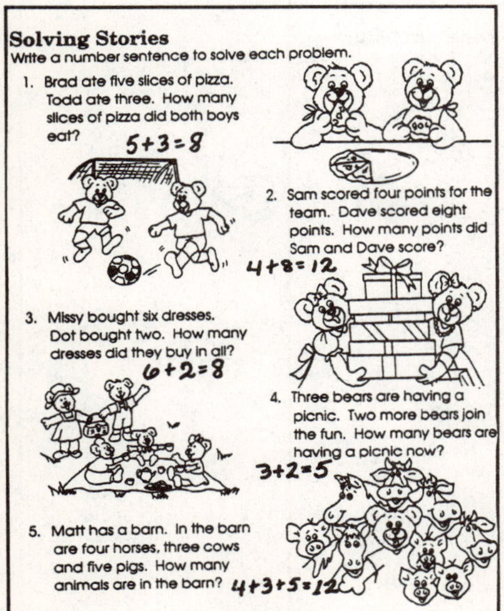

Solving Stories

Write a number sentence to solve each problem.

1. Brad ate five slices of pizza. Todd ate three. How many slices of pizza did both boys eat? 5+3=8
2. Sam scored four points for the team. Dave scored eight points. How many points did Sam and Dave score? 4+8=12
3. Missy bought six dresses. Dot bought two. How many dresses did they buy in all? 6+2=8
4. Three bears are having a picnic. Two more bears join the fun. How many bears are having a picnic now? 3+2=5
5. Matt has a barn. In the barn are four horses, three cows and five pigs. How many animals are in the barn? 4+3+5=12

Page 97

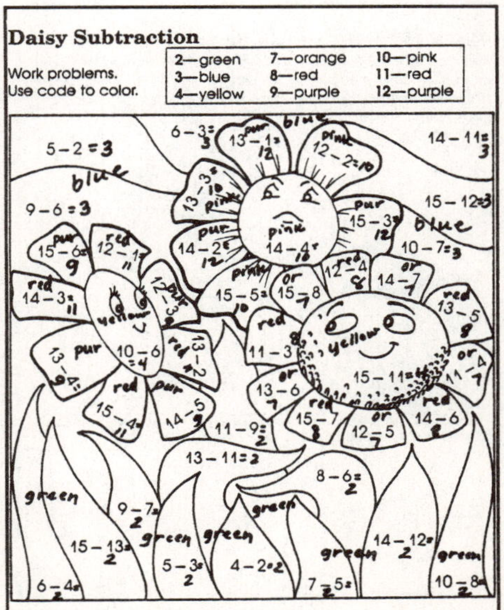

Daisy Subtraction

Work problems. Use code to color.

2—green	7—orange	10—pink
3—blue	8—red	11—red
4—yellow	9—purple	12—purple

Page 98

Pick a Picnic

Subtract. Write each answer. Then draw a line to show where three answers are the same in a row.

12 − 9 = 3	11 − 2 = 9	9 − 8 = 1
8 − 6 = 2	7 − 4 = 3	7 − 5 = 2
7 − 3 = 4	10 − 1 = 9	11 − 8 = 3

10 − 7 = 3	12 − 3 = 9	11 − 2 = 9
12 − 7 = 5	9 − 0 = 9	8 − 5 = 3
11 − 4 = 7	9 − 2 = 7	12 − 5 = 7

10 − 4 = 6	8 − 3 = 5	8 − 4 = 4
12 − 4 = 8	12 − 8 = 4	8 − 2 = 6
11 − 7 = 4	10 − 3 = 7	11 − 3 = 8

9 − 7 = 2	11 − 9 = 2	10 − 2 = 8
11 − 5 = 6	9 − 3 = 6	12 − 6 = 6
8 − 1 = 7	12 − 7 = 5	9 − 5 = 4

7 − 7 = 0	11 − 6 = 5	9 − 1 = 8
10 − 3 = 7	9 − 4 = 5	10 − 0 = 10
8 − 8 = 0	10 − 5 = 5	12 − 4 = 8

Page 99

Connect the Facts

Subtract. Write the answer.

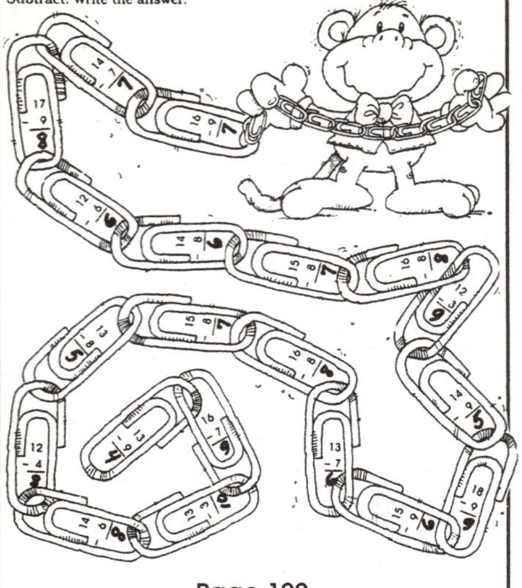

Page 100

How Many Animals Are Left?

The key word left tells you to subtract. Circle the key word left and solve the problems.

1. Bill had 10 kittens, but 4 of them ran away. How many kittens does he have left?

10 – 4 = 6

2. There were 12 rabbits eating clover. Dogs chased 3 of them away. How many rabbits were left?

12-3=9

3. Bill saw 11 birds eating from the bird feeders in his back yard. A cat scared 7 of them away. How many birds were left at the feeders?

11-7=4

4. There were 14 frogs on the bank of the pond. Then 9 of them hopped into the water. How many frogs were left on the bank?

14-9=5

5. Bill counted 15 robins in his yard. Then 8 of the robins flew away. How many robins were left in the yard?

15-8=7

Page 101

Maggy at School

Circle the subtraction key word left and solve the problems.

1. In Maggy's classroom there are 12 girls. One day 4 of the girls went home with the flu. How many girls were left in school that day?

12-4=8

2. Maggy is in 10 different clubs. This week 5 of them will not meet. How many of Maggy's clubs are left to meet this week?

10-5=5

3. Maggy had 16 crayons. She broke 9 of them. How many crayons does Maggy have left?

16-9=7

4. There are 13 boys in Maggy's classroom. One morning 8 of the boys went to the gym. How many were left in the classroom?

13-8=5

5. One day 4 of the 13 boys were called in from the playground. How many of the boys were left on the playground?

13-4=9

Page 102

A Hidden Message

Add or subtract. Use the code to find out your new motto!

Code:	9	18	6	15	13	12	16	11	8	7	14	17
	H	Y	D	E	V	T	S	O	A	M	N	I

9	
+8	
17	
I	

16	14	8	6
-7	-6	+5	+9
9	8	13	15
h	a	v	e

14	9
-7	+9
7	18
m	y

17	15	9	13	8
-8	-7	+5	-7	+8
9	8	14	6	16
h	a	n	d	s

4	6
+7	+8
11	14
o	n

12	17	6	15
-5	-9	+6	-6
7	8	12	9
m	a	t	h

Page 103

All Aboard!

Add or subtract. Match the related facts.

5 + 9 = 14 — 14 – 9 = 5
8 + 7 = 15 — 15 – 7 = 8
15 – 9 = 6 — 6 + 9 = 15
17 – 8 = 9 — 9 + 8 = 17
7 + 7 = 14 — 14 – 7 = 7

Add or subtract. Color spaces with answers greater than 12 brown. Color the rest green.

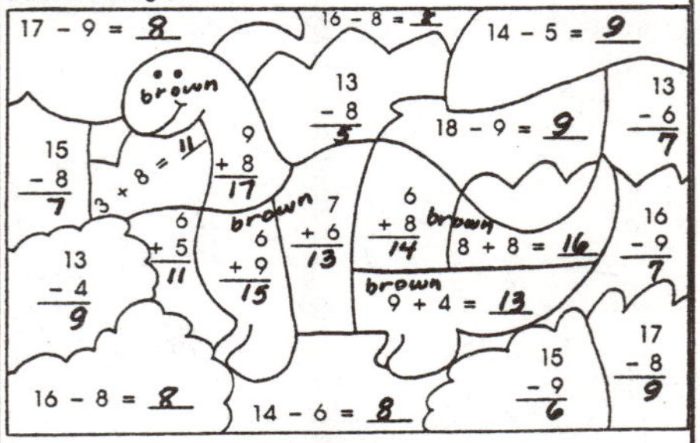

Page 104

Add or Subtract?

The key words in all tell you to add. The key word left tells you to subtract. Circle the key words and solve the problems.

1. The pet store has 3 large dogs and 5 small dogs. How many dogs are there in all?

3 ⊕ 5 = 8

2. The pet store had 9 parrots and then sold 4 of them. How many parrots does the pet store have left?

9 ⊖ 4 = 5

3. The pet store gave Linda's class 2 adult gerbils and 9 young ones. How many gerbils did Linda's class get in all?

2 ⊕ 9 = 11

4. At the pet store 3 of the 8 myna birds were sold. How many myna birds are left in the pet store?

8 ⊖ 3 = 5

5. The monkey at the pet store has 5 rubber toys and 4 wooden toys. How many toys does it have in all?

5 ⊕ 4 = 9

Page 105

Training with Facts

Use the numbers on each train to write the fact families.

8 + 6 = 14
6 + 8 = 14
14 - 6 = 8
14 - 8 = 6

6 + 9 = 15
9 + 6 = 15
15 - 9 = 6
15 - 6 = 9

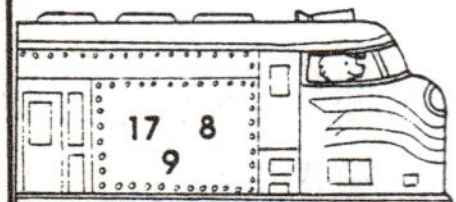

8 + 9 = 17
9 + 8 = 17
17 - 8 = 9
17 - 9 = 8

9 + 5 = 14
5 + 9 = 14
14 - 9 = 5
14 - 5 = 9

Page 106

Adding Strategies

When adding three numbers, add two numbers first, then add the third to that sum. To decide which two numbers to add first, try one of these strategies.

Look for doubles.

8 + 3 + 3 (3 + 3 = 6) = 14

4 + 4 + 5 (4 + 4 = 8) = 13

2 + 9 + 2 (2 + 2 = 4) = 13

Look for a ten.

7 + 3 + 4 (7 + 3 = 10) = 14

8 + 4 + 6 (4 + 6 = 10) = 18

1 + 5 + 9 (1 + 9 = 10) = 15

Try these. Look for a 10 or doubles.

5	2	7	3	6
5	6	1	7	2
+ 4	+ 8	+ 7	+ 4	+ 6
14	16	15	14	14

7	7	6	5
6	8	7	5
+ 6	+ 3	+ 4	+ 3
19	18	17	13

Page 107

Sum Ice Cream

Add. If the sum is 11 or more, color the cone brown. If the sum is less than 11, color the cone yellow.

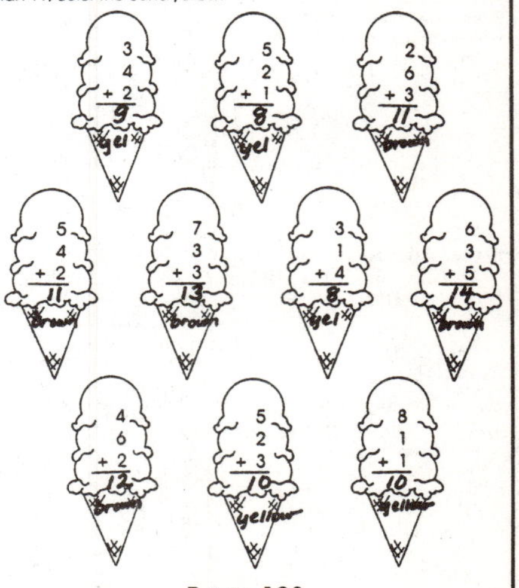

Page 108

Path Problems

Add. Show the detective the correct path. Color the path with sums of 13.

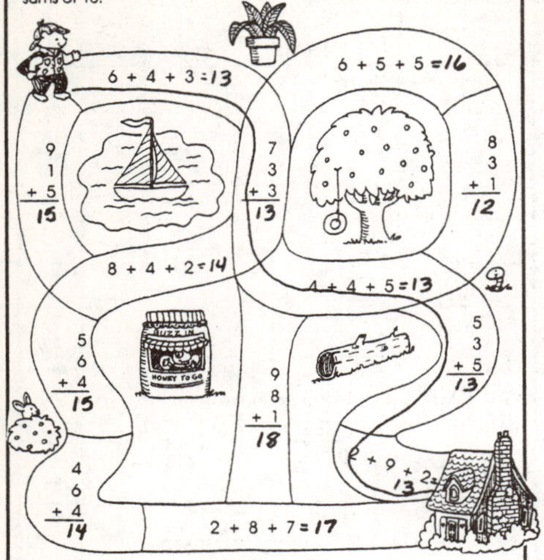

6 + 4 + 3 = 13
6 + 5 + 5 = 16
9 + 1 + 5 = 15
7 + 3 + 3 = 13
8 + 3 + 1 = 12
8 + 4 + 2 = 14
4 + 4 + 5 = 13
5 + 6 + 4 = 15
9 + 8 + 1 = 18
5 + 3 + 5 = 13
4 + 6 + 4 = 14
2 + 9 + 2 = 13
2 + 8 + 7 = 17

Page 109

Something's Missing

In the forest, 13 animals have a picnic. Skunk brings 8 sandwiches. How many sandwiches should Raccoon bring so that each animal can have one?

8 + ? = 13

What number added to 8 equals 13?

To find the missing addend, find the difference of 13 and 8. That is, subtract the given addend (8) from the sum (13).

13 − 8 = 5

Since 13 − 8 = 5, then 8 + 5 = 13.

Raccoon should bring 5 sandwiches.

Try these. Find the missing addends.

9 + 6 = 15 | 6 + 7 = 13

9 + 5 = 14 | 8 + 6 = 14

8 + 8 = 16 | 9 + 9 = 18

Page 110

Food Fun

The table below tells what each animal brought to the picnic. Fill in the missing numbers.

Animal	Vegetables	Fruits	Total
Skunk	8	6	14
Raccoon	9	8	17
Squirrel	7	8	15
Rabbit	6	7	13
Owl	7	9	16
Deer	9	9	18

Write the name of the animal that answers each question.

1. Who brought the same number of vegetables as fruits? deer
2. Who brought two more fruits than vegetables? owl
3. Who brought two more vegetables than fruits? skunk
4. Which two animals brought one more fruit than vegetables? rabbit and squirrel
5. Which two animals brought the most vegetables? deer and racoon
6. Which two animals brought the most fruit? deer and owl
7. Which animal brought the least vegetables? rabbit
8. Which animal brought the least fruit? skunk
9. Who brought more fruit, Skunk and Squirrel, or Raccoon and Rabbit? racoon & rabbit

Page 111

Circus Fun

Add. Remember to add the ones first.

25 + 14 = 39
53 + 32 = 85
71 + 28 = 99
44 + 32 = 76
51 + 37 = 88
26 + 52 = 78
26 + 42 = 68
37 + 51 = 88
19 + 30 = 49

Page 112

Anchors Away

Add. Use the code to find the answer to this riddle:

What did the pirate have to do before every trip out to sea?

48	36	58	96	69	75	89	29
O	H	G	B	T	E	N	A

42 + 16 = 58 G; 34 + 41 = 75 E; 60 + 9 = 69 T

17 + 31 = 48 O; 55 + 34 = 89 N

26 + 43 = 69 T; 14 + 22 = 36 H; 52 + 23 = 75 E

83 + 13 = 96 B; 24 + 24 = 48 O; 5 + 24 = 29 A; 52 + 17 = 69 T

Page 113

Digital Addition

Add ones first. 4 + 2 = 6 — 24 + 32 = 6

Then, add tens. 2 + 3 = 5 — 24 + 32 = 56

17 + 21 = 38 | 34 + 52 = 86 | 5 + 62 = 67 | 6 + 52 = 58

20 + 40 = 60 | 51 + 8 = 59 | 72 + 17 = 89 | 47 + 21 = 68

25 + 62 = 87 | 42 + 24 = 66 | 83 + 14 = 97 | 32 + 25 = 57

44 + 31 = 75 | 8 + 31 = 39 | 62 + 17 = 79 | 82 + 7 = 89

Page 114

Nutty Addition

Sam Squirrel and his friend Wendy were gathering acorns. When they got 10 acorns, they put them in a bucket. The picture shows how many acorns Sam and Wendy each gathered. Write the number that tells how many.

tens 3, ones 6 — 36

tens 2, ones 7 — 27

How many acorns did Sam and Wendy gather in all? To find out:

1. Put numbers on ten's and one's table. 36 + 27
2. Add ones first. 36 + 27 = 3 (Ring 10. Regroup 13 ones as 1 ten 3 ones.)
3. Add tens. 36 + 27 = 63

Sam and Wendy gathered 63 in all.

Try this. Add. Regroup as needed.

38 + 46 = 84 | 54 + 27 = 81 | 49 + 13 = 62 | 26 + 17 = 43

Page 115

Keep On Truckin'

Write each sum. Connect the sums of 83 to make a road for the truck.

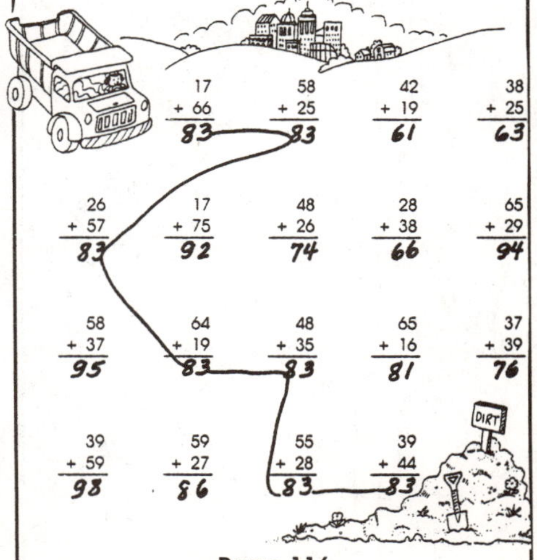

17 + 66 = 83 | 58 + 25 = 83 | 42 + 19 = 61 | 38 + 25 = 63

26 + 57 = 83 | 17 + 75 = 92 | 48 + 26 = 74 | 28 + 38 = 66 | 65 + 29 = 94

58 + 37 = 95 | 64 + 19 = 83 | 48 + 35 = 83 | 65 + 16 = 81 | 37 + 39 = 76

39 + 59 = 98 | 59 + 27 = 86 | 55 + 28 = 83 | 39 + 44 = 83

Page 116

Just Like Magic

Add. Write each answer.

a 25 + 49 = 74
i 54 + 26 = 80
r 36 + 19 = 55
o 58 + 17 = 75
e 16 + 18 = 34
y 28 + 37 = 65
s 29 + 32 = 61
w 62 + 29 = 91
t 18 + 35 = 53
u 38 + 12 = 50
m 46 + 25 = 71
h 47 + 29 = 76
c 69 + 27 = 96
l 39 + 49 = 88

Use the answers and the letter on each lamp to solve the code.

May (71 74 65) all (74 88 88) your (65 75 50 55)

wishes (91 80 61 76 34 61) come (96 75 71 34) true! (53 55 50 34)

Page 117

Squirrelly Fun

Add. Regroup as needed. Match the squirrels to their trees.

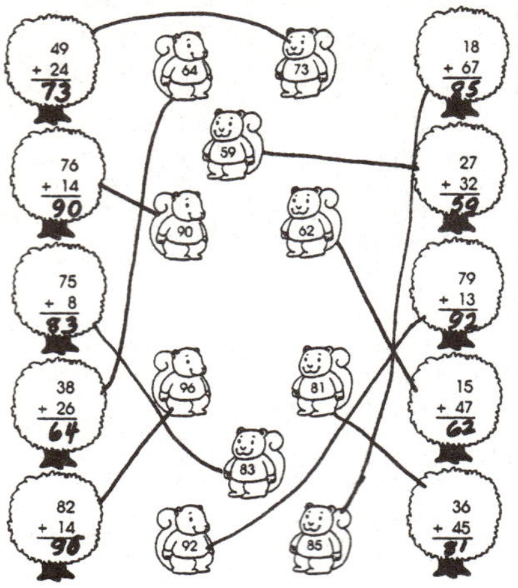

Page 118

Fishy Business

Write the numbers and subtract.

tens	ones		tens	ones
4	2		5	6
- 2	1		- 3	3
2	1		2	3

tens	ones		tens	ones
7	3		7	5
- 4	1		- 4	0
3	2		3	5

tens	ones		tens	ones
6	8		8	3
- 5	2		- 5	1
1	6		3	2

tens	ones		tens	ones
4	7		5	6
- 2	7		- 4	4
2	0		1	2

Page 119

Cookie Mania

There are 46 cookies.
Bill eats 22 cookies.
How many are left?

46
− 22

1. Put numbers on ten's and one's table.
2. Subtract ones.
3. Subtract tens.

tens	ones
4	6
− 2	2
2	4

There are 24 cookies left.

Try these. Subtract the ones first. Then subtract the tens.

78 − 25 = 53; 59 − 36 = 23; 83 − 61 = 22; 67 − 43 = 24

Rewrite in column form. Subtract ones, then tens.

97 − 14 = 83 54 − 30 = 24

Page 120

Prehistoric Problems

Work problems. Use color code. 25—blue, 31—yellow, 57—green, 14—orange, 21—brown, 11—red

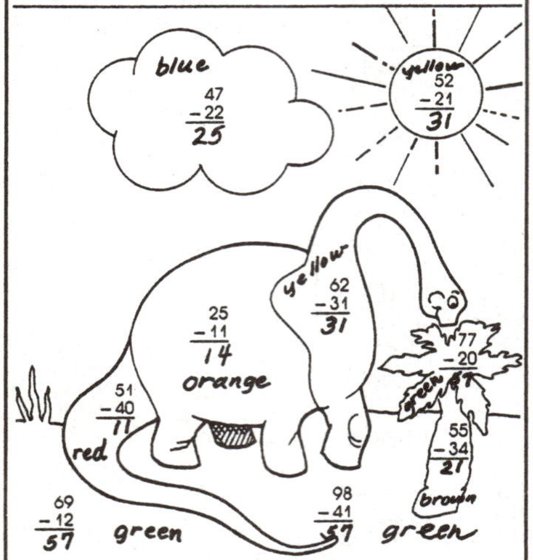

Page 121

Cookie Craze!

Subtract. Circle the difference. Color the cookies with differences greater than 30.

49 − 23 = 26 (16, 26, 25)
67 − 41 = 26 (26, 15, 62)
58 − 37 = 21 (81, 11, 21)
75 − 50 = 25 (20, 25, 35)
86 − 21 = 65 (67, 86, 65) color
64 − 52 = 12 (12, 26, 16)
97 − 65 = 32 (31, 33, 32) color
77 − 43 = 34 (34, 43, 39) color
49 − 13 = 36 (56, 36, 37) color

Page 122

Shell Subtraction

Ellen found 32 shells on the beach. She gave 15 shells to Cindy. How many shells does Ellen have now? To find out:

1. Put numbers on ten's and one's table.
2. Subtract ones. Ask: Do I need to regroup?
3. Subtract tens.

32 = 2 tens and 12 ones

tens	ones
~~3~~ 2	~~2~~ 12
− 1	5
1	7

Ellen has 17 shells now.

Try this. Subtract. Regroup as needed.

31 − 17 = 24; 45 − 38 = 7 (3 | 7); 40 − 26 = 24; 36 − 19 = 17

Page 123

Driving You Crazy

Match the drivers to their cars.

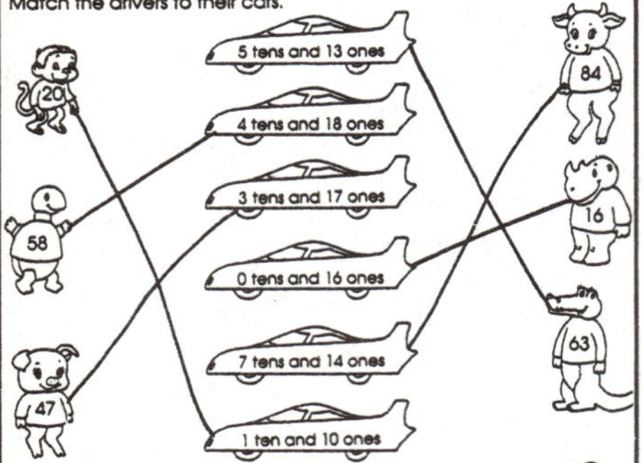

Regroup. Write how many tens and ones.

Answers may vary.

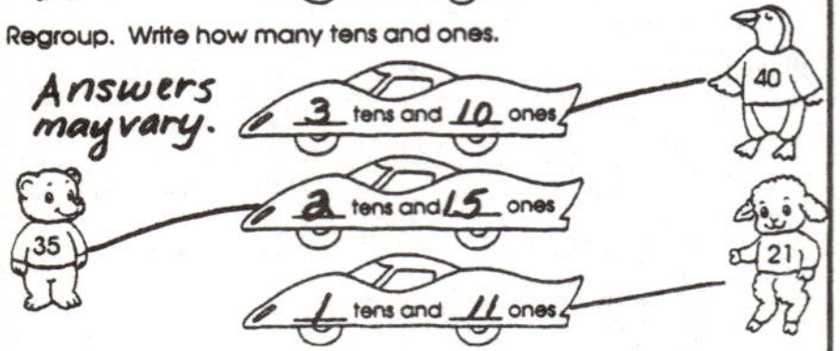

Page 124

Hatta Boy!

Subtract. Regroup as needed. Write your answers on the hats.

Page 125

Subtraction on the Beach

Subtract. Regroup as needed. Color the spaces with differences of:

10-19	red	30-39	green
50-59	brown	20-29	blue
40-49	yellow	60-69	orange

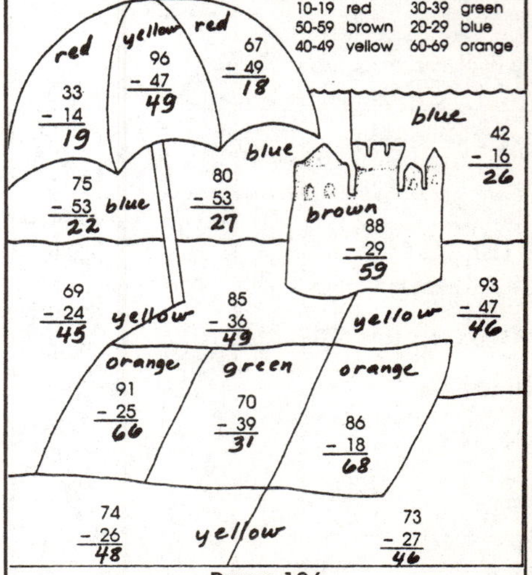

Page 126

How's Your Pitch?

Subtract. Write each answer.

Letter	Problem	Answer
u	95 − 19	76
n	64 − 47	17
t	80 − 28	52
r	71 − 38	33
a	83 − 58	25
h	94 − 26	68
y	75 − 39	36
i	90 − 29	61
c	93 − 36	57
o	81 − 37	44
e	71 − 18	53
g	84 − 45	39
s	50 − 38	12
p	72 − 44	28

Use the answers and the letters on the baseballs to solve the code.

your (36 44 76 33) pitch (28 61 52 57 68) is (61 12)
right (33 61 39 68 52) on (44 17) target (52 25 33 39 53 52)!

Page 127

Airport Action

To find out if the answer to a subtraction problem is correct, add the answer to the number taken away. If the sum is the same as the first number in the subtraction problem, then the answer is correct.

Example 1

$43 - 27 = 16 \rightarrow 16 + 27 = 43$

Since the sum is the same as the first number in the subtraction problem, the answer to the subtraction problem must be correct.

Example 2

$71 - 28 = 43 \rightarrow 43 + 28 = 71$

Check the subtraction by adding.

$52 - 37 = 25 \rightarrow 25 + 37 = 62$

Is the subtraction problem correct? no
How do you know? Answer does not match first number.

Subtract. Then add to check.

$52 - 37 = 15 \rightarrow 15 + 37 = 52$ | $80 - 26 = 54 \rightarrow 54 + 26 = 80$ | $64 - 48 = 16 \rightarrow 16 + 48 = 64$

Page 128

Playing in the Park

Circle **Add** or **Subtract**. Then, write a number sentence to solve each problem. Think and check to see if your answer makes sense.

1. There are 6 swings. Four children are swinging. How many swings are empty?
   Add (Subtract) — 6−4=2; 2 swings
2. The slide has 8 steps. Craig climbed 3 steps. How many more steps must he climb?
   Add (Subtract) — 8−3=5; 5 steps
3. Ellen went across the monkey bars 5 times. So did Brooke. How many times did both girls go across?
   (Add) Subtract — 5+5=10; 10 times
4. Three girls sat on one park bench. Three boys sat on another bench. How many children are sitting on both benches?
   (Add) Subtract — 3+3=6; 6 children

Page 129

Superstar Students

Fill in the table using the information given. Then answer the questions.

Second Grade Students at Superstar School

Class	Boys	Girls	Total
A	11	17	28
B	12	15	27
C	9	14	23
Total	32	46	78

1. Which class has the most students? A
2. Which class has the least students? C
3. How many more girls than boys are in second grade? 14
4. Which class has the most boys? B
5. Which class has the least girls? C
6. If each boy in class A gave his teacher an apple, how many apples would she get? 11
7. How many students are in second grade at Superstar School? 78 Outline in red the box that tells this.
8. How many more students are in class A than class C? 5
9. If each boy in class B gave a girl in class A an apple, how many girls would not get an apple? 5
10. If 9 students move away, how many students would be in second grade then? 69

Page 130

Tree Troubles

Help the squirrels get to their trees. Add or subtract in your head. Write the final answer on the tree.

- 3 + 4 + 5 − 3 − 2 = 7
- 5 − 2 + 6 + 3 − 4 = 8
- 9 − 3 + 5 − 4 + 2 = 9
- 6 + 6 − 5 + 3 − 2 = 8
- 8 + 4 − 6 + 5 − 3 = 8

Page 131

Roll Call

Look at the animals at the top of the page. Write the correct word to tell where each animal is standing in the line.

1. eighth
2. tenth
3. ninth
4. sixth
5. second
6. fifth
7. third
8. seventh
9. first
10. fourth

Word Bank
first
second
third
fourth
fifth
sixth
seventh
eighth
ninth
tenth

Page 132

My First Treat Will Be . . .

Circle the ordinal number word for each treat.

- third, sixteenth, (fifth)
- fifteenth, (fourth), first
- (twelfth), second, seventh
- third, eleventh, (fifteenth)
- eighth, first, (tenth)
- (sixteenth), thirteenth, third
- ninth, second, (thirteenth)
- sixth, (seventh), ninth,

Page 133

Two by Two

Finish counting.

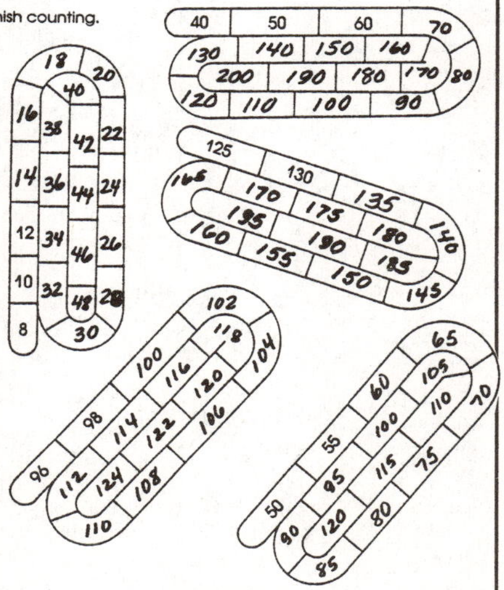

Page 134

Critter Count

Number of turtles's found. turtle = 5

= 20
= 35
= 15

Number of snail's found. snail = 10

= 50
= 60
= 30

Number of worm's found. worm = 2

= 16
= 6
= 10

Page 135

Who Has the Most?

Circle the right answer.

1. Jane has 3 's.
Bob has 4 's.
Bill has 5 's.

Who has the most 's?

Jane Bob **(Bill)**

2. Pam has 7 's.
Joe has 5 's.
Jane has 6 's.

Who has the most 's?

(Pam) Joe Jane

3. Amy has 23 's.
Sandy has 19 's.
Jack has 25 's.
Who has the most 's?

Amy Sandy **(Jack)**

4. Ann has 19 's.
Burt has 18 's.
Brent has 17 's.
Who has the most 's?

(Ann) Burt Brent

5. The boys have 14 's.
The girls have 16 's.
The teachers have 17 's.

Who has the most 's?

boys girls **(teachers)**

6. Rose has 12 's.
Betsy has 11 's.
Ann has 13 's.
Who has the most 's?

Rose Betsy **(Ann)**

Page 136

Who Has the Least?

Circle the right answer.

1. Pat had 4 's.
Charles had 3 's.
Jane had 5 's.

Who had the least number of 's?

Pat **(Charles)** Jane

2. Jeff has 5 's.
John has 4 's.
Bill has 6 's.

Who has the least number of 's?

Jeff **(John)** Bill

3. Jane has 7 's.
Peg has 9 's.
Fred has 8 's.
Who has the least number of 's?

(Jane) Peg Fred

4. Charles bought 12 's.
Rose bought 6 's.
Mother bought 24 's.
Who bought the least number of 's?

Charles **(Rose)** Mother

5. John had 9 's.
Jack had 8 's.
Jeff had 7 's.
Who had the least number of 's?

John Jack **(Jeff)**

6. Alma bought 12 's.
Nina bought 16 's.
Marty bought 13 's.
Who bought the least number of 's?

(Alma) Nina Marty

Page 137

Munch a Bunch

Gertrude Goat and her friends Ginger, George, and Gus are making special popcorn balls. Each piece of popcorn has a number on it.

Read the clues to find out which pieces of popcorn each goat will use for his/her popcorn ball. Write the numbers on the popcorn.

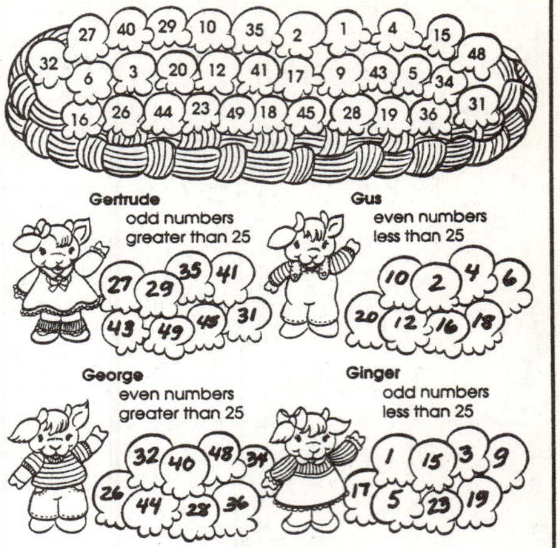
27 40 29 10 35 2 1 4 15
32 6 3 20 12 41 17 9 43 5 48 34
16 26 44 23 49 18 45 28 19 36 31
Gertrude
odd numbers greater than 25
27 29 35 41 43 49 45 31
Gus
even numbers less than 25
10 2 4 6 20 12 16 18
George
even numbers greater than 25
32 40 48 34 26 44 28 36
Ginger
odd numbers less than 25
1 15 3 9 17 5 23 19

Page 138

"Mouth" Math

Write < or > in each circle. Make sure the "mouth" is open toward the greater number!

36 (<) 49	35 (<) 53
20 (>) 18	74 (>) 21
53 (<) 76	68 (<) 80
29 (>) 26	45 (>) 19
90 (>) 89	70 (>) 67

Page 139

Right on Time

Cut out the time signs at the bottom of the page. Paste each sign on the engine next to the correct clock.

5:00
8:00
4:00
9:00
3:00
10:00
2:00
1:00
12:00
11:00
7:00
6:00

Page 140

Space Time

What time is it?

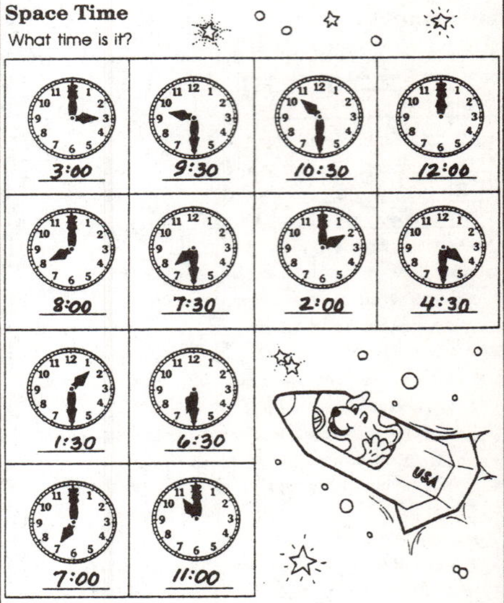
3:00
9:30
10:30
12:00
8:00
7:30
2:00
4:30
1:30
6:30
7:00
11:00
USA

Page 141

Turtle Time

What time is it?

9:10
8:25
10:05
8:20
1:45
7:55
8:15
3:50
2:35
7:30
2:40

Page 142

My Family Time Tree

Write the time.
Draw the hands on each clock.

I get up at_____ I go to bed at_____

School starts at_____ I watch TV at_____

Lunch is at_____ Answers will vary. Dinner is at_____

Recess is at_____ School ends at_____ I play at_____

Page 143

Time to Clean Up

Match the digital time with each clock face by cutting and pasting each lid on the correct trash can.

9:05
12:25
5:40
11:20
4:15
7:35
8:00
2:55
1:30
10:50
3:10
6:45

Page 144

It's About Time!

Trace each mouse with red if it has a time word.

minute, day, week, catch, flower, second, month, patch, hour, year

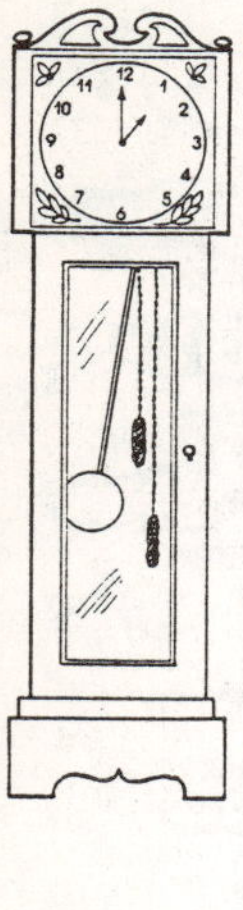

Draw a circle around the correct answer.

1. There are sixty seconds in a minute. / year.
2. There are sixty minutes in an second. / hour.
3. There are 24 hours in a minute. / day.
4. There are 365 days in a year. / week.
5. There are seven days in a week. / hour.
6. There are twelve months in a year. / week.

Page 145

Postage Stamp, Please

Add up the coins on each envelope. Write the total on the stamp.

10¢, 10¢, 1¢, 5¢, 1¢, 1¢ — 28¢	10¢, 10¢, 10¢, 10¢, 1¢, 5¢, 1¢ — 47¢
10¢, 10¢, 5¢, 5¢, 5¢, 1¢ — 36¢	10¢, 10¢, 10¢, 10¢, 10¢, 10¢, 5¢, 1¢ — 66¢
10¢, 10¢, 10¢, 10¢, 10¢, 5¢, 1¢ — 56¢	10¢, 10¢, 10¢, 10¢, 10¢, 10¢, 10¢, 1¢, 5¢ — 71¢
10¢, 1¢, 5¢, 1¢, 1¢ — 18¢	5¢, 5¢, 5¢, 5¢, 1¢, 10¢, 10¢, 1¢ — 42¢

Page 146

Pencil Topper Purchases

Peggy wants to buy three different pencil toppers. Look at the cost of each topper.

bear 5¢, penguin 3¢, elephant 2¢, mouse 6¢, pig 1¢, duck 8¢, cat 4¢, monkey 7¢

Peggy has 12¢ to spend. Write the names of the different pencil topper combinations she might pick.

1. bear	1. monkey	1. bear
2. penguin	2. cat	2. mouse
3. cat	3. pig	3. pig
1. cat	1. duck	1. monkey
2. mouse	2. pig	2. penguin
3. elephant	3. penguin	3. elephant

Page 147

Mall Mania

Count the coins in each purse. Then draw a line from each coin purse to the store where that amount is given.

Birthday Boutique — Cards 16¢
Fish World — Goldfish 11¢
Traveler's Helper — Mini-Travel Games 22¢
Soda Shop — 12¢
Young Scientist's Wonderland — All Rocks 41¢

Purses: 5¢, 5¢, 1¢, 1¢ | 25¢, 10¢, 5¢, 1¢ | 10¢, 1¢, 1¢, 10¢ | 10¢, 1¢, 5¢

In which store did you not spend any money? Fish World

Page 148

So Many Choices!

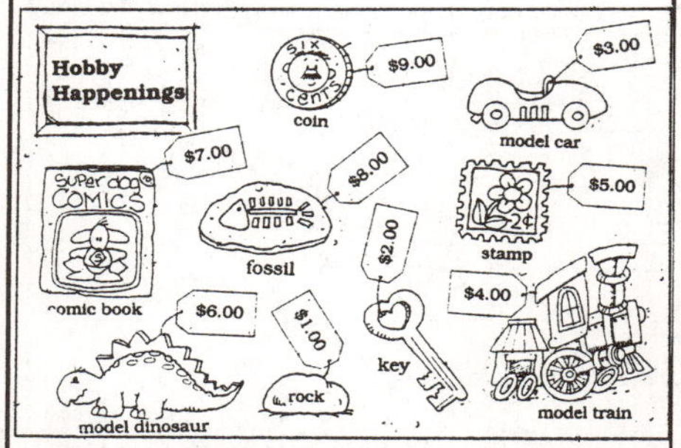

Hobby Happenings
coin $9.00
model car $3.00
comic book $7.00
fossil $8.00
stamp $5.00
$2.00
key
$4.00
$6.00
$1.00
rock
model dinosaur
model train

You want to buy 3 **different** items in the hobby store. You have $16.00. Write all the different combinations of items you can buy using the entire $16.00.

1. comic book	1. comic book	1. model train	1. coin
2. dinosaur	2. rock	2. stamp	2. key
3. model car	3. fossil	3. comic book	3. stamp
1. coin	1. fossil	1. model car	1. coin
2. model car	2. key	2. stamp	2. rock
3. model train	3. dinosaur	3. fossil	3. dinosaur

Page 149

Earnings Add Up!

Help Wanted

Wash dishes $1.50 | Feed cat $.95 | Mow lawn $3.50
Mop floors $1.25 | Pick tomatoes $2.75 | Wash windows $2.85

Use the Help Wanted poster above to help you find out how much you can earn by doing each set of jobs. Write the total amount for each set.

1. feed cat 2. pick tomatoes 3. wash dishes $5.20	1. wash dishes 2. mow lawn 3. wash windows $7.85	1. wash windows 2. mop floors 3. mow lawn $7.60	1. feed cat 2. wash windows 3. mop floors $5.05
1. pick tomatoes 2. wash windows 3. feed cat $6.55	1. feed cat 2. wash dishes 3. mop floors $3.70	1. pick tomatoes 2. wash windows 3. mow lawn $9.10	1. mop floors 2. pick tomatoes 3. wash windows $6.85

Page 150

Here's Your Order

Count the money on each tray. Write the name of the food that costs that amount.

hamburger .. $2.45	milk .... $.64	cake $2.85
hot dog $1.77	soda pop $1.26	pie $2.25
sandwich $1.55	milkshake ... $1.89	sundae ...... $.95

50¢, 1¢, 25¢, 10¢, 1¢, 1¢, 1¢, $1.00 — milkshake	$1.00, 5¢, 10¢, 5¢, 5¢, 5¢, 25¢ — sandwich
$1.00, 1¢, 5¢, 25¢, 10¢, 1¢, 25¢, 10¢ — hot dog	10¢, 10¢, 50¢, 5¢, 5¢, 5¢, $1.00, $1.00 — cake
25¢, 10¢, 25¢, 10¢, 10¢, 10¢, 5¢ — sundae	10¢, 5¢, 10¢, 5¢, 5¢, 5¢, $1.00, $1.00, 5¢ — hamburger

Page 151

Flowers That "Measure" Up

Cut out the centimeter ruler at the bottom of the page. Use the ruler to measure how tall each flower is from the bottom of the stem to the top of the flower. Write the answer below the bee.

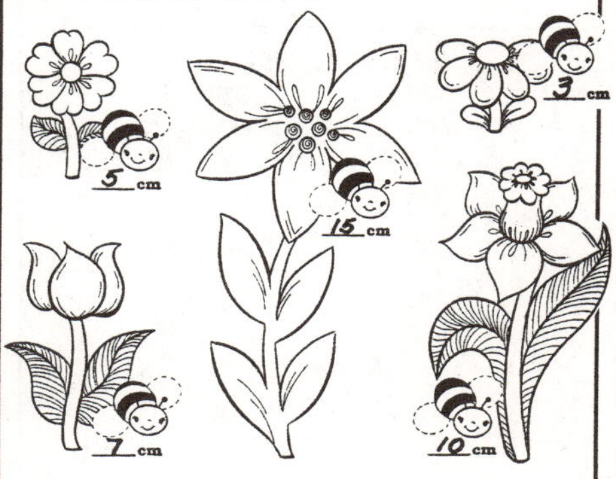

5 cm
15 cm
3 cm
7 cm
10 cm

Page 152

Brush Up on Measuring!

Use your centimeter ruler to measure these brushes to the nearest centimeter.

about 9 centimeters — about 6 centimeters

about 4 centimeters — about 11 centimeters

about 8 centimeters — about 3 centimeters

about 14 centimeters

about 10 centimeters — about 2 centimeters

about 17 centimeters

Page 153

Jungle Journey

Use a centimeter ruler to measure the line segments. Write the total length on each hut.

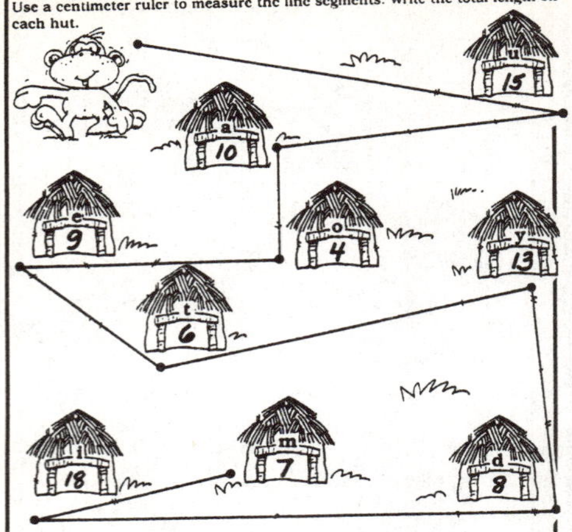
15
a
10
c
9
o
4
y
13
t
6
i
18
m
7
d
8

Use the numbers and the letters on the huts to solve the code.

y o u   m a d e   i t !
13 4 15   7 10 8 9   18 6

Page 154

Jumping Jellybeans

Use an inch ruler to measure the line segments. Write the total length on each candy jar.

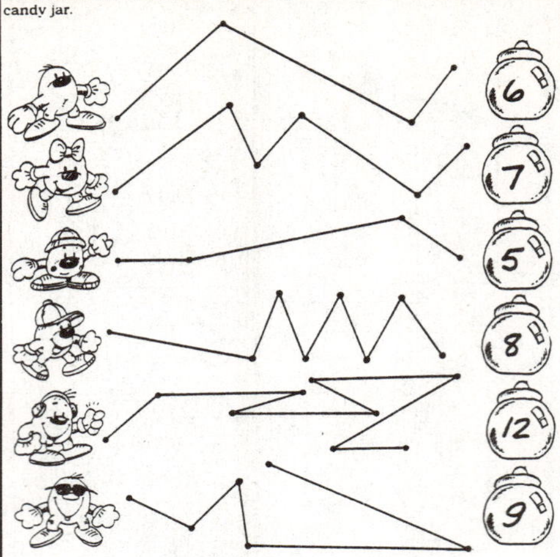
6
7
5
8
12
9

Page 155

The Inch Worm

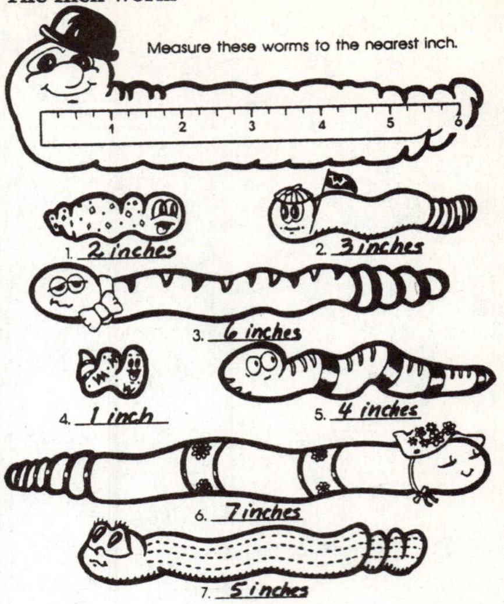
Measure these worms to the nearest inch.
1 2 3 4 5 6
1. 2 inches
2. 3 inches
3. 6 inches
4. 1 inch
5. 4 inches
6. 7 inches
7. 5 inches

Page 156

How Big Are You?

You are getting so big! Every day, you grow a little more. Estimate how long some of your body parts are. Then, using a ruler, work with a friend to find the actual measurements.

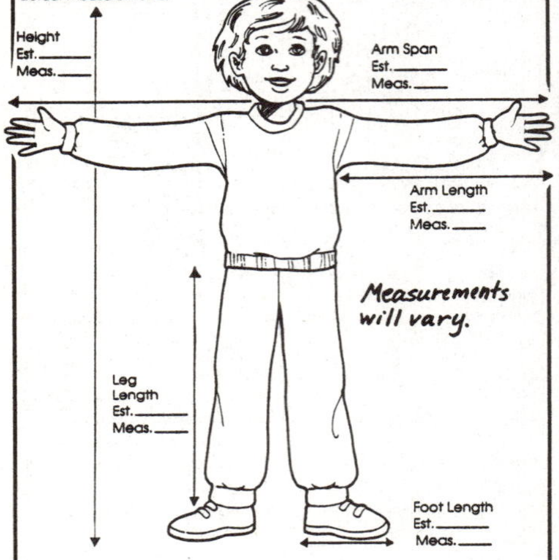
Height
Est.
Meas.
Arm Span
Est.
Meas.
Arm Length
Est.
Meas.
Measurements will vary.
Leg Length
Est.
Meas.
Foot Length
Est.
Meas.

Page 157

How Far Is It?

Use your ruler to measure each distance on the map. Then use the letters on the tires and your answers to solve the message at the bottom of the page.

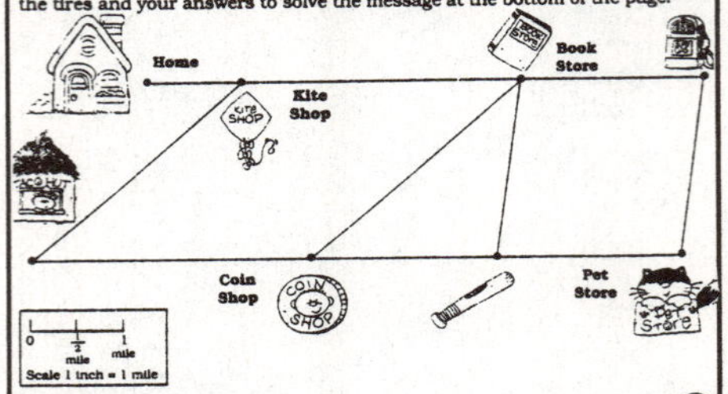
Home
Kite Shop
Book Store
Coin Shop
Pet Store
0 ½ mile 1 mile
Scale 1 inch = 1 mile

How far is it from . . .

1. home to the Kite Shop? *1 mile* (s)
2. home to the Book Store to the Gas Station? *6 miles* (e)
3. home to the Kite Shop to the Taco Hut? *4 miles* (p)
4. the Taco Hut to the Coin Shop to the Book Store to the Gas Station? *8 miles* (a)
5. the Taco Hut to the Coin Shop? *3 miles* (u)
6. the Baseball Field to the Book Store to the Kite Shop? *5 miles* (d)
7. the Pet Store to the Gas Station? *2 miles* (r)
8. the Gas Station to the Pet Store to the Baseball Field to the Coin Shop to the Taco Hut? *9 miles* (m)

You *m e a s u r e d   u p* !
9 6 8 1 3 2 6 5   3 4

Page 158

Liquid Limits

Draw a line from the containers on the left to the containers on the right that will hold the same amount of liquid. **Hint:** 2 pints = 1 quart.

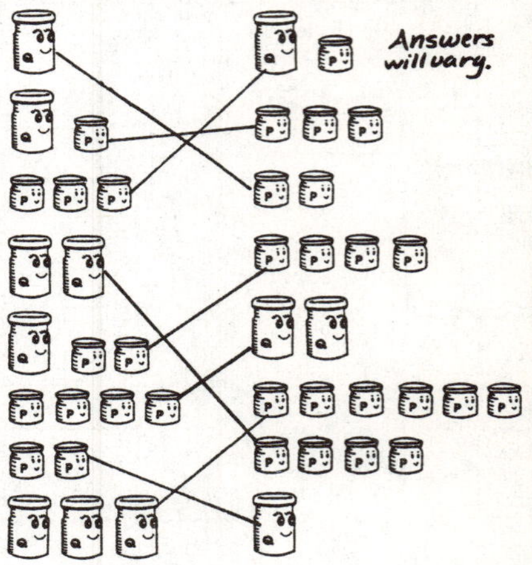
Answers will vary.

Page 159

Shape Sort

Color the ones in each row that are the same size and shape. Write T for triangle, R for rectangle and S for square.

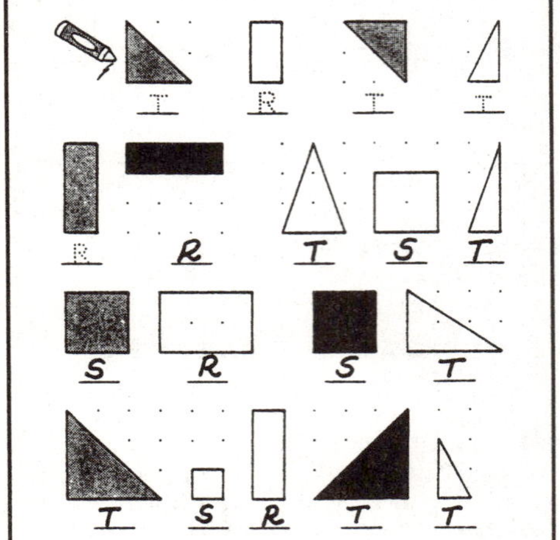
T R T T
R R T S T
S R S T
T S R T T

Page 160

Sea Shapes

Find the shapes and color them using the code.

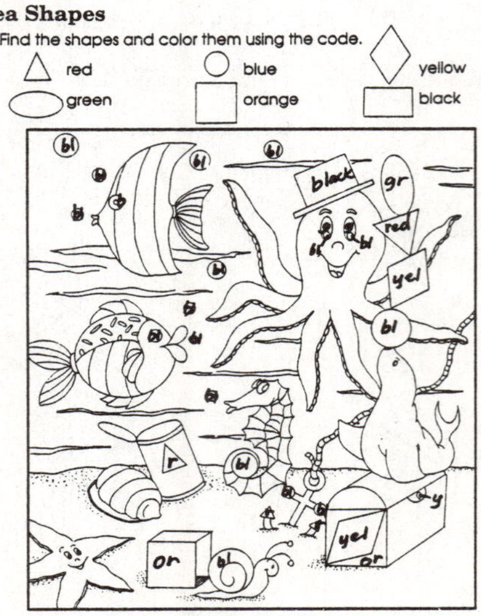
red
blue
yellow
green
orange
black
black
gr
red
yel
bl
yel
or

Page 161

Equal and Unequal Parts

Cut out each shape below along the solid lines. Then fold the shape on the dotted lines. Do you get equal or unequal parts? Sort the shapes into two piles: those with equal parts and those with unequal parts.

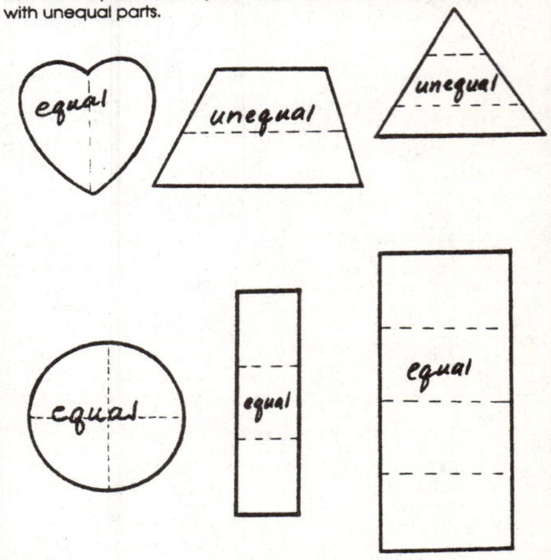
equal
unequal
unequal
equal
equal
equal

Page 162

Mean Monster's Diet

Mean Monster has to go on a diet. He is so fat he popped all the buttons off his shirt. Help him choose the right piece of food.

1. Mean Monster may have 1/4 of this chocolate pie. Color in 1/4 of the pie.

2. Mean Monster may eat 1/3 of this pizza. Color in 1/3 of the pizza.

3. For a snack, he wants 1/3 of this chocolate cake. Color in 1/3 of the cake.

4. For lunch, Mean Monster gets 1/2 of the sandwich. Color in 1/2 of the sandwich.

5. For an evening snack, he can have 1/4 of the candy bar. Color in 1/4 of the candy bar.

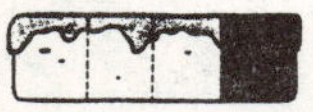

6. He ate 1/2 of the apple for lunch. Color in 1/2 of the apple.

Page 163

Shaded Shapes

Draw line from fraction to correct shape.

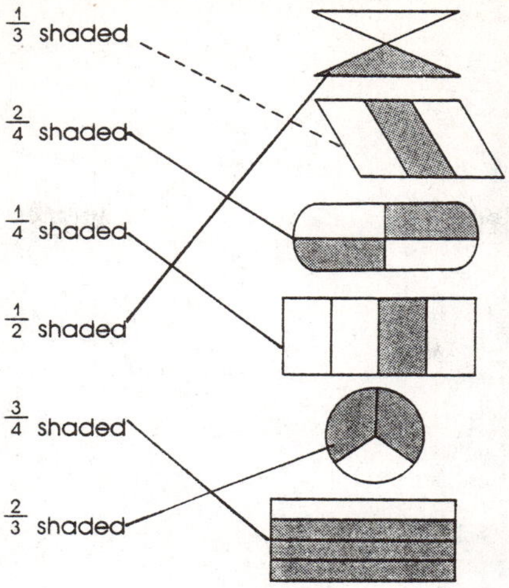

Page 164

Fraction Food

Count the equal parts. Circle the fraction that names one of the parts.

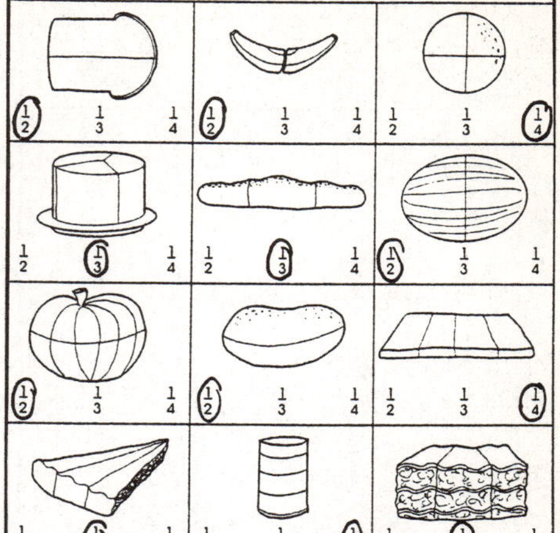

(1/2) 1/3 1/4	(1/2) 1/3 1/4	1/2 1/3 (1/4)
1/2 (1/3) 1/4	1/2 (1/3) 1/4	(1/2) 1/3 1/4
(1/2) 1/3 1/4	(1/2) 1/3 1/4	1/2 1/3 (1/4)
1/2 (1/3) 1/4	1/2 1/3 (1/4)	1/2 (1/3) 1/4

Page 165

Fortunate Fractions

Read the fraction on each tray. Color the correct number of fortune cookies to show each fraction.

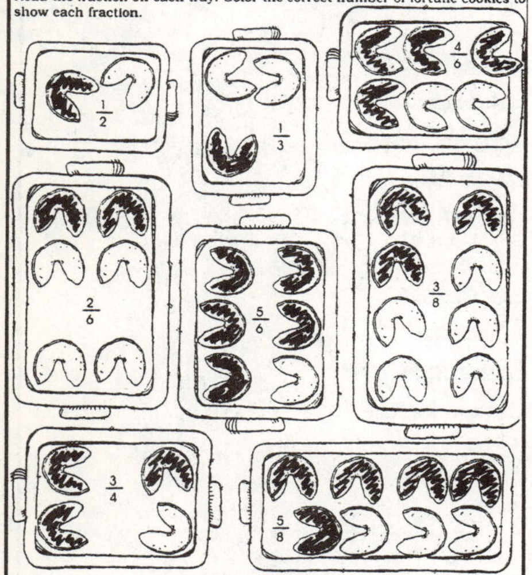

Page 166

Turtle Spots

Count the spots on the turtles.
Color the boxes to show how many spots.

Page 167

Wormy Apples

Color the boxes to show how many worms.
Answer the questions.

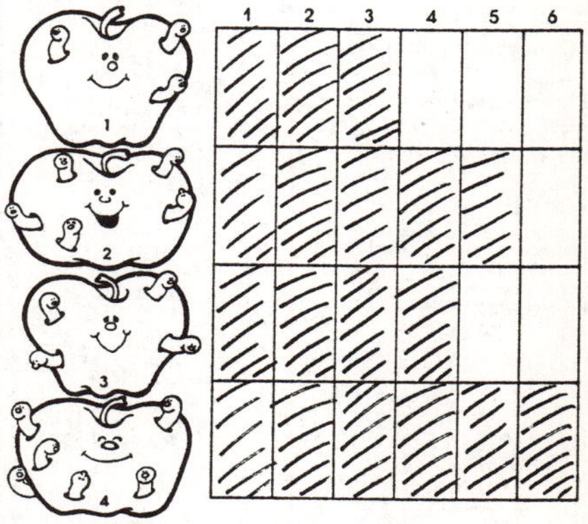

How many worms in apple 1? 3 2? 5 3? 4 4? 6
In apples 1 and 3? 7 In apples 2 and 4? 11
How many more worms in apple 4 than in apple 2? 1
How many more worms in apple 3 than in apple 1? 1

Page 168

Pat's Fish

This picture graph shows how many fish Pat caught.

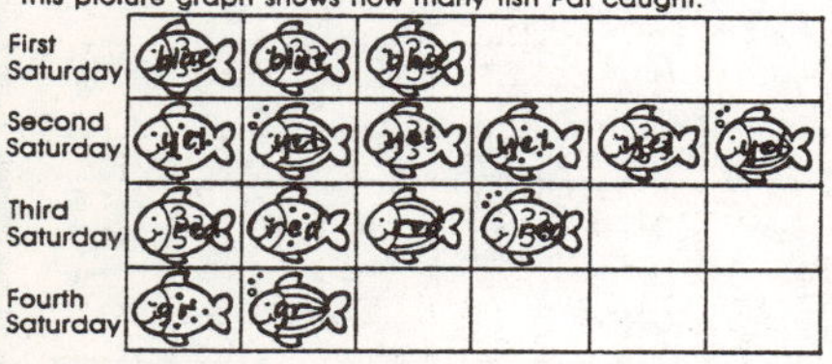

Color the fish Pat caught on the third Saturday red.
Color the fish he caught on the first Saturday blue,
the second Saturday yellow, and the fourth Saturday green.
How many fish did he catch on the first Saturday? 3
second Saturday? 6 third Saturday? 4 fourth Saturday? 2

Page 169

Honey Bear's Bakery

Look at the picture of the bakery. Fill in the graph to show how many of each treat are in the picture.

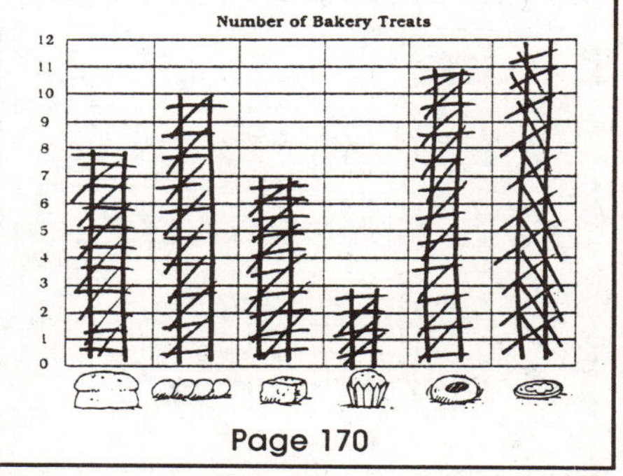

Page 170

Treasure Quest

Read the directions. Draw the pictures where they belong on the grid.
Start at 0 and go . . .

over 2, up 5. Draw a
over 9, up 3. Draw a
over 8, up 6. Draw a
over 5, up 2. Draw a
over 1, up 7. Draw a

over 7, up 1. Draw a
over 6, up 4. Draw a
over 2, up 3. Draw a
over 3, up 1. Draw a
over 4, up 6. Draw a

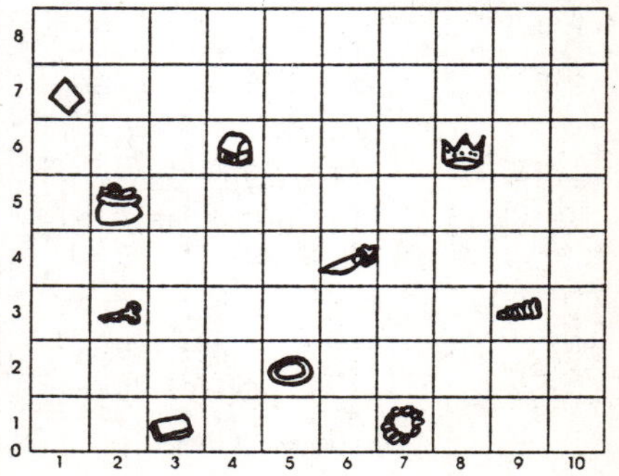

Page 171

0-7682-3792-0 Skills & Practice Gr. 2

Multiplying Rabbits

7 + 7 = 14
2 sevens = 14
2 × 7 = 14

8 + 8 = 16
2 eights = 16
2 × 8 = 16

2 + 2 + 2 + 2 = 8
4 twos = 8
4 × 2 = 8

3 + 3 + 3 + 3 + 3 = 15
5 threes = 15
5 × 3 = 15

4 + 4 + 4 = 12
3 fours = 12
3 × 4 = 12

9 + 9 = 18
2 nines = 18
2 × 9 = 18

5 + 5 + 5 = 15
3 fives = 15
3 × 5 = 15

6 + 6 = 12
2 sixes = 12
2 × 6 = 12

3 + 3 + 3 + 3 = 12
4 threes = 12
4 × 3 = 12

4 + 4 = 8
2 fours = 8
2 × 4 = 8

Page 172

Mr. X and His Cookies

Draw a line from each picture to its matching problem.

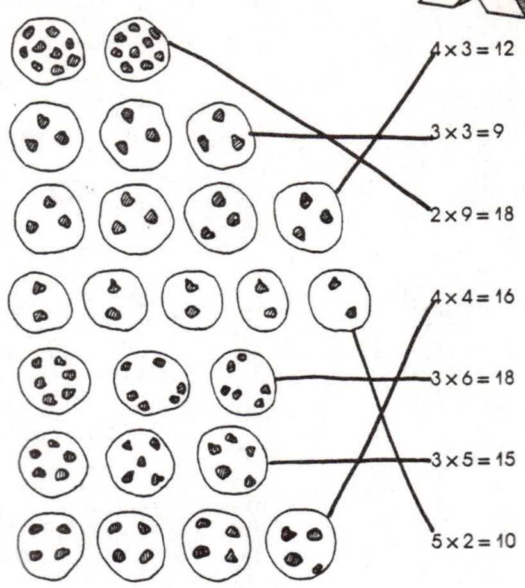

4 × 3 = 12
3 × 3 = 9
2 × 9 = 18
4 × 4 = 16
3 × 6 = 18
3 × 5 = 15
5 × 2 = 10

Page 173

Move That Body

Read a task on the chart. Color the spaces on the chart which show the parts of the body that would be used for the task.

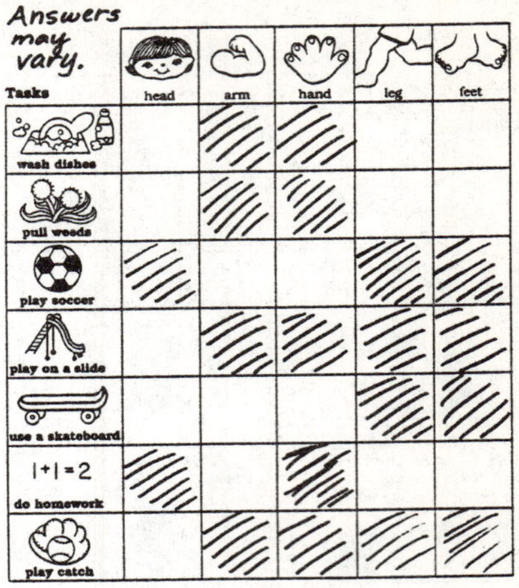

Answers may vary.
Tasks
head
arm
hand
leg
feet
wash dishes
pull weeds
play soccer
play on a slide
use a skateboard
1 + 1 = 2
do homework
play catch

Page 174

Body Works

Read the clues. Write the words in the puzzle.

Across:

2. You use these to breathe.
4. You need to do this when you're tired.
5. This breaks down food.
7. This tells your body what to do.
9. A gas you breathe.
10. It pumps blood.

Down:

1. It carries oxygen to your body.
3. Microscopic living things that can make you sick.
6. This helps when you are sick.
8. These support and shape your body.

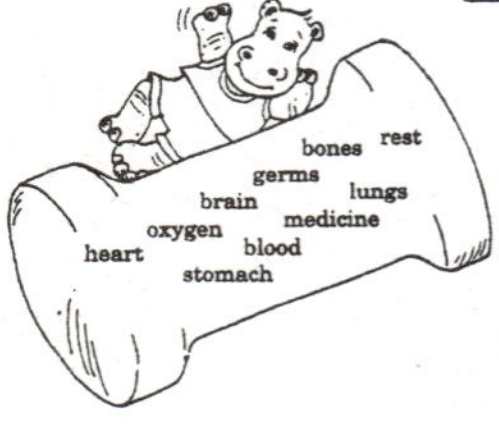

bones
rest
germs
brain
lungs
medicine
oxygen
blood
heart
stomach

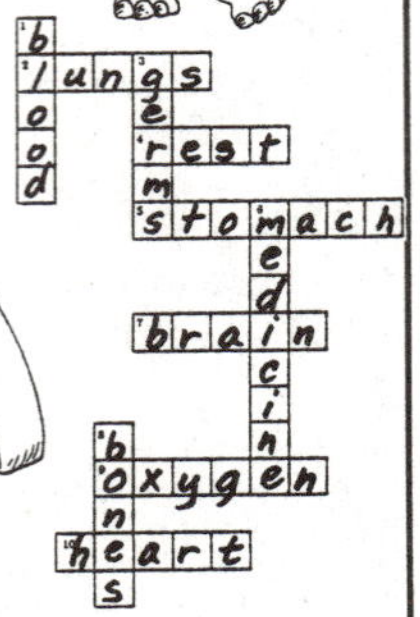

blood
lungs
germs
rest
stomach
medicine
brain
bones
oxygen
heart

Page 175

My Bones

Bones give your body shape. They let you stand up tall. You cannot see your bones. But you can feel many of your bones under your skin.

Draw a line from each bone to the part of the body where it is found. Write the name of the bone(s).

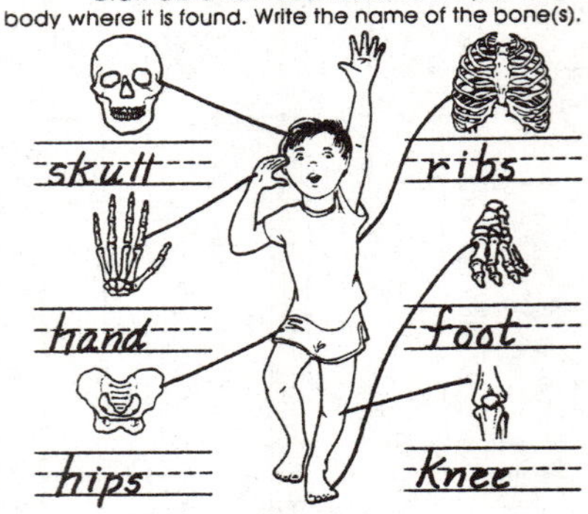

skull
ribs
hand
foot
hips
knee

Word Bank

skull, ribs, foot, hand, knee, hips

Page 176

Name That Bone

Name these bones of your skeleton.

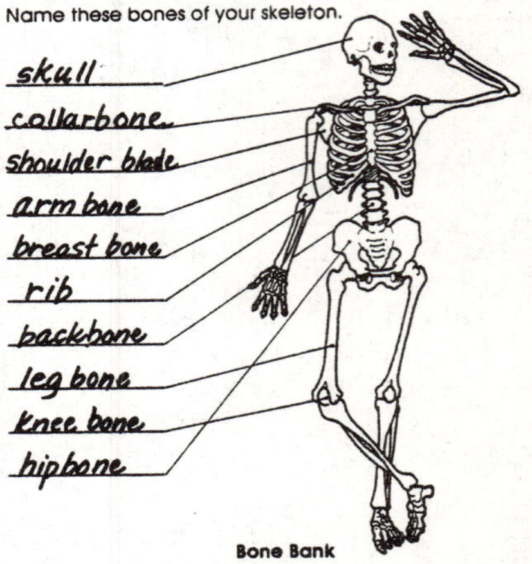

skull
collarbone
shoulder blade
arm bone
breast bone
rib
backbone
leg bone
knee bone
hipbone

Bone Bank

hipbone, arm bone, backbone, rib, collarbone, breastbone, leg bone, skull, knee bone, shoulder blade

Page 177

Crossbones

Across

3. protects your heart and lungs
6. all of your bones
7. connects your leg and foot

Down

1. on the end of your hands
2. on the end of your feet
4. spine
5. makes your leg bend
6. protects your brain

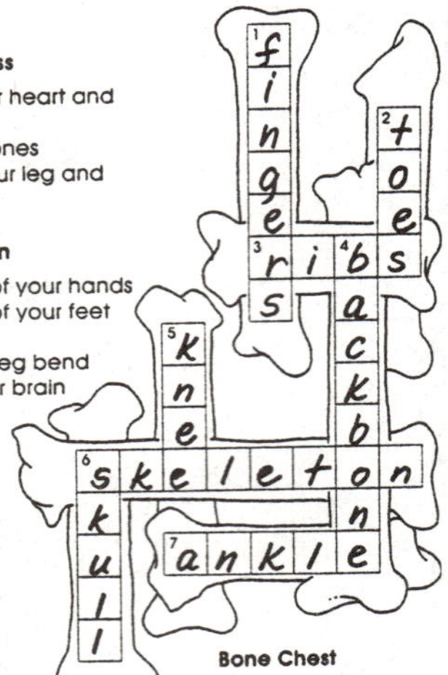

fingers
toes
ribs
backbone
knee
skeleton
skull
ankle

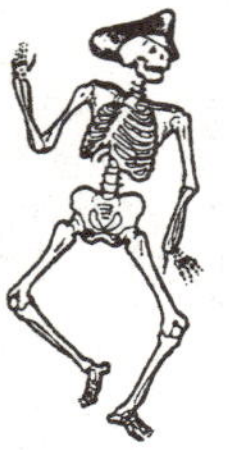

Bone Chest

ribs, toes, fingers, knee, skull, backbone, ankle, skeleton

Page 178

Outfitted for Health

Read the phrases in the Word Bank. Write only the **good** health habits on the lines.

Word Bank			
	Take a bath. Drink water. Sit all day. Exercise.	Eat a lot of sweets Get plenty of sleep. Never wash your hands. Eat healthy foods.	Stay up all night. Keep cuts clean. Brush your teeth.

1. Take a bath.
2. Drink water.
3. Exercise.
4. Eat healthy foods.
5. Get plenty of rest.
6. Keep cuts clean.
7. Brush your teeth.

Page 179

A Delicious Dinner

Pretend that you get to plan a healthful dinner for your family. Write the menu, choosing items from the lists.

Meats	Vegetables	Side Dishes
barbecue chicken	steamed broccoli	brown rice
hamburgers	creamed corn	mashed potatoes
grilled pork chops	buttered peas	baked beans

Answers will vary.

Page 180

A "Sense"-ible Arrangement

Cut out the flowers at the bottom of the page. Pick one flower and look at the object and word on it. Paste the flower on the vase that tells which sense you would mainly use with the object on that flower.

cake
watermelon
taste
knock
bell
hear
perfume
ammonia
smell
star
cloud
see
wind
raindrops
feel

Page 182

Identifying Prints

Cut out the fingerprints at the bottom of the page. Use a magnifying glass to match the cut-out fingerprints to those on the page. Paste each fingerprint next to the one it matches.

Exhibit D
Exhibit C
Exhibit B
Exhibit A
Exhibit F
Exhibit E

Page 183

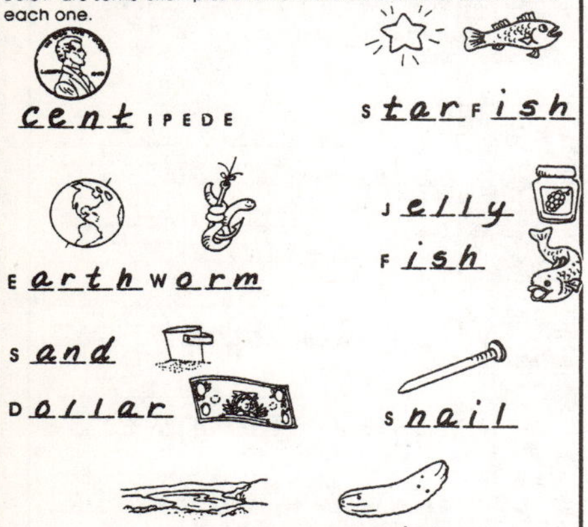

Interesting Invertebrates

Invertebrates are animals that have no backbone or inside skeleton. Some have soft bodies protected by shells. Others have soft bodies that are not protected. Some invertebrates are so small that they can only be seen with a microscope.

Below are some examples of invertebrates. Use the clues to name each one.

cent IPEDE
s tar f ish
J elly
F ish
E arth worm
s and
D ollar
s nail
s ea c ucumber

Page 184

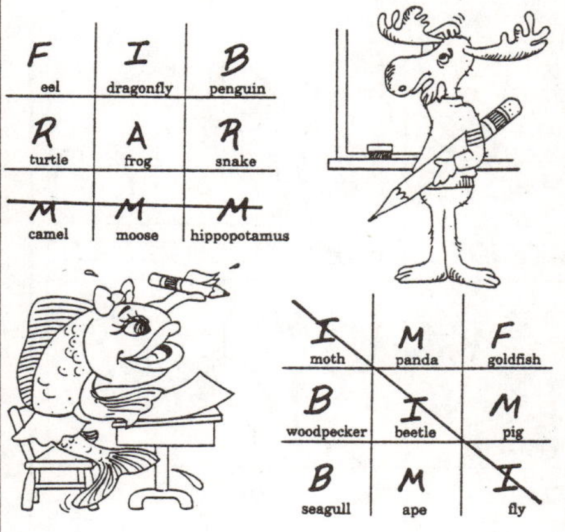

A "Class"-y Group

Read a word. If it names a mammal, write M above the word. If it names a reptile, write R above the word. If it names an amphibian, write A above the word. If it names an insect, write I above the word. If it names a bird, write B above the word. If it names a fish, write F above the word. Then draw a line to show where three of these letters are the same in a row.

F eel	I dragonfly	B penguin
R turtle	A frog	R snake
M camel	M moose	M hippopotamus

I moth	M panda	F goldfish
B woodpecker	I beetle	M pig
B seagull	M ape	I fly

Page 185

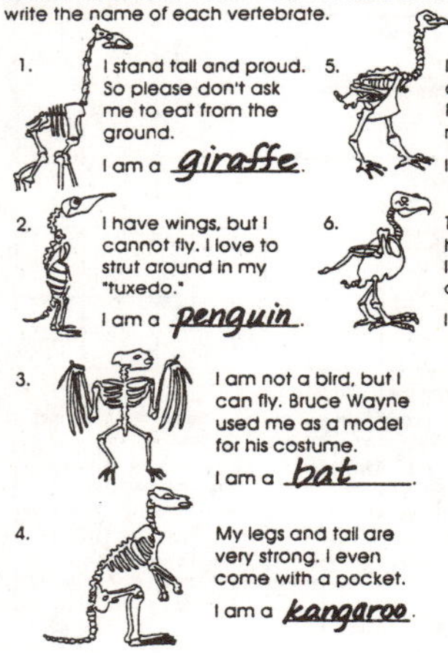

From the Inside Out

Animals whose skeletons have backbones are called **vertebrates**. The backbone, or spine, is made up of bones called **vertebrae**.

Look at the skeletons below. Use the riddle and the Word Bank to write the name of each vertebrate.

1. I stand tall and proud. So please don't ask me to eat from the ground. I am a *giraffe*.
2. I have wings, but I cannot fly. I love to strut around in my "tuxedo." I am a *penguin*.
3. I am not a bird, but I can fly. Bruce Wayne used me as a model for his costume. I am a *bat*.
4. My legs and tail are very strong. I even come with a pocket. I am a *kangaroo*.
5. I am thankful to be alive at holidays. People might "gobble" me up! I am a *turkey*.
6. They say I have no hair, and they're right. I represent a great country. I am a *bald eagle*.

Word Bank
bald eagle
kangaroo
turkey
penguin
giraffe
bat

Page 186

Fine, Feathered Friends

Do the puzzle about birds.
Color only the birds.

1 feathers
2 warm
3 eggs
4 bill
5 lungs

Down
1. __________ keep a bird's body warm and dry.
4. A bird uses its _________ to pick up food.

Across
2. A bird is a _________ -blooded animal.
3. Baby birds are hatched from __________.
5. Birds breathe with their __________.

Word Bank
feathers bill lungs eggs warm

Page 187

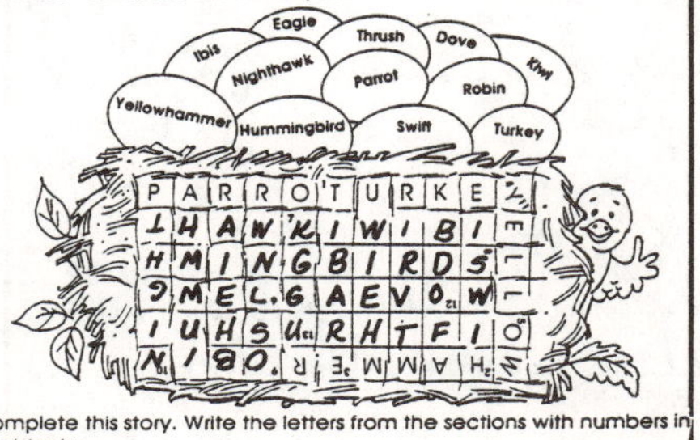

Birds of a Feather

Birds are the only animals that have feathers. All birds have wings, but not all can fly. They all hatch from eggs, have backbones, and are warm-blooded.

The eggs in the nest contain names of different birds. When filling in the puzzle, the last letter of one name becomes the first letter of the next name. Write the names of the birds in the puzzle in the correct order. Start at the outside edge and spiral in toward the center. The first three names are written for you.

Eagle
Ibis
Thrush
Dove
Nighthawk
Kiwi
Parrot
Robin
Yellowhammer
Hummingbird
Swift
Turkey

Complete this story. Write the letters from the sections with numbers in the blanks.

A sly and hungry fox quietly crept into the hen house one night. Carefully, he took a basket and began filling it with eggs. As he turned to leave, he tripped on a rake and went tumbling down, eggs and all. The hens awoke, laughed loudly, and said,

"*The yolks on you*!"

Page 188

A Fish Story

Fish live almost anywhere there is water. Although fish come in many different shapes, colors, and sizes, they are alike in many ways.

- All fish have backbones.
- Fish breathe with gills.
- Most fish are cold-blooded.
- Most fish have fins.
- Many fish have scales and fairly tough skin.

Professor Fish teaches a *school* of fish in the ocean. He decided that he would make name tags for everyone. But, he decided to have some fun, and he jumbled the fish' names on their name tags.

Use the clues to unscramble the fish names. Write each name correctly at the top of the name tag. Then use your imagination to draw each fish.

Pictures will vary.

parrot fish rparto fish (a talking bird)	*lionfish* oinlfish (king of the beasts)	*kingfish* gknifish (opposite of queen)
butterfly fish tbtureifly fish (an insect with colorful wings)	*goatfish* ogatfish (a nanny – or a billy –)	*porcupinefish* opprucneifish (animal with quills)

Page 189

A Mixture of Mammals

Mammals live in many different places. They are a special group because they . . .

- can give milk to their babies.
- protect and guide their young.
- are warm-blooded.
- have hair at some time during their lives.
- have a large, well-developed brain.

Below are some silly pictures made from two mammals put together. Write the names of the two real mammals on the lines. The last letter(s) in the name of the first animal is the first letter(s) in the name of the second animal. The first one is done for you.

1. whale — leopard
2. porpoise — seal
3. zebra — racoon
4. bear — armadillo
5. elephant — anteater
6. skunk — kangaroo
7. tiger — rabbit
8. camel — elephant

Page 190

The Reptile House

There are about 6,000 different kinds of reptiles. They come in all sorts of shapes and colors. Their sizes in length range from 2 inches to almost 30 feet. Reptiles can be found on every continent except Antarctica. Even though reptiles can seem quite different, they all . . .

- breathe with lungs.
- are cold-blooded.
- have dry, scaly skin.
- have a backbone.

In the Reptile House at the zoo, each animal needs to be placed in the correct area. Read the information about each reptile. Then use the clues and the pictures to write the name of each reptile in its area.

Giant Tortoise can live over 100 years. It can hide under its shell for protection.

Reticulated Python is the longest snake. One was almost 33 feet long.

Saltwater Crocodile is one of the largest reptiles. It can weigh 1,000 lbs.

Komodo Dragon is a dragon-like reptile. It is the largest living lizard.

Tuatara is closely related to the extinct dinosaur.

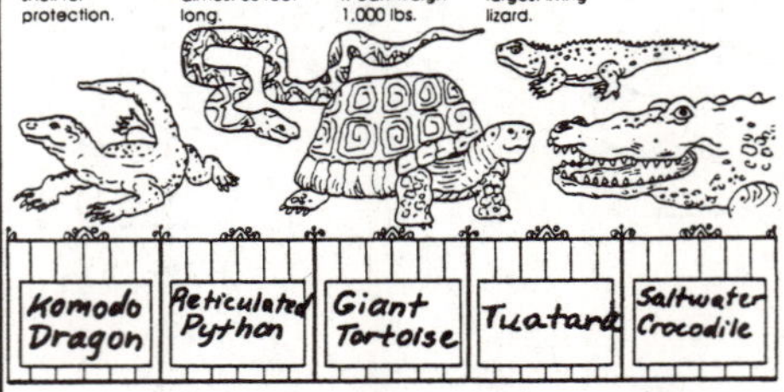
Komodo Dragon
Reticulated Python
Giant Tortoise
Tuatara
Saltwater Crocodile

Clues:
- The snake is between the largest lizard and the largest member of the turtle family.
- A relative of the alligator is on the far right side.
- The reptile who carries its "house" is in the middle.

Page 191

Amazing Amphibians

Amphibians are cold-blooded vertebrates (animals with backbones). They have no scales on their skin. Most amphibians hatch from eggs laid in water or on damp ground. Many amphibians grow legs as they develop into adults. Some live on land and have both lungs and gills for breathing. Frogs and toads are examples of amphibians.

Santjie, a South African sharp-nosed frog, holds the record for the longest triple jump. He jumped a total of more than 33 feet!

The frogs below won 1st, 2nd, and 3rd place in a recent triple-jump contest. Each jump after each frog's first jump was two feet shorter than the jump before. How many total feet did each frog jump? Fill in the answers on the trophies.

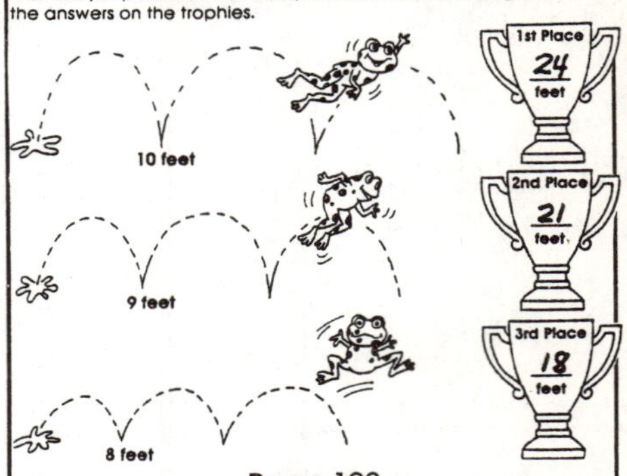
10 feet
9 feet
8 feet
1st Place
24
feet
2nd Place
21
feet
3rd Place
18
feet

Page 192

Plotting Plants

Follow Rupert Rabbit as he learns about plants. Use the words in the Word Bank to help you.

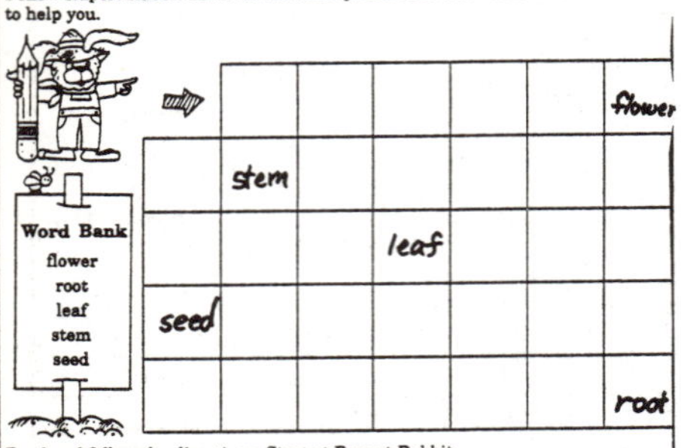
Word Bank
flower
root
leaf
stem
seed
flower
stem
leaf
seed
root

Read and follow the directions. Start at Rupert Rabbit.

1. Go right 5 spaces. Then go down 3 spaces and left 5 spaces. Write the word that names what grows into a new plant here.
2. Now go up 2 spaces. Then go right 6 spaces and down 3 spaces. Write the word that names the part of the plant that is underground here.
3. Now go up 3 spaces. Then go left 3 spaces and down 1 space. Write the word that names the part of the plant that makes the food here.
4. Now go right 2 spaces. Then go up 1 space and left 4 spaces. Write the word that names the part of the plant that carries food and water to the rest of the plant here.
5. Now go down 2 spaces. Then go right 5 spaces and up 3 spaces. Write the word that names the part of the plant that makes the seeds here.

Page 193

Those Nutty Seeds

Seeds are found in different parts of the plant. Some seeds are found in the flower. Some seeds are found in the fruit or the nut.

Circle the part of the plant that has the seed. Write the name of the seed.

Word Bank	
pine	maple
apple	acorn
corn	dandelion

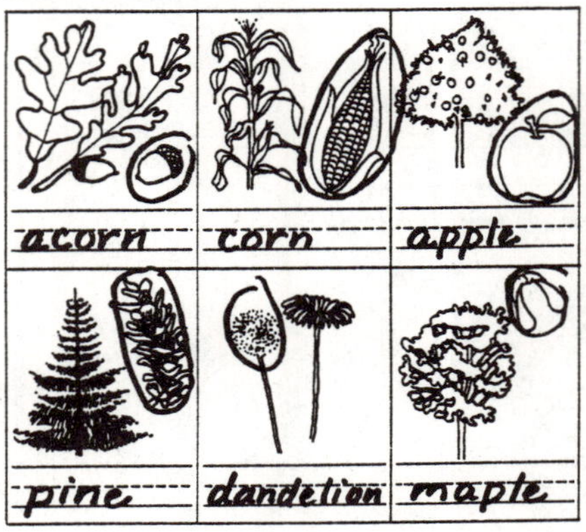
acorn
corn
apple
pine
dandelion
maple

Page 194

Traveling Seeds

Seeds travel from one place to another. Sometimes people move the seeds. Sometimes they are moved in other ways.

Finish the sentences to tell how seeds travel.

Word Bank
people
animals
animals
wind
water

Seeds travel with people.

Seeds travel in water.

Seeds travel on animals.

Seeds travel in animals.

Seeds travel in the wind.

Page 195

Eyes in the Dark

What has eyes, but cannot see? A potato! The little white bumps that grow on a potato's skin are called "eyes." An eye can grow into a new potato plant.

You will need:
potato
potting soil
flowerpot or plastic glass

1. Put the potato in a dark cupboard or closet. Check it daily for small bumps called "eyes."

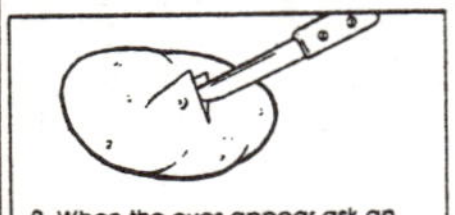

2. When the eyes appear ask an adult to cut them off the potato.

3. Fill a flowerpot half full of potting soil and lay the piece of potato on it with the "eyes" facing up.

1"

4. Cover the "eyes" with 1 inch of soil. Water. Keep moist–but not wet. Watch closely for about two weeks.

Record what happened after . . .

1 week

Answers will vary.

2 weeks

What happened?

A potato is a tuber. A tuber is a fat underground stem with little buds that can grow into new plants. The "eye" that you planted was really a potato bud that grew into a new plant.

Page 196

Dynamic Dinosaurs

Dinosaurs were reptiles that lived millions of years ago. Some of them were the biggest animals to ever live on land. Some were as small as chickens. Some dinosaurs ate plants, while other were meat-eaters.

Scientists have given names to the dinosaurs that often describe their special bodies, sizes, and habits.

Look at the object(s) placed in the picture with each dinosaur. Use the objects as clues to fill in the blanks and finish each dinosaur's name.

SCHOOL
TRICERA TOPS
LAMB EOSAURUS
DIME TRODON
SALT ASAURUS
PLATE OSAURUS

Page 197

Dial a Dinosaur

Danny loves dinosaurs. In fact, he loves them so much that everyone calls him Dinosaur Danny! Find out what Dinosaur Danny's favorite dinosaur is by decoding the message below. To do this, use the numbers on the telephone and the directional markers.

For example: 3 points to the letter D.

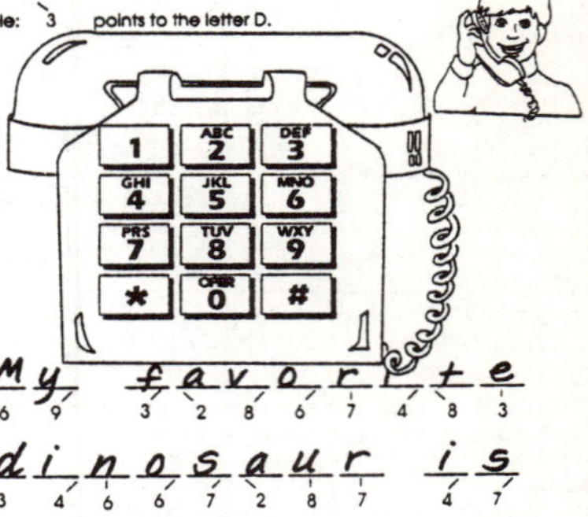
1
ABC 2
DEF 3
GHI 4
JKL 5
MNO 6
PRS 7
TUV 8
WXY 9
*
OPER 0
#

My favorite dinosaur is stegosaurus

Write your own message and share it with a classmate.

Page 198

Magic Square Mania

Did you know that the word dinosaur comes from two Greek words meaning terrible lizard? Dinosaurs were not lizards at all! To further improve your dinosaur vocabulary, read Column A. Choose an answer from Column B. Write the number of the answer in the Magic Square. The first one has been done for you.

Column A
- A. Person who studies fossils
- B. Petrified remains of animals and plants
- C. Meat-eating dinosaurs
- D. Plant-eating dinosaurs
- E. Movement of animals over long distances
- F. Large bony plates on dinosaur's neck
- G. Bones on the top of a dinosaur's head
- H. The Age of Dinosaurs
- I. Large groups of animals that live together

Column B
1. skeleton
2. Mesozoic Age
3. carnivores
4. herbivores
5. paleontologist
6. migration
7. herds
8. frills
9. crest
10. fossils

A 5	B 10	C 3
D 4	E 6	F 8
G 9	H 2	I 7

Add the numbers across, down and diagonally. What answer do you get? 18

Why do you think this is called a magic square? ______

Page 199

Weather Watch

Weather is the condition of the air around the earth for a period of time. The weatherman's job is to predict the weather.

There were some very unusual weather patterns recorded for a recent month. Use the key to draw the correct weather symbols for each day.

- Every Monday and Tuesday it rained. Then it was sunny for the following three days.
- On the first and third weekends, the first day was cloudy, and the second day was snowy.
- On the second and fourth weekends, it was just the opposite.

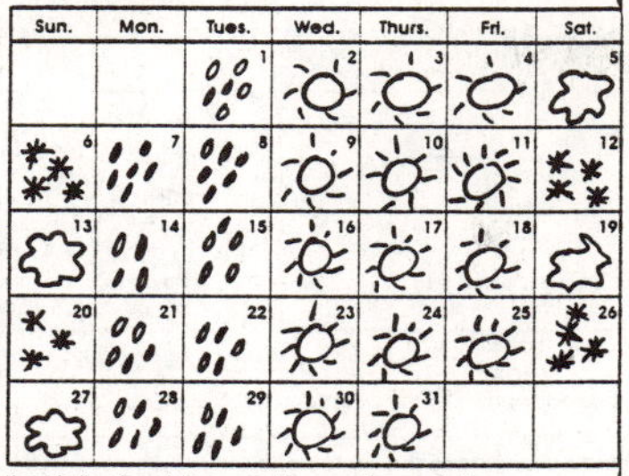

Write the word that tells about the weather on these dates:
- 6th day of the month snowy
- 13th day of the month cloudy
- last day of the month sunny

Page 200

Gauging the Weather

Cut out the centimeter ruler at the bottom of the page. Use the ruler to measure the amount of rainfall from the bottom of the gauge to the top of the water. Write the measurement on the raindrop.

Page 201

A Cloudy Day

Clouds bring us many kinds of weather. Some clouds give us fair weather. Other clouds bring rain.

Paste the picture of the cloud next to its description.

	How the Clouds Look	Weather
 Cumulus	Big, puffy clouds	Nice day, but there might be a small shower.
 Cumulo-nimbus	Tall, dark, piles of clouds.	Thunderstorm
 Cirrus	Whispy clouds that look like feathers.	Fair
 Stratus	Layers of gray clouds that cover the whole sky.	Steady drizzle.

Page 202

Lacy Patterns

Kim likes to look at the lacy patterns of snowflakes with her magnifying glass. Most of them have six sides or six points. But she has never seen two snowflakes that are alike. Kim catches them on small pieces of dark paper so that she can see them better. Some of the snowflakes are broken because they bump into each other as they fall from the clouds.

Color. What does Kim use to make the snowflakes look bigger?

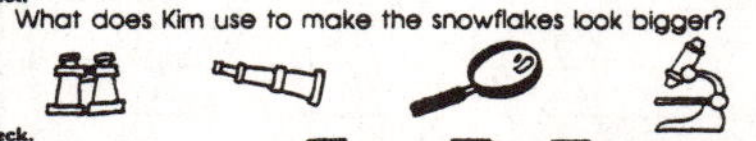

Check. Most snowflakes have ☐ seven ☑ six ☐ five sides or points.

Kim looks at them on dark pieces of paper so that she can...
☐ take them to school. ☐ make a picture. ☑ see them better.

Write. Why are some of the snowflakes broken?

They bump into each other.

• Finish the snowflake.

Page 203

Sink or Float?

Why do some objects float? Why do other objects sink? Is it because of their shape? Is it because of their color? Let's find out!

You will need:
large bowl of water
test objects such as –
apple, nail, orange, eraser, wood, stone, egg, penny, crayon

Sinker or Floater?

1. List your objects.
2. Make guesses. Will they sink or float?
3. Test your objects to find the actual results.

Object	Guess	Actual Results
Answers will vary.		

What happened?

If an object is heavy for its size, it will sink. If it is light for its size, it will float. A brick is heavy for its size so it will sink. A piece of wood the same size will float.

Page 204

Salty Water Evaporation

1. With a partner, decide which of you will be responsible for each job below.
   Experimenter—responsible for following the given directions, gathering materials, and cleaning up.
   Recorder—responsible for reading the directions and questions out loud and for recording the answers.
2. Gather the following materials:
   spoon
   salt
   paper cup
   1/4 cup water
3. Stir the salt into the water.
4. Put the cup in a warm place.

5. Use what you already know about science to predict:
   What do you think will happen to the water? Answers will vary.
   What do you think will happen to the salt? ______
6. Check the cup in a few days and record:
   What has happened to the water? ______
   What has happened to the salt? ______
   What do you think happens to ocean water when it is exposed to the sun? ______
   What do you think happens to the ocean salt when the water evaporates? ______

Page 205

Anti-Freeze

Water turns into a solid at a temperature of 32°F. This is called the freezing point. Does all water freeze at 32°F? Let's find out!

You will need:
2 small paper cups
4 teaspoons of salt
water
marking pen
freezer

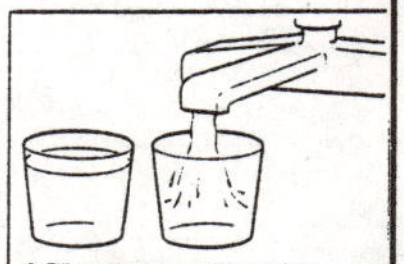

1. Fill both cups with water.

2. Mix 4 teaspoons of salt in one of the cups. Write "salt" on that cup.

3. Put both cups in the freezer. Check on them every hour for four hours.

I found out . . . Answers will vary.

the cup of plain water ______

the cup of salt water ______

What happened?

When the temperature of water gets very cold, the particles of water hook together to make ice crystals. Salt gets in the way of this process, and an even lower temperature is needed before ice crystals will form.

Page 206

Layers of the Ocean Floor

Have you ever wondered what is under the sand on a beach? Some beaches are really layers of rock, pebbles, shells, and sand. Work in a group of four students and choose one of these materials to bring to school for your group. Write your name next to the material that you will bring:

sand ______ shells ______

rock ______ pebbles ______

Your teacher will provide a glass jar and water.

1. Gather the materials and take turns adding them to the jar. Add the same amount of each material.
2 Fill the jar to the top with water.
3. Close the lid tightly!
4. Take turns shaking the jar 10 times each.
5. Set the jar aside for one day.
6. Each student should draw and label one layer of the jar on the worksheet. Then put your names on the paper.
7. For follow-up, draw a picture of the layers of the ocean floor. Think about the layers you saw in your jar.

Page 207

Ocean Temperatures

Where do you think the ocean temperatures are the warmest? Do you think the salt makes the ocean warmer or cooler? Do you think the sun makes the ocean warmer or cooler? Try this experiment to find out!

1. Get 4 clear glasses of water.
2. Add salt to 2 of the glasses and stir well.
3. Set one freshwater glass and one saltwater glass in the shade outside.
4. Set the other 2 glasses in the sun outside.
5. Set thermometers in each of the 4 glasses.
6. Divide into 4 equal groups and start at a different glass.
7. Wait 15 minutes, then read the thermometer and record below.
8. On signal, rotate to the next glass.

Fresh/Shady
Fresh/Sunny
Salty/Shady
Salty/Sunny
Answers will vary.

_______ °C _______ °C _______ °C _______ °C

The Dancing Coin

You can make a coin dance on the top of a bottle as if a ghost were pushing on it. Let's try!

You will need:
glass soft-drink bottle
coin

1. Wet the rim of an empty bottle and one side of the coin.
2. Place the wet side of the coin on rim of the bottle.
3. Hold the bottle with your warm hands. Watch closely!

What happened to the coin? *Answers will vary.*

What happened to the temperature of the air in the bottle when you put your hands around the bottle? ________

What happened?

Your warm hands heated the cool air in the bottle. The air expanded and tried to escape. It pushed on the coin and made it dance.

The Crusher

I'll bet you can crush a plastic soft-drink bottle without even touching it. Of course there is a little trick. Let's try it!

You will need:
plastic soft-drink bottle
hot water
cold water

1. Fill the bottle with hot water from the faucet. Be careful. Let the bottle stand for a minute.
2. Pour out the hot water. Quickly screw on the cap. Make sure the cap is on tight.
3. Pour a pitcher of very cold water over the bottle or hold the bottle under the cold water faucet. Watch what happens!

What happened?

The hot water made the air in the bottle very warm. The bottle cap captured the warm air in the bottle. The cold water made the warm air become cold. Cold air takes less space and the air pressure outside the bottle pushed in the sides of the bottle.

Powerful Push-Up

Can air hold up water? It can with a little help from you. Let's find out how!

You will need:
drinking glass
card the size of a postcard
water

1. Fill the glass to overflowing.
2. Lay the card on top of the glass.
3. Hold the card down with one hand. Turn the glass over. Remove your hand. Wow!

What happened to the water in the glass? *Answers will vary*

What happens if you tilt the glass? ________

What happened?

Air pushes in all directions. The air pressure pushing up under the card is greater than the pressure of the water pushing down. The card stays in place.

High and Dry

Can you put a piece of paper under water without getting it wet? You can do it with a little help from air pressure. Let's try!

You will need:
drinking glass
sheet of paper
sink full of water

1. Crumple a sheet of paper. Push it into the bottom of a glass so that it stays in place.
2. Hold the glass upside down.
3. Push it straight down into the water.

What happens to the paper if you pull the glass straight up? *Answers will vary.*

What happens if you tilt the glass when putting it in the water? ________

What happened?

The glass is full of air. The air cannot come out because it is lighter than the water. If you tilt the glass, the air escapes and water enters.

The Last Straw

Sodas, milkshakes and root beer are all fun to sip through a straw. It would be fun to sip them through two straws. Could you sip liquid through three straws? four straws? What is the most you could use? Let's find out!

You will need:
plastic straws
clear tape
plastic pop bottle
water

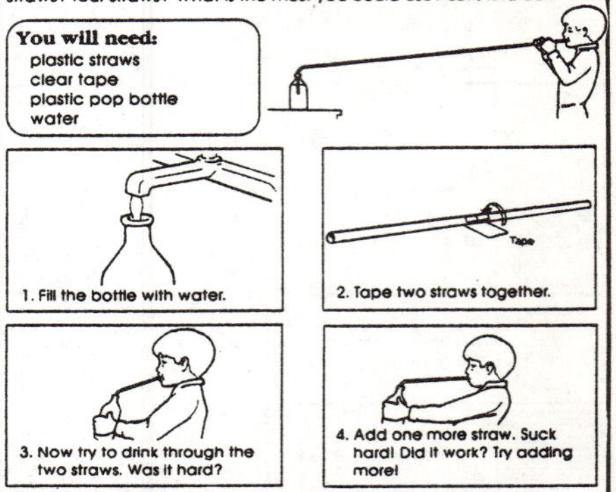
Tape

1. Fill the bottle with water.
2. Tape two straws together.
3. Now try to drink through the two straws. Was it hard?
4. Add one more straw. Suck hard! Did it work? Try adding more!

How many straws can you tape together and still drink through? ________

What happened?

Air pressure pushes down on the water in the bottle and also down on the water in the straw. When you suck the air out of the straw there will be no air pressure pushing down on the water in the straw, only air pressure pushing on the rest of the water in the bottle. The air pressure in the bottle pushes the water up the straw.

What's the Matter?

All things are made of **matter**. Matter takes up space. It can take three forms – solid, liquid or gas.

Solids have shape and volume. They do not change shape easily.

Liquids have volume, but they have no shape of their own. They take the shape of the container they are in.

Gases have no shape or volume. Most gases are invisible.

Find and circle the words in each wordsearch that are examples of each kind of matter. Then write the words on the lines.

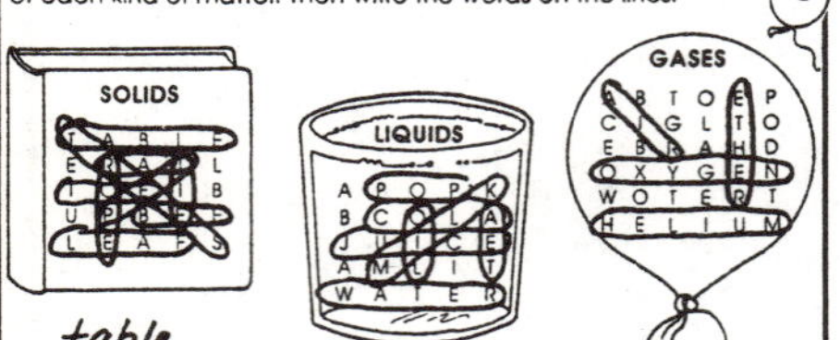
SOLIDS
LIQUIDS
GASES
O X Y G E N
W O T E R T
H E L I U M
W A T E R

Solids	Liquids	Gases
table	*pop*	*oxygen*
tree(s)	*cola*	*helium*
leaf	*milk*	*air*
pet	*juice*	*ether*
bee	*water*	
tie	*oil*	
toe	*tea*	
rope		
rat		

"Shadowing" Shadows

Cut out the pictures at the bottom of the page. Read the directions and paste the objects where they belong.

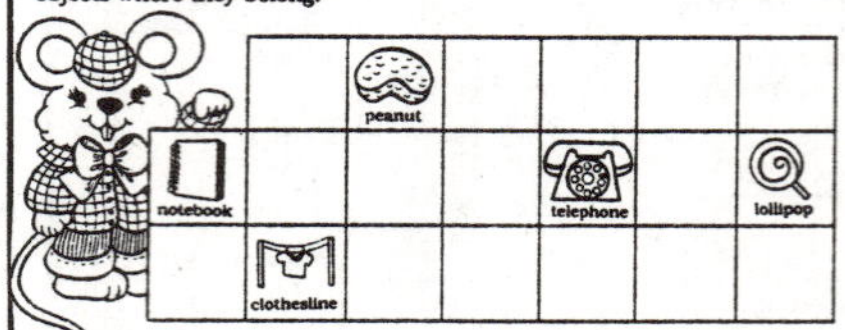
peanut
notebook
telephone
lollipop
clothesline

Start at Detective Mouse.

1. Go down 1 space and right 4 spaces. Paste the picture here of what you would make this shadow.
2. Now go left 3 spaces and down 1 space. Paste the picture here of what would make this shadow.
3. Then go right 5 spaces and up 1 space. Paste the picture here of what would make this shadow.
4. Go up 1 space and left 4 spaces. Paste the picture here of what would make this shadow.
5. Go down 1 space and left 2 spaces. Paste the picture here of what would make this shadow.

Volume Control

If the words name something that makes a loud sound, color the space gray.
If the words name something that makes a soft sound, color the space red.

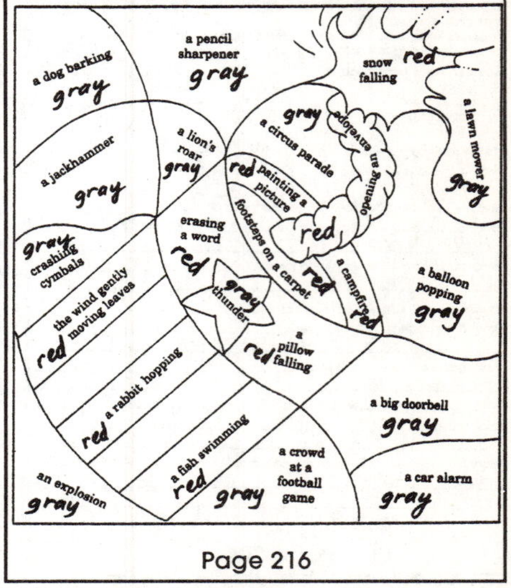
a dog barking gray
a pencil sharpener gray
snow falling red
a lawn mower gray
a jackhammer gray
a lion's roar gray
a circus parade gray
opening up red
painting a picture red
footsteps on a carpet red
erasing a word red
crashing cymbals gray
the wind gently moving leaves red
thunder gray
a campfire red
a balloon popping gray
a pillow falling red
a rabbit hopping red
a big doorbell gray
a fish swimming red
a crowd at a football game gray
an explosion gray
a car alarm gray

0-7682-3792-0 Skills & Practice Gr. 2

Gravity: The Force Is with You

Before you drop the pairs of objects, predict which of each pair will reach the ground first. Drop the two objects at the same time from a height of 5 feet (1.5 m). Record the result after each drop.

Objects	Prediction	Result
pencil and piece of chalk		
piece of chalk and chalkboard eraser	Answers will vary.	Results should be that both objects land at the same time.
pencil and empty cup		
tissue box and textbook		
textbook and basketball		
encyclopedia and thick rubberband		

Page 217

Keep It Clean!

Have you ever cleaned a penny? Let's try it!

Materials:

4 dirty pennies, salt, vinegar, soap, water, taco sauce, window cleaner, steel wool pad, paper towels

Directions:

1. In the "I predict . . ." section on the chart, explain what you think each penny will look like after you clean it with one of the materials.
2. Your teacher will place a small amount of each material in the center of each table.
3. Try cleaning one penny using window cleaner. Explain what it looks like in the "I observed . . ." section.
4. Now try cleaning another penny using soap, water, and the steel wool pad. Explain what it looks like.
5. Clean a different penny in salt and vinegar. Explain what it looks like.
6. Now clean the last penny in taco sauce. Explain what it looks like.

Materials	I predict . . .	I observed . . .
window cleaner	Answers will vary.	
soap, water, and steel wool pad		
salt and vinegar		
taco sauce		

Page 218

Magnetic Attraction

The word **magnet** begins with the same three letters as the word magic, and sometimes magnets do seem a little magical.

Every magnet has two poles — north and south. The north pole of one magnet attracts and pulls toward the south pole of another magnet. Two poles that are the same (two north poles or two south poles) do **not** attract each other. Instead, they push away from each other.

Using the information above, continue labeling the horseshoe and bar magnets below with **N** (for north) and **S** (for south).

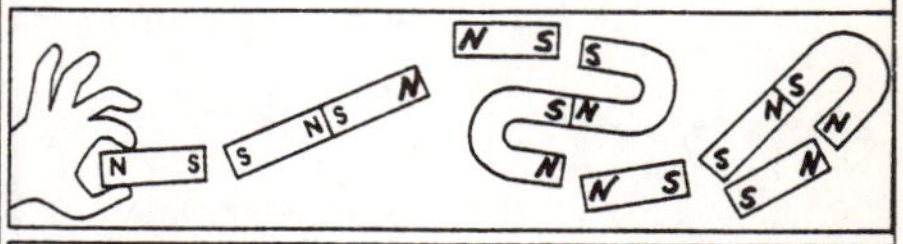

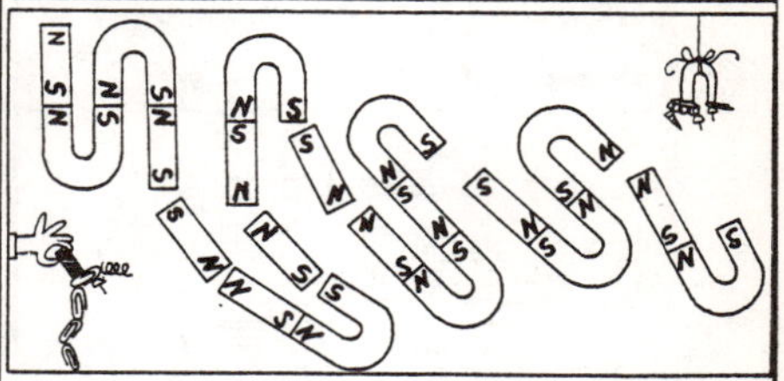

Page 219

"Attractive" Magnets

Cut out each object and paste it on the chart where it belongs. Use a crayon to graph the results.

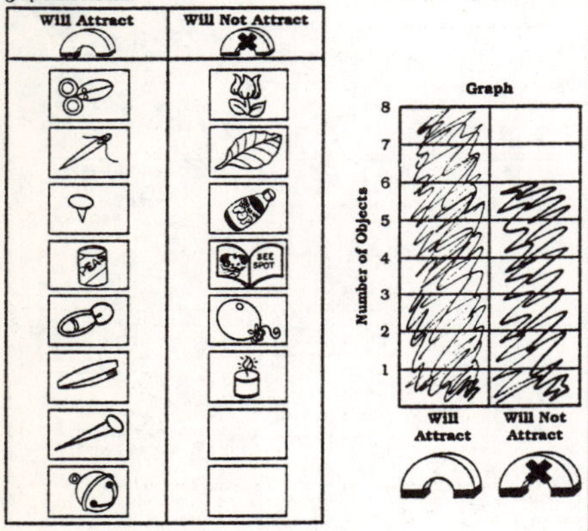

Will Attract
Will Not Attract
Graph
Number of Objects
1
2
3
4
5
6
7
8
Will Attract
Will Not Attract

Page 220

Lifting with Levers

A lever is a simple machine used to lift or move things. It has two parts. The **arm** is the part that moves. The **fulcrum** supports the arm and does not move.

Name the parts of this lever.

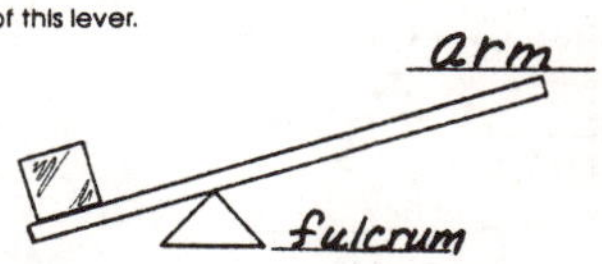

arm
fulcrum

Unscramble the names of these levers.

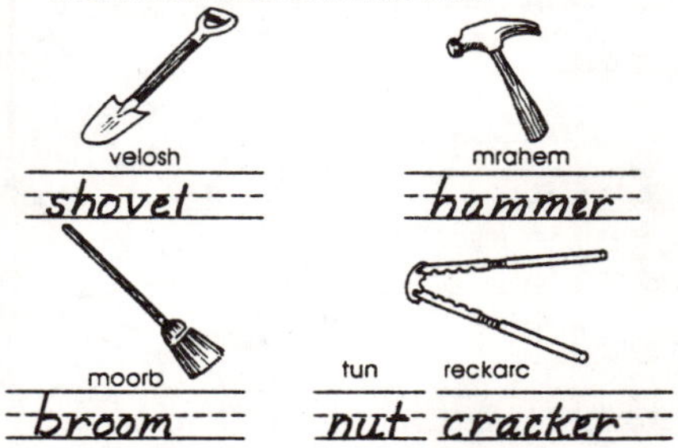

velosh
shovel
mrahem
hammer
moorb
broom
tun
nut
reckarc
cracker

Page 221

Levers at Work

Levers help make our work easier. Circle all the levers. Then find their names in the wordsearch.

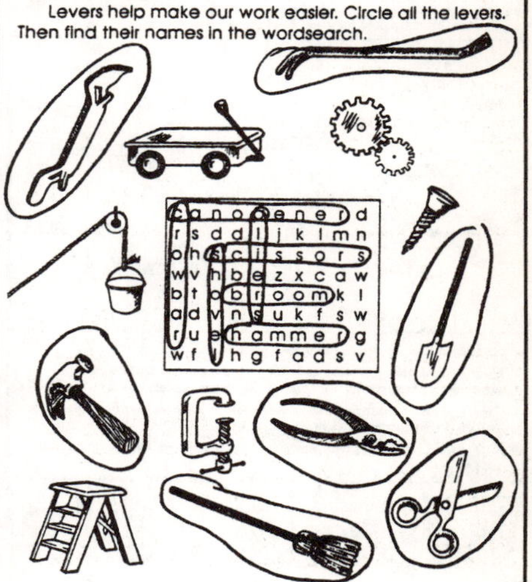

Page 222

The Right Tool for the Job

Mother gave Tyrone and Kim a list of jobs. Help them pick the right tool for each job. Draw a line from the job to the tool.

What will help Kim raise the flag up the flagpole?

What will Tyrone use to help him get the cat out of the tree?

What will Kim use to carry sand to her new sandbox?

What will Tyrone use to get the nail out of the board?

What will Kim use to hang the mirror on her bedroom door?

What will Tyrone use to slice the turkey?

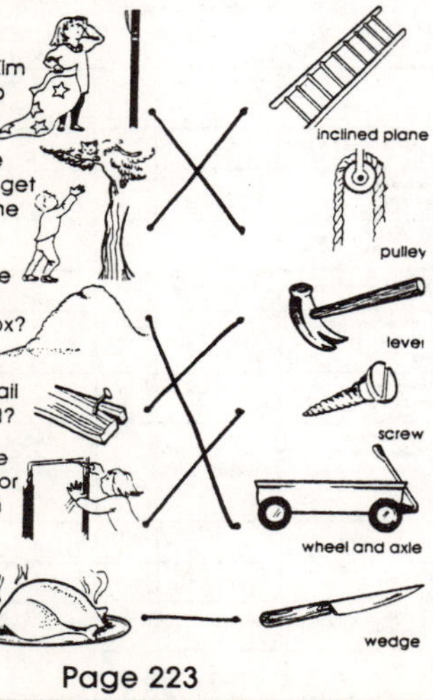

inclined plane
pulley
lever
screw
wheel and axle
wedge

Page 223

Slanted Machines

An inclined plane has a slanted surface. It is used to move things from a low place to a high place. Some inclined planes are smooth. Others have steps.

Color the inclined planes in the picture.

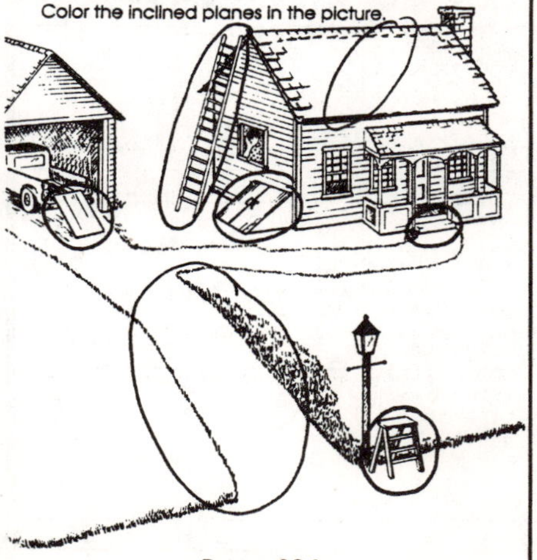

Page 224

The Wedge

A wedge is a type of inclined plane. It is made up of two inclined planes joined together to make a sharp edge. A wedge can be used to cut things. Some wedges are pointed.

Color only the pictures of wedges.

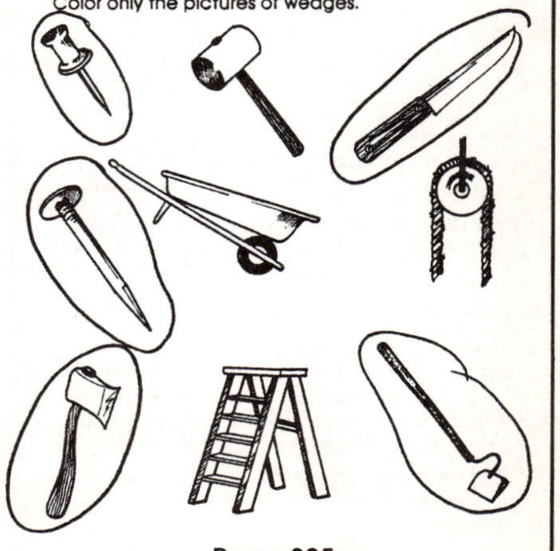

Page 225

Ready for Work!

Read the names of the objects in the Word Bank. Write the objects under the correct kind of simple machine.

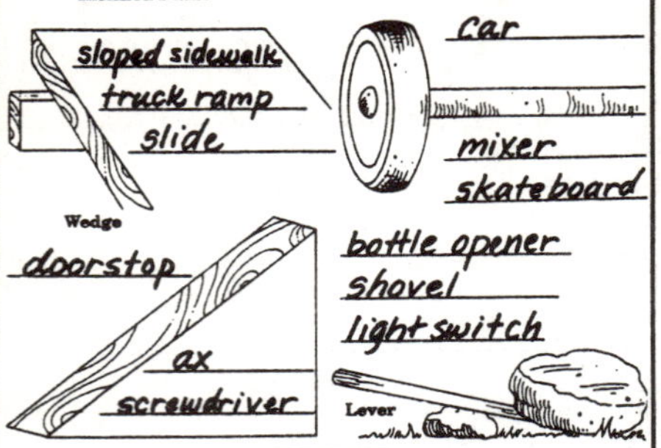

Inclined Plane
sloped sidewalk
truck ramp
slide
Wheel and Axle
car
mixer
skateboard
Wedge
doorstop
ax
screwdriver
bottle opener
shovel
light switch
Lever

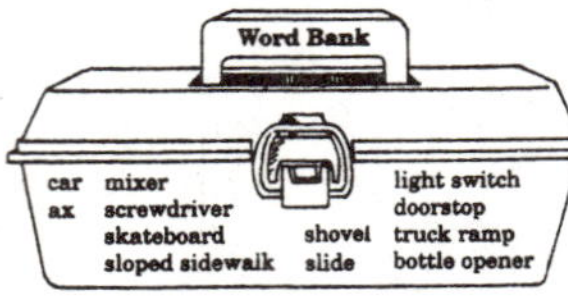

Word Bank
car mixer ax screwdriver skateboard sloped sidewalk shovel slide light switch doorstop truck ramp bottle opener

Faraway and Close Up

Kim's favorite subject is science. She has a telescope and a microscope in her bedroom. At night, she looks through her telescope. Things that are far away, like the moon, stars and planets, look bigger. When she looks through her microscope, she can see tiny things close up, like a drop of water or a bit of salt.

Unscramble and write.

Kim's favorite subject is science. (niecsec)

Circle.

She has a bicycle / (telescope) and a (microscope) / planet in her bedroom.

Color.

What faraway things look bigger with a telescope?

color
color
color

Check.

When Kim looks through her microscope, she can see ...

- [x] tiny things close up.
- [ ] big things far away.

• SOMETHING EXTRA •

What is your favorite subject? Why?

Planets

There are eight planets that move around the sun. Our planet is Earth. Earth is closest to Mars and Venus. Jupiter is the largest planet. It is many times larger than Earth. Saturn is the planet with seven rings around it. The smallest planet is called Mercury!

Circle. How many planets are there? three nine (eight)

Mercury	Earth	Jupiter	Mars	Venus	Saturn

Write.

Earth I am your planet.

Mars
Venus } We are closest to Earth.

Jupiter I am the largest planet.

Saturn I am the planet with seven rings.

Mercury I am the smallest planet.

Color. Draw three red rings around Saturn.

• Draw what you think you would find on the planet Mercury.

Position the Planets

Write the names of the planets on the lines according to their distance from the sun. Use the Word Bank to help you spell the words correctly.

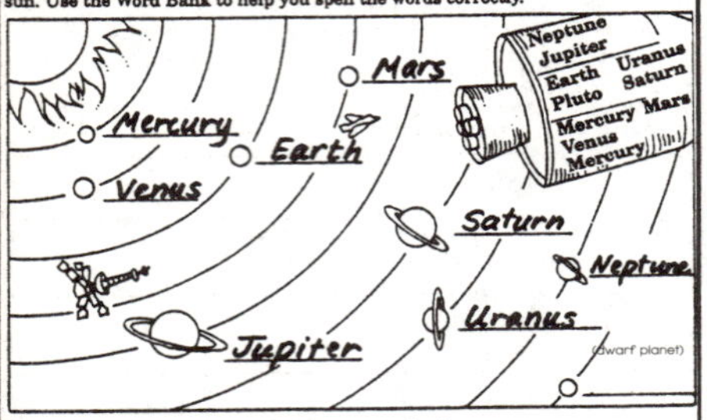

Neptune
Jupiter
Uranus
Earth
Saturn
Pluto
Mars
Mercury
Venus
Mercury
Mars
Venus
Earth
Saturn
Neptune
Uranus
Jupiter
(dwarf planet)

Read the sentences. Record the information on the chart.

1. *Viking 2* took close-up pictures of Mars on September 3, 1976, but scientists still are not sure if there is life on the planet.
2. Two of Saturn's outer rings were very clear in pictures taken by *Pioneer-Saturn* on September 1, 1979.
3. In March of 1979, the probe *Voyager 1* discovered that Jupiter has a thin ring around it.

Name of Probe	Planet Destination	Date	Results or Discoveries
Viking 2	Mars	Sept. 3, 1976	took pictures, still not sure of life
Pioneer-Saturn	Saturn	Sept. 1, 1979	pictures clearly showed Saturn's rings
Voyager 1	Jupiter	March 1979	discovered Jupiter has a thin ring

Spacing Out

Read a clue. Find the matching word in the puzzle and write it on the line. Then connect the puzzle dots in the same order as your answers.

Clues

1. The planet we live on Earth
2. The closest star sun
3. They shine in the sky at night stars
4. Earth is a planet
5. Planets, stars, and moons are in space
6. Time when the sun shines day
7. A group of stars constellation
8. A person who travels in space astronaut
9. The path a planet follows to travel around the sun orbit
10. It gives us light at night moon
11. People who study the stars astronomers
12. You use this to see the stars close up telescope
13. Time when the sun does not shine night
14. We feel this from the sun heat

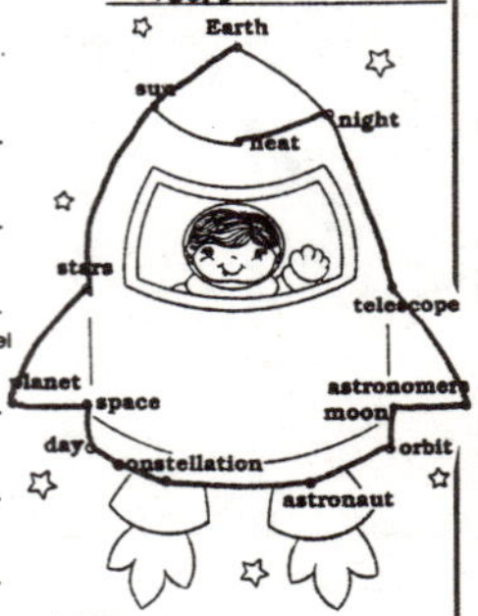

Earth
sun
night
heat
stars
telescope
planet
space
astronomers
moon
days
orbit
constellation
astronaut

Birthday Surprise!

1. Complete sentences 1 and 2.
2. Connect the numbers in the dot-to-dot.
3. Color 2 presents red and 3 presents blue.
4. Draw candles on the dot-to-dot picture to show how old you are.
5. Color the dot-to-dot.

Answers and pictures will vary.

1. My birthdate is ________ ________ ________
   month date year
2. I am ________ years old.

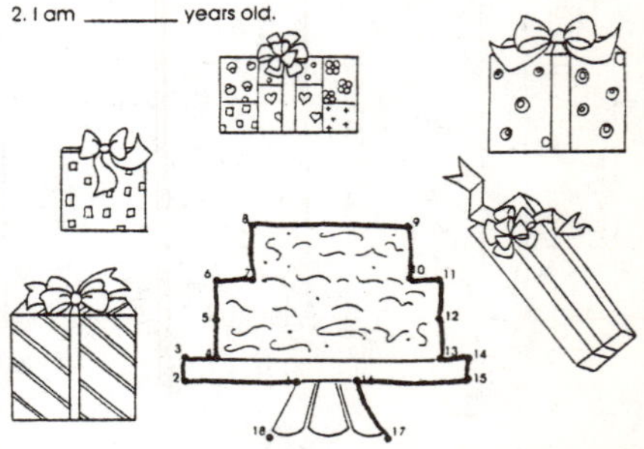

I Like Me!

Complete the sentences below to tell about you.

Most people like the way I Answers will vary.

I feel happy when ________

The thing I like best about me is ________

I feel sad when ________

I feel special when ________

At home I ________

At school I ________

Featuring the One and Only Me

In each box write about a different event in your life. Draw a picture to go with each event. Answers will vary.

I was born.		

My Body Homework

You know how special your body is! To keep your body working and looking its best, you should start developing good habits now and keep them as you grow older. Use this check list to keep yourself on track for the next week. Keep it on your bathroom mirror or next to your bed where it will remind you to do your "homework!"

	Sun.	Mon.	Tues.	Wed.	Thurs.	Fri.	Sat.
I slept at least 8 hours.							
I ate a healthy breakfast.							
I brushed my teeth this morning.							
I ate a healthy lunch.							
I washed my hands after using the bathroom.							
I exercised at least 30 minutes today.							
I drank at least 6 glasses of water.							
I stood and sat up straight.							
I ate a healthy dinner.							
I bathed.							
I brushed my teeth this evening.							

0-7682-3792-0 *Skills & Practice Gr. 2*

People Scavenger Hunt

Get to know the kids in your class. Find someone to fit each description. Try not to use the same name twice!

How We Look

1. ________ has freckles on his/her arms.
2. ________ is wearing a watch, ring or necklace.
3. ________ has red on his/her socks.
4. ________ has 3 buttons on his/her shirt.
5. ________ is missing 3 baby teeth.

How We Feel

1. ________ likes green beans.
2. ________ wants a baby brother or sister.
3. ________ is scared during thunderstorms.
4. ________ would like a snake as a pet.
5. ________ would like his/her room painted blue.

What We Do

1. ________ ate cereal for breakfast.
2. ________ played a sport last weekend.
3. ________ can dive into a swimming pool.
4. ________ made his/her bed today.
5. ________ is taking lessons to learn how to do something.

Page 235

Shooting for My Goals

What is something new you want to do? Maybe you want to improve at something you already do. Fill in the sentences below.

There are two goals I have for the rest of the school year.

One is *Goals will vary.*

Two is ________

I will do this by

day ________

month ________

year ________

________ signed

Page 236

My Personal Shield

Let your friends learn more about how special you are. Complete each sentence and draw a picture to go with it.

Answers and pictures will vary.

My proudest moment is ________

I am good at ________

I helped ________

I try very hard at ________

Page 237

Interview a Friend

Interview your friend and then fill out the information below.

My friend is ________

Answers will vary.

Favorite Colors

Favorite Book

Favorite Activities

Favorite Foods

Page 238

Create a Comrade!

Imagine that you could create a perfect friend. Describe your "creation" on the lines below.

Name ________

Age ________

Favorite Pastime ________

Personal Qualities

Answers will vary.

Special Interests/Hobbies

Talents

What we could do together

Page 239

Friendly Favorites

Think of the names of favorite animals, food and places that begin with the letters in the word FRIENDS. Write the names in the correct boxes below. One word in each column has already been done for you. For extra fun, play with a friend. The one who can think of the most names is the winner.

NEW YORK

	Animal	Food	Place
F	*Answers will vary.*		
R			
I		ice cream	
E			
N			New York
D	dog		
S			

Page 240

Buddy's Lists

Buddy likes to make lists. Yesterday, he wrote a list of his favorite things to do with friends. Today, he wants to divide this list into three more lists. Help Buddy by filling in these three lists with one-syllable, two-syllable and three-syllable words from his word list. The first word has been done for you.

One-syllable words

1. golf
2. *swim*
3. *camp*
4. *skate*
5. *swing*

Buddy's Word List
Things to Do with Friends

golf	basketball
Ping-Pong™	camp
swim	snorkeling
backpacking	biking
volleyball	skate
baseball	canoeing
fishing	soccer
swing	

Two-syllable words

1. *Ping-Pong*
2. *baseball*
3. *fishing*
4. *biking*
5. *soccer*

Three-syllable words

1. *backpacking*
2. *volleyball*
3. *basketball*
4. *snorkeling*
5. *canoeing*

Page 241

Cars and Colors

What is the color of your family car? *Answers will vary.*

If you have more than one car, what are the other colors? ________

Record the colors of all the cars in your class on the bar graph below. If a color is not shown, include it in "Other."

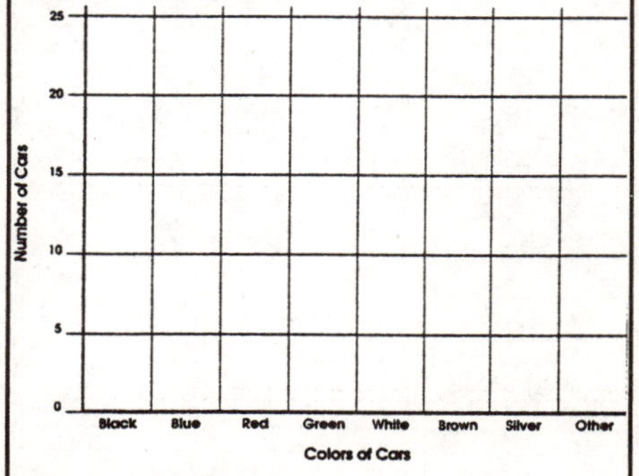
25
20
15
10
5
0
Number of Cars
Black
Blue
Red
Green
White
Brown
Silver
Other
Colors of Cars

1. What is the most popular color of car? ________
2. What is the least popular color of car? ________
3. What is the total number of cars that were counted? ________
4. Were there any colors that were equally popular? ________

Page 242

Comparing a Car and a Truck

In some ways, cars and trucks are alike. In other ways, they are different. On the car, write words and phrases that are true about it but are not true about the truck. Do the same with the truck. Where the car and the truck overlap, write words and phrases that are common to both of them.

Answers will vary.

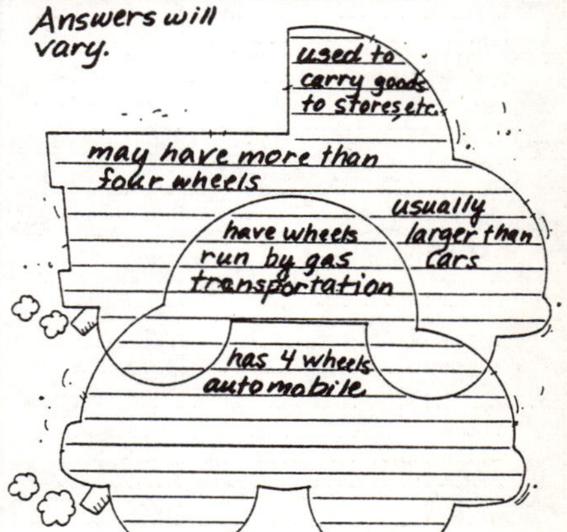
used to carry goods to stores etc.
may have more than four wheels
usually larger than cars
have wheels
run by gas
transportation
has 4 wheels
automobile

Page 243

Sightseeing by Train

Follow the train as it travels through the countryside.
Identify by number the places where the train:

goes through a forest	14	goes through a covered bridge	8
comes to a stop	16	passes through a plowed field	11
crosses a high bridge	1	comes down the mountain	4
passes a water tower	12	passes a volcano	10
exits a tunnel	3	goes through rocks	6
crosses a low bridge	7	crosses a lake	5
passes a school	13	goes by a small town	9
enters a tunnel	2	passes cows	15

Page 244

Sights and Sounds of Travel

Look at the numbered pictures below. Write the numbers of the pictures by each question.

What can carry more than one person?	1,2,3,4,5,6,7,8,11
What moves on wheels?	3,4,6,7,9,10,12
What moves on just two wheels?	3,9
What makes a very loud noise?	1,2,3,5,8,12
What moves through water?	1,11
What has a motor to make it run?	3,1,2,4,5,7,8,12
What can hold large, heavy objects?	1,2,4
What can travel very fast?	1,2,3,4,5,7,8
What has to be pushed or pulled?	6,10

Answers may vary.

Page 245

Transportation Sort

Study the examples of transportation below. Sort the objects into three groups. Think how each type travels.

Draw a ○ around objects in group one.
Draw a △ around objects in group two.
Draw a □ around objects in group three.

Answers will vary.

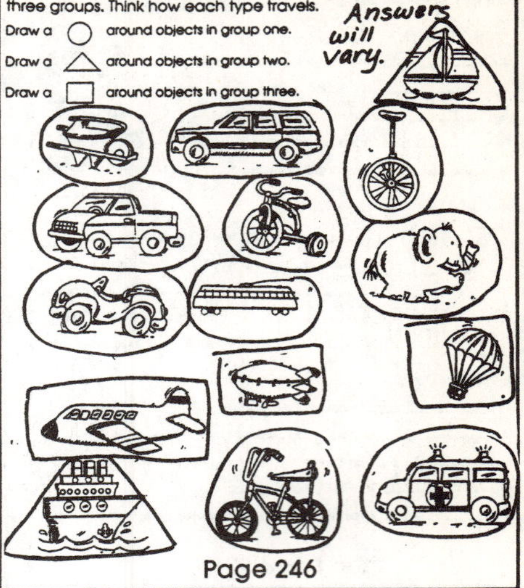

Page 246

How Many Wheels?

Cut out the pictures of the vehicles at the bottom of the page.
Paste the vehicles with no wheels in section 1.
Paste the vehicles with two wheels in section 2.
Paste the vehicles with three wheels in section 3.
Paste the vehicles with four wheels in section 4.
Paste the vehicles with more than four wheels in section 5.

Page 247

Transportation Magic Square

1. Read Column A. Choose an answer from Column B. Write the number of the answer in the correct square. The first one has been done for you.

Column A	Column B
A. Filled with helium	1. jet plane
B. Runs on gasoline	2. rowboat
C. Powered by wind	3. sailboat
D. Burns coal or wood	4. steam locomotive
E. Runs on nuclear energy	5. blimp
F. Moves on snow or ice	6. submarine
G. Moves by pedals	7. wagon
H. Powered by oars	8. sled
I. Pulled by horses or oxen	9. bicycle
	10. car

A 5	B 10	C 3
D 4	E 6	F 8
G 9	H 2	I 7

2. Add the numbers across, down, and diagonally. What answer do you get? 18

Why do you think this is called a magic square? ______

Page 248

Traveling to a Large City

1. Circle the correct answer. Then follow the directions.

A large truck used for moving furniture is called a:
a. dump truck - Mark out all letter M's below.
(b.) van - Mark out all letter C's below.
c. pickup truck - Mark out all letter I's below.

A large vehicle for transporting children to school is called a:
(a.) bus - Mark out all letter B's below.
b. yacht - Mark out all letter A's below.
c. jet - Mark out all letter F's below.

A vehicle pulled by horses or oxen is called a:
a. hot air balloon - Mark out all letter D's below.
b. tricycle - Mark out all letter O's below.
(c.) wagon - Mark out all letter P's below.

A long line of boxcars that runs on a track is called a:
a. submarine - Mark out all letter L's below.
(b.) train - Mark out all letter N's below.
c. bicycle - Mark out all letter R's below.

A vehicle that sails through water is called a:
(a.) ship - Mark out all letter E's below.
b. tank - Mark out all letter M's below.
c. sled - Mark out all letter A's below.

~~N~~	M	~~B~~	~~N~~	I	~~P~~	~~E~~	~~B~~
A	~~C~~	~~E~~	M	~~B~~	~~C~~	~~E~~	I
~~E~~	F	~~N~~	~~C~~	~~P~~	~~E~~	~~B~~	~~N~~
~~P~~	~~C~~	L	~~E~~	~~N~~	~~B~~	~~E~~	~~B~~
~~E~~	~~B~~	~~C~~	P	~~B~~	O	~~E~~	~~N~~
R	~~E~~	~~N~~	~~E~~	I	A	~~P~~	~~E~~
~~E~~	D	~~B~~	~~P~~	~~N~~	~~B~~	A	~~B~~

2. Start at the top. Write the name of the remaining letters in the spaces below.

I will travel to what city? M i a m i F l o r i d a

Page 249

By Land, by Sea, and by Air

Write the first letter of the names of the objects below.
The letters form words.
Underline the word in red if it travels "By Land."
Underline the word in green if it travels "By Sea."
Underline the word in orange if it travels "By Air."

air H O T A I R

B A L L O O N

sea R A F T

land S U B W A Y

Page 250

Follow That Sign!

Look at the road sign symbols below. Each sign is matched to a letter. Use the road sign code to find the names of four vehicles that travel on roads.

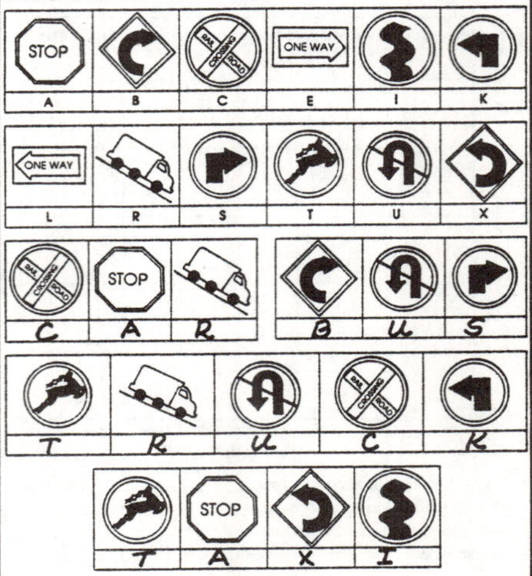

Page 251

The Subway

Some big cities have a subway. A subway is a railroad that is under the ground. The trains carry people from one part of the city to another. The trains stop often to let people off and on. Many people ride to work on a subway. Others ride to school or to go shopping. Subways are nice because they do not take up space in a city.

Write.

A subway is a railroad that is under the ground.
shop subway

Circle.

Yes or No

The subway takes people to parts of the city.	(Yes)	No
The subway stops only one time each day.	Yes	(No)
The subway stops to let people off and on.	(Yes)	No

Circle.

Where are some people on the subway going?

Color the subway train red.

- Draw where you would go on the subway.

Page 252

A Helicopter

Would you like to ride in a helicopter? A helicopter flies in the air. It can fly up and down. It can fly **forward** and **backward**. It can fly **sideways**. A helicopter can even stay in one spot in the air! Helicopters can be many sizes. Some helicopters carry just one person. Some carry 30 people. Helicopters can be used for many jobs.

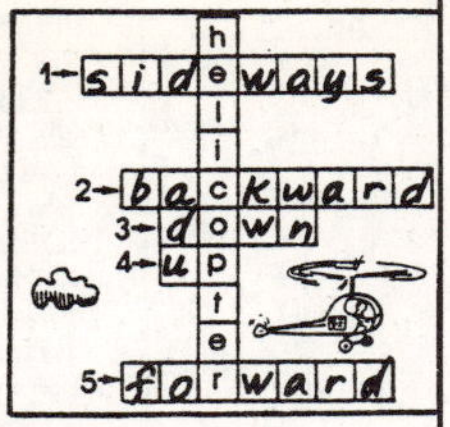

h e l i c o p t e r
1→ s i d e w a y s
2→ b a c k w a r d
3→ d o w n
4→ u p
5→ f o r w a r d

Write. A *helicopter* flies in the air.
trailer helicopter

Write. Which way can a helicopter fly? (Look at story.)
4→u*p* 3→d*own* 5→f*orward*
2→b*ackward* 1→s*ideways*

Write the answers in the puzzle above.

Circle. Yes or No
A helicopter can stay in one spot in the air. (Yes) No
Helicopters come in many sizes. (Yes) No
All helicopters can carry 10 people. Yes (No)

• Draw a big green helicopter.

Page 253

Hot Air Balloons

Would you like to fly in a hot air balloon? A hot air balloon can fly when it is filled with hot air or a gas, called helium. Most hot air balloons use helium to fly. People can ride in a basket that is tied to the balloon. The wind moves the balloon in the sky. To come down, the people must let some of the air or gas out of the balloon.

red
purple
green
red
purple
green
1 2 3 1 2 3

Circle. What does a hot air balloon need to fly?
(hot air) music (gas)

Write. Most hot air balloons use *helium* to fly.
helmets helium

Circle. What do people ride in?
cart (basket)

Circle. The moon / (wind) moves the balloon in the sky.

Color. 1 - red 2 - purple 3 - green

• Draw a hot air balloon with two people in the basket.

Page 254

What's New?

Inventions help to make life easier. Various inventors from all around the world try to come up with ways to improve upon things presently used.

Below are pictures of inventions that have changed as inventors improved them. Number them in the correct order each version appeared by writing 1, 2, and 3 in the boxes.

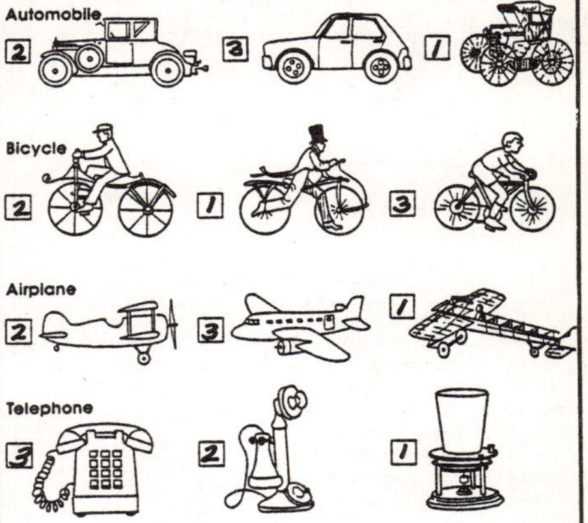

Automobile
2
3
1
Bicycle
2
1
3
Airplane
2
3
1
Telephone
3
2
1

Page 255

Selecting Supplies

Read each word in the Word Bank. If a word names a **need**, write it on the sack of flour. If a word names a **want**, write it on the pickle barrel.

Word Bank
videotape milk bracelet
kite soda pop bed candy bar
soccer ball home backpack
vegetables balloon fruit
bread coat hat
Want
videotape
bracelet
kite soda pop
candy bar
soccer ball
backpack
balloon
Need
milk bed
home vegetables
fruit bread
coat hat

Page 256

"Good Service" Delivery

Read each word. If it names an occupation that provides goods, mark **G** on the word. If it names an occupation that provides a service, mark **S** on the word. Then draw a line to show where three answers are the same in a row.

S television salesperson	S veterinarian	S beekeeper
S receptionist	G pizza parlor owner	S lawyer
S crossing guard	S school bus driver	G kite manufacturer

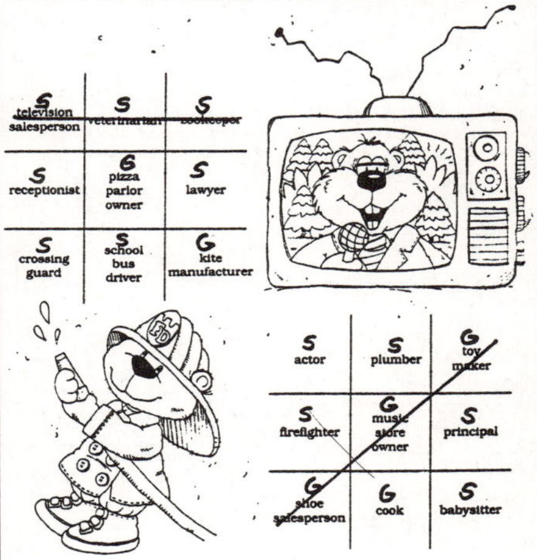

S actor	S plumber	G toy maker
S firefighter	G music store owner	S principal
G shoe salesperson	G cook	S babysitter

Page 257

Brought to You from . . .

Look at each picture. If the picture shows something that comes from a farm, mark **X** on the picture. If it shows something that comes from a factory, mark **O** on the picture. Then draw a line to show where three answers are the same in a row.

chair
book
SEE SPOT
carrot
bow
strawberry
football
potato
glass
pencil
Made in the U.S.A.
U.S.A.
nail
backpack
peanuts
lettuce
swimsuit
apple
radish
paintbrush
pillow

Page 258

My Community

Finish the sentences. Draw a picture to match.

The name of my community is *Answers will vary.*

One place I like to visit is *Answers will vary.*

Here is a picture of the place.
MAIL
DAIRY PRODUCTS

Page 259

About My Community

Write about your community.

I live in *Answers will vary*

It is in the state of *Answers will vary*

I live in or near a *Answers will vary*

suburb city farm town

This is a picture that shows me shopping at the market.

In winter the weather is *Answers will vary*

In summer the weather is *Answers will vary*

My community is in or near
☐ mountains.
☐ a desert.
☐ a plain.
☐ a valley.
☐ hills.

The water nearest my community is
☐ an ocean.
☐ a river.
☐ a lake.
☐ a swamp.

Page 260

Build a Community

Cut out the pictures at the bottom of this page. Read the directions. Paste the pictures where they belong.

Train Station

1. Place the school **west** of the house and **east** of the row of trees.
2. Place the train at the **southwest** edge of the railroad tracks.
3. Place the Police Station **west** of the Train Station and **east** of the train.
4. Place the Grocery Store **east** of the house and **south** of the rising sun.
5. Place the Bank **north** of the train.
6. Place the Fire House **south** of the Grocery Store and **east** of the Train Station.

Page 261

Just Being Neighborly

Go along with Percival Porcupine as he delivers the Welcome basket.

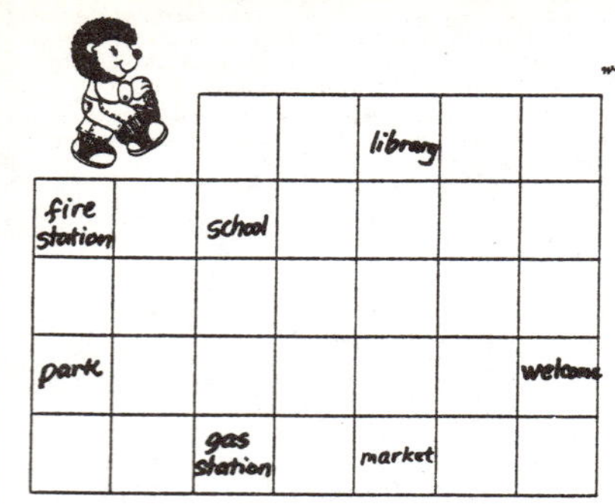

N
W
E
S
library
fire station
school
park
welcome
gas station
market

Follow the directions. Trace a path from one place to the next.

1. Start at Percival and go east 3 spaces. Write **library**.
2. Then go south 4 spaces. Write **market**.
3. Next go west 2 spaces. Write **gas station**.
4. Now go north 3 spaces. Write **school**.
5. Go west 2 spaces. Write **fire station**.
6. Go south 2 spaces. Write **park**.
7. Go east 6 spaces. Write **welcome**.

Page 262

Find the Ring

Look at the map. Read each clue and write the correct word on the line. Then draw a line from one place to the next to show where each clue takes you.

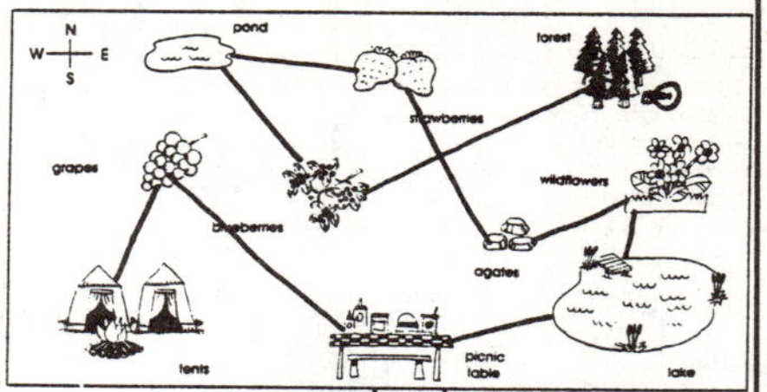

N
W
E
S
pond
forest
strawberries
grapes
wildflowers
blueberries
agates
tents
picnic table
lake

1. Begin where campers sleep. *tents*
2. Go north to a fruit that makes a purple-colored juice. *grapes*
3. Go southeast to a place where you can sit and eat. *picnic table*
4. Then go east where you can row a boat. *lake*
5. Turn north to the small plants with colored petals. *wildflowers*
6. Go southwest to find some special rocks. *agates*
7. Now go northwest to pick some sweet, red berries. *strawberries*
8. Go west to a place where you can swim. *pond*
9. Then go southeast and pick some round, blue-colored fruit. *blueberries*
10. At last, go northeast to a place where there are many trees. *forest*
11. Look closely to find the missing ring. Draw a circle around it.

Page 263

Follow the Map

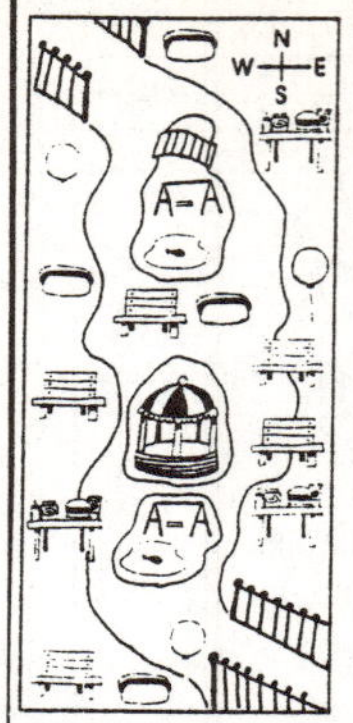

N
W
E
S
A-A
A-A

Use the map to answer the questions.

1. How many entrances do you see? *two*
2. How many ponds are in the park? *two*
3. How many picnic areas are there? *three*
4. How many picnic areas are near a playground? *three*
5. How many bridges do you see? *one*
6. How many balloon sellers are there? *three*
7. How many benches can you find? *five*
8. How many places are there to buy food? *four*
9. How many carousels are there? *one*

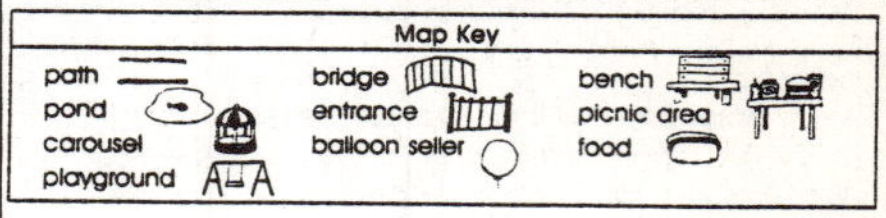

Map Key
path
pond
carousel
playground
bridge
entrance
balloon seller
bench
picnic area
food

Page 264

The Adventure Begins

One rainy Saturday morning, Patrick, Brenda, and Jamie decided they needed something new and exciting to do that morning. They took out the telephone book and turned to the yellow pages. In it they found these advertisements for special places to visit.

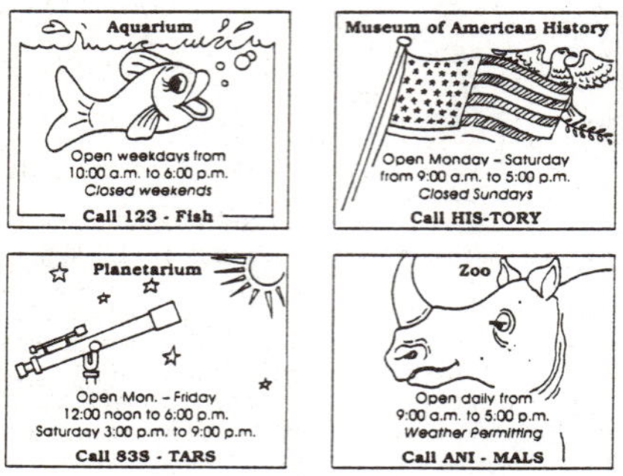

Aquarium
Open weekdays from 10:00 a.m. to 6:00 p.m.
Closed weekends
Call 123 - Fish
Museum of American History
Open Monday – Saturday from 9:00 a.m. to 5:00 p.m.
Closed Sundays
Call HIS-TORY
Planetarium
Open Mon. – Friday 12:00 noon to 6:00 p.m.
Saturday 3:00 p.m. to 9:00 p.m.
Call 83S - TARS
Zoo
Open daily from 9:00 a.m. to 5:00 p.m.
Weather Permitting
Call ANI - MALS

The children looked carefully at the ads. Which place did they choose to visit and why?

They chose to go to the *Museum of American History*

because *it is open Saturday morning.*

Page 265

Home Sweet Home

At the Museum of American History, Patrick, Brenda, and Jamie saw large exhibits of Native Americans and their homes.

Use the rebuses below to discover the different types of houses various nations of Native Americans lived in. Your answers will sound right, but the spellings won't be right. Get the correct spellings from the Word Box.

–P + –TCH

The *Chippewa* Indians lived in domed bark lodges.

–P + –ARTER + –B

The *Iroquois* Indians lived in long houses.

S + BLUE –BL

The *Sioux* Indians lived in buffalo-hide tepees.

–T + V + –P +

The *Navajo* Indians lived in hogans.

P + + SLOW –S

The *Pueblo* Indians lived in adobes.

Word Box		
Pueblo	Iroquois	Sioux
Navajo	Chippewa	

Page 266

Whose House?

Use the pictures of the Native American houses to answer the riddles.

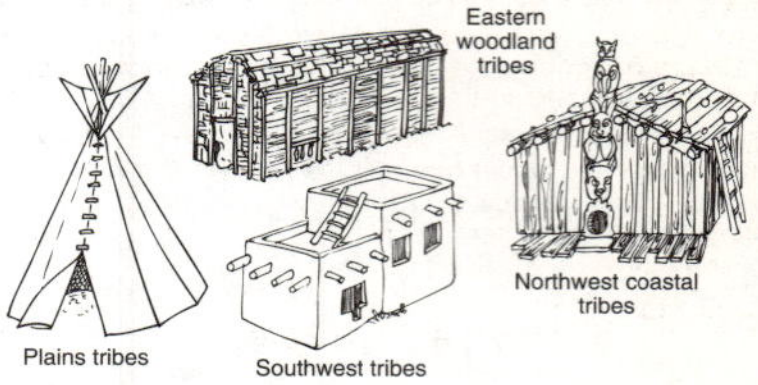

Eastern woodland tribes
Northwest coastal tribes
Plains tribes
Southwest tribes

This house has no beds. Many families live in it. It is made of adobe brick. It has no doors, only windows. Whose house is it? Southwest tribes	This is called a plank house. Many families live in it. It is made of large beams and trees. It has a totem pole in front. Whose house is it? Northwest coastal tribes
This is called a long house. It has bunk beds. It is made of branches and bark. Fire burns in the center of it. Whose house is it? Eastern woodland tribes	This house can be set up in 10 minutes. One family lives in it. It is made of poles and animal skins. A fire burns inside. Whose house is it? Plains tribes

Page 267

A Family of Friends

There was a great exhibit at the Museum of American History of figures of Native Americans and Pilgrims sharing the first Thanksgiving feast. When the Pilgrims came to Plymouth, Massachusetts, in 1620, they had a very difficult year. Native Americans helped the Pilgrims hunt and harvest food.

Read each riddle. Use the Word Box to write each food that the Native Americans helped the Pilgrims find or grow.

1. Water doesn't stick –
It rolls off my back;
And when it does,
I loudly say, "Quack, quack!"
I am *a duck*.

2. I'm not inside a whale,
But I'm found in a "wheel."
You'll also find me
In a piece of "steel."
I am *an eel*.

3. When your roof "leaks,"
You may want to cry.
You'll do the same thing
When I'm near your eye.
I am *a leek*.

4. Boil me or pop me
When I am ripe.
Cook me in bread
Or use my cob as a pipe.
I am *corn*

5. I like to "honk,"
And I can fly.
Ask the lady who rode me,
Reciting rhymes in the sky.
I am *a goose*

Word Box		
a goose	a leek	a duck
corn	an eel	

Page 268

Then and Now

The museum had great examples of things the colonists used. Although their lives were different than ours today, many of their needs were the same.

Unscramble the names of objects we use today. (The first letter is underlined.) Then write the correct letter to match similar objects of the past and present.

Present | **Past**

a. cetelrci *electric* nkablte *blanket* — *b.* candles

b. mapl *lamp* — *a.* bed warmer

c. satemhc *matches* — *e.* quill and ink well

d. tlpea *plate* — *d.* wooden trenche[r]

e. epn *pen* — *c.* tinder box

Page 269

Down on the Farm

At the museum the children learned that though the colonists worked very hard, they also took time for some fun. One favorite form of fun was corn-husking competitions.

In the cornfield below, Thomas picked and husked corn from the cornstalks that have circles around the numbers.

Jonathon picked and husked corn from the cornstalks that have squares around the numbers.

James did the same with the cornstalks that have triangles around the numbers.

1
2
3
4
5
6
7
8
9
10
11
12
13
14
15
16
17
18
19
20
21
22
23
24

Using the pattern started above, finish drawing the circles, squares, and triangles. Then answer these questions.

1. Who picked and husked corn from cornstalk #20? *Jonathon*
2. Who picked and husked corn from cornstalk #22? *Thomas*
3. If all of the even-numbered cornstalks had two ears of corn, and all of the odd-numbered cornstalks had one ear of corn, how many ears of corn did each boy husk?
Thomas *12* Jonathon *12* James *12*

Page 270

Sew What?

A favorite activity of colonial women and girls was getting together for a quilting bee. The quilts, made from scraps of linen, wool, and cotton, were frequently sewn together in a pattern.

Look carefully at the pattern in the unfinished quilt below. Then continue the pattern by drawing pictures in the blank sections to complete the quilt.

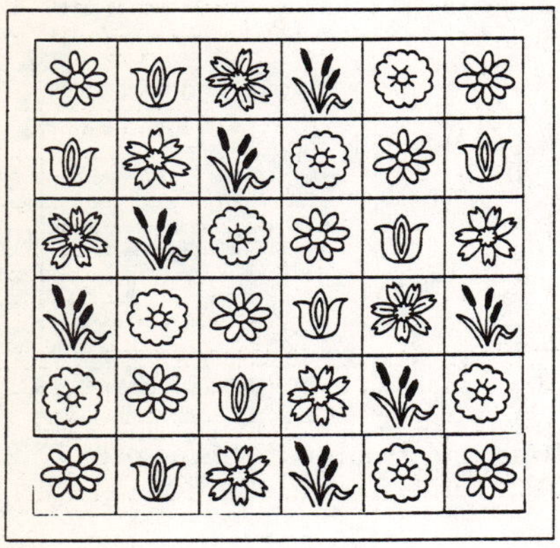

Page 271

Go West, Young Man!

From about 1760 to 1850, pioneers moved westward across the United States. They traveled in big covered wagons called **Conestoga** wagons.

Some of the trails that the pioneers took in their Conestoga wagons are marked on the map below.

Look closely at the trails. Then answer the questions.

1. If the pioneers started at Nauvoo and traveled **west**, how many different trails could they take? 5
2. If the pioneers began at Independence and traveled **west**, how many choices of trails would they have? 9

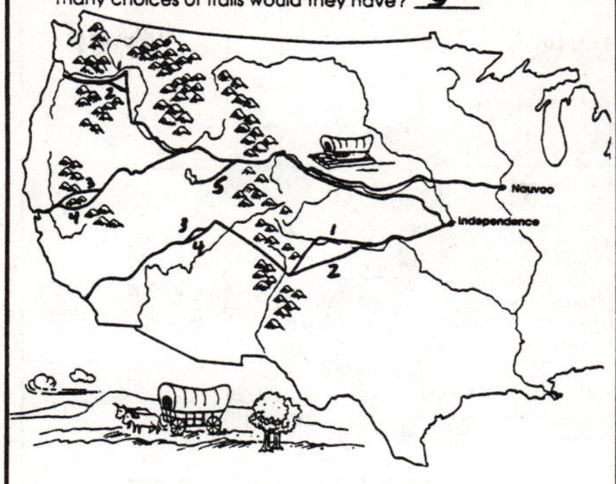

Page 272

A Man of Peace

A large picture of the Lincoln Memorial was on display at the museum. Abraham Lincoln was our 16th president. Shortly after he became President in 1861, America's Civil War began between the people living in the South and the people living in the North.

Abraham Lincoln made a famous speech in which he said that all people are created equal. He wanted all people in our country to live together in peace.

Look carefully at the tall columns around the outside of the building. If you walked around the whole building, how many columns would you pass? 36

Page 273

What's Your Brand?

The Museum of American History had a great display on cowboys who lived from the 1860's to the 1880's. These cowboys went on cattle drives for two to three months at a time and sometimes traveled 1,000 miles! They were often in danger from rattlesnakes, quicksand, cattle stampedes, and wild horses.

During cattle roundups in the spring and fall, cowboys branded the newborn calves to show what ranch they belonged to.

Look at the brands below. Use the Word Box to write what each brand meant.

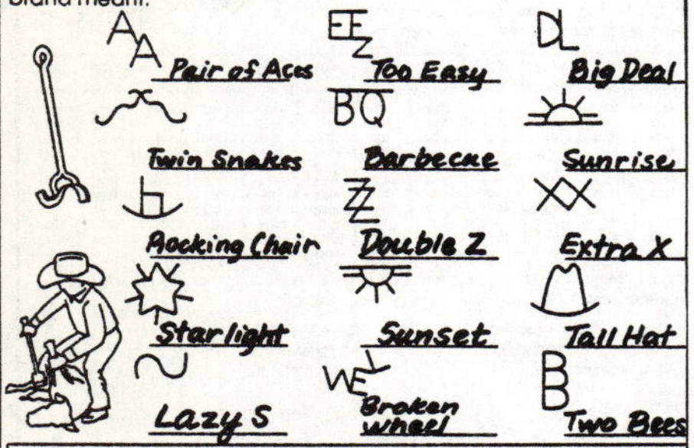

Pair of Aces — Too Easy — Big Deal
Twin Snakes — Barbecue — Sunrise
Rocking Chair — Double Z — Extra X
Starlight — Sunset — Tall Hat
Lazy S — Broken wheel — Two Bees

Word Box

Twin Snakes	Double Z	Pair of Aces	Sunrise	Too Easy
Rocking Chair	Extra X	Big Deal	Sunset	Barbecue
Broken Wheel	Lazy S	Starlight	Tall Hat	Two Bees

Page 274

News Flash!

One large room in the museum had pages from calendars on its walls, listing events from America's past. Pretend that you were a newspaper reporter in the year 1888. You wrote a story about each event on the day it happened, as shown on the calendar below.

October – 1888

Sunday	Monday	Tuesday	Wednesday	Thursday	Friday	Saturday
	1	2	3	4	5	6
7	8	9 National Monument to George Washington opened	10	11	12	13
14	15	16	17	18 First school for agriculture set up in Minnesota	19	20 American baseball teams go on world tour
21	22	23	24	25 Double-decker ferry-boat launched in New York	26	27
28	29	30 J.J. Loud develops ball-point pen in Plymouth, Mass.	31			

Here are headlines for your newspaper stories. Write the date each story was written.

"Piggyback Ride Across River" October 25
"A Hit 'Round The World" October 20
"First President Honored" October 9
"New Invention Makes Mark" October 30
"Learning to Farm Is Fun" October 18

Page 275

Help Wanted

America has often been called a "Land of Opportunity." Its people may choose from many types of careers.

Use the Word Box to write two different careers that have the following characteristics in common. Answers may vary.

1. Place importance on books	teacher	librarian
2. Consider water an important tool	farmer gardener	fireman
3. Work with needle and thread	seamstress	tailor
4. Work with food	chef	gardener farmer
5. Make sure people follow rules	police	umpire
6. Deliver mail and packages	delivery person	mail carrier
7. Takes care of medical needs	nurse veterinarian	doctor
8. Work with animals	veterinarian	farmer zookeeper
9. Use numbers quite often	mathematician	accountant
10. Provide entertainment	musician	actor

Word Box

mathematician	veterinarian	teacher	chef
actor	police officer	nurse	doctor
accountant	mail carrier	seamstress	gardener
musician	fireman	librarian	tailor
delivery person	farmer	umpire	zookeeper

Page 276

Geography Magic Square

Read column A and choose an answer from column B. Write the number of the answer in the correct magic square. The first one has been done for you.

Column A

A. Large areas of water
B. A flat area of land that is higher than the land around it
C. One of the seven areas of land on Earth
D. A hot, wetland area of thick trees, plants and animals
E. A sun-dried clay brick used for building
F. A piece of land with water on three sides
G. A cone-shaped mountain made of ash and melted rock
H. A hot, dry area of land covered with sand
I. A group of mountains

Column B

1. peninsula
2. volcano
3. plateau
4. desert
5. continent
6. rain forest
7. ocean
8. adobe
9. range

A 7	B 3	C 5
D 6	E 8	F 1
G 2	H 4	I 9

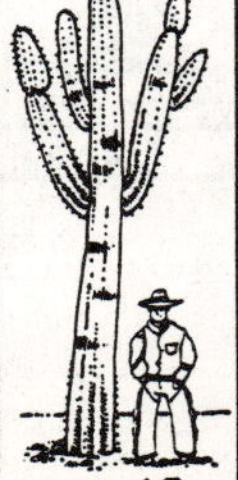

Add the numbers across and down. What answer do you get? 15

Page 277

Landform Riddles

Use the Word Bank to solve the riddles. Then color the pictures.

Word Bank

lake island plain river mountain peninsula

I have water on three sides. I am a peninsula	I have water all around me. I am an island	I am wet and have land all around me. I am a lake
I am long and narrow and flow through the land. I am a river	I am raised land, larger than a hill. I am a mountain	I am low and flat. I am a plain

Page 278

Seeking the Sights

Read each clue. Use the map to locate the matching state. Write the abbreviation on the line.

1. The Space and Rocket Center is in the state south of Tennessee, **east** of Mississippi and **west** of Georgia. AL
2. Buffalo Bill's home is in the state **west** of Iowa and **south** of South Dakota. NE
3. Elephant Rock is in the state **southeast** of Oregon and **west** of Utah. NV
4. Casey Jones Railroad Museum is in the state **north** of Alabama and **south** of Kentucky. TN
5. Fossil National Monument is in the state **east** of Idaho and **south** of Montana. WY
6. The Corn Palace is in the state **southeast** of Montana and **northwest** of Iowa. SD
7. A life-size model of one of Columbus' ships, the *Santa Maria*, is in the state **west** of Pennsylvania and **east** of Indiana. OH
8. Gillette Castle is in the state **east** of New York and **south** of Massachusetts. CT

Page 279

The Seven Continents

Pretend you are a pilot. Your job is to land on each continent for a top-secret mission. You must learn what each continent looks like.

Write the name of each continent below its picture. Use the word bank below.

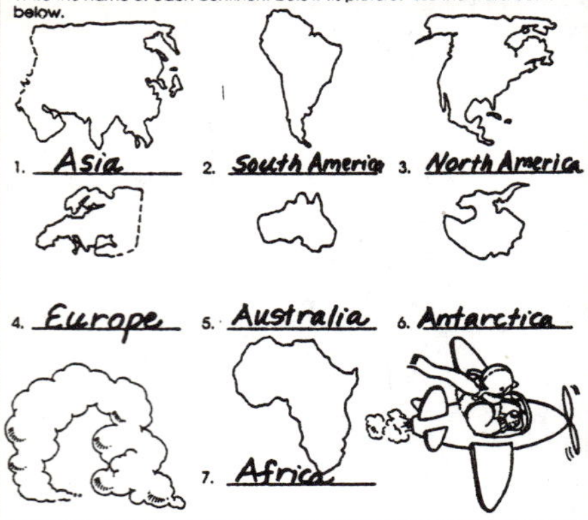

Africa	Asia	Europe	South America
Antarctica	Australia	North America	

Page 280

Animals Around the World

Color the animals and the continents.

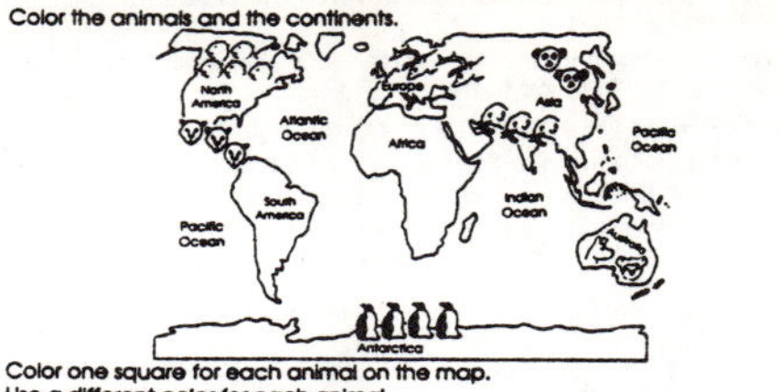

Color one square for each animal on the map.
Use a different color for each animal.

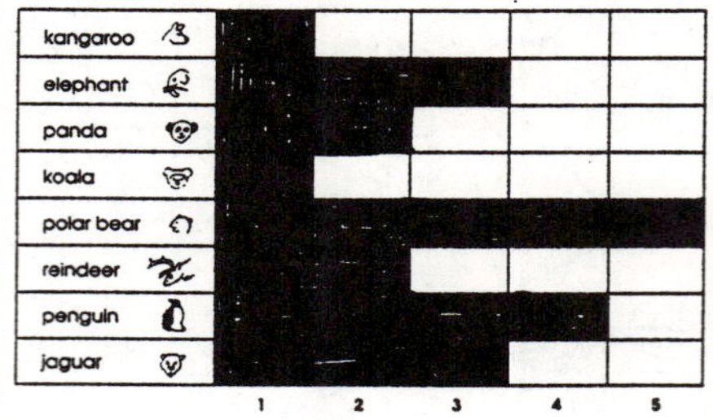

Page 281

Hawaii

Hawaii was the last state to become part of the United States. It is the 50th state. Hawaii is made up of eight large islands and many small islands. The islands are mountains that were made long ago under the ocean. Some mountains in Hawaii still shoot out steam and melted rock. Sugar cane and pineapples grow in Hawaii. People in Hawaii enjoy warm weather and colorful flowers.

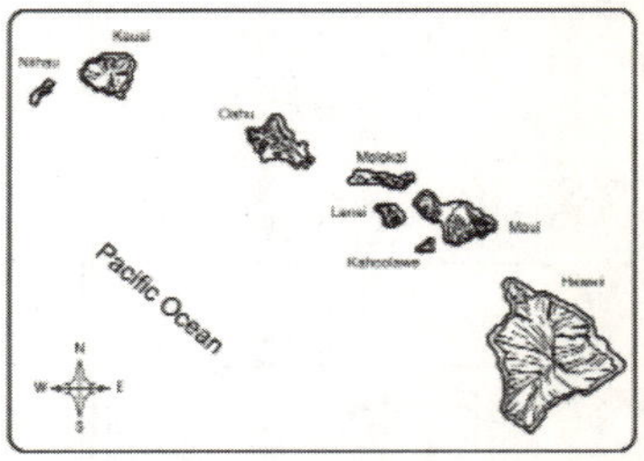

Read to answer questions on page 283.

Page 282

Hawaii (continued)

Use facts from the story to fill in the crossword puzzle. The Word Box will help you

Word Box
Hawaii
mountains
islands
sugar
pineapple
flowers
eight

Across
2. Colorful ______ grow in Hawaii.
4. The 50th state.
6. ______ cane grows on the islands.
7. Hawaii has ______ large islands.

Down
1. The islands are__________.
3. ______ grows in Hawaii.
5. Hawaii is made up of many ______.

Page 283

Speaking Strine

Australians, like Americans, have their own "language" called Strine. An Aussie might say something like this, "I'm going to take my swag and tucker down to the billabong while my jumbucks are resting." That sounds like a foreign language!

In the box to the left below is a Strine dictionary so you can translate what the "bloke" said. "I'm going to take my bedroll and belongings and food down to the water hole while my sheep are resting."

Using the dictionary, write and illustrate two sentences of your own.

How to Speak Strine
billabong - water hole
billy - container for boiling tea
bloke - man
bonzer - great, terrific
bush - country away from the city
chook - chicken
dingo - Australian wild dog
dinkum, fair dinkum - honest, genuine
dinki-di - the real thing
fossick - to prospect for gold or gems
grazier - ranch
jumbuck - sheep
make a good fist - do a good job
ocker - basic down-to-earth Aussie
outback - remote bush
pom - English person
roo - a kangaroo
shout - buy a round of drinks
station - sheep or cattle ranch
Strine - what Aussies speak
swag - bedroll and belongings
tucker - food
ute - utility or pickup truck
waltz matilda - carry a swag

Sentences will vary.

Page 284

Happy New Year!

In China, the most celebrated holiday is the New Year. The Lantern Festival is part of the celebration. That is when Chinese people welcome the first full moon of the year. The Chinese New Year is fixed according to the lunar calendar. It occurs somewhere between January 30 and February 20. Each Chinese year is represented by one of 12 animals.

Look at the chart below to see what animal represents the year you were born.

RAT	OX	TIGER	HARE (RABBIT)	DRAGON	SNAKE	HORSE	RAM	MONKEY	ROOSTER	DOG	PIG
1900	1901	1902	1903	1904	1905	1906	1907	1908	1909	1910	1911
1912	1913	1914	1915	1916	1917	1918	1919	1920	1921	1922	1923
1924	1925	1926	1927	1928	1929	1930	1931	1932	1933	1934	1935
1936	1937	1938	1939	1940	1941	1942	1943	1944	1945	1946	1947
1948	1949	1950	1951	1952	1953	1954	1955	1956	1957	1958	1959
1960	1961	1962	1963	1964	1965	1966	1967	1968	1969	1970	1971
1972	1973	1974	1975	1976	1977	1978	1979	1980	1981	1982	1983
1984	1985	1986	1987	1988	1989	1990	1991	1992	1993	1994	1995
1996	1997	1998	1999	2000	2001	2002	2003	2004	2005	2006	2007
2008	2009	2010	2011	2012	2013	2014	2015	2016	2017	2018	2019

The Festival of the Lanterns is celebrated on the third day of the New Year. Make a colorful lantern to hang in your classroom.

1. Fold a bright-colored piece of construction paper vertically.
2. Cut strips from the folded side stopping 2" from the open edge.

3. Open, bend in circle, and staple.

4. Cut out a long paper strip and staple to make a handle.

Page 285

The "Boot"

From America, Italy is across the Atlantic Ocean. It is part of a continent called Europe. Most of Italy is shaped like a boot. It also has two islands named Sicily and Sardinia. Its "boot," or mainland, extends into the Mediterranean Sea. The shape of the mainland is called a peninsula because it has water around three of its sides. Rome is Italy's capital and largest city. It has been an important city for more than 2,500 years. Italy got its name from the Romans who called its southern part Italia, meaning "land of oxen" or "grazing land."

Color Italy green.
Color the Mediterranean Sea blue.
Use the map to unscramble the names of some Italian cities below it.

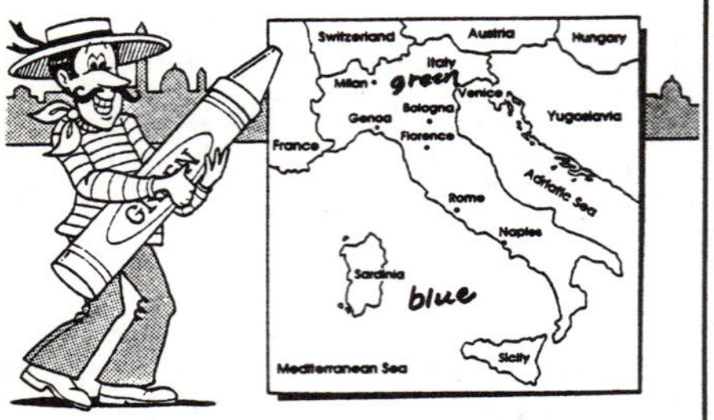

ALSNEP Naples ENCLEOFR Florence MERO Rome
LMNIA Milan AENOG Genoa NCVEIE Venice
OGBNLOA Bologna

Page 286

The American Alphabet

The United States attracts people from all over the world. We are sometimes called a nation of immigrants.

Write the alphabet in order in the boxes. Then use the Word Box and the letter in each box to write the name of each country where it belongs.

Answers for 5 and 18 may be transposed.

1. India
2. Mozambique
3. China
4. Ireland
5. France
6. Afghanistan
7. Egypt
8. Netherlands
9. Israel
10. Japan
11. Korea
12. Philippines
13. Germany
14. Canada
15. Poland
16. Puerto Rico
17. Iraq
18. Greece
19. Australia
20. Italy
21. Cuba
22. Vietnam
23. Norway
24. Mexico
25. Kenya
26. Venezuela

Word Box
Afghanistan
Australia
Canada
China
Cuba
Egypt
France
Germany
Greece
India
Iraq
Ireland
Israel
Italy
Japan
Kenya
Korea
Mexico
Mozambique
Netherlands
Norway
Philippines
Poland
Puerto Rico
Venezuela
Vietnam

Page 287

A Capital Idea

This is what Tommy's suitcase might have looked like after visiting the eight countries on his adventure. Color and cut out the travel stickers below. Paste them on the suitcase so each capital matches its country.

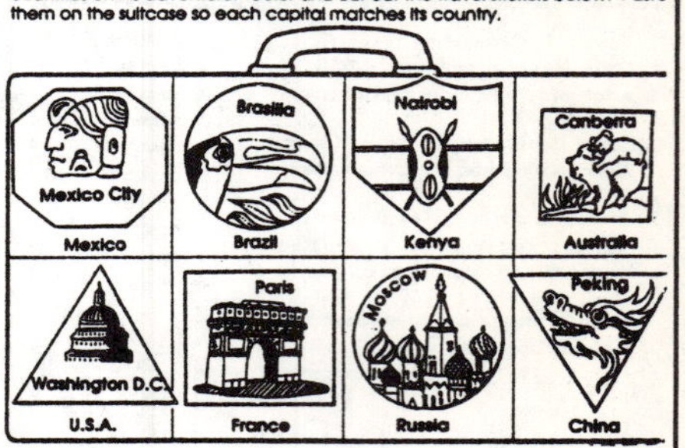

Page 288

Notes

Notes

Notes

Notes